THE GENERALSHIP OF MUHAMMAD

UNIVERSITY PRESS OF FLORIDA

Florida A&M University, Tallahassee
Florida Atlantic University, Boca Raton
Florida Gulf Coast University, Ft. Myers
Florida International University, Miami
Florida State University, Tallahassee
New College of Florida, Sarasota
University of Central Florida, Orlando
University of Florida, Gainesville
University of North Florida, Jacksonville
University of South Florida, Tampa
University of West Florida, Pensacola

THE GENERALSHIP OF
MUHAMMAD

Battles and Campaigns of the Prophet of Allah

RUSS RODGERS

University Press of Florida

Gainesville · Tallahassee · Tampa · Boca Raton
Pensacola · Orlando · Miami · Jacksonville · Ft. Myers · Sarasota

17 16 15 14 13 12   6 5 4 3 2 1

All maps by Russ Rodgers

LIBRARY OF CONGRESS CATALOGING-IN-PUBLICATION DATA
Rodgers, Russ
The generalship of Muhammad : battles and campaigns of the Prophet
of Allah / Russ Rodgers.
p. cm.
Includes bibliographical references and index.
ISBN 978-0-8130-3766-0 (alk. paper)
1. Muhammad, Prophet, d. 632—Military leadership. I. Title.
BP77.7.R64 2012
297.6'3—dc23
2011037547

The University Press of Florida is the scholarly publishing agency
for the State University System of Florida, comprising Florida A&M
University, Florida Atlantic University, Florida Gulf Coast University,
Florida International University, Florida State University, New
College of Florida, University of Central Florida, University of Florida,
University of North Florida, University of South Florida, and University
of West Florida.

University Press of Florida
15 Northwest 15th Street
Gainesville, FL 32611-2079
http://www.upf.com

To my wife and daughter, who continue to teach me joy and gratitude.

Contents

Introduction

It is necessary to provide you, the reader, with an idea about the scope and nature of this military analysis of the campaigns of Muhammad, along with a few of the important specialized terms and the types of sources used. In the modern world of military historical literature there are a number of terms used to describe how weaker movements engage and defeat stronger opponents. Today such terms as insurgency, asymmetric warfare, and irregular warfare are commonly used to explain such movements, and yet these terms were unknown to military thinkers until most recent times. When one speaks of insurgency today, they typically refer to a weaker group that uses methods of warfare often cited as irregular, unconventional, or asymmetric, and that strives to overcome what is considered an established government or organization. But even such a definition raises the question of what irregular, unconventional, or asymmetric warfare is. Such terminology can actually engender confusion among readers and military practitioners alike.

For the purposes of this work, "irregular" or "unconventional" warfare refer to organizational methods that eschew clear and deliberate organization and operations, especially one that clearly defines the differences between combatants and civilians. But more importantly, terms such as "insurgency" or "asymmetric warfare" highlight a difference in actual tactics and operational techniques used by a particular movement. Therefore, irregular warfare should not be confused with insurgency, or unconventional warfare confused with asymmetric warfare. So what do these terms actually mean, and what is the best way to define them?

In the context of the modern world, "insurgency" refers to any movement bent on overthrowing an established government or organization. With this said, we must next understand the difference between a symmetric and an asymmetric insurgency. While it is fashionable for some to think that insurgency and asymmetric warfare are the same thing, to do so does violence to the strict definition of the word "asymmetric." Symmetric or asymmetric refer simply to methods. To be symmetric simply means to use methods nearly identical to one's enemies, while to be asymmetric would be to move outside an enemy's realm of experience. In this manner we can see that anyone in history can engage in both, perhaps even simultaneously, while also engaging in insurgency or conventional military operations. However, such a definition did not exist in the ancient world, and certainly not in the world of Muhammad's seventh-century Arabia. Therefore, for the sake of this study, these terms have been superimposed over the historical activities of Muhammad and his companions to help us understand how he campaigned and won. Therefore, to clarify, an insurgency is a movement to overthrow an existing or established government or organization while asymmetric or symmetric warfare are merely techniques to achieve this end.

With this in mind, it can be seen that any form of warfare can be asymmetric or symmetric. During World War II, Germany used an asymmetric doctrinal approach of mobile warfare to defeat France in 1940, the latter organizing its defense around the idea of positional military thought. Popularly known as the blitzkrieg, or lightning war, the Germans were able to overrun France and defeat an army that was larger and better equipped than their own. By using an asymmetric approach, they were able to defeat a doctrinally ill-prepared opponent. In contrast, the Allies largely used a symmetric approach to defeat Germany three years later. Allied forces mirrored the German army in almost every aspect, and defeated them by often overwhelming them with material superiority. By the time the Allies reached the western border of Germany, the war devolved into an attritional contest as the forces slugged it out for months along the German frontier.

While few would argue against the idea that conventional warfare can be symmetric or asymmetric, it becomes more controversial when discussing insurgency. Once the shooting starts, insurgencies are typically asymmetric, but this is more out of necessity than a matter of choosing the best technique to achieve victory. If given a choice and the resources necessary, almost any leader in history would chose to achieve victory more quickly through conventional means than to opt for the drawn-out lengthy conflict called insurgency or guerrilla warfare. Insurgencies cannot face an established government on equal terms, or, put another way, symmetrically. This is the portion of insurgency that most see and that is written about in the popular texts of today.

But what is typically missed is that insurgencies are far more about philosophical and worldview transformation than about ambushing government forces from a jungle or mountain sanctuary. The initial phase of an insurgency strives to alter the mind of people, particularly key leaders, to support a new worldview that is in contrast to their established one. Indeed, this is arguably the most important aspect of any insurgency, and it is almost exclusively symmetric, apart from the differences in the worldviews. Once the fighting begins, much of an insurgency movement has already passed by the snoozing leaders of a targeted culture. In this way, the insurgency moves from a symmetric to an asymmetric approach in order to build the force necessary to push a sleepy majority of a culture into succumbing to the insurgency's demands. Once having achieved the level of force necessary, the insurgency transforms once again from an asymmetric to a symmetric approach to bring about the final triumph. When looking at insurgency from this perspective, one can see that the dictum of Carl von Clausewitz that war is the extension of politics by other means can be flipped to its inverse, that politics is an extension of war by other means.[1] Insurgency starts in the realm of philosophy and ideology to lay the foundation and is followed by the physical violence necessary to impose its principles on a culture that otherwise would not have accepted such views.

This book deals with Muhammad's insurgency campaign to gain dominance over Makkah, and ultimately Arabia. It examines how he organized his philosophical insurgency while residing in Makkah, and how he altered his techniques to engage in a more active insurgency that applied economic and social pressure on the people of Makkah to eventually succumb to his call to the sole worship of Allah and acceptance of himself as Allah's last prophet. While military operations are a significant part of this work, the philosophical aspects are not neglected. Both are examined to see how they influenced the course of events and the decision making of the antagonists. Muhammad's early life is examined to set the stage for the direction he chose for himself and his followers. This is followed by a discussion of the operations he undertook to achieve dominance over Arabia. Finally, an analysis is made of Muhammad's generalship and how he performed in light of past and more recent contemporaries.

It must be noted that there are some aspects of Muhammad's life that do not receive a detailed examination because these would be peripheral to the intent of the text. The primary focus of this work is to analyze how Muhammad campaigned and won, and just as importantly, how the Quraysh, the dominant tribe that controlled Makkah, lost, bringing with it the subjugation to the Prophet of most of Arabia.

Researching and writing a military biography of Muhammad, the Prophet of Allah, encounters a number of challenges. These challenges deal with sources, terminologies, and the emotions aroused by any analysis of a leading figure of a major world movement. For example, it should be noted that early Islamic sources on which this biography is based clearly note that there was a difference between what Muhammad knew as a man and what he presented as the Prophet of Allah. In the context of the former, such sources stress that Muhammad, like other men, grew in knowledge and learning, gaining valuable experience as he conducted his military operations. This is not inconsistent with the Islamic tradition.[2] Because it was necessary for him to develop knowledge based on experience, this also implies that he had strengths and weaknesses as a military commander.

Regarding the theories of warfare already discussed, there is presently much debate swirling about the nature of insurgency conflict, and so it is necessary to attempt to clarify the finer points as to how they relate to Muhammad and his times. We find that Muhammad used both symmetric and asymmetric techniques during the twelve years of his insurgency against Makkah and Arabia. In the early days of Muhammad's movement, his approach was symmetric, as he largely used the same principles and concepts available to the Quraysh to leverage them. For example, since they believed in tolerance, he early on appealed to their notions of tolerance to limit persecution against his followers as he preached the initial passages of the Qur'an among the people. As Muhammad's followers migrated to Madinah, his approach became increasingly asymmetric, using techniques unfamiliar to the Quraysh.

Besides the difficulties encountered in understanding symmetric or asymmetric insurgencies and how they apply to the Prophet, another problem involves who is actually the insurgent. In many cases, the one labeled the insurgent could arguably be called the counterinsurgent. For example, it is a general article of faith that the American Indian waged an insurgency against European American settlers in the 1800s. Yet, it can be argued with more relevance that it was the settlers who were engaged in an insurgency while the Indians fought a counterinsurgency. From this perspective, one must be careful about using labels. In the case of Muhammad, it would seem that he and the Muslims were engaged in an insurgency, but on the other hand, he probably would have argued the opposite, claiming that it was the Quraysh who were the insurgents against the ancient faith of Islamic monotheism. This book takes the position that the Muslims were the insurgent, but it is always worthwhile to at least entertain an opposing viewpoint and examine how it would impact our interpretation of events.

Regarding sources used, they are almost all Islamic, and are from the Sunni perspective, no less. There is next to nothing from the viewpoint of Muhammad's key opposition, the Quraysh of Makkah, and there is even less from the outlying tribes in Arabia. Therefore, any attempt to reconstruct Muhammad's military life can encounter the problem of being one-sided. Nevertheless, it is still an area deserving serious research. While taking a critical view of the Islamic sources, certain portions of *sira* and hadith literature have been generally taken at face value unless some aspect of the information demands additional analysis questioning the nature of the source. In dealing with these texts and documents, one must differentiate between plausibility and probability. Many events may be plausible on the surface but not necessarily probable in the realities of the mountains and deserts of Arabia. While an accusation can be laid by some that this makes any project on Muhammad's life a problematic mixture of myth and reality, the analysis within this work will demonstrate that the well-accepted early Islamic texts are reasonably accurate to events that could have happened.

With this said, it is important to briefly discuss the problems inherent in the sources and recent scholarship that critiques these items. The work of Fred Donner that describes the basic approaches to the Islamic source documents offers an excellent departure point for this analysis.[3] It is not the intent here to reproduce his examination of these approaches in their entirety, but a few key points can be made that will assist the reader unfamiliar with these processes. Moreover, some analysis will follow that critiques these processes in their examination of early Islamic sources. Donner divides the way recent scholars view the early Islamic documents into four approaches. The Descriptive Approach is explained as being the most fundamental and earliest method in examining the documents. This method accepts much of the corpus of early material, particularly the Qur'an and *sira* literature, at face value. However, it tended to downplay the hadith literature as being more religious in nature than historical. Donner cites this method as having value because it represented a move away from the earlier polemic approach that sought to assail Islam without referencing Islamic sources. Nevertheless, he faults this method for being too accepting of the early material.[4]

The second method is the Source-Critical Approach. This view was influenced by the positivism that was in vogue in the late-nineteenth and early-twentieth centuries. Positivism stressed the notion that facts could be demonstrably known if a researcher engaged in careful criticism of sources through comparative analysis. This method assumed that extant historical accounts and documents contained a large measure of accurate information that needed to be sifted from inaccurate material that had infiltrated though poor transmission of the accounts. Like the Descriptive Approach, the Source-Critical Approach excludes the hadith literature as being of a religious, not historical, motif. Regarding early Islamic historical records, scholars who took this approach tended to divide the sources into various historical "schools," such as the Madinan, Syrian, or Iraqi schools. When analyzing the sources, some have even gone so far as to postulate that the early Islamic historical sources were based on an earlier and now lost primary written source,[5] much like the approach taken by some Biblical scholars that the synoptic New Testament Gospels, at least the books of Matthew and Luke, were based on a now non-extant single primary document called "Q."

The third view is what Donner calls the Tradition-Critical Approach. It began at the end of the nineteenth century and emphasized an analysis of the hadith literature. Scholars following this approach have attempted to analyze the accepted hadith sources to show that many were actually late-date forgeries intent on advocating one political viewpoint over another during the upheavals in the Islamic world years after the Prophet Muhammad's death. Thus, in this view the traditions of Islam developed over a significant amount of time, culminating in the settled dogmas of today. The core of this argument is contained in Ignaz Goldziher's work in the 1890s, and although it attempted to discount a large amount of hadith material accepted by the Islamic world, Goldziher remained convinced that much of the source material was still quite factual.[6] The core of this approach was borrowed largely from Biblical studies involving textual and form criticism, the latter often referred to as "higher criticism" in an effort to somehow determine what material was accurate and what was not. Connected to this is the problem of oral traditions and maintaining accurate information over generations. What makes this approach unique is that Western scholars began to examine the hadith literature more seriously as the basis for historical events. Donner notes that a key problem with this method is that it tends to reduce the so-called kernel of historical material within the sources to a logical vanishing point.[7] Put another way, how can one be sure what material is factual and what is concocted by some malicious person at a later date?

The last method explained is the Skeptical Approach. This viewpoint comes under severe criticism by Donner, and for sound reasons. This concept denies that there is even a measure of historical fact in the early documents, stating that the material is largely an ahistorical junkyard with no meaning. Some of the more prominent recent scholars of this viewpoint include John Wansbrough, Michael Cook, Patricia Crone, and Suliman Bashear.[8] The Skeptical Approach essentially states that early Muslim believers placed a gloss on the Qur'anic material, practically from whole cloth, and then expanded this to include hadith literature. Although Donner does not use the term, he is implying that there had to be some form of massive ancient conspiracy to rid the Islamic world of any documents that might contradict the fabricated version of events.

What is most fascinating about the Skeptical Approach is that even in our so-called modern era, with our massive communications network that seemingly could help to destroy competing ideas, it has been proven impossible to invent whole stories without some form of serious critique offering competitive and contradictory information. Moreover, it would appear that those holding this viewpoint are in essence templating the modern era into the past. Since our current world has fallen victim to a host of falsehoods and hoaxes—among them that come readily to mind are some of the scandals that have rocked the scientific community such as Piltdown Man—it is assumed that such hoaxes were perpetrated in the past. Donner provides an excellent examination of the problems with this approach, and it would be best to refer the reader to his work for a more complete view.[9]

However, with that said, it would be worthwhile to examine the approach of one scholar in particular to demonstrate some of the problems when dealing with the early Islamic sources. While the late Albrecht Noth would be considered by many to reside within the Source-Critical Approach, his work carries with it a strong element of the Skeptical Approach. What Noth pioneered is an attempt to describe early Islamic writings under the heading of various themes, or overarching constructs that would delineate the development of the early source material. In many ways, the essence of Noth's argument is that early sources of Islam followed various themes, grouped together gradually over time by those who transmitted the information orally. With this in mind, let us allow Noth to speak for himself: "These documents, as we have them in the early compilations, can at most allow us to discern the faded outlines of the originals, barely perceptible after a long process of (most likely oral) transmission, in the course of which they have been subjected to all sorts of changes."[10] Having thus explained his key position, Noth proceeds to highlight the problem of literary forms, topoi, and schemata, all within the context of the various themes he had previously outlined. With this premise established, let us examine a few problems with each of these concepts that are often neglected when analyzing historical documents.

The first involves Noth's use of themes. A theme is a basic subject area around which various pieces of data are grouped. According to Noth, there are two basic types, primary and secondary. The first involves a set of subject matter that appears to be based on a "genuine topic of early interest." The second involves topics expropriated from material used in previous themes.[11] What does he mean by this? Regarding the secondary themes there is little to say here, for Noth summarily dismisses these out of hand, saying these are either embellishment or outright fiction. This does not mean that they do not represent an important aspect of later development within Islam, such as dealing with systems of dating and the development of law and governmental administration. Instead, he is simply saying that these secondary themes have little to no foundation in the early sources; thus, the outgrowth of any ideas from them is not based on early Islam.

As to the primary themes, Noth lends more credence. However, this does not help, for it would appear that on the basis of his quote noted earlier there is little to go on regarding the veracity of the early sources, even in the primary themes. His careful choice of words implies that the themes came first, and then various hadith were developed to match those themes, a contention to which scholars such as Donner do not largely concur. In contrast to Noth's almost universal skepticism, Donner approaches the notion of themes by indicating that people will recall what is important to them about different aspects of their cultural heritage, and will gradually organize such recollections into convenient categories, or themes.[12]

The distinction between the two views should not be dismissed lightly. A point that Donner raises is that life is loaded with themes, and that even the typical person's life can be grouped into themes of family, work, recreation, and intellectual and spiritual development. Just because one sees a system of themes in a culture does not necessarily mean that the historical data grouped by later analysts, arguably arbitrarily in many cases, is fictitious. Indeed, the notion of themes does nothing in determining whether a set of historical data is really legitimate or a fanciful fiction. As such, engaging in such an analysis provides us little real information about what can be accepted and what should be rejected in the data. While the use of themes helps us to organize the raw data and sort it for later analysis and use, it proves to be an inadequate tool for evaluating the validity of the sources.

The issue of literary forms is more problematic within Islam, at least on the surface, to scholars ensconced within academia but not exposed to the overall world at large.[13] Early Islamic sources have their origin almost exclusively within the oral tradition and as such are often rejected out of hand by some analysts. For example, Noth views any speeches recorded in early Islamic histories as "fictitious from beginning to end."[14] The key rationale inherent in such a view is that the typical person in our current era cannot remember five words in sequence let alone five sentences or a few paragraphs strung together. However, this does not mean others in a previous era devoid of television, radio, recorded music and speeches and inundated with the written word could not do this. Put more directly, just because Noth could not memorize the majority of what a person said does not mean a Bedouin tribesman in

Arabia in the seventh century could not. A few examples will suffice to demonstrate this point.

All of us remember the little exercise done by our teachers in elementary school, where the instructor would whisper a fairly long and complicated story into the ear of one student who would then pass the story down. At the end of the line, we would all listen in amazement at how garbled the story had become, proof positive that oral tradition is a poor means to communicate anything factual. But not so fast! First, the story was only uttered once by the teacher, with the expectation that an eight year old should memorize it out of hand. The catch here is that a typical child of today is not disciplined enough for initial lengthy memorization. The second problem with this method is that in almost all oral traditions, the stories were recited repetitively, a form of rote drill that achieves the same objective of rote drill in memorizing mathematical formulae. Demonstrative of this are two famous individuals from the days of World War II, George S. Patton Jr. and Erwin Rommel. As a child, Patton was read to constantly, and he absorbed the material he heard repetitively until he could recite entire chapters of the Bible and classical writers by heart.[15] In similar fashion, but in a different subject, Erwin Rommel memorized the entire logarithmic table, allowing him the ability to perform critical calculations without notes.[16] People can memorize lengthy amounts of material if they have developed the disciplined mind to do so, and if they hear the material repetitively.

Moreover, Noth's summary rejection of early Islamic speeches raises another problem. Should we now summarily toss out any speech allegedly uttered by other ancient personalities as recorded in the writings of the likes of Tacitus or Thucydides? It is a curious world of scholarship that accepts on the one hand the recorded musings of ancient Greek and Roman leaders brought forth by the pen of men who did not necessarily see the actual event, but on the other hand rejects forthwith a short speech made by a Muslim leader. Even if not remembered exactly word for word, could one accept the real possibility that the essential subjects raised in the speech were raised by the speaker in question? For some scholars on Islamic sources to overtly reject oral tradition opens a Pandora's box that can lapse into other fields of study, reducing the ancient source record to a world of mere fables.

The third area needing some discussion is that of the notion of topoi. Topoi (sing. topos) is the abbreviated form of a Greek literary phrase *topos koinos*, which means "commonplace."[17] In essence, topoi are commonplace phrases, constructs, or ideas that analysts see in historical writings, particularly ancient ones. Moreover, when classified as topoi, the analyst is implying that the data is largely invented for some reason, usually to teach some moral lesson or religious dogma. Donner is cautious regarding the classification of topoi, but Noth is excessive. To Noth, almost everything is a topoi, something that was probably invented to suit somebody's moral or religious bias and frame of mind. Thus, names are simply inserted into battle narratives because it is necessary to list the commanders in the action to emphasize a personality's heroic efforts. Or a person whose family is later famous in the Islamic community is credited with the capture of an important enemy, to establish a basis for why that family is now important. Or the emphasis is placed on feats of arms in battle, once more to accentuate the heroic aspect of a prominent family.[18] According to Noth, none of these are ultimately reliable because some hidden hand either invented the historical record or at least altered it, usually for some nefarious reason such as inflating the veterans' pension lists or to have a later event measure up to some previous feat of arms.[19]

One example Noth cites as a topos is the motif of Muslim armies placing mountains to their backs. The cases he cites are those involving operations during the post-Muhammad conquests, where Muslim armies used this technique in imitation of the Prophet. In this case, Noth displays a serious lapse regarding his knowledge of the military art and history. Using terrain features as psychological and physical obstacles and anchors in battle is a point well known to students of military history, and a point emphasized by such ancient military thinkers as Frontinus, Vegetius, and Polyaenus.[20] Noth simply states that the "reports which convey this information cannot be considered authentic."[21] In this case, he allows his ignorance of military theory, practice, and history to color his analysis and to summarily reject historical information. None of the points mentioned imply that topoi never show up in ancient writings, or for that matter even in modern ones. However, the tendency of some to summarily write off historical data as topoi does a disservice to historical research. Indeed, in large measure it makes such research pointless.

Finally, there is the issue of schemata. "Schemata" is simply a catch-all term to group concepts such as transitional formulae and pseudo-causes into a useful category.[22] The issue of transitional formulae will suffice to explain how far afield some have gone to dismiss early historical evidence. Noth noticed that there are plenty of examples in the early Islamic literature of transitional statements, repeated almost verbatim time and again, to offer transition from one concept to the next. As such, the early Islamic writers will say that a person will go to place A, then they will go to place B, and then finally go to place C. Noth criticizes this formula because it does not provide any notion of the passage of time and what caused certain events. In other words, the early sources do not explain to us the movements of people and armies in space and time. What is Noth's solution to this problem? He discards the information forthwith. Again, let us allow Noth to speak for himself: "Given their 'fast-forwarding' quality, the transitional formulae are incapable of depicting the temporal dimensions of events and developments. But if this is so, then they are equally devoid of reliable information about the origins and motives behind those events and developments. They tell us stories, but they tell us no history."[23] One of the items he cites regards the Muslim conquests of Sijistan and Khurasan, indicating that Muslim writers place the campaign within one year. Yet Noth fails to note that Alexander the Great conquered the same area in just over a year, and virtually the entire known world east of Greece in seven. Again, it is curious scholarship when a group of scholars accept the rapid conquests of Alexander but reject out of hand the possibility that an unlearned army of tribal people could perform similar feats of arms.[24] We shall later see that Muslim forces almost certainly did engage in the operations they are credited with, and within the timeframes offered in the early accounts.

It is worth noting that such methods of analysis are not used to examine modern history. For example, nobody would reject World War I German aviator Ernst Udet's claim that the famous French ace Georges Guynemer allowed him to live after a furious aerial action simply because the former's guns jammed.[25] Why not just pass this off to data created later to reflect the theme of chivalry that was now dying out in the world of modern battle? Or what of the deaths in aerial combat of the German flyer Werner Voss and the American pilot Wilbert White, both killed in separate actions on the very day they were to head home on leave?[26] Should we not pass that off as a topos, a commonplace notion that reflects the pathos we all feel regarding the losses incurred in war? One can see how techniques used to evaluate ancient sources could take modern events and turn them into mere myth.

While Donner is more credulous than Noth regarding the early sources, he still attempts to downplay various anecdotes in the historical record by referencing the concept of historicization. This notion postulates that while some accurate information may be included under a given theme, additional spurious or false material is placed there as well. While the concept is legitimate in generality, it becomes a tricky matter when one deals with actual situations. For example, Donner cites an incident related by the Islamic historian al-Tabari in which a few Muslim ambassadors, having arranged a meeting with the Persian emperor just prior to the Muslim invasion of Persia, are rebuffed by being given a load of earth to lay on the neck of the most noble of the representatives present. Intended as an insult, the Muslims would take this as a good omen for their future conquest. Donner's contention is that this account is most likely spurious, having been placed in the chronicle by someone because of its symbolism.[27] The problem here is that Donner is assuming, because of the symbolism, that the story is probably false. However, it is quite possible, and I dare say probable, that the incident actually occurred, and that it was seen as a symbolic moment after the Muslim conquest. In this context, part of Donner's contention is that too many events related in ancient documents are simply too miraculous to be authentic.[28]

And this brings us to the point that history is often more bizarre than fiction. Take, for example, another illustration from World War I aviation. In May of 1915, British captain Louis Strange pushed his Martinsyde S.1 to its maximum ceiling of 8,500 feet to engage a German two-seat reconnaissance plane over the French town of Menin. The German observer fired off a few shots with a pistol at Strange's aircraft, so Strange emptied the drum of his Lewis machine gun at the German plane. Unfortunately, this had no apparent effect, and because the Lewis gun was mounted above the top wing, Strange had to struggle to remove the drum to change it out. In the process, he lost control of his machine, with his aircraft flipping inverted and tossing him from his seat. Strange, who had no parachute, was saved by clinging to the very Lewis gun's ammunition drum he had just been struggling to disengage from the weapon. His plane went into an inverted spin, falling 5,000 feet as the British pilot dangled precariously, desperately struggling to get back into the cockpit. At last he was able to pull himself into his seat and regain control of his aircraft with just enough altitude to avoid the trees of the forest below.[29]

Should we accept such a bizarre incident as genuine? While Strange indicates that a German pilot claimed to have seen him completely thrown from the cockpit, and thus claiming an aerial victory, Strange is the only one to record this incident, and eighteen years after the fact. While unique and bizarre, the incident has the ring of truth, partly in the way in which Strange relates it, and partly from the fact that Strange does nothing to embellish his combat record, having claimed a solitary aircraft downed in late 1914. While this does not provide us with a perfectly scientific certainty as to the event, it offers us enough to conclude that the action probably did happen largely as he described. Having said this, we must wonder why historians dealing with more recent history readily accept such anecdotal claims as this but then quickly reject seemingly odd and improbable incidents as related in ancient history.

The problem demonstrated in the proceeding pages highlights the issue of not only credibility of early historical evidence but more tellingly the attitude of almost total solipsism of many modern analysts when they examine such material. It is one thing to have a healthy level of doubt regarding such material. It is wholly another to develop constructs to summarily reject material for whatever personal bias that individual may have. The process outlined here contrasts the difference between a historian and what Ludwig von Mises would call "historicism." In Mises' thinking, a historian is primarily tasked to examine past events and conditions, explaining key facts and their impact. In contrast, "Historicism is an epistemological doctrine";[30] that is, it is a quest to establish some type of new "truth" outside of the historical evidence. This is a trend engaged in by some scholars for the past two hundred years, a trend that has actually hampered balanced historical enquiry. As Donner noted, the foundation for the latter three approaches he outlined was largely based on the textual and form criticism approaches that scholars had developed over the last hundred years regarding Biblical sources, an approach largely pursued to alter the long-accepted views of the Bible as a source of religious truth.[31] Afterward, this method was used to assail other religious traditions.

With these thoughts in mind, are we possibly seeing examples in the critiques of some writers not only a religious bias but also forms of cultural and chronological chauvinism? Why are Western documents such as Tacitus' *Histories* or Caesar's *Gallic War* accepted largely at face value, but sources couched in religious constructs are so eagerly rejected out of hand? For example, Tacitus' *Histories* as handed to us today are based on a few manuscripts dated approximately 900 years after the time he allegedly wrote the work.[32] Caesar's *Gallic War* suffers from the same problem, being based on a few manuscripts dated 900 to 1,000 years after the fact.[33] Yet these are almost universally accepted as truly written by these individuals, and are even considered largely factual. Moreover, if they are the only source for an event, they are typically accepted as is. Why is such a benefit of the doubt not accorded to early Islamic sources? In contrast to these two Western classics, the materials of early Islamic sources date anywhere from 120 to 300 years after the events described, and these in *written* form handed down from the previous oral transmission since that time.[34]

This does not imply that ancient sources do not require scrutiny to examine them for error and contradictions. Indeed, it is fascinating that Noth claims that Muslim forces could not conquer a particular area in one year, yet he apparently never actually calculated the ability of armies to move, supply, and coordinate themselves in such an area. If his analysis of the *barid* system of postal riders is any indication, he has not done this. He grossly underestimated the ability of postal riders to maintain a system of rapid communication, despite the prime example that we have just in the last few hundred years in the Pony Express system in the United States. Pony Express riders could cover a 2,000-mile distance in as little as eight days while carrying twenty pounds of mail. This implies that the *barid* system could cover 625 miles in fewer than four days, and yet Noth claims that there simply was no possible way that the *khalifa* in Madinah could communicate so rapidly with his armies in al-Irak during the conquest of Persia.[35]

The proceeding has not been engaged in simply as a critique of Albrecht Noth's work but instead as an explanation of how some analysts of ancient writings have steered far afield in their efforts, for whatever motives, to discredit ancient sources. Noth does have his strengths, and when he has corroborating evidence, he does provide good analysis of some topoi.[36] Moreover, it is important to apply rigorous tests to determine what information is valid and what is not. However, such tests are not a matter of mere judgment, personal subjectivity, or the result of formulating new approaches to sources. Instead, they come from analyzing claims and determining validity on the basis of what could be accomplished in a real world. When studying military subjects, especially in ancient history, this requires an understanding of logistics, economics, military technique, and fundamental human nature. By simply rejecting the early sources, we lose a valuable collection of insightful material into the military world of a culture vastly different from that of the West.

This brings us to an examination of how I have approached the sources. Using Donner's categories as a point of origin, one could say that my approach has been largely Descriptive with a strong dose of the Source-Critical Approach. However, I have not engaged in the latter in the way that many Orientalists may. For example, scholars of Arabic and its associated fields of study focus largely on the language and then on the customs of the people. Instead, I have focused on customs of the people and factors of space and time. In this sense, I have approached the sources empirically rather than linguistically. When examining an operation, a string of raids, or the way the Prophet Muhammad organized his polity, the question is constantly asked, could these things happen in real space and time? Do we have examples and illustrations of incidents that corroborate such activities, even if from other cultures? Concurrently, efforts are made to analyze the logistical factors of the operations and compare them to the anecdotal sources to see if there is a correlation. If the early sources indicate that so many camels were used for transport, could these camels carry sufficient resources to keep an army supplied in the field? And if the information indicates that the logistics were weak, do the anecdotal accounts bear this out?

Due to my Descriptive Approach, I tend to accept the sources initially at face value unless other material demonstrates that there is a problem with those sources. The Source-Critical Approach then allows for an examination of the evidence and any corroboration from other sources, which is certainly a far cry from the Skeptical or even Tradition-Critical Approaches. Neither of these two approaches can stand up to scrutiny in the end and, therefore, should be rejected. After all, if one accepts either of these viewpoints, why bother to continue studying ancient historical material of any type, let alone Islamic?[37] Within the context of starting from the sources largely accepted as genuine within the Islamic movement, I depart from the approaches outlined by Donner by accepting the received collections of hadith literature, particularly regarding the military campaigns and operations. This naturally places my approach in contrast to the Tradition-Critical Approach, which sees much of the hadith literature as late-date forgeries. The reason for my acceptance is both internal and based on the logistical analysis of the events. In this context, forgeries would not have been able to match anecdotal recollections to the realities of the logistics involved.

Besides the aforementioned logistic issues, there are concepts related within the early sources that imply authenticity. For example, why would the resistance in Makkah, and even Madinah, be highlighted rather than glossed over? After all, both cities became the base for the Islamic movement. Would it not make sense, if the material was simply created out of whole cloth, to highlight Muhammad's acceptance and not discuss resistance at all? And as for battles, why would we see Muhammad and his followers endure such troubles and trials? If forged, Muhammad would not have been surprised at Badr, and Uhud would have been transformed into a victory. Makkah would not have been conquered by the Prophet, but he would have instead merely returned to the acclamation of the people. Instances where Muslims were ambushed and defeated would have been glossed over or disappeared altogether. The assassination plot against Kʿab bin al-Ashraf would have gone smoothly, with only one man killing him instead of three struggling to do so. Al-Abbas, the Prophet's uncle, would be transformed into a full-fledged believer from the start, not a seeming latecomer to the Prophet's cause. Moreover, any evidence of Muslims complaining about Muhammad's gentleness with al-Abbas would have been excised from the record.

Naturally, those who take the Skeptical Approach would state that all of these instances are elements of the mythos that was developed to justify certain portions of Qur'anic verse. But could one just as easily say that the incidents were real and that the Qur'anic verses were recited to reflect what actually happened? This does not mean I accept the early sources without reservations or critique, but I allow the corpus of literature, in lieu of having other sources available, to be self-critical. When contradictions do occur within this source material, these are explained if they have bearing on the operations analyzed.

Among the specific sources employed, it is important to discuss the value of a few of these and the nature of their organization. Foremost, it is important to note that the sources used follow the Sunni tradition of Islam, with only a few references made to Shi'ite sources, because the Sunni interpretation predominates within Islam and these sources are more readily accessible. Ibn Ishaq's *sira*, reconstructed by

Guillaume, is a valuable asset. However, it should not be taken alone, as there are a number of hadith passages and events that are not included in his work. Moreover, in doing the reconstruction, Guillaume at times failed to maintain proper sequencing, placing some events obviously out of order or in limbo. Nevertheless, one cannot pursue an examination of Muhammad's life without referencing Ibn Ishaq. Regarding Ibn Hisham's recension of Ibn Ishaq's work, I have chosen to only reference passages that Ibn Kathir uses in his *sira* when they supplement material from other sources. Otherwise, Ibn Hisham either simply repeats Ibn Ishaq or, worse, removes important material.

As for al-Waqidi, a number of analysts have indicted him for problems in his writings, and this has been carried forth to his scribe and disciple Ibn Saʿd. Yet to not consult either of these sources is to miss a vast amount of material on the Prophet's military life that others simply do not discuss. Another good supplemental work is the massive historical effort of al-Tabari. This work has been edited and translated, and for reference purposes I have used the Leiden manuscript's pagination retained in the multivolume collection published by the State University of New York. As a consequence, I have dispensed with the cumbersome listing of each separate volume of the work. Al-Tabari adds valuable information from obscure or lost sources that shed additional light on what others wrote.

Overall, I have chosen to follow Ibn Ishaq's organization and chronology, turning to Ibn Saʿd, al-Waqidi, Ibn Kathir, al-Tabari, and the accepted hadith literature for added material of relevance. I have also turned to resources of the classical and medieval period of Islam to provide additional insights and concepts thinly discussed by the primary sources. In doing this, my attempt is to offer a comprehensive analysis of Muhammad's military life and his use of asymmetric and symmetric principles in his campaigns. And since my work is an analysis of Muhammad's military acts, there are naturally some aspects of the Prophet's life that are overlooked as being irrelevant to the text. I would refer the reader to Ibn Ishaq for the most complete single source to know and understand Muhammad's life and to gain insight about these peripheral incidents.

Regarding the organization of the hadith sources, the hadith literature has different standards for indexing. Al-Bukhari's materials are largely standardized, but others, such as Imam Muslim, have differing systems for organization. This may cause some minor confusion to some but overall should not present any serious difficulty. Additional hadith sources, such as an-Nasa'i and al-Tirmidhi, have only recently been published in English editions, which will probably set the standard for their indexing in any future editions. As for referencing, al-Bukhari's collection was examined first, with supplemental material taken from the other collections as necessary. This would conform to the standards established by traditional usage within Sunni Islam regarding the veracity of the *sahih* hadith collections.

The Qur'an has only been referenced sparingly because it is not the best source regarding the life of Muhammad but is instead more of a devotional text meant to be chanted as a part of worship. As such, it has passages that are incredibly cryptic, even to those who are native readers of ancient Arabic. However, the Tafsir, or commentary, of Ibn Kathir sheds tremendous light on such passages, as does the collection of hadith literature, and these provided additional historical information to highlight critical situations.

We now come to the problem of technical terms. Arabic, particularly the ancient dialect, has some unique and tricky aspects to it that lead to interesting results when texts are translated. For example, some texts vary in calling Muhammad apostle, messenger, or prophet. I have chosen to use the latter consistently throughout unless quoting a passage from a translated source that uses one of the other terms.[38] Readers should not let this confuse them but simply make the mental transference as necessary. I have also chosen to leave out many diacritical marks for the sake of textual simplicity, and leave in those only if necessary to differentiate words that translate in like manner. This, of course, can create some confusion with specialists, and with this in mind there is a technical lexicon at the end of the book to help the reader with these terms.

When using the plural of an Arabic term, I have chosen to anglicize it rather than using the Arabic form. The rationale for this is simple. I wrote this book for the reader of military history and not for specialists among Orientalists. For example, the plural of "*sunnah*" is "*sunan*," but if referencing "*sunnah*" in plural, I write "*sunnahs*." While this is obviously not technically correct, it is easier for the reader not versed in Arabic to readily identify the terms. I have also chosen to consistently use "bin," rather than "ibn," when listing a person's name. The term simply references that someone is the son of another, a concept still in use in the Arabic world. Thus, 'Ali bin Abu Talib translates as 'Ali, the son of Abu Talib. The only time "ibn" is used is when it is in quoted text or part of a widely accepted name usage, such as Ibn Ishaq. "Bint" is used to reference a woman in the same fashion.

The nature of Arabic grammar dictates that when the word "Abu," which means father, such as in the names ʿAli bin Abu Talib or Saʿd bin Abu Waqqas, is preceded by another word it is changed to "Abi." However, so as not to engender confusion, I have chosen to leave the word as "Abu" throughout the text, unless found differently in quoted material. In addition, I have chosen to follow more recent Muslim practice of calling such cities as Mecca, "Makkah," and Medina, "Madinah," contrary to the practice of Orientalists. In like manner, I use the term "Allah" to reference the god of Islam and not "God," as do the Orientalists. Some noted lexicographers state that "Allah" is a proper name and thus should not be translated, a practice followed by most Muslims in their works.[39] I have chosen to follow their standard of practice rather than that of Orientalists. I have only referenced Allah as "God" when quoting works translated by Orientalists, such as Guillaume's translation of Ibn Ishaq.

Another issue that can confuse the reader of Islamic history involves the dating scheme. Islamic cultures, much like the Christianized West begins the dating of events with a seminal event in their history—in the case of Islam, the migration of the Prophet Muhammad from Makkah to Madinah. However, to reduce confusion I have decided to follow the dating scheme of Fazlur Rehman Shaikh in his book *Chronology of Prophetic Events* to render these dates into the Western format. This scheme does differ some with traditional dates accepted by Orientalists, but the latter is dated and Rehman Shaikh's research more recent and comprehensive. I also realize that there is much historical and current discussion as to the exact dates of various events, and that even the chronology of events is still being questioned. However, readers should not let the problems of dating and chronology cause alarm, for the purpose of this book is to analyze Muhammad's techniques and generalship in light of the historical events rather than engage in contentious debate about the exact date of a particular battle. Naturally, this can become an issue when the time of year would impact the weather, but I believe readers will find these issues addressed adequately in the text.

In consideration of the controversy that revolves around some aspects of Islam largely due to recent historical events, some have attempted to label Islamic aspects of warfare, such as jihad, to be irrational and devoid of reasoned judgment. This is a hasty and inaccurate portrayal. These critics merely assume that if one appears to be emotive in their premises, that they are thus unable to make rational decisions based on such emotions. Yet even the rational can begin with an emotive premise, and to simply dismiss the ideas and decisions that come from such a process is to fail to understand why a particular group of people act as they do. Instead, it is critical to understand the foundational ideas that generate the actions of others, even if emotional, and to see how they can make step-by-step logical assessments that lead to a particular course of action. In light of recent Islamic revival movements, it is incumbent on all to examine and ascertain why such groups behave as they do. While the primary goal of this book is to provide the most in-depth discussion yet accomplished of the Prophet's campaigns, it has also been written partly so that the student of military history can understand how a warrior for Islam thinks and acts.

Lastly, I wish to offer thanks to a few individuals who helped to make this project happen. Charles E. White provided constant encouragement and ideas that helped develop the project and focus on unique aspects of Muhammad's campaigns. David Cook offered some excellent insights to help clarify problems that he identified in the manuscript. A very critical reviewer helped by highlighting a few serious holes in the argument that needed to be refined; while seemingly harsh on the surface, some of these comments were the most useful and enlightening. I also need to thank my wife, Alina, for her patience as she endured long months of being a "research widow." Finally, there are many individuals who provided little pieces of advice and counsel that all added up to be a large piece of support and help in evaluating the sources, seeking out additional ones, and placing everything into perspective. To all of these people I owe a tremendous debt of gratitude. Nevertheless, as always, any omissions and errors are my own.

1

Revolution

Muhammad's life did not start out remarkably. He was born in the Hashim clan of the Quraysh, the leading tribe that controlled Makkah. However, the Hashim clan had fallen on hard times and was in decline.[1] This was exacerbated by Muhammad's own immediate circumstances, for his father died around the time he was born and his mother died six years later. His father hailed from Makkah, and his mother, via previous generations, from Madinah. Due to the latter, the young lad was taken by his widowed mother at times to visit his maternal relatives. When Muhammad's mother died, his grandfather, ʿAbd al-Muttalib, took charge of the orphaned boy to ensure he was raised in Makkah. Thus, Muhammad had a foot in two worlds, and both would play a significant role in his life.

His tutelage under his grandfather would last but two years. With ʿAbd al-Muttalib's death, Muhammad was taken under the wing of his paternal uncle, Abu Talib, to be raised as one of his own. However, while Muhammad was certainly cared for, his future looked bleak. He was an orphaned child now cared for by an uncle who himself had sons. Therefore, Muhammad could lay no legitimate claim to any inheritance because the lion's share of such would typically go to the eldest natural-born son. Abu Talib's two sons, Jaʿfar bin Abu Talib and ʿAli bin Abu Talib, would have priority of any inheritance and family blessing, leaving little for their cousin.

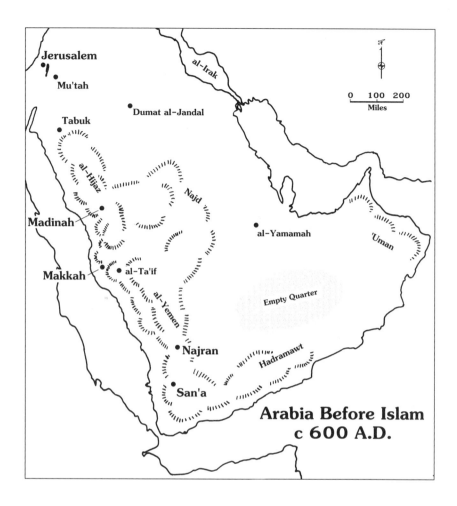

Jerusalem

Mu'tah

al-Irak

Tabuk

Dumat al-Jandal

0   100   200
Miles

al-Hijaz

Najd

Madinah

al-Yamamah

'Uman

Makkah

al-Ta'if

al-Yemen

Empty Quarter

Najran

Hadramawt

San'a

**Arabia Before Islam
c 600 A.D.**

This did not mean that Abu Talib did not teach important lessons to his adopted child, for the early evidence indicates that Muhammad was taught the merchant's vocation. He learned to ply the trade routes northward to Syria and certainly traveled to the various trade fairs in the region. If we are to accept the early evidence at face value, Muhammad gained a reputation for shrewd but honest bargaining.[2] His reputation became sufficiently well known that he even began to act as a small banker for a number of the Quraysh in Makkah.[3] As both a merchant and banker, Muhammad developed significant contacts, but these appear to be largely confined to the area of Makkah because people of the surrounding tribes did not know who he was once he announced his prophetic calling.[4] His contact and support base was therefore primarily local to Makkah, yet still retaining familial ties to Madinah.

Muhammad's slow mercantile rise within Qurayshi circles mirrored the apparent gradual decline of the propertied *shaykhs*. The tribal *shaykhs* were local and regional leaders who established law and order and served as the judges of disputes. Their power was largely based on landed wealth, making them property rich but cash poor. One of their roles was that of the dispenser of welfare within their tribe, and this welfare was usually disbursed in kind rather than in any type of monetary instrument. But, as Makkah began to rise in importance as a waypoint for mercantile trade along the western caravan route, the authority of the *shaykhs* became subject to challenge.

It has largely been accepted as an established fact that the Quraysh were great traders of western Arabia who controlled the trade route between the eastern Byzantine Empire and the riches of the east.[5] This interpretation has been effectively challenged by some, but this does not diminish the role of Makkah.[6] Instead, it actually highlights more effectively what was probably taking place. The ascendancy of Islam in Arabia as a Qurayshi-dominated religious creed has possibly led to the influx of information that emphasized their trade while ignoring that of others. What we do know is that Qurayshi trade was largely regional, and that they were probably not the purveyors of eastern riches to expectant Byzantine markets. However, the fact that they were respected for maintaining law and order at various trade fairs indicates that they may have had a significantly different role than what has been portrayed by some.[7] While being small traders themselves, the Quraysh may have gained a reputation as the guardians of caravans for others, such as the Yemenis from the south, a point attested to by some during the fairs.[8] This would help to explain their significance while being consistent with what evidence we have regarding their trade.

Makkah and the Quraysh found themselves at an interesting crossroads between the Byzantines and the Sasanid Persians. For several centuries both empires had engaged in intermittent conflict along their nebulous frontiers, thereby disrupting life and trade in the lands between the two powers. Most of this fighting took place in northern Arabia, Syria, and Armenia. However, both powers became increasingly interested in southern Arabia, partly due to efforts by merchants to continue trading despite the disruption caused by ongoing wars. While such eastern trade was not the staple of the Byzantine Empire, it was

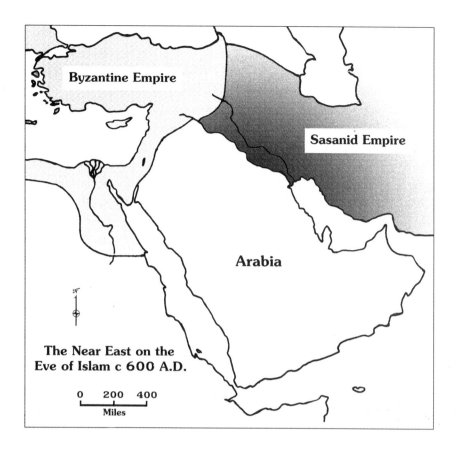

The Near East on the
Eve of Islam c 600 A.D.

0   200   400
Miles

of some interest, and merchants sought ways to avoid the dangers of war and the high cost of tariffs imposed by local nobles, not to mention issued orders from Byzantine officials that such trade should cease. It would appear that they found this route by going through southern Arabia.[9]

The Persian nobles, in an effort to control what they may have regarded as illicit trade—that is, trade that circumvented their imposed tariffs—and spurred on by the decision of the Byzantine Emperor Justin to cease tribute payments, decided to invade Yemen around 572, only two years after the traditional birth date of Muhammad.[10] Prior to this, the Abyssinians had conquered the region, and now the small army of invading Persians destroyed the occupying Abyssinian force and took control of the territory.[11] This placed them in an ideal position to control both the Red Sea and the western caravan trade routes, and to impose tariffs or blockade these routes altogether. However, as a sidelight of the greater Byzantine-Persian conflict, the occupation of Yemen languished as the Persians found themselves under intense pressure from renewed Byzantine operations. By 591, the Byzantines had helped Khusrau II, deposed son of the Persian emperor, seize the throne and, as the price for victory, imposed an exacting toll upon the Persians—the surrender of the disputed lands of Armenia.[12]

When Heraclius seized the reins of the Byzantine Empire in 610, the Persians would dispute his claim to the throne and engage in a massive offensive into Syria, Anatolia, and Egypt, marching to within a mile of Constantinople. The Persian conquests were so significant that it supposedly influenced one of the Qur'anic recitations.[13] By a brilliant ruse and employing an indirect approach, Heraclius sailed from Constantinople in 614, and landed on the coast of Syria to invade the hinterlands of the Persian army then camped on the doorstep of his throne.

The combination of internal turmoil and external conflict meant that the Persians in Yemen withered on the vine. Intermarrying with Yemeni women, they settled in the territory and developed the government and trade of the region. By the time Muhammad had declared his prophethood, these Persian soldiers and their descendants in Yemen had become known as the 'Abna, who would play an interesting and largely unexamined role in the Riddah, or Apostates War, after Muhammad's death.[14] The 'Abna seemingly regulated the southern portion of the western caravan trade route but, with less control from Persia, probably decided that flourishing trade was far more in their interest than the vagaries of imperial politics. As a result, the trade routes began to expand, which led to the rise of the merchant class in western Arabia and Makkah.

Because the tribal *shaykhs* were cash poor, their only influence over the people of their tribes was through general consensus upheld by tradition and the in-kind largess they lavished upon their people. The growing wealth of merchants meant that these traders could break free of the politics and social strictures of the *shaykhs* and chart their own course, capable of buying virtually anything they needed to support them in their endeavors. As a consequence, the more wealthy merchants began to build their own small fortifications that were separate from their tribal kinsmen, employed small bands of men as retainers to protect their lives and property, and used their wealth to ignore selected decisions coming from the body of tribal leaders. Makkah was governed by a tribal council called the *mala'*, in which the *shaykhs* held sway.[15] However, they had little power to force any clan of the Quraysh to accept a decision, and this lack of authority trickled down to the merchants, who rose like a phoenix in the towns to demand a level of independence unheard of in Arabian life.

Most Arabian municipalities were a series of small fortified communities interlocked by regional self-interest. While these small communities, not much larger than a modern suburban block, were walled with limited means of ingress and egress, few towns and cities in Arabia had a single fortified wall encompassing the totality of the residents.[16] Although without an outer wall, the towns and cities still represented a measure of unity in a given region due to some common interest. Some merchants challenged this approach and began to build small castles on the outside of the towns and cities, asserting their independence not only economically but physically as well. This was a direct challenge to the traditional authority of the *shaykhs*. When Muhammad was a young man, he was able to witness and participate in some of events that were generated by the conflicts between propertied and moneyed classes. The question must be asked: on which side was Muhammad?

Muhammad's state of affairs must be recalled. He was an orphaned son raised by an uncle from a clan that was apparently in decline. By all measures of traditional Qurayshi or Arabian life, Muhammad's future was bleak. Nevertheless, by the time he was twenty-five years old, he had at least gained some status as a merchant, although he was still unmarried and without a son, both issues that were of critical importance to enhance one's stature in the community. This naturally placed a considerable stress on his life as he struggled to choose between the individualism of the merchant class and the collectivism of the tribe. Two issues can illustrate this conflict.

Muhammad's circumstances clearly highlight that he had difficulty with the traditional concept of inheritance.[17] Since the eldest son received the lion's share of the family wealth, it meant that Muhammad, an adopted orphan, had no claim to any inheritance at all, relegating him to obscurity and relative poverty within the clan. For this reason he would individually empathize with those of like circumstance, desirous to change the customary means of allotments. Yet in contrast, he obviously liked and accepted the traditional concept of tribal welfare, along with the largess that was distributed by the *shaykhs* to their people as a means of wealth redistribution and collective social control.[18] The merchants, in their push for independence, were neglecting the perceived role of spreading their rising wealth to others, and this was indeed one of Muhammad's primary criticisms of them in the early days of his prophetic ministry.[19] But while he criticized what he viewed as the stinginess of the merchants, he did not demand that they at this early stage endorse the collective notion of the worship of Allah alone, and for several years there was some acceptance of his message among the Quraysh.[20] These two issues of inheritance and welfare largess offer examples of how Muhammad approached the tension between individual and collective prerogatives. While he sided with individuals in cases where he felt personal empathy, he tended to lean toward demands regarding a more collective outcome.

The world of the Quraysh had developed over several hundred years until they had gained control of Makkah and its important religious shrine, the *ka'bah*. Tradition had it that Adam had built the *ka'bah* and then implanted into its eastern corner the *hajaru al-aswad*, or black stone that had been thrown from heaven to land at his feet. The Noahic flood destroyed the *ka'bah*, and it was subsequently rebuilt by Abraham and his son Ishmael. It was supposed to be, according to the traditions, an exact replica of the one in paradise, and positioned exactly beneath its location as well.[21] The *ka'bah*, as important as it was, was not without competitors. Another shrine, apparently calling itself *ka'bah*, had been built in Najran in Yemen, to the south of Makkah, while the Christian Abyssinians who later conquered Yemen built a church there to draw pilgrims away from Makkah.[22] A well-respected and time-honored religious shrine meant economic activity; thus, competitors to the *ka'bah* in Makkah meant a loss of economic status and wealth, a point not to be forgotten in the context of Muhammad's later message and his focus on the *ka'bah* of Makkah.

With the shrine came responsibilities and privileges that were to be shouldered by selected groups in Makkah. After some internecine struggles, the Qusay clan of the Quraysh seized control of the five offices that had developed connected to the care and maintenance of the *ka'bah*, and the pilgrims that came with it. These responsibilities also entailed privilege, another point critical to Muhammad's mission. The offices involved holding the keys to the *ka'bah*; exercising authority over governing assemblies; handing out war banners, or *liwa'*; watering the pilgrims from the sacred well of Zamzam, or *siqayah*; feeding these pilgrims, or *rifadah*.[23] Of these offices, only one involved the direct contribution of money, or a tax, to a treasury, that being the *rifadah*.

The *rifadah* was in essence a property tax paid by key members of the Quraysh to Qusay and his descendants.[24] The importance of this tax cannot be understated, for it was for all intents and purposes the only tax levied on the Quraysh on property and paid in kind to provide food for destitute pilgrims. In other words, the ones who primarily paid this tax were the landed *shaykhs*. While there is marginal evidence that the merchants paid some other type of tax, this is only inferred because there are no specifics.[25] This would imply that if merchants ever did contribute money to the treasury, it was done on a voluntary basis. Makkah itself had no agriculture, which meant that the landed *shaykhs* drew their payments from other sources, such as sales and rents on land they owned in either Makkah or the resort city of al-Ta'if, or fees they charged merchants and pilgrims to use facilities in the city.[26] As a property tax, the *rifadah* was regressive, meaning that as the wealth of individuals grew, the tax often did not. Thus, over time, the wealth of the *shaykhs* used for largess shrank in comparison to the wealth gained by individual merchants.

In addition, the right to water and feed pilgrims implied something more than just caring for those who were destitute, for it is only logical that the Quraysh were not going to feed the throngs of pilgrims for free. Therefore, the control of the *siqayah* and *rifadah* seems to indicate that the clan who controlled these offices had a government-granted monopoly to sell water and food to pilgrims. This meant not only a large influx of outside wealth to this clan but also the power to distribute some of it as they saw fit to garner support in Makkah and perhaps beyond. While modern analogies can be risky, the best one that can be made would be to compare a suburbanite with a small farmer. The suburbanite, on the one hand, lives off an income earning job and obtains his necessities through local stores. The small farmer, on the other hand, develops most of his necessities from his land and works with a group of employees that live as clients on or near his property. Of the two, only the latter pays taxes, while the former, save for any indirect taxes that may come his way from his shopping activities, pays none. The stress that would develop between these two groups would be obvious.

Thus, one particular landed group was the recipient of the benefits of tax collection and monopolistic sales associated with the *rifadah* during the pilgrimages. By the time Muhammad was a young man, Makkah was beginning to feel the strain of one group believing they were overtaxed and cut out of the wealth generated by such a monopoly, with growing animosity against another group they thought was escaping largely unscathed regarding such exactions. To compound this strain, a third group was living off the revenues of this taxation and their monopoly sales. In essence, there was the rising tension between taxed property owners, nontaxed merchants, and a noble but relatively unproductive bureaucracy with exclusive rights to easy wealth.

The tension within Makkah had boiled over several times in the past to open warfare. When Qusay died around AD 470, he left the five offices to one of his sons, ʿAbd al-Dar, even though he was neither the eldest nor most talented. His two brothers, ʿAbd al-Manaf and ʿAbd al-Uzza, certainly looked upon this state of affairs with jealously, for ʿAbd al-Dar's clan now controlled the key source of tax revenue and enjoyed the monopolistic privileges during the pilgrimages. It did not take long for the families of the excluded brothers to organize against this situation. Around AD 500, the families of ʿAbd al-Manaf and ʿAbd al-Uzza, along with a collection of allies from other clans excluded from power, embarked in an effort to overthrow the clan of ʿAbd al-Dar to seize the offices for themselves. The sons of ʿAbd al-Manaf—ʿAbd al-Shams, Hashim, Naufal, and al-Muttalib—took the lead in this movement, pledging their loyalty to one another by dipping their hands into a bowl of perfume. These "Scented Ones" were the revolutionaries against the "Confederates" who organized to defend the inherited rights of the ʿAbd al-Dar. These groups managed to create a state of near open warfare in the city. This compelled a general popular consensus that some agreement had to be reached before swords were drawn, and the clan of ʿAbd al-Dar, apparently finding their confederation too weak, surrendered the most important offices, that of watering the pilgrims and providing them food. As a consequence, the *rifadah* tax and the monopolistic rights during the pilgrimages shifted to one of the sons of ʿAbd al-Manaf, al-Muttalib. This right would be passed down into the Hashim family through ʿAbd al-Muttalib, and then to Muhammad's uncle al-Abbas (see figure 1.1).

Caught in the middle of this ongoing tension were the average workers, clients of others who, for all intents and purposes, were little more than serfs. Arabian life had in essence three social classes. There were the propertied *shaykhs* who represented the nobility, and the moneyed merchant middle class who used their liquid assets to finance and bankroll select people who received their favor. After these two groups were

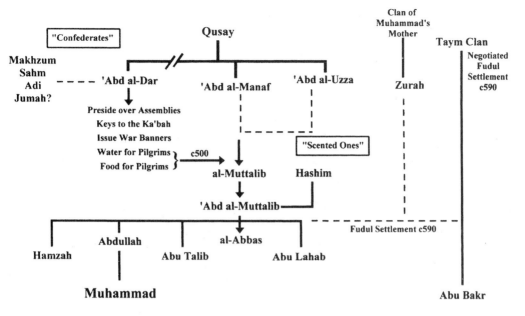

The Revolution of the Scented Ones. Power shift in Makkah, c. AD 500–590.

those without land or money, who lived day to day as indentured employees to their masters. While the term "slave" might be preferred by some, there is a significant difference between a *mawla*, or client, and a slave. Some *mawlas* were actually freed slaves but had retained their social and economic ties to their former masters. Having no property or wealth, they had nowhere to go and little chance for upward mobility. Socially, slaves were much worse off than *mawlas*, for at least the latter could do some independent traveling and attempt to earn additional money from side jobs if time permitted. While some sources describe *mawlas* as non-Arabs, it is apparent from the nature of contracts made that this was not always the case.[27] Conversely, slavery was connotative of either non-Arabs or blacks, and early traditions, possibly even before Islam, indicated that no Arab could be enslaved.[28] This discussion of the status of clients, or day-workers, is important in understanding Muhammad's message and strategy. In the early years in Makkah, he apparently strove to secretly reach selected financial moneyed individuals while he openly preached to reach the *mawlas* who were employed as laborers by the propertied elite. Caught in the middle and the principle target of his criticisms were most middle-class merchants. While it could be argued by some that these generalities are too simplistic, and that exceptions invalidate the rule, it can also be argued that modern interpretations of class warfare in Marxian terms demonstrate the same weaknesses. While there certainly were exceptions, the evidence available suggests a growing level of class conflict within Makkah, a class conflict that could be exploited for the particular benefit of any group with the wherewithal to organize and use it. Moreover, productivity was relatively low, which meant that the margin between mere subsistence and abject poverty was slim. Any tax, no matter how small, could be seen as a serious burden, and this was made even more offensive by the special monopoly rights enjoyed by one small group primarily for their own benefit, for such a monopoly would naturally drive up prices. For the *mawlas*, scratching to make ends meet daily and supplementing this with the welfare largess of their landed *shaykhs*, it had to be galling to see a small but growing element developing moneyed wealth that gave them a standard of living beyond the norm, yet they paid next to nothing to the public weal to help out those who were struggling. Moreover, some *shaykhs* would be irritated by the taxes because it took in-kind wealth out of their hands and allowed a bureaucracy to do the distribution, thus granting the latter the favor of the recipients. Within Arabia it was generally considered essential to be seen as generous with others if one was to have the status of *shaykh*, and to lose some of this to a central bureaucracy, no matter how small in relative terms, meant a significant loss of prestige.[29]

Another aspect of governance within Arabia that should be understood is that regarding crime and punishment. While not having what many would consider the refined justice system of present-day cultures, tribes in Arabia had a system of maintaining law and order that was reasonably effective. This revolved around the principles of *lex talionis*, bloodwit, and the blood feud. These three tiers interlaced to create a deterrent against crime, at least crime that was not sanctioned by tribal leaders, as Arabia was renowned for the *razzia*, or tribal raid. Within Arabic culture the principle of bravery in battle was highly prized, and the *razzia* served as an outlet for such urges in what one called Arabia's national sport.[30] Moreover, these raids served to assist tribes in redistributing some wealth from one group to another. It also allowed individual warriors to exhibit shrewdness and courage in what could be best described as low-intensity simulated warfare, for it was rare that any were killed in such raids.

If deaths occurred in *razzias*, then the three-tiered system of justice came into play. The *lex talionis* allowed the offended tribe to demand a life for life, limb for limb, and eye for eye.[31] While this smacks of reciprocity, negotiations were not always even, especially if the offended tribe was weak. Nevertheless, if the tribe that conducted the raid did not want to engage in a wider war, they would negotiate a settlement to pay the bloodwit. The bloodwit, or *diya* in Arabic, was a payment, typically in kind such as goats, sheep, camels, or horses, although payment in horses was very rare due to their scarcity, to provide recompense for a human life that was taken during the raid.[32] But if the offended tribe refused to pay the bloodwit, it could easily lead to a blood feud, in which the offended tribe would wage war until satisfied.

This system of justice has led many observers to conclude that Arabia was a land of violence and bloodshed, especially in the days of *jahiliyah*, or ignorance prior to Islam, for it is tempting to template present-day notions of law and justice as the norm and all other systems as barbaric.[33] While there were periods of time when this was true, it would seem that this was not the case just prior to Muhammad announcing his prophetic calling. Rather than accept simplistic statements from many Islamic sources, it is far better to use examples that demonstrate that Arabia—or at least its western half—had settled into a form of a legalistic balance of power. Some of these examples will be examined in more detail later when placed in their appropriate context regarding Muhammad's military operations, but it is necessary to review a few here.

The most obvious piece of information that western Arabia had become far more settled than is often admitted can be found in the minimum deployment of guards for a caravan at Nakhlah, just east of Makkah. When this caravan was surprised by Muhammad's men, it was guarded by only four men, despite its apparent value.[34] That a caravan going into Makkah should be so poorly guarded is indicative of the improving level of order in the region. While some may argue that other caravans had several hundred guards, it should be noted that this was after Muhammad's *hijrah*, or migration, to Madinah and after indications that he intended to raid such caravans. Often overlooked is that guards cost money, both in pay and maintenance, and therefore to use an excessive number of guards well beyond what was needed would eat away at the profits to be gained in the caravan. It would seem more indicative that the caravan at Nakhlah, at that time believed to be safe and a considerable distance from Muhammad's raiders, was more representative of the level of protection offered to caravans prior to the beginning of Muhammad's raids.

Another point that demonstrates the growing level of peace and stability in Arabia is the dearth of raids inflicted on the Muslims by other tribes. While the Muslims were based in Madinah, there were only a few attempts at raiding them, and these were generally feeble. In only one did the raiders escape, but the wealth seized was minimal. If *razzias* were the common order of the day, one would expect to see the Muslims suffering extensive raids against their own flocks and herds just as they inflicted on others. Moreover, one would expect to see the Quraysh of Makkah, the most offended tribe regarding Muslim raids, to have responded with a vengeance. Instead, it will be demonstrated later that the Qurayshi response was lackadaisical at best, while the Muslims would engage in a form of raiding warfare far beyond what other tribes were familiar, and thus outside of the norm of the day.

An additional item that demonstrates this increasing stability was the nature of Muhammad's special operations against other tribes, and the fact that those who were victimized by such raids were caught so unprepared. Whether the targets were poets or tribal leaders, special operatives from the Muslims would infiltrate and kill opponents almost at will. Moreover, the responses of both the victims and those around them, which will be examined in more detail later, indicate that such assassinations were outside of their own experience. The nature of these responses demonstrates the novelty of Muhammad's approach in engaging in such special operations. Had *razzias* and other forms of violence been the norm, those victimized by the Prophet's special operations would not have been so surprised or upset by these tactics. These examples will suffice for the moment to illustrate that western Arabia was not the land of violence and mayhem often assumed by many commentators.

Another point of conflict would revolve around the status of *shaykhs* and prophets. *Shaykhs* had some specific criteria that defined them and were usually limited to the clans and tribes they represented. Moreover, their claim to authority had little to do with forcefulness of command but, as noted previously, revolved around their wealth.[35] But a claim to prophethood presented a different challenge. A prophet could represent a single lesser deity or idol and thus be limited in scope much like a *shaykh*. Naturally, a clan or tribe that followed a particular god would not be interested in the competing claims of a prophet from another group representing a mere contender of an equal or lesser status. However, Muhammad's claim was beyond this, for he proclaimed that he was the Prophet of Allah, who was implicitly understood to be the highest of the gods in western Arabia. While his claim was initially limited to the Quraysh, it is clear in the early sources that he soon expanded this claim well beyond the limits of Makkah.[36]

With this in mind, a prophet of this stature could become a powerful tool or weapon in the hands of *shaykhs* and moneyed men who wished to expand their influence to other tribes. Such expansion would involve the collection of additional revenues that such powerful men could then use to enhance their prestige through distribution to the needy. It would appear that this was the reason key men of the Hashim clan supported Muhammad, seeing in him an instrument to revive their clan's flagging fortunes and give them the status they needed to control Makkah—and possibly beyond.[37] This could also have served as a key reason why some propertied *shaykhs* were encouraged to support Muhammad early on in competition to others who might try to gain his support.[38] This would fit well with Muhammad's prophetic call. While the problems of his family lineage could prevent him from being a *shaykh*, the prophetic calling from Allah would give him a scope of influence beyond that of a local tribal leader.

It is not necessary to recount how Muhammad became the Prophet of Allah, or to discuss every aspect of his ministry. However, some important points of his calling that influenced his later choices as a military leader should be noted. Early traditions generally agree that he was forty years old when he received his vision of the angel Jibril, Arabic for Gabriel, in a mountain cave above Makkah. This placed it around December 609.[39] A few observations are important at this point. The fact that Muhammad was able to spend significant time in the cave of Hira' above Makkah indicates that at this phase in his life he had attained sufficient wealth to be able to spend large amounts of time in what could be described by some as nonproductive activity. He had done this largely by marrying a wealthy widow, Khadijah, who had a mercantile business inherited from her late husband. Her wealth allowed Muhammad the free time to engage in these leisure activities and still be able to eat and pay his rent or mortgage. Khadijah was forty years old when Muhammad married her, but he was twenty-five.

This reverse age disparity is unique in almost all cultures, and especially in Semitic ones, and thus it is clear that Muhammad married her largely out of economic and social considerations. While sources describe Khadijah as noble, gracious, and wealthy, no source of significance ever cites her beauty, unlike descriptions of other women he married after the *hijrah*.[40] That Muhammad found it necessary to marry her, rather than having offers of women from other clans, is illustrative of his social and economic plight. A large portion of the early hadith literature discusses the wonderful aspects of their relationship, and while this is not in dispute, this literature mostly ignores Muhammad's difficulties prior to their marriage. Khadijah's wealth gave Muhammad two things: the independence he needed to spend leisure time planning for the future, and children, including two sons. Unfortunately, these two sons died in infancy, a tragedy that would haunt Muhammad the rest of his life because the need to have a son was critical for anyone wanting to claim the status of a nobleman.[41]

Nevertheless, this economic foundation gave Muhammad the freedom to exercise his calling as a prophet, though he held his new-found status a closely guarded secret for three years. During that time, he discussed this with only his family and a few close friends, developing a small cadre of followers, many of whom circulated among family and friends as secret Muslims.[42] Maintaining such secrecy was necessary for him to at least establish some foundation for his insurgency movement. And an insurgency was exactly what it was, for Muhammad worked to establish the necessary building blocks to provide some modicum of expectation of success to gain a status of power beyond the reach of his limited social situation.

As noted earlier, there was a growing level of tension within the Quraysh of Makkah. This tension not only revolved around class issues but also involved clan jealousy. Two sides of the Qusay line were vying for authority to control the economics and politics of the city, while other clans outside of the Qusay line were certainly concerned about their lack of political power. Muhammad's immediate family was once part of the Qusay line that was excluded from power, and this made them possible allies of those clans on the outside, at least so long as Muhammad's Hashim clan would gather in the reins of power when the dust settled. It should be noted that there were elements within Muhammad's family and clan who were very supportive, though some possibly secretly, of Muhammad's claim to prophethood. Thus,

Muhammad reached out in two directions, to his family and clan, and to those outside of the line of Qusay, with the target being those currently in power or those who had wealth.

One of those he reached early was Abu Bakr, of the Taym clan. The Taym were excluded from the most important elements of power in Makkah.[43] While Abu Bakr was a reasonably wealthy merchant, he apparently had a broader conception of what life could be like in Makkah and Arabia, and for this reason he accepted Muhammad's claims. There is some divergence of understanding regarding his wealth. On the one hand, some early sources indicate that he devoted his entire life savings and income to furthering Muhammad's cause, but on the other hand, there is some evidence that this may not have been very much.[44] Regardless, Muhammad would later indicate that Abu Bakr was to receive one of the greatest blessings for his financial support.[45] Moreover, he had some historical reasons to back Muhammad, as Abu Bakr's ancestors had helped to negotiate the Fudul settlement of ca. AD 590, an agreement that reduced conflict in and around Makkah and helped to set the Quraysh on the path of being a protector of other's property.[46] To solidify the power of Makkah under the Prophet would provide Abu Bakr and his clan considerable advantages, both political and economic.

Another person who became an early supporter of Muhammad, albeit secretly, was his uncle al-Abbas. Muhammad had four uncles, of which al-Abbas was arguably the wealthiest, in large measure because of his control of the *rifadah* and monopoly rights during pilgrimages. He was principally a merchant and banker, and his connection to the Hashimite clan would allow him to be a conduit to the *shaykhs* and other wealthy merchants. As such, he had the means and ability to organize capital and focus it where he wished, and there are indications that he used this money to support his nephew as the newly proclaimed Prophet of Allah.[47]

Some may wish to argue that hadith literature about al-Abbas were later inventions to support the claims of his descendants to the *khalifate*. However, it should be noted that these traditions were probably well established in the corpus of early Islamic oral tradition long before the rise of the Abbasid dynasty in AD 750. Moreover, it would make little sense if these traditions were forged by such historians as al-Tabari and Ibn Ishaq, for the leading imams of the time continued to validate these traditions even when they were more than willing to stand up to the Abbasid *khalifas* as the latter attempted to manipulate other oral traditions for their own advantage.[48] If forgeries could be created to establish the rule of the Abbasids, it would make sense that the imams would simply have created more forgeries to avoid Abbasid persecution on other issues. In addition, some of the earliest reciters of these traditions had sympathies that were outside the realm of the Abbasid dynasty with leanings to Shi'ite claims to leadership of the *ummah*, the community of Muslim believers. Therefore, it would seem more possible that the early Islamic historians would have forged hadith to support the Shi'ia rather than the Abbasids.[49] To simply assert that literature supportive of al-Abbas were forgeries creates problems that are difficult to surmount.

Muhammad's reach outside of the elite would extend to the day laborers who struggled to make ends meet. Once he made himself known, he would spend significant time reaching those considered underprivileged in the city, and this would set them against their masters and leaders.[50] In addition, the underprivileged were often the young and idealistic, while their masters were considerably older, thus exploiting a generational gap as well as class division.[51] It is here that one needs to understand exactly what type of message the newly proclaimed Prophet of Allah was preaching. As idol worshippers, the Quraysh allowed the placement of 360 idols in the *ka'bah*. The origin of these idols is obscure, but it appears that many were once pieces of the *ka'bah* itself, with clans taking them to their communities as a sort of vicarious substitute for the real thing. This allowed them to perform their religious rites without the need to travel to the primary source. It also would make sense that these idols roughly corresponded to the days of the lunar calendar, with an additional four idols as higher gods in a form of loose hierarchy. However, to see this as a form of Greek pantheon would be in error, for Makkah was far too democratic for this. Each of these 360 gods was adopted by various families, clans, and tribes, who saw in them a representation of their own connection to the *ka'bah* and the basis of their own political and social prominence and power, and thus their right to choose their own destiny.[52] In this context, one way to describe Makkah was as a loose confederation of families and clans that had surrendered a minimum of their freedom to be bound in a common association yet maintaining most of their autonomy. This came largely after the death of Qusay, when there was a decline in the authority of centralized government, a decline that threatened to dissolve the social fabric of Makkah.

Muhammad's message revolved around the declaration that only Allah was to be worshipped. When he initially went public, he only focused on his prophetic calling and his attacks against the greed of the merchants. But after a few years he began to stress the centrality of Allah and its exclusive claim that those who worshipped others were in the hellfire.[53] Allah was not unknown to the Quraysh, for even they considered him to be the high god over the *ka'bah*, and it was in his name that they took oaths in the days of *jahiliyah*.[54] What was new about Muhammad's message was that he, as the Prophet of Allah, was calling on people to follow Allah only. And as the declared exclusive Prophet of Allah, this meant that he alone was Allah's messenger and lawgiver. The implications are obvious here, and were not lost on the leaders of the Quraysh. In essence, Muhammad was calling upon them to follow and obey him, as he alone was the conduit of Allah's message and law.

This message was truly revolutionary, for it meant that anyone following Muhammad would surrender their loyalty to their idols and thus submit themselves to another's authority outside their family and clan. For those *mawla'* without property, this was a form of liberation, for if what the Prophet was saying was true, then they would no longer serve their former masters but be bound only to Muhammad. For *shaykhs* and merchants, this message was largely seen as a threat, for their authority and independence was called into question. But a few within the Quraysh, especially in the Hashimite clan, saw opportunity. Here was a chance to reverse declining fortunes and to seize power within Makkah, and possibly beyond. Here was the chance to take the *rifadah* and to make themselves the elite of the city, and perhaps more. This vision would certainly have only been local initially, but as Muhammad's influence spread, naturally the vision would spread with it. It was for this reason that key members of Muhammad's clan would shelter and protect him, providing his followers with food, clothing, money, and intelligence. To them, Muhammad and his small band of followers were the vanguard of a new revolution. If he succeeded, they would advance with him, but if he failed they could wash their hands of him and claim they had no part.[55]

There were others who also had some inkling of this, and they resisted Muhammad's claims. However, it must be pointed out that this resistance was relatively mild, despite the claims made by many Muslim authorities even in some of the earliest sources. For example, early historical, or *sira*, literature states that the first Muslims were terribly persecuted by those who hated Muhammad and Islam. However, when one examines actual examples of such persecution, one discovers that the primary means of persecution was ridicule.[56] While some Muslims were beaten, and a few even tortured, such as Bilal, the early record shows that only one, possibly two, Muslims were killed, and even these are questionable.[57] This is not to mitigate the difficulties of the early Muslims but to demonstrate the true lack of resistance to early Islam. Had the Quraysh responded with greater vigor and decisiveness, Muhammad's nascent movement would have been crushed and relegated to a footnote in history. However, it was their own legal system that failed them, and it is here that we must return to the issue of *lex talionis* and the blood feud.

With people intertwined in family, clan, and tribe, only a select few could claim true independence. But with dependence also came protection; one of the most ancient of doctrines in any culture is the notion that protection and allegiance are reciprocal.[58] If one is to gain the allegiance of another, they must grant something in return, and that was usually some form of protection. Those claiming to be Muslims in the early days in Makkah were still affiliated with their families and clans, and for anyone outside those groups to make aggressive moves against such people would risk the imposition of the *lex talionis* and the blood feud. The only ones who could overtly assault a Muslim would be one within that Muslim's family or clan, and even this could cause problems between the different families of the clan. As a consequence, Qurayshi culture was a relatively tolerant one, for while one could ridicule the opinions of another, they could not use serious force to impose their will on that person to stop their opinions unless there was some obvious threat to the entire leadership structure of the society. Even in the latter case, the *mala'* would find it difficult to impose their decisions on the rest of the city. Put another way, while the system of justice in Arabia could place limits on murder and theft, it failed miserably in defining treason and stopping a philosophical revolution.

From where did this failure come? This failure was based on the very essence of Qurayshi society and their laws. Polytheism leads to a notion of tolerance for many things and eliminates the idea that if a culture is to survive there must be some foundational absolute on which that culture is based. For the Quraysh and the people of Makkah, as well as many of the surrounding tribes in Arabia, the most fundamental absolutes were only two: their growing affluence and their desire to be left alone to enjoy their expanding wealth. Beyond these two primary principles, there were ultimately no other "rights and wrongs" that demanded their attention to the point that one should fight, kill, or die for. With this in mind, one can see that when the chips are down, there are few people willing to sacrifice, fight, and possibly die simply to retain some personal affluence, especially if they are finally offered the option of at least keeping most of their wealth if they compromise or surrender to the will of another. Had the Quraysh any other key principles that they considered fundamentally important, Muhammad's rising movement would have encountered more effective resistance.

The best way to describe Qurayshi government in Makkah was that it was a form of democratic republic.[59] It was a republic in that clans still maintained a level of independence within the city and made many of their own decisions, but the clans were also represented by their leaders who could make some key decisions in the *mala'*. It was democratic in that the worship of a multitude of idols brought adherence to a multitude of paths to the right way, and people could largely choose their own path, at least within the context of their families and clans. Of course, these two aspects would create a level of tension within the culture. On the one hand would be the principle that each could follow their own light as seen in their idols, but this could run into the restraint that the *mala'* and leading men of the city would want to impose to prevent a rising tide of anarchy. Yet the very nature of the democratic ideals within polytheism would run counter to such restraints, and is one of the reasons why the leading men could only govern by consensus. Therefore, while the leading men of Makkah might wish to prevent an increase in anarchy, the contradictions within their own worldview represented a significant obstacle to this effort.

These issues are critical to understanding what Muhammad was attempting to do, and why he encountered such little resistance not only in the early days in Makkah but also later when he was in Madinah. He was trying to create a unified system of governance, where the leader would not have to seek a consensus for important decisions. The call for worshipping Allah alone was a call to strip Makkah and the Quraysh of democratic notions to create a united system of law and government. Such a system would ultimately bypass the authority of the family, clans, and tribes, and would place the final authority in the hands of the Prophet. As the Prophet of Allah, Muhammad would have far more authority and control than any *shaykh*, although, as we shall see, this system was not foolproof. For example, we will later find the Prophet constrained by popular opinion to engage the Quraysh outside of Madinah, a battle against his own better judgment that would almost lead to catastrophe. Nevertheless, what Muhammad was attempting to do was return Makkah to the days of old, when Qusay unified and ruled the city with such authority that the people considered it a religious legal absolute.[60]

About midway through Muhammad's ministry in Makkah, two events helped to solidify his position, encouraging him to shift his stance regarding the Muslims from one of nonviolent passivism to that of self-defense. With the conversions of his uncle Hamzah and 'Umar bin al-Khattab of the 'Adiy clan, two powerful men, physically and financially, came to the cause of Islam. Their status in Makkah elevated the Prophet's position, with these two men functioning as bodyguards for the Muslims, and in particular for the Prophet. The conversion of Hamzah will be instructive in this regard.

One day when Muhammad was walking to al-Safa, a hill next to Makkah that was considered sacred during the hajj, his archenemy, Abu Jahl, tried to block his movement, insulting him and reviling his religion. To this the Prophet said nothing. When Muhammad's uncle Hamzah was returning from hunting in the hills about the city, he heard of what happened and found Abu Jahl sitting near the *ka'bah*. Filled with rage over how he had treated his nephew, Hamzah came up to Abu Jahl and hit him violently with his bow, possibly fracturing his skull. Several of Abu Jahl's friends stood up to defend him, accusing Hamzah of "turning heretic." Hamzah hotly replied, "And who's going to prevent me?" Before the men came to blows, Abu Jahl interceded, telling his friends to leave Hamzah alone, for he had "insulted his nephew deeply." Ibn Ishaq later recorded that "the Quraysh recognized that the apostle had become strong, and had found a protector in Hamzah, and so they abandoned some of their means of harassing him."[61]

Several items of importance emerge from this account. The first is the exponential response of Hamzah to the insults delivered against his nephew. Instead of trading insult for insult, he traded serious blows for an insult. This ramp-up of violence almost led to a fisticuff between

Hamzah, who was now claiming status as a Muslim by identifying with the Prophet, and Abu Jahl's supporters. The second item of interest in this account is the restraint demonstrated by Abu Jahl. While his friends may have been able to overwhelm Hamzah, it was obvious that Muhammad's uncle had more than just physical strength on his side. As a prominent family member of the Hashimite clan, a fistfight at the *ka'bah* would have had serious repercussions among the Quraysh. This leads to the third issue, the ability of Muhammad to now deter most of the persecution leveled at him, along with many of the other Muslims. While Muhammad still enjoyed the protection of Abu Talib, his uncle Hamzah would be able to intervene, both physically and politically, to provide protection and strengthen the position of the Prophet and the Muslims in general. This, along with the conversion of 'Umar bin al-Khattab, provided Muhammad the foundation to transform his movement from simple passivity to a more aggressive posture of self-defense. This represented the first decisive shift in the Muslim movement, and it was after these two events that the Qurayshi leaders decided to increase pressure on the entire Hashimite clan in an effort to silence Muhammad.

For a period of almost ten years, Muhammad continued to teach and preach his position largely under the protection of his uncle Abu Talib. Some among the Qurayshi leadership attempted to stop him, but the principles of the *lex talionis* limited their means. Initially, they offered Muhammad the kingship of Makkah, but to accept would be to take power at their hands, which would still leave the Hashimite clan in a lesser position. Moreover, he would now be their creation, and they would naturally strive to exercise control over his decisions. Muhammad declined this offer with good reasons. Next, they attempted a boycott of the Hashim clan, but some key leaders of the Quraysh violated the boycott and secretly supplied the clan with badly needed food while others conspired to undermine the boycott legally to finally force its revocation.[62] While such persecution was not necessarily deadly, apparently it was sufficiently strong enough even with the intervention of the likes of Hamzah to convince some of Muhammad's followers, particularly those without any tribal protection, to flee Makkah and migrate to Christian Abyssinia where they received asylum. The Quraysh sent a delegation in an effort to get the Negus, or ruler, of Abyssinia to expel them. This confrontation provides some interesting details, though much of it may very well be apocryphal. Nevertheless, a portion of the reported exchange between the Negus and the Muslims offer an insight into tactics used by Muhammad and his followers at this time.

The Quraysh sent two men to the court of the Negus, ʿAbdullah bin Abu Rabiʿa and ʿAmr bin al-As bin Waʾil, to demand that he extradite the Muslims. Even though some Qurayshi leaders wanted them sent back, Abu Talib tried to preempt the effort by sending his own messenger to flatter the Negus and convince him not to heed the demands of the two men to follow. The emissaries then arrived with gifts for the Negus and his generals and proceeded to explain why he should not continue granting asylum to the Muslims. The Abyssinian leader determined that he would not send them back until the Muslims were given a chance to defend themselves. They were summoned, and Jaʿfar, the son of Abu Talib who had been one of those to go into exile, stepped forward to be their spokesman. After explaining how they had become Muslims, the Negus asked Jaʿfar to explain what they believed about Jesus Christ. Jaʿfar recited generalities from Surah 19 Maryam, the chapter regarding Mary, the mother of Jesus. When he was pressed for more specifics Jaʿfar stated that "we say about him that which our prophet brought, saying, he is the slave of God, and his apostle, and his spirit, and his word, which he cast into Mary the blessed virgin."[63]

It is obvious that Jaʿfar did not quote much of Surah 19, for this particular chapter of the Qurʾan unequivocally denies that Jesus was God's son, a key principle of the Christian faith and a point that the Negus could not have been ignorant of. This doctrine regarding the position of Jesus had long ago received wide publicity within early Christian theology. At one time, Abyssinia had even been a place of contention between the Arians and the Trinitarian formula that had been preached there by the Christian bishop Frumentius.[64] Jaʿfar's additional explanation provided numerous adjectives regarding Jesus, but he never did reiterate the Christian position that Jesus was God's son. This was a critical omission, for in his presentation Jaʿfar presented only part of the Qurʾanic message, enough to convince the Negus into believing that the Muslims he was protecting were simply another Christian sect. As a consequence, the two Qurayshi representatives were sent away and the Muslims were not extradited.

This incident before the Negus highlights the nature of the Prophet's early tactics when in Makkah. Prior to the Prophet's *hijrah*, Muhammad taught and emphasized tolerance and freedom of religion. This was necessary because he and his followers were an extremely small minority within the midst of one of the more powerful tribes in Arabia. If the numbers that migrated to Abyssinia and later to Madinah are any indication of the true strength of the Prophet's movement in the early days, there may have been no more than 75 to 100 Muslims within a population of over 7,500, or no more than 1 percent. Being such a minority placed the young movement in serious jeopardy if the Muslims had resorted to force in an effort to impose their will on others, a point clearly noted by some observers.[65] Moreover, it was critical to appeal to the notion of freedom of choice to curtail the ridicule and minor attacks of some of the Quraysh, particularly to keep them from escalating to the point that the Prophet's movement would be crushed. Part of Muhammad's strategy was to play for time as he attempted to broaden his base while enjoying the direct protection of his uncle and clan. However, when Abu Talib died, Muhammad lost his champion who backed his agenda and thus had to search elsewhere for this badly needed support.

What is interesting here is that at this time, probably about one year before his migration from Makkah, Muhammad was essentially fair game. For the most part, he had no direct protection, though at one point he would be offered this by al-Mut'im bin 'Adiy, the same clan from which 'Umar bin al-Khattab hailed.[66] It was here that the *lex talionis* kept the enemies of the Prophet in check, for even without such protection most were afraid to directly assault him, especially since he had the likes of Hamzah and 'Umar to provide an effective retaliation for any attack. The *sira* material cites an instance where Abu Jahl thought of making such a move, but divine intervention was cited as the reason why he backed off.[67] Nevertheless, Muhammad must have realized that such restraint imposed by the cultural norms was about to wear thin, and he continued to aggressively seek protection from other tribes outside of Makkah. He first attempted to reach the elite of other tribes, but these early efforts were rebuffed; in one case, he was driven out of al-Ta'if by a mob.[68] Concurrently, his own preaching was possibly undermining his position because his declarations were becoming more direct, as when he told the Quraysh that not much time would pass "before you will enter unwillingly into that which you dislike."[69] Needless to say, some of the leading men of the Quraysh were losing their patience with a man they saw as subverting their culture and attacking their place in society.[70]

One example of Muhammad being denied protection is revealing as to what may have been the Prophet's ultimate objective. He went to preach to the Banu ʿAmir bin Saʿsaʿa, explaining Islam and asking for their protection. One of the members of the tribe, Bayhara bin Firas, realized how useful the Prophet would be for a group desirous of power: "By God, if I could take this man from Quraysh I could eat up the Arabs with him." He then asked the Prophet what would happen after they gave the *bayʿah*, or oath of loyalty, and pledged to protect him. Would they have authority over the Arabs once the Prophet was victorious? Muhammad's answer was evasive: "Authority is a matter which God places where He pleases." At this, Bayhara suspected Muhammad's motive and rebuffed him, stating that they would not place themselves at risk for nothing, for they would expect to receive some power and authority if they put their lives in danger for him.[71]

Muhammad's answer was more than just vague religious jargon. If he was to retain credibility he could not openly pledge to a tribe that they would be in charge of the Quraysh after his death, especially if his intention was to actually entrench the Quraysh in power not only in Makkah but perhaps even in western Arabia. As shall be seen, he never made such an offer of power to any who pledged to help him, including those of Madinah. If Muhammad was the vanguard of a segment of the Quraysh vying for political and economic hegemony in the region, it was important for him not to make such promises, especially in a culture that could be so fickle.

Still needing protection, Muhammad managed to make contact with tribal representatives from Madinah, his maternal home. These men had come for one of the trade fairs and knew of Muhammad through the family of his mother. Once presented with the Prophet and what he espoused, these men quickly understood how useful he could be to solidifying their own position in Madinah, especially against the Jews.[72] Madinah, at that time known as Yathrib, had been engaged in a small civil war for a number of years, with the two leading tribes, the al-Aws and al-Khazraj, vying for control of the city. The initial meeting with Muhammad involved but six men of the al-Khazraj. After accepting Islam, these six men returned to Madinah to become such aggressive conveyors of the Prophet's message that soon every household knew of Muhammad's mission. This could be considered Muhammad's first truly effective propaganda effort as he prepared his base. It did not take long before it bore fruit.

In February 621, twelve men met the Prophet outside of Makkah, ten from al-Khazraj and two from al-Aws. They met at the mountain pass of al-'Aqaba, located just north of Makkah near the caravan road. There they took the "pledge of women," that is, a commitment that involved no fighting.[73] This pledge, among other issues, called on them to revoke their idols, thus making Allah their only god and Muhammad their lawgiver whom they were to obey. After the men returned to Madinah, Muhammad sent them Mus'ab bin 'Umayr, a reciter of the Qur'an, to teach them the ways of Allah, and to several others who preached Muhammad's essential message from house to house.

The method of preaching and teaching illustrates subtlety in technique. While done fairly openly, no effort was made to use any compulsion at this time because the Muslims were a miniscule element within the city. The early Muslims in Madinah, being only a few, had no strength to call for the use of force, nor does it appear that any massive popular appeal was made. Instead, men of middle rank and not tribal *shaykhs* were invited to sit and listen to the doctrines espoused by the Prophet, and were told that they could take it or leave it, if they so desired.[74] Therefore, in the early days in Madinah, moral suasion was used to bring selected persons to Islam, with efforts to quietly bypass the most senior leadership.[75] However, a few leaders of clans were reached and converted, largely through hearing of the activities of the Muslim preachers from those of lesser rank. One of these men was Sa'd bin Mu'adh, a clan leader of the al-Aws and probably the most senior man converted in these early days, who would later play a pivotal role in the destruction of one of the Jewish tribes in the city. The Prophet, having first made his person known in Madinah, now moved to have his ideology taught, initially to the lower and middle ranks of society. This infiltration to gradually win over the city from within and below would last one year before the next meeting of men from the Madinah tribes.

The Second Pledge of al-'Aqaba occurred one year after the first, during the hajj in March 622, and involved seventy men and two women from the al-Aws and al-Khazraj. While it appears some efforts were made to now reach the leading *shaykhs*, it would seem that once again those represented were leaders of middle rank within their tribes.[76]

They met in the same location, but this pledge was very different from the one before, for it now involved a pledge of war. They met secretly, stealing away from their campsites to rendezvous with the Prophet who was accompanied by his uncle al-Abbas, there to ensure that Muhammad received a firm guarantee of security but perhaps also to weigh the possibilities of how he would invest his money and information to assist in the Prophet's cause.[77] Before the pledge was given, al-Abbas delivered a speech of political theater to cement the deal, making two claims, one that was at best dubious while the other was patently false. The first was that Muhammad was "the most respected person in his kinsmen." While possible, this seems unlikely considering the vehement opposition he had received from his uncle Abu Lahab, not to mention the opposition from Abu Jahl and other Qurayshi leaders. But the second statement was clearly fictitious: al-Abbas stated that "Muhammad has rejected (the offers of) all people other than you."[78] This was simply not true, being a twist of facts to convince the men of Madinah that they held a special place in the Prophet's heart. In reality, they were one of the last that Muhammad had attempted to reach, having no other offers to consider.[79] Nevertheless, Muhammad received the commitment of these men to support him, providing the Prophet with a desperately needed base to carry on the revolution against the elements of the Quraysh that needed to be humbled and suppressed.

Its declaration to wage war against Muhammad's enemies was one crucial aspect of the Second Pledge of al-'Aqaba. While the men of the Madinah delegation knew it meant war with everyone, it also meant war specifically with the Jewish tribes of their city.[80] This issue, which is very important regarding later events surrounding the defeat of the major Jewish tribes in Madinah, is largely overlooked in many biographies of the Prophet, although it is clearly discussed in the earliest sources.[81] During the negotiations before the pledge was made, one of the members of the Madinah delegation asked the Prophet about previous alliances they had made with the Jews, expressing his concern that once Muhammad was victorious, he might leave them to face the defeated Jews alone. To this the Prophet declared that "I will war against them that war against you and be at peace with those at peace with you."[82] The implication was clear. The Second Pledge of al-'Aqaba was a pledge of war against any who opposed Islam, and this pledge would invalidate previous treaties—principally those with the Jews of Madinah. At this point, Muhammad indicated he had clear permission from Allah to engage in fighting.[83] The Quraysh heard rumors of this meeting and saw it at once for what it was: a clarion call to war. The Qurayshi leaders went to their counterparts of the Madinan pilgrims to confront them only to hear plausible denial since they had not been apprised of those who had crept away to give their *bay'ah* to the Prophet. Those among them who had become Muslims kept it a secret, a few even striving to deceive the non-Muslims that they were still part of their pagan culture and not involved in the gathering at al-'Aqaba.[84]

Abu Bakr realized "there would be fighting" the moment he heard Muhammad reciting Surah 22:39–40, a passage he vocalized just prior to the *hijrah*.[85] Surah 22:39 states that "Sanction is given unto those who fight because they have been wronged." Another translation states that "Permission (to fight) is given to those (believers) who are fought against."[86] It is important to note that, up to the Pledge of Second al-'Aqaba, there is no indication that the Qurayshi opponents to Islam were engaged in fighting the Muslims, unless of course one accepts the notion that verbal opposition and ridicule is fighting. If the latter is accepted, then using combat as a means to oppose ridicule and verbal opposition demonstrates another exponential response to the Quraysh. Moreover, this passage in the Qur'an goes on to say that the believers had been "expelled from their homes unjustly," but there is no indication that any of the Quraysh actually physically drove the Muslims from their residences.[87] Instead, there is evidence to show that the Quraysh were actually trying to keep some Muslims from leaving of their own accord, albeit in an effort to get them to recant their Islam.[88]

Immediately after the Prophet's *hijrah*, or migration, to Madinah he would recite Surah 2, one verse encouraging the Muslims to "fight them until persecution is no more, and religion is for Allah. But if they desist, then let there be no hostility except against wrongdoers."[89] There would seem to be some indication that the Prophet was beginning to suffer some defections because of the pressure placed upon them by the Quraysh, and it might very well be one of the reasons why he wanted his followers to migrate. By removing them from their homes and placing them in a strange environment, this would enhance their need to bind themselves closer together as strangers in a strange land, determined to maintain their own identity in the midst of new and unfamiliar surroundings. Thus, the claim by some early Muslim writers that the Quraysh were forcing some to abandon Islam may not be totally accurate. Instead, there may have been some who had second thoughts as they weighed their circumstances and thought of leaving hearth and home for the sake of the Prophet of Allah.

Confronted by this new state of affairs, the Qurayshi opposition attempted to organize an assassination attempt against the Prophet. It was obviously poorly coordinated, for Muhammad easily escaped, along with Abu Bakr, to make his migration to Madinah. On the night of 21 June 622, the Prophet and his friend, guided by a pagan shepherd, departed for the city of his maternal relatives.

The Insurgency Grows

As Muhammad's camel approached Madinah, most traditional accounts state that the people poured forth in acclamation. However,
there are sources that suggest the people were more frightened than
jubilant, a sure indication of the tension brought by the Prophet and his
intent on waging war with the Quraysh.[1] For a few days he remained in
the small village of Quba to the south of the city, arriving in Madinah
proper around 2 July 632. Muhammad's migration to Madinah not only
represented a seminal event for that city; it also presented the Quraysh
of Makkah with a serious situation. They were fully aware of what Muhammad's departure meant, and while many were certainly happy to
be rid of the Prophet of Allah, some leaders of the Quraysh knew that
with Muhammad gaining a base of operations, it was only a matter of
time before he would begin some form of offensive raids against them.[2]

The Quraysh were now faced with a set of choices that demanded
immediate attention. However, the *mala'* apparently could make no
firm decision regarding what to do. Muhammad had already proph-
esied that those of the Arabs who followed him would one day rule
the Arabs and Persians, while those who did not would be slaughtered
and burn in the fires of hell. Such utterances offered much to those
who had little to lose and much to gain by Muhammad's triumph, and
this, coupled with the counsel of spies in their midst, confused their
decision making process, making them irresolute.[3] This lack of resolution was apparent in their unwillingness to track Muhammad down.

While the *sira* literature implies that some of the Quraysh knew of the Prophet's departure, with one even attempting to hunt him down, the very fact that Abu Bakr's son, servant, and daughter traveled at different times outside of Makkah to feed Muhammad and Abu Bakr in their hiding place without being followed demonstrates the confusion reigning within the counsels of the Quraysh. Had they been decisive in their plans, they could have easily followed these individuals to the cave at Mount Thawr and killed Muhammad and his companion.

As such, the Quraysh had four options. They could decisively track down the Prophet and kill him in the desert. They could wait until the Prophet got to Madinah and then attack that city with all of their resources until he was delivered up to them. They could attempt to make peace with the Prophet, finding whatever ground to make a compromise with him. Or they could ignore the situation and make no real decision at all. The last obviously represents the worst of the four, but this was the very path they chose, largely because their leadership was divided and confused. It would appear that the only decision they could come to was to increase the guards on the caravans they escorted. By choosing this option, they handed the initiative to the Prophet who was at that moment critically weak in his new base.

Unlike Makkah, Madinah was an agricultural city that produced dates as its principle produce. At around 2,700 feet above sea level, it was significantly higher in elevation than Makkah and offered a vertical drop of more than 2,400 feet to the western coastal plain and its trade route. The city lay within a geographical bowl, with mountains on the west and north, and elevated terrain of basaltic lava to the east. Thus, it had only four access routes, one from the north around Mount Uhud, one to the northeast toward al-Irak, one to the south into the blazing table rock of the Harrat Rahat, and one to the southwest toward the oasis way station of Badr. Of these, the Quraysh only had two available access routes, and the one from the south would be difficult for any large army due to its lack of wells along the way, a situation that has changed significantly today. Moreover, the elevation difference meant that Muhammad held the operational high ground. Each time he launched an operation, his men would work downhill while any counteroperation would require the Quraysh to work uphill.

Madinah's layout was similar to many others in the region, with a series of small towns loosely grouped together around an oasis field and lacking a single wall about the circumference. Each of these small

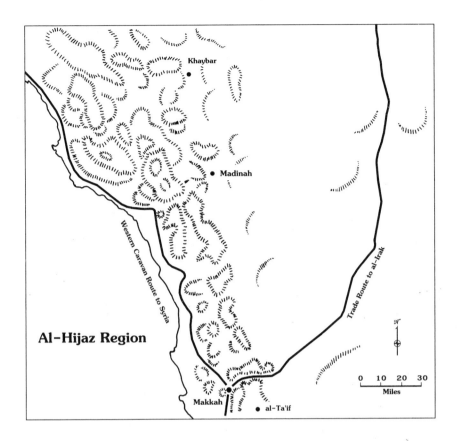

Al-Hijaz Region

Khaybar

Madinah

Western Caravan Route to Syria

Trade Route to al-Irak

Makkah

al-Ta'if

0 10 20 30
Miles

towns represented a tribe or clan tightly interwoven with walls and narrow corridors between the stone buildings. They also had their own towers for defense, often built above a well to provide immediate access to water if the area ever came under siege. As such, each town was a miniature fortress capable of defending itself and possibly assisting an immediate neighbor if needed. The principle weakness of this layout was in its inability for these towns to maintain a united front against a determined enemy, for each town could be defeated in detail if an attacker could maintain a sufficient supply base to conduct each siege. However, this last point represented a two-edged sword, for obtaining supplies while engaged in a siege was typically a difficult matter.

Penetrating the towns of Madinah looked deceptively simple, for without any outer wall the various sections appear to lay open for the taking. However, any attacker that would attempt to quickly force a decision would find themselves trapped in a maze of walled, winding streets no wider than a cart, with no way to focus the attack in any given direction. And all the while, the attacker would be subjected to missile fire from the roofs of the houses and towers lining the way. In such a circumstance, an attacker would most likely be compelled to engage in siege operations to overcome each of the towns in turn, and this would require a base of supply to maintain their forces in the field. This would be difficult to obtain locally, for while the tribes and clans of Madinah may not be united politically, they would be more likely to unite should they be attacked as a group by an outsider.

With this in mind, we now come to understand the true weakness of Madinah and other towns like it—being a weakness within. Should any one tribe or clan in the city determine to engage in low-frequency operations against its neighbors, this tribe could conduct a locally supplied and supported siege operation to a successful conclusion. Therefore, it would be incumbent on the people of Madinah to not allow within their midst any group that would attempt to upset any balance of power or undermine the status quo. Madinah had in once before encountered such a problem, but it is apparent that they learned little from their experience.

The political situation of Madinah prior to Muhammad's arrival was precarious. The town was divided into five principle tribes and a number of small subtribes or clans. Of these, two were pagan, the al-Khazraj and the al-Aws, which were each a stem of a tribal group called the Banu Qaylah.[4] The al-Khazraj was apparently the largest of the two, a fact hinted at by the number of representatives granted to Muhammad's council of advisors after the Second Pledge of al-ʿAqaba.[5] These two tribes had been in competition as to who would rule Madinah, for with such rule came special privileges to wealth. Each turned to the three other tribes, all Jewish, to tip the scales in their favor. These three tribes, the Banus Qaynuqa, al-Nadir, and Qurayzah, were either remnants from the Diaspora caused by the destruction of Jerusalem in AD 70, Arab converts, or a combination of both. The smallest was probably the Qaynuqa while the largest would appear to have been the Qurayzah.[6] Besides these three Jewish tribes, there were a number of small Jewish clans who typically attached themselves to a more powerful group as *mawla*. The evidence available indicates that these small clans associated with the al-Khazraj and al-Aws, leaving the three major Jewish tribes distinct.

Over the years tribal authority waxed and waned, with each group seeking alliances with others to maintain a strong and semi-independent

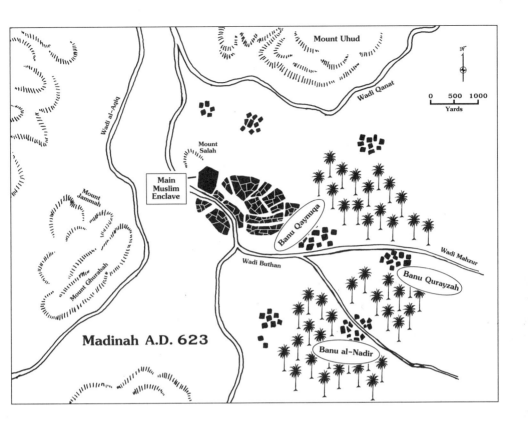

Madinah A.D. 623

status in the city. This culminated in the battle of Bu'ath around AD 617 that may have possibly involved most of the city's inhabitants.[7] With no clear victor, an uneasy truce prevailed, and it was into this situation that Muhammad made his covenant with tribal members at al-'Aqaba. His arrival in Madinah now upset the balance of power, for his first move was to consolidate the al-Khazraj and al-Aws into one tribal group through the Covenant, or Constitution, of Madinah.

There is much confusion surrounding interpretations of the Covenant of Madinah in many Western and Islamic historical works. The most important that must be clarified is the contention of many that the three major Jewish tribes were participants in this agreement. However, before examining this issue it is necessary to first provide an overview of the Covenant's provisions. There are several extant versions of the treaty, and it has been extensively covered in another work.[8] These differ in only minor details, and the version that will be used here is reproduced in the *Letters of the Holy Prophet Muhammad*, edited by Sultan Ahmed Qureshi.[9] The Covenant had fifty-one paragraphs,

Table 2.1. The Covenant of Madinah

Major Sections of the Covenant of Madinah, AD 622

Part I	Introduction; definition of the Muhajirun
Part II	Subtribes of al-Khazraj and al-Aws delineated along with their basic responsibilities
Part III	Deals with murder and the payment of bloodwit
Part IV	Instructions to provide mutual support when needed
Part V	The exclusive nature of the treaty; shunning outsiders
Part VI	Muhammad to act as final arbiter and judge
Part VII	Various Jewish subtribes delineated along with their basic responsibilities; much like part II
Part VIII	No military action without Muhammad's concurrence
Part IX	No aid or comfort to be given to the Quraysh of Makkah

according to Ibn Hisham, and these can be grouped into nine major parts.

Within this covenant are a few important provisions that must be examined. The first and most obvious is the place of Muhammad as the final judge and arbiter of disputes between those agreeing to the pact. Because of the ongoing civil war that had been fought in the city, many had grown weary of the conflict and sought an outsider to settle their problems. This is not necessarily unusual or even remarkable, but with one exception. Muhammad brought with him a very important proviso that formed the core of the ninth part, which stated his intent to wage war on the Quraysh of Makkah. While many early Islamic sources attempt to indict the Quraysh as being the first to engage in hostilities, the very nature of the Covenant of Madinah makes it clear that the Prophet had already declared that a state of war existed with them.[10]

The next critical provision involved the signatories to the Covenant. It is usually accepted that a portion of vague language in the document references the three major Jewish tribes. Moreover, it is also assumed that these Jewish tribes had lost their independence and were now clients of either the al-Khazraj or al-Aws. However, there is internal evidence in the *sira* literature to prove otherwise, evidence largely ignored by most of the analysis that has been done. One important piece was discussed briefly earlier and now must be examined again in light of the Covenant.

When members of the al-Khazraj and al-Aws met with Muhammad to make the Second Pledge of al-'Aqaba, some noted that they had certain alliances with the Jews that would need to be broken. The logical import would state that if the three major Jewish tribes were clients of the two pagan tribes, they would simply be drawn into the covenant. For members of the al-Khazraj and al-Aws to indicate that they had to break these treaties makes it very clear that they, and not the Jews, were the ones in a subservient political posture, or at best equals. To understand this in a different way would do violence to the sense of the passages in the literature. It would appear that scholars such as Julius Wellhausen and others simply assumed that the Jews were in the subservient role, probably from a personal philosophical or historical bias.

The next piece of evidence involves the incident that touched off the siege of the Banu al-Nadir. The details of this operation will be covered later, but a few important points will be discussed here. When one of Muhammad's men unwittingly killed two men belonging to another tribe with whom the Prophet had just concluded an alliance, Muhammad was compelled according to the Covenant to provide bloodwit for the deceased. At this point he did a curious thing. He went to the Banu al-Nadir to request that they help him pay the bloodwit. This is not necessarily unusual, for tribal leaders would occasionally go to other tribes for such help. But to make such a request was typically done only between allies, and this is where the Covenant of Madinah failed, for the provisions of that agreement called on each tribal signatory to pay the bloodwit for offenses by their own people.[11] Thus, had the Banu al-Nadir been party to the Covenant, it would have been a clear violation of the treaty for the Prophet to go to them and ask for assistance with the bloodwit. Some have tried to contend that Muhammad had some additional treaty arrangements with the Jewish tribe, but there is no conclusive evidence to support this.[12] Instead, it would appear that these attempts have been made to cloud the real issue at hand, that the al-Nadir and the other two Jewish tribes had no real agreement with the Muslims, save for a mutual nonaggression pact at best, and that when the Prophet went seeking financial aid, he was possibly attempting to create an incident for a casus belli against the Jewish tribe.[13]

However, the most obvious indicator that the three major Jewish tribes were not part of the Covenant is because of their absence from the agreement. Efforts have been made to imply that a vague Arabic phrase, essentially referencing generic tribal groups under the label of the "Banu so-and-so," was in fact a reference to the three major Jewish tribes.[14] However, this contention hinges on the notion that these tribes were now clients of the two pagan tribes, a notion that cannot be supported by the internal evidence. For Wellhausen to simply assert that "it is inconceivable that the indigenous Jews who formed nearly half the population of Medina should be totally excluded from a document designed to make Medina an indivisible unity" demonstrates Wellhausen's lack of understanding of the purpose of the Covenant as well as his own philosophical bias.[15] Put simply, it is inconceivable to Wellhausen that the Prophet would set up a situation that would lead to civil war in a community. The purpose of the Covenant of Madinah was to unite the Muslims and any others that would surrender their independence to join them on the terms set by Muhammad, but it was not to create an indivisible unity in Madinah on the terms of other groups. If the latter was the case, Madinah would represent the situation then present among the Quraysh of Makkah. Instead, it was to unite only the Muslims so that they could become their own tribal group that would wage war against all others who opposed them. This contention was clearly understood by those who took the Second Pledge of al-'Aqaba, which then led to the Covenant.[16] The major Jewish tribes were clearly not in the Covenant, and this would later become a serious point of conflict when the Prophet would expel or destroy them in turn.

This now leads us to a discussion of Madinah, its population, and, in particular, the number of Muslims in the city in the early days after Muhammad's arrival. There are no sources telling us how many people lived in Madinah around AD 620, although there have been attempts by a few to make estimates. A similar attempt will be made here, extrapolating from the slender evidence that can be culled from the early sources. Muhammad Hamidullah estimated that around 10,000 people lived in the various towns of Madinah, and this number seems reasonable.[17] Some of the early sources provide us some insight into the population, allowing a basic estimation of the overall population, and even a possible breakdown. The initial migration of the Muslims of Makkah to Madinah numbered approximately 80 men and 35 women. An additional 35 children can be added as a reasonable estimate, for a total of 150 Muhajirun, or emigrants.[18] Estimates of the remaining population can be extrapolated from the information regarding the number of fighters available to some of the Jewish tribes. For example, we know that the Banu Qaynuqa had approximately 700 adult men. We also know that the Banu Qurayzah had anywhere from 600 to 900 fighting men, and for this estimate we shall use 800.[19] We can also estimate the

Table 2.2. Population of Madinah

	Men	Women	Children	Totals	% of Total
Muhajirun	80	35	35	**150**	**1**
Al-Khazraj	1,100	1,125	1,000	3,225	28
Al-Aws	600	625	550	1,775	15
Total Ansar				**5,000**	**43**
Qaynuqa	600	625	650	1,875	16
Al-Nadir	700	725	750	2,175	19
Qurayzah	700	825	900	2,425	21
Total				**6,475**	**56**
Totals	3,780	3,960	3,885	**11,625**	**100**

possible number of fighting men for the al-Khazraj and al-Aws as fewer than 2,000.[20] Finally, it is probable that the Qaynuqa was the smallest of the Jewish tribes. A possible rationale for this can be found in the fact that they were allied to the larger al-Khazraj while the al-Nadir and Qurayzah were allied to the smaller al-Aws.[21] This would make sense because during the civil war fought before Muhammad arrived in Madinah there was no clear victor, though some sources imply that the al-Aws won. Apparently, the arrangement of allies created a fairly even balance between both sides.

With these numbers in mind, and including estimates for women and children, a table can be created to show the approximate population breakdown of Madinah.

These numbers are naturally just estimates, and they are not intended to spark contentious debate.[22] What they do is provide a snapshot into the demographics of Madinah during the Prophet's first months there, allowing us to understand some of the dynamics between the various groups. It would readily be assumed by many that Muhammad had Madinah well under control early on, but in reality the most committed element of the Muslims were a small percentage of the total. The number of participants at the battle of Badr in 623 can also provide a clue as to the number of men truly committed to the cause, that is, those who were willing to drop domestic work and engage in a major raid. During this raid, the Ansar, composed of men from the al-Khazraj and al-Aws and who were considered to be the helpers to the Muhajirun, numbered 231.[23] If we were to extrapolate from that number and estimate that perhaps 700 of the Ansar were the most dedicated of the Muslims, this would lead to approximately 800 in Madinah who were seriously committed to following the Prophet's orders, or only 7 percent of the population.

Even if this estimate were considered low, it could still be argued that only about 10 percent of the population of Madinah was fully devoted to supporting Muhammad and his mission during his early days there. It is worth noting that at one point the Muslims of Madinah were numbered, with the count coming to 1,500 souls, or about 13 percent of the total estimated population.[24] No details are offered as to when this census was taken, but the narrator of the hadith asked "should we be afraid (of infidels) although we are one thousand and five hundred in number?" The implication was that the Muslims were a small minority in Madinah and as such were vulnerable to a vigorous counterinsurgency campaign. But, during the *ummah's* most vulnerable days, there was no counterinsurgency against them worthy of note.

Because of the vulnerability of this small Muslim contingent, it was essential for the Prophet to develop his base of operations and solidify as much support as possible. It would be necessary to establish a firm logistical base and to recruit fighters to expand his fledgling army. It would also be essential to nurture and expand his intelligence service, something that he obviously was working on while still in Makkah. One of the first things he needed to do was establish a unified front for the Muslims. He initiated this partly through the Covenant of Madinah, but he finalized this through his efforts to join his Muhajirun and Ansar followers into a new tribal group.

Each emigrant from Makkah was pledged to a Madinan brother, and each became a son and heir to each other's property and fortune. This immediately stirred up controversy because the emigrants had no property to speak of. Muhammad had to have known this, and it would appear that he was attempting to insinuate the unemployed of his followers into the wealth of the settled people of the town. With conflict bubbling to the surface, the Prophet hastily withdrew the charge, and the brotherhood became one in name only, with no other rights and privileges.[25] Nevertheless, it still provided the foundation for a united *ummah* that would serve the Prophet well in his task. Come what may, he now had a super tribe that would back and protect him from his enemies.[26]

Since the Muhajirun represented a group largely composed of unemployed young men, most of them were without a formal place in society.

When the Prophet had his residence and mosque constructed, he had a portico built that became known as the *suffah*. The *suffah* became the residence for the transient and unemployed of the Muhajirun, thus also becoming the recruiting station for the Prophet's raids.[27] This was ideal, for the mosque was in essence the center of the Islamic community not only politically but also with regard to welfare largess so necessary for an Arabian nobleman, or sayyid, to engage in. A register was maintained in the mosque, and those desirous of going on a raid placed their name in the register and awaited a summons to mobilize.[28]

The Ansar were the Muslim believers who were natives of Madinah. The word literally means "a strong helper" and is based on the root *nasara*, which is to assist.[29] There is an important reason why the Prophet chose to call the Madinan Muslims Ansar, for they were to provide the support base for the Muhajirun who were to engage, at least initially, in all of the fighting. While the Muhajirun were largely dispossessed and unemployed, the Ansar owned property and primarily harvested dates, along with barley as a supplemental grain.[30] Muhammad knew that the migrant Muslims needed assistance, which is why he ordered the well-to-do Ansar to take in one of the Muhajirun as a part of their families, thereby ensuring initial minimal logistical support for the core of his fighters.[31] For their part, the Muhajirun were supposed to work with their Ansar hosts, doing whatever labor was necessary to harvest crops, though this part of the arrangement never materialized.[32]

In addition to having the Ansar provide this support, the Prophet also quickly instituted the payment of *sadaqah*, or "charity." During the Makkan period, *sadaqah* and its specific cousin *zakat* were voluntary and without specifics. *Sadaqah* represented a generic form of charitable giving while *zakat* gradually became an obligatory tax. When Muhammad became the judge for at least half of the city of Madinah, it was only a matter of time before he would realize that voluntary taxation was insufficient. Sometime during the second year after the *hijrah*, *zakat* became mandatory, and its minimum requirements and exemptions were detailed.[33] Simply stated, *zakat* was a 2.5 percent tax paid by each Muslim on their accumulated wealth at the end of each year.[34] Thus, it was not an income tax but an accumulated wealth tax. Anyone with assets, crops, livestock, or other valuables stockpiled at the end of the year, except for what passed as the minimum exemption, paid *zakat* on those items. According to the Prophet, *zakat* was to be "taken from the rich amongst them and given to the poor amongst them."[35]

These regulations on *zakat* had several interesting effects. The first was the tendency for some, due to a lack of planning, to simply try to avoid the tax at the end of a given year by giving away any significant surplus beforehand. Not only would they avoid the watchful eye of the tax collector and the stigma that would come with being labeled as one who hoarded wealth, which was a serious wrong in the eyes of the Prophet, but they could also paint themselves as being very generous, thus garnishing favor with others. Early Islamic literature is replete with illustrations of how the generous man would be rewarded both in this life and in paradise, and how the stingy would be punished.[36] This in turn had the effect of probably raising more support and revenue for various Muslim individuals than what the 2.5 percent tax would raise on its own, and would concurrently see some of this wealth brought in throughout the year, rather than being held to the end.

Zakat during the Prophet's day had a variety of uses, including supporting widows and orphans, helping the indigent, and supporting the warrior for Allah. Interestingly, while the rich normally could not receive *zakat*, this stipulation was waved if they were engaged in fighting in the cause of Allah.[37] This was clearly elaborated by the Prophet in one of the last Surahs he recited, Surah 9 al-Tawbah. By this point, the collection of *zakat* had become institutionalized and its details fleshed out. Among them was the importance of supporting the warrior in the cause of Allah.[38]

On the basis of how *zakat* was paid, it is obvious that most if not all of the Muhajirun did not pay *zakat*, at least initially. Therefore, the burden of *zakat* fell upon the Ansar, and the primary beneficiaries were the Muhajirun, who ranged from the destitute to the warriors. Naturally, most of the former, without any other livelihood, would be encouraged to join the ranks of the latter. Nevertheless, it is apparent that not many were very interested in risking their lives for the sake of nebulous plunder, for the Prophet found it necessary to recite verses imploring their participation in fighting, even though it was something they did not like.[39] These recruits, raw and nervous, would have to be trained—largely through on-the-job experience—to learn how and when to fight, raid, and escape. While individual weapons' training was conducted, oftentimes on the grounds of the Prophet's mosque, there is no evidence that Muhammad or any of his companions ever exercised the men in unit formations and battle drills such as found in Greek or

Roman armies.[40] It was to be in the furnace of battle where they would gain their understanding of troop movements and maneuver.

With the issue of how to initially support the Muhajirun settled, the Prophet next had to turn to the political problems of the city. Satisfactory resolution of these problems would help his men secure the logistical resources of the area. Essentially, the Prophet had two major problems. The first involved the three major Jewish tribes already discussed, and the second involved a group of Muslims who were apparently stingy with their support. These became known as the *munafiqun*, or hypocrites. Both had to be handled effectively for Muhammad to expand his insurgency operations and to triumph over the Quraysh. He could either confront these problems head on or find ways to negotiate through the labyrinth of Arabian tribal politics to keep these groups relatively inactive, but more importantly to keep them from uniting. It is here that Muhammad probably developed his most intricate and elaborate fifth column by creating his own opposition party.

The *munafiqun* are much discussed in the early writings and documents, and within these sources are some hints as to what may have actually been happening. Invariably, each source cites 'Abdullah bin Ubayy bin Salul as the leader of the *munafiqun*. There appears to be no source that overtly states that 'Abdullah's role may have been much more supportive of the Prophet. Not only will that be the contention here, but it can be submitted that it is very possible that 'Abdullah bin Ubayy was, at least after some initial resistance, an active secret supporter of Muhammad's political operations within Madinah. To make this case, it will be necessary to review some circumstances without delving too deeply into the specifics, these being covered in more detail in later chapters.

One technique of asymmetric insurgency that is both largely unappreciated and even less understood is the concept of creating one's own opposition. Put simply, because one will always incur some opposition to one's policies, the best technique for dealing with this opposition is to co-opt and then control the leadership of this movement to ensure that they can never attain any measure of true effectiveness. Naturally, this is easier said than done and does incur risks. For example, what happens if the leadership of this opposition decides to become a real opposing force on policy issues? If this occurs, then all of the labor and money spent on developing the opposition is lost, and one now has a real opponent to face—and one of their own making, no less. However, if the plan is even largely successful, it will bear tremendous fruit.

How does this work in practical terms? Social and political movements tend to coalesce around particular leaders and in organizations. Since man is a social being, the individual must unite with others of like mind to exponentially increase their capabilities, for when organized, people as a group are more effective than the sum of the individuals. Therefore, rather than wait for opponents to organize secretly, it is best to surreptitiously provide such giddy minds with an organization that is controlled. In this way, the individual within the organization can be steered to issues and tactics of the creator's choosing. Should individuals decide to push out on their own, they will be cited as schismatic from the movement, and thus working now as individuals or small and ineffective groups. There are examples in history when this has been done, but most can only be made by inference. However, Machiavelli does refer to this concept in his work *The Prince*, noting that one of the best ways to control a foreign state is to set them under their own laws with people in charge who are friendly to the conquering power.[41]

'Abdullah bin Ubayy, as part of the al-Khazraj, played a pivotal role in Madinah prior to, and after, Muhammad's arrival. Prior, he had played a role in the civil war that had been fought between the al-Khazraj and al-Aws.[42] When Muhammad arrived in Madinah, he learned that the people were on the verge of crowning 'Abdullah king as a way to settle their ongoing disputes, and Muhammad learned that he should deal with 'Abdullah gently because of his status and his loss of prestige by the arrival of the Prophet as the city's newly accepted judge.[43]

There are indications that 'Abdullah initially resisted Muhammad in subtle ways and was occasionally verbally harsh with him. However, beyond that, 'Abdullah took no direct measures against the Prophet. Furthermore, there is evidence to suggest that his position with Muhammad changed over time, and that he became the lightning rod for opposition, thus keeping the opposition from boiling over into full rebellion. He also played a pivotal role in assisting Muhammad in overcoming some of the Jewish tribes. The evidence that 'Abdullah was eventually a fifth columnist supporting Muhammad is in seven parts and will be organized chronologically where known.

Prior to the battle of Badr in December 623, the Quraysh wrote a letter to 'Abdullah asking him and his supporters to join them in a war against Muhammad. 'Abdullah went so far as to mobilize forces against the Muslims and forced Muhammad to negotiate with him. Muhammad convinced 'Abdullah's supporters to demobilize, but we do not know if the two leaders made any secret agreements.[44] What is important about this incident is that Muhammad apparently did nothing to punish 'Abdullah or his followers for such an obvious breach of the Covenant of Madinah. While early hadith and *sira* literature cite breaches of treaty for reasons to expel or destroy the three Jewish tribes, there was no effort to do the same with 'Abdullah and his key supporters. The most logical reason for this is obvious: Muhammad and his most faithful supporters were a small percentage of the population in Madinah, and he needed to exercise care in not antagonizing a substantial element of those who claimed to still support him, at least in part. It may have been at this time that he decided to nurture a relationship with 'Abdullah to develop him as either a witting or unwitting partner in controlling any opposition in the city. This may have developed sufficiently to allow Muhammad to leave Madinah just a few months later in the expedition that culminated in the battle of Badr.

'Abdullah's role at the battle of Uhud just over one year later in December 624 is often cited as one of duplicity where the *munafiqun* deserted the Muslims, thus aiding in their defeat at the hands of the Quraysh.[45] While Muhammad was maneuvering his men into position north of Madinah, 'Abdullah took three hundred men and returned to the city. But while many see this as desertion, one early source casts doubt on this interpretation, instead noting that 'Abdullah may have departed to ensure the security of Madinah from attack should the Muslims be defeated, a contention seemingly supported by al-Waqidi.[46] It should also be noted here that 'Abdullah had sided with Muhammad's initial plan to stay in Madinah and force the Quraysh to engage in a costly siege operation, a plan far from indicative of a man who wanted Muhammad to be ruined. If 'Abdullah did desert the Muslims prior to the battle of Uhud, it is strange that Muhammad took no action against him, either then or later, when his hand over public affairs was strengthened. Not long after the battle of Uhud, Muhammad would actually place 'Abdullah in charge of Madinah when the Prophet went on another raid to meet the Quraysh again at Badr, and he would later campaign with him during the Tabuk operation, something that would appear strange if he could not be relied upon at a critical time.[47]

While 'Abdullah would openly oppose Muhammad's plan to execute the Banu Qaynuqa, the first Jewish tribe to be expelled from Makkah, when it later came to the Banu al-Nadir, 'Abdullah would engage in a curious episode of subterfuge. When the al-Nadir tried to determine whether to stand firm in their fortifications, 'Abdullah and several other leaders of the al-Khazraj sent them a message that they and their supporters would defend the al-Nadir, thus urging them to remain in place. But when the al-Nadir chose to defend in place, the promised help did not materialize, in which case "God cast terror into their hearts," compelling them to ask Muhammad for terms to be deported as the Qaynuqa before.[48] One may ask what practical result such a false promise had. It can be found in the plan of the al-Nadir to stay in place, thus allowing them to be besieged. Instead of deciding to break out and fight with desperation, they remained behind their walls passively trusting on a false hope until their supplies ran low.

Secret support to Muhammad can also be found in 'Abdullah's posture that stymied any real opposition to the Prophet from others within the al-Khazraj, for they would have awaited the word from their leader to move on the Muslims, an order that of course never came. In this regard, 'Abdullah provided Muhammad with exceptional service.

In 627, Muhammad launched a raid against a tribe near Makkah, the Banu al-Mustaliq. When the raid was complete, the Muslim army began the trek back to Madinah, and in the process one of Muhammad's wives, the youthful 'Aisha, became separated from the column. She had gone into the desert to relieve herself and in the process lost her necklace, causing her to return to the secluded spot to find it. When the column moved out, the men watching her camel and *howdah*, the enclosed basket used for women when traveling, assumed she was asleep within and began their march north. Now alone in the desert but used to the environment, the woman did not panic, deciding to wait in place until they discovered her absence and came back for her. She had just wrapped herself in her cloak and laid down when one of the Muslim men, operating as rear security, came upon her. This was a seriously awkward moment, for the man suddenly realized that the woman alone before him was none other than the Prophet's wife! Uttering "truly to Allah we belong and truly to Him we shall return," a statement made when a Muslim is confronted with some form of calamity, the man placed 'Aisha on his camel and brought her back to the Muslim army.[49]

Despite the man's obvious efforts to prevent any affront to 'Aisha's honor, the incident precipitated a major scandal that almost led to

'Aisha being stoned for adultery. A number of individuals engaged in a whispering campaign against her, including 'Ali bin Abu Talib, the Prophet's cousin and son-in-law, and Hassan bin Thabit, the Prophet's court poet. The former actually urged the Prophet to take another wife, essentially alluding to having 'Aisha stoned.[50] However, 'Aisha later indicated that the leader and key instigator of the slander was none other than 'Abdullah bin Ubayy, who was cited as one of the "greatest offenders" in the matter.[51] Nevertheless, when the matter was at last settled, several others, including Muhammad's court poet, were flogged for defacing 'Aisha's honor; as for 'Abdullah, no punishment was given. Indeed, this aspect of the issue was largely deflected when the Prophet asked others to impose punishment on 'Abdullah, a request that almost brought the al-Khazraj and al-Aws to blows as it played upon their tribal prejudices. With the Madinan Muslims in an uproar, the Prophet was able to simply drop the matter, having lesser individuals including one woman beaten for the gossip.

'Abdullah's role in the Tabuk campaign, conducted around July 630, also sheds light on his relationship to the Prophet. When Muhammad organized this operation, he had to empty the city of Madinah of men and call on allies to raise the thirty thousand deemed necessary for the operation. 'Abdullah commanded half of the men, maintaining them in a separate camp from the rest of the army, which was directly under Muhammad's command.[52] While the army did not engage in any fighting, the incident reveals two possible situations, first, that Muhammad still had to rely upon 'Abdullah to help organize a significant ground force, and second, that it is possible that 'Abdullah was used to mobilize the disaffected and debouch them from Madinah, thus effectively eliminating the possibility of a coup. The best way to ensure that nobody attempted to revolt was to bring them along on the campaign, keeping them in a separate army under the leadership of a significant personage in whom the disaffected would look for direction, albeit mistakenly, should a possible coup emerge.

When the Tabuk campaign was completed and 'Abdullah bin Ubayy died in February 631, Muhammad prayed secretly over his grave during the night and ensured that 'Abdullah was buried in Muhammad's shirt, acceding to a request for this by 'Abdullah's son.[53] Even though Muhammad had previously commanded that no Muslim was to offer prayers for an unbeliever or one who harmed the Muslims, Muhammad now indicated that Allah had granted him a choice to do so if he so desired, an issue that initially upset one of his closest companions.[54] Thus, Muhammad secretly honored 'Abdullah not only by praying for him but by also shrouding him in the Prophet's shirt, a significant honor reserved for only a few.[55] Since the burial was at night, there was no need to provide such honors because no one else was present. Nevertheless, the Prophet consented to these things, and did so for a reason not readily known. This, despite the fact that 'Abdullah bin Ubayy had been the leader of the *munafiqun*, who had vied for control of Madinah prior to Muhammad's arrival, who deserted the Prophet's army at the battle of Uhud, who slandered his wife 'Aisha, and who even maintained two female prostitutes to bring in extra income, a practice to which Muhammad even recited a verse of the Qur'an against, though he apparently did nothing to stop.[56] Although one report states one of the girls refused this demand and appealed to the Prophet, there appears to be no evidence that 'Abdullah stopped this practice merely on the Prophet's recitation of a Qur'anic passage.[57]

The material cited regarding 'Abdullah bin Ubayy bin Salul is here to demonstrate not only the complexity of Muhammad's situation in Madinah, but also the possibility that Muhammad was, at minimum, using 'Abdullah as the rallying point of discontent so he could track it more openly. Indeed, some of the evidence implies strongly that 'Abdullah was a willing participant in such a strategy for which he received special rewards, such as the Prophet looking the other way to allow him to do largely as he pleased. While condemned as the leader of the *munafiqun* openly, it could have easily been conceivable that 'Abdullah had become the Prophet's secret ally, both taking blame for things that went wrong and holding dissenters enthralled as the Prophet gradually expanded his control of the city.[58]

There are naturally passages in hadith and *sira* literature that can cast doubt on this theory, such as 'Abdullah's comments that Islam was overwhelming the people of Madinah and driving out their traditional ways, and that immediately after the scandal with 'Aisha, the Prophet contemplated having 'Abdullah assassinated.[59] There may even have been efforts by some of the *munafiqun*, with 'Abdullah possibly leading the way, to reduce the amount of money given in *sadaqah* and *zakat*, thus hurting the Muslim cause.[60] Yet these passages must be seen within the wider context of the entire period of Muhammad's life in Madinah. As such, many of the sayings that place 'Abdullah in a different light are difficult to understand if he was the wicked hypocrite that he is assumed to be.

It is important to highlight that at one point ʿAbdullah's own son, ʿAbdullah bin ʿAbdullah bin Ubayy, approached the Prophet and asked for permission to kill his father to remove him from the scene. Instead, Muhammad calmed the young man, saying "nay, but let us deal kindly with him and make much of his companionship while he is with us," clearly indicating his intent to at minimum use ʿAbdullah bin Ubayy politically.[61] However, the material presented earlier has made the case that at one point ʿAbdullah crossed over from being politically used to becoming a willing, though secret, partner in the Prophet's revolution. If this were so, then it would represent arguably the most brilliant and successful asymmetric fifth column operation Muhammad conducted.

One aspect of Muhammad's early operations in Madinah cast light on this contention regarding ʿAbdullah bin Ubayy, for it appears he had attempted the same thing with the three major Jewish tribes. When the Prophet was still in Makkah, he had chosen to turn his direction of prayer toward Jerusalem. After the *hijrah*, Muhammad used this point, along with the way he dressed and combed his hair, to make himself acceptable to the Jews in an effort to co-opt them.[62] This political strategy began to crumble when the leaders of the Jews confronted Muhammad with their Scripture rolls, asking the Prophet of Allah to discuss Hebraic history and prophecy.[63] If the nature of Qurʾanic passages were any indication, Muhammad could not relate the same information as contained within the Jewish scriptures, for there are extensive variations between Muhammad's recitation of such Biblical events and those contained in the Torah.[64] As a consequence, the Jews rejected him. It took about eighteen months before Muhammad declared that Muslims should now turn to face the *kaʿbah* to the south, rather than Jerusalem to the north. This alteration of the *qiblah*, made on 15 November 623, about one month before the great victory at Badr, was an open indication that the Prophet's efforts to co-opt the Jews had failed.

This led the Prophet into an intense psychological campaign for the hearts and minds of the people in Madinah. This campaign included subtle propaganda and overt threats, followed by even more blatant acts of aggression within a period of about five years that were directed at both the Madinans at large and the Jews in specific. Each was organized with the intent of gradually marginalizing and destroying opposition while concurrently bolstering the morale of the Muslims, its most

Table 2.3. Muhammad's Early Asymmetric Campaign and Targets

Events toward Madinans	Events toward Jews	Date
The *hijrah*		July 622
Increasing length of prayer		July 622
	Changing the *qiblah*	15 November 623
First fast during Ramadan		November 623
Victory of Badr		16 December 623
	Direct threat to the Jews	December 623?
Killing of Asma' bint Marwan		24 December 623
First 'Id al-Fitr festival		30 December 623
Killing of Abu 'Afak		January 624
	Expulsion of Qaynuqa	January 624
	Killing of Ka'b bin al-Ashraf	4 September 624
Defeat at Uhud		29 December 624
	Expulsion of al-Nadir	July 625
Victory of al-Khandaq		January 627
	Destruction of Qurayzah	February 627
Failure at al-Hudaybiyah		January 628

committed element still a significant minority in the city. A timeline will help to illustrate these efforts, with each event oriented toward the group it primarily impacted.

Most of these issues will be explored in more detail later, but some initial observations can be made. It can be seen that in the first year, Muhammad was primarily concerned about enhancing the unity of the *ummah* against competitors. As such, efforts were made to avoid integrating the Muslims into the city's cultural milieu, and actually creating a sharp distinction between themselves and their primary threat, the three major Jewish tribes. Such a maneuver is counterintuitive to the typical political response to opposition, for in most instances political operatives search for common ground in which to create a synthesis of compromise. By presenting his movement as an absolute, much as he had done in Makkah, the Prophet developed what could be best described as a form of defensive philosophical interior lines. Just as conventional forces will often effectively defend a position by exploiting the principle of interior lines, so did the Prophet create such a defensible ideological position for his movement, a posture often used by asymmetric insurgencies. Though his movement was small, this insulated them from foreign philosophical assaults while enhancing the unity and cohesion of his own movement. As the change of *qiblah* placed the *ummah* in opposition to the Jews, other factors, such as increasing the length of the daily prayers, fasting at Ramadan, and the celebration of the ʿId al-Fitr festival, served to bring the *ummah* closer together. Add to this the inclusion of the *adhan*, the call to prayer; collection of *zakat* from the believers; and the requirement to attend Friday prayer services, and it can be seen that Muhammad had made decisions all geared toward turning the outnumbered *ummah* into a small and disciplined body. In this way the *ummah* became an insurgency in the midst of Madinah, even as they began to embark on an offensive insurgency against the Quraysh. Engaging in what amounted to a two-front war would require tremendous political and military dexterity as well as significant support.

One aspect of insurgency warfare often lost in analysis is the critical need for logistical support. While a budding insurgency can initiate hostilities on a shoestring, it is necessary to secure sufficient support to not only defend itself but most importantly to expand operations to engage in a decisive offensive to overwhelm the targeted culture or group. Once in Madinah, Muhammad needed to secure the necessary supplies and financing to support the *ummah*, especially the fighters who did little to no productive work, and to provide the weapons and transport necessary to move considerable distances in a very hostile environment. Fighting men and their families must be fed, along with any mounts used in battle, while the extensive panoply of war must be obtained. While some of the Muslims did have their own weapons, many hailed from the lower class of Makkan society, while many of those of Madinah, though staunchly middle class, had been focused more on agriculture than war.

The first order of business was food, and the evidence available indicates that for many of the Muhajirun the rations initially were quite thin, though apparently Muhammad did eat reasonably well for the first seven months after the *hijrah*.[65] The problem involved the agricultural production of Madinah and the willingness of the Madinans to surrender some of this food for the sake of the Muhajirun. If the population figures cited earlier are reasonably correct, then the people of Madinah needed approximately 10 million pounds of food annually, along with an additional 18.2 million pounds for their animals of various sizes and types, to ensure basic survival and sufficient strength to work their fields and date palm groves.

What happened after this would depend on how much land was truly arable at the time of the Prophet, and this is where calculations can become sketchy. It is largely assumed that Madinah provided at least some of their agricultural crop for export, but there is little record that cites this city as a major producer of such goods for the region. Khaybar, to the north, on the other hand, was far more productive in this manner because their date palm groves were situated in the wide valley of a wadi. This provided better production that allowed them the ability to export close to 50 percent of their annual production.[66]

An analysis of the terrain around Madinah would suggest that no more than 10 square miles, or 6,400 acres was arable. However, the amount of land actually cultivated at any one time was certainly less than this, probably closer to 7 or 8 square miles, or between 4,500 and 5,100 acres. The principle crop of the region was dates, but some wheat and barley were grown as well. This production was then supplemented marginally by camel by-products and some limited protein from sheep and goats. Calculating the amount of land worked to be around 5,100 acres, along with the production of animal products, would bring an annual yield of approximately 36.5 million pounds of food, after assuming that production methods then were not as efficient as today. After assessing for wastage of 5 percent, a surplus of around 6.1 million pounds would be available for sale, or about 17 percent of the total produced.[67]

This does not leave much to support a group of professional soldiers, for to support just 300 fighters and any marginal administrative personnel would require a bare minimum about 328,500 pounds of food annually, or about 5.38 percent of the surplus. It is worth noting that this number is above the *zakat* rate of 2.5 percent, which indicates the need for additional contributions by the people to support the fighting element. However, if the arable land was only 4,500 acres, this surplus would fall by half, thus requiring 11 percent of the surplus to support this small professional force. One can see that if the agricultural production was strained in a given year, this would place considerable economic stress on the Madinans and the professional force they were required to support. The available evidence suggests that such economic stress was prevalent within the region during Muhammad's initial tenure in Madinah.[68]

This situation was complicated by another contingency: the land and produce of the Jewish tribes. If this represented approximately 35 percent of the annual production of Madinah, a supposition extrapolated from the stated number of date palms available to the people in Khaybar,[69] then the strain on the surplus of the non-Jewish population would be considerably greater, anywhere from 4.13 percent to 8.32 percent of the surplus. This amount is far above the *zakat* rate and would help to explain the problem of food shortages and economic stress in the city. For example, when carrying out the assassination of one of the leaders of the al-Nadir, Ka'b bin al-Ashraf, the Muslims complained that Muhammad's arrival had caused them considerable economic stress and that they wished to buy food from him.[70] This attempt to set up Ka'b would not have worked had the situation presented not been plausible.

What did this mean for the Prophet and his small contingent of professional fighters? It certainly meant that supplies for the early raids would be considerably strained, and this is supported by the hadith literature.[71] Raids of neighboring tribes and Qurayshi caravans would be necessary to at least supplement the food supply, a point that certainly weighed on the Prophet's mind. Put another way, the Muhajirun were either going to have to find employment in the fields and trades, or they were going to have to gain support through the means of offensive actions against any and all in the region, and this was going to have to occur soon. Therefore, Muhammad had little time to organize and prepare his closest supporters to engage in combat against what was arguably one of the most prominent and powerful tribal groups in western Arabia, the Quraysh.

Furthermore, Muhammad needed to find a means to raise his army. Largely due to the low productivity of the culture, it was difficult to raise large professional armies. As a consequence, most fighters were militia recruited for brief campaigns to then return to their civilian work. Only a small portion of the army would be professional, and Muhammad organized these from the Muhajirun who had migrated from Makkah. Since many of the Muhajirun were unemployed, as noted earlier, the

Prophet retained a large number of these men in a veranda of his newly built mosque called the *suffah*. Men remained here waiting for the summons from the Prophet to sign a registry in the mosque indicating their willingness to go on a raid. Muhammad would then select the men needed from this list for a particular mission. Thus, the core of fighters for Muhammad's initial operations came from the underemployed and unemployed Muhajirun. Only when the Prophet determined to engage in a more aggressive raid did he turn to the Ansar of Madinah to assist.

Besides food, another key problem of supply was that of weapons. While weapons for ancient warfare may appear to be simple in comparison to modern combat systems, it must be borne in mind that the means of production was exceedingly crude, and that the manufacture of quality weapons was a craft performed by skilled artisans. The concepts of interchangeable parts and mass production were not yet understood, necessitating that each spear, sword, and shirt of chain mail had to be crafted individually at considerable expense and time. Crude spears were relatively easy to produce, but more quality weapons required real skill and were therefore quite costly. While there is evidence of smiths and skilled craftsmen operating in Makkah and Madinah, there is no evidence that such craftsmen existed among the early Muslims. Moreover, such skilled craftsmen were in very short supply in Madinah, regarding the production of not only weapons and armor but even clothing because the city had to import such items.[72] They would have to rely upon others to provide their weapons and armor, either seized as plunder or purchased locally or abroad. In the medieval European marketplace, a coat of chain mail could cost as much as a horse, although there are indications due to prevalence that such chain mail shirts were cheaper and more readily available to Muhammad.[73] Nevertheless, the process of creating chain mail shirts was labor intensive and costly, thus limiting the supply to only a few who could afford them.

Other weapons could be even more difficult to obtain or use. During Charlemagne's era, a quality sword could cost half as much as well as the chain mail in European markets, though there are instances where these were much more costly, making them a treasured possession as the primary offensive weapon.[74] Because they were so treasured, it was not uncommon for swords to be named, a practice engaged in by both Christian Europeans and Arabian Muslims.[75] Contrary to what many might think, bow and arrow weapons were quite complex, for they required not only skill to produce as a weapons system but also proficiency in the hands of the user. The bow had to be crafted to handle the stress of being drawn while also being used as a staff and rod when unstrung. The shafts had to be fashioned straight and true to allow for reasonably accurate flight while the head had to be produced to penetrate various types of armor, especially chain mail.[76] This was compounded by the necessity of the user to train incessantly with such a system to become adept and effective in battle. References of Muhammad's men pelting their enemies with stones, especially early on during such engagements as Badr, is indicative of their initial lack of proficiency with the bow.

For Muhammad to simply go out and purchase these items would require him to have a financial base he simply did not possess, at least to our knowledge, when he first arrived in Madinah. While some of the Muhajirun and Ansar would have had their own personal weapons, the lack of quality weapons within the overall population would have limited the number of men the Prophet could initially field, thus providing one explanation why the first raids were manned by so few. Although the weapons were personal in nature, they still required basic maintenance and replacement, as the wastage of battle could lead to broken and lost material. So while food was the first essential need for the Muslims, Muhammad also had to contemplate how he would equip his men to fight.

Beyond the basic weapons, horses were simply out of reach for most, and only the wealthiest individuals had these during the early days of Muhammad's tenure in Madinah. Overall, these were exceedingly rare in the Hijaz, and in Arabia in general, and were thus highly prized by their owners. Their cost was exorbitant, going as high as four thousand dirhams, well beyond the price of a slave.[77] In the battles that will be examined in the following chapters, one will see a dearth of horses in action. It is only near the end of the Prophet's life, with the Tabuk campaign, that we see a significant deployment of horse cavalry by anyone in Arabia at that time. Considering their previous scarcity, this raises the question of where these came from, a point that will be explored later.

Because horses were scarce, the camel could at least provide Muhammad's men some measure of mobility. However, even these initially seemed to be relatively scarce for the Muslims, for during the earliest raids it was not uncommon for Muhammad to have two of his men alternately ride one camel. Camels were cheaper than horses, typically purchased for around four hundred dirhams, although in one case a man sold a camel to the Prophet for only forty dirhams, an obvious example of a token price for a gift.[78] Female camels were more emotionally stable and not prone to stubbornness when heavily taxed, so they were preferred for riding.[79] Although used for riding, camels were typically not used as fighting platforms, for it was extremely difficult to fight from a camel. Instead, camels were typically used as beasts of burden, or to provide men operational mobility, in which case the men would dismount to fight once in contact with an enemy.[80]

While men, equipment, and food supplies were critical to Muhammad's mission, the Prophet determined early on that he would need an excellent intelligence service. Details of specific intelligence missions will be covered later, but a few points need to be stressed here. An effective intelligence service does not just happen, for it requires recruitment and extensive maintenance to have such a service, and both require some type of expenditure. With this in mind, it is apparent that the Prophet was developing an intelligence service long before he migrated from Makkah, and this involved four distinct groups. The first two were within Makkah, with one being Muslims who remained behind. These would engage in active disinformation operations, such as after the raid on Nakhlah. The next group in Makkah would be those who were secret supporters. These would conduct information gathering, organization of financial support, and engage in discreet disinformation operations within the very counsels of the Qurayshi leadership.

The third group would involve those outside of Makkah who were usually secret supporters of the Prophet, whether city dwellers in places like Madinah, or Bedouin tribesmen scattered throughout Arabia. These provided Muhammad with information about the movement of Qurayshi caravans and forces, and they operated as double agents, which indicates that they were supportive of the Quraysh when actually working for Muhammad so as to sow disinformation regarding the Prophet's movements. In at least one instance, one agent would create arguably the most significant intelligence operation of Muhammad's insurgency, a point we will explore later in chapter 7. The last group would be some within Madinah who operated in a counterintelligence role. These kept the Prophet informed regarding the details of the behaviors of his followers, the *munafiqun*, and the opposition in the town.

After Muhammad had politically organized the town and started to build his small army, it was necessary to provide them with the training to engage the Quraysh of Makkah, considered one of the more important tribes in western Arabia. Therefore, it was necessary to initiate a series of raids and operations not only against Qurayshi caravans but also against some of the local tribes so as to pull them away from any tribal alliances with the Quraysh and to draw them into the orbit of the *ummah*. But before launching these raids, the Prophet ensured that he would not allow any obvious insurgents within the midst of his own mosque. He ordered his closest companions to expel the *munafiqun* "with some violence," these being punched, slapped, knocked down, and dragged violently from the Prophet's mosque, a level of persecution that at least equaled if not eclipsed that inflicted on the Muslims by the Quraysh when the former were still in Makkah.[81]

The Road to Badr

It took the prophet about seven months to organize his first expedition.[1] While there is some disagreement among the sources as to which expedition came first, for our purposes here this is immaterial. For the sake of clarity, the analysis made of these operations will generally follow the timeline established in al-Waqidi's *Kitab al-Maghazi* and Ibn Saʿd's *Kitab al-Tabaqat*, unless other sources demand differently. Muslim chroniclers divide these expeditions into two types, the *ghazwah* and *sariyah*. The former represented a mission led by the Prophet personally while the latter was led by a lieutenant. An interesting aspect about the *sariyah* is that the term normally referred to a reconnaissance or forage collection mission.[2] However, when used by such writers as al-Waqidi, the term took on the additional meaning of a raid, though probably still retaining some of the prior connotation of being a reconnaissance.

These early raids were tasked to intercept Qurayshi caravans, and in this regard all were failures regarding their primary mission. Only one of these expeditions, with up to two hundred men, was led by Muhammad himself to recover some animals lost to a raid by a neighboring tribe. The raiders fled to the mountains, and Muhammad was unable to find them. Thus, this expedition also met with no success. Typically, the early expeditions sent out by the Prophet consisted of anywhere from seven to two hundred men, with almost all on foot, as there were few camels and even fewer horses.[3] Only one small mission was sufficiently

Table 3.1. Early Raids Prior to the Battle of Badr

Date	Mission	Enemy	Muslims	Leader	Result
July 622	Hijrah				
Jan 623	Sif al-Bahr; Quraysh	200	30	Hamzah	No Fighting
Feb 623	Rabigh; Quraysh	unknown	60–80	'Ubaydah	No Fighting
Mar 623	Al-Kharrar; Quraysh		8–20	Sa'd bin Abu Waqqas	No Contact
July 623	Buwat; Quraysh	100	200	Muhammad	No Contact
Aug 623	Al-Abwa; Quraysh		60	Muhammad	No Contact
Aug 623	Al-'Ushayrah; Quraysh		150–200	Muhammad	No Contact
Aug 623	Safwan; Kurz bin Jabir	unknown	150–200	Muhammad	Failure
Oct 623	Nakhlah; Quraysh	4	8–12	'Abdullah bin Jahsh	Victory
Dec 623	Badr; Quraysh	700+	314	Muhammad	Victory

Sources: The tables of battles presented were developed from Watt, *Muhammad at Medina*, Excursus B, 339–43, and Rehman Shaikh, *Chronology of Prophetic Events*, both cross referenced to Ibn Sa'd's *al-Tabaqat* and Ibn Ishaq's *Sirat*.

mobile on camelback, but this one was too heavily outnumbered by enemy cavalry to achieve any real results.[4] Although these preliminary expeditions against the Qurayshi caravans could be considered failures, they did succeed in their secondary purpose, to elevate the concerns of the Quraysh and serve notice that their economic interests were being tracked and threatened. Moreover, while seemingly insignificant, they would incite the Quraysh to react. Some biographers of the Prophet attempt to state or imply that these operations were never meant to attack the caravans, only to threaten them, and that Muhammad had war forced upon him.[5] The early hadith and *sira* literature are more conclusive on this issue and clearly indicate that Muhammad was the one who started open combat with the Quraysh, these consisting of minor raids against Qurayshi caravans, their economic lifeline.[6]

In the list of actions used, the dates and numbers of enemy, where recorded, are approximations, and there is a modest measure of dispute about the dates. However, these do not alter the analysis as to what happened prior to the battle of Badr. After the *hijrah*, Muhammad strove to organize the community of believers and to prepare for offensive action against the Quraysh to the best of his ability and as resources would allow. His campaign against the Quraysh would focus on two axes of attack. The direct axis would be to hit the Qurayshi caravans in the field. The second would be to intimidate neighboring tribes especially those who had agreements with the Quraysh, to either rally under his banner or at least take a neutral posture. While the latter would not be as immediately efficacious as the former, it would still raise the level of threat to the caravans sufficiently to force the Quraysh to spend more resources to protect them. This is even more serious if the Quraysh functioned largely as a caravan security force, as noted in a previous chapter, for this would be a blow to their prestige and another threat to their livelihood.

It was about this time, not long after his arrival in Madinah, that Muhammad called upon his followers to engage in the struggle against the enemies of the Muslims. This is often called jihad in many sources, a term widely used but so often misinterpreted. To engage in jihad was merely to partake in a struggle. However, the contemporary misunderstanding regarding jihad involves what some classical sources have labeled as the "greater versus the lesser jihad." This confusion centers on an oft-quoted hadith that says that the Prophet, when returning from a battle, told his followers that they had completed "Jihad Asghar (the lesser Jihad) to strive in Jihad Akbar (the greater Jihad)." When his companions asked what this meant, Muhammad is reported to have said that the greater jihad was "the Jihad of someone against his desires."[7] This tradition is based on a weak hadith narration, and some such as Ibn Taymiyyah considered it a forgery.[8]

Regardless, even if the tradition is accepted as accurate, it remains that the term "jihad" is largely interpreted in early Islamic literature as physical combat, both defensive and offensive in nature. Even the Sufi tradition, which is largely connected to this hadith, accepts physical fighting as being immensely important, with one tradition implying that the battle against the inner self can only be waged after fighting and defeating real-world enemies on the field of battle. Indeed, the word

"Sufi" comes from the Arabic *suffa*, which is a raised platform that was the origination of the *suffah*, the veranda where many of the Prophet's early fighters resided.[9] When analyzing Muhammad's methods of warfare, the term "jihad" will be largely avoided in these pages to avoid the confusion that surrounds the term. Whether or not it is called jihad, it is clear from the historical record that Muhammad engaged in warfare, and much of this offensive in nature. It was necessary for the Prophet, as the leader of an insurgency, to go on the offensive, for change could not be imposed on the Quraysh and the neighboring Bedouin tribes without placing serious pressure on them, and this could only be done through combat.

Muhammad's uncle Hamzah led the first raid departing Madinah in January 623, with his objective being the western caravan route near Al-'Is, located almost due west from Madinah. At nearly the same time, the Prophet sent 'Ubaydah bin al-Harith with sixty to eighty men to the southwest, also intent on hitting the same caravan route but further to the south. Some sources assert that 'Ubaydah's was the first raid, but here it is not critical which one departed before the other. It would appear that the Prophet intended this operation to be a two-pronged assault to hit the same caravan, possibly to ensure that if the Quraysh slipped by one group, they would be intercepted by the next. While it is not explicitly stated, it would appear that both missions were driven off by a Qurayshi escort that numbered from two hundred to three hundred men.[10] Hamzah's mission was saved by the intervention of a local *shaykh* who was friendly to both antagonists, after both forces had hobbled their camels with the intent of fighting within arrow-shot of each other. Had Hamzah's small force actually fought the Quraysh that day, they would surely have been obliterated. As for 'Ubaydah's group, they had to deploy a rearguard and engage their foe with archers, a sure indicator that they were hard-pressed to escape.[11]

Undeterred, the Prophet sent Sa'd bin Abu Waqqas with a small band to once more interdict the coastal road, this time near al-Kharrar. In planning for this operation, the Prophet apparently suspected that he had enemy agents within the midst of his *ummah*, and thus he had instructed Sa'd to travel by night and remain concealed by day. Traveling by night not only concealed movement, but it also allowed the men to move during the coolest part of a day, conserving strength and reducing water usage.[12] While night movement sounds simple enough, it must be noted that movement through any desert terrain, even mountainous, is extremely difficult during darkness, and that it takes special skills and practice to navigate effectively by the stars.[13] Every mountain and every little track looks the same to the uninitiated, and one could become hopelessly lost within a few hours. Moreover, movement by night was a significant novelty for the rural Bedouin, who found the darkness both dangerous and frightening.[14] Saʿd's mission failed to engage the caravan as it slipped by them the previous day. This may have been in large measure due to the difficulties they had with efficient night travel at that time.

Despite this effort to conceal the movement of his men, Muhammad realized that somehow the Quraysh were apprised of his operations. He now decided, as the sayyid of the *ummah*, to personally lead the next mission. In July 623, the Prophet organized about two hundred men and traveled approximately eighty miles to set up an ambush site near Buwat, a small village along the coastal route not far from Hamzah's earlier objective. There is no indication of why his force did not intercept the Qurayshi caravan of 2,500 camels, which was unfortunate for him as he outnumbered the guards by two to one.[15] Cheated of a possible triumph, the caravan slipped away and the Prophet brought his force back to Madinah.

One month later, the Prophet tried again, this time leading two separate raids to the caravan route. The first to Waddan or al-Abwa had him deploy 60 men and march south, then west to intercept the coastal route. While he failed to make contact with a Qurayshi caravan, he did present a sufficient threat to a tribe in the area to convince them to agree to a nonaggression treaty.[16] The second raid, with about 150–200 men, was initiated when he learned through his agents in Makkah that a Qurayshi caravan had departed Makkah for Syria.[17] His objective was al-ʿUshayrah and involved Muhammad taking a circuitous route, first northward and then into the mountains of the Hijaz to emerge in the valley of Yanbu. This approach march was certainly conducted in an effort to confuse spies in Madinah as to his destination. However, by this point his operations had become predictable and one dimensional, and his general direction and objectives were obvious. Most of the men moved on foot and traveled about 110 miles, the expedition having only 30 camels on which the men rode in turn. Once there, he learned that the caravan had already passed by several days prior. Little did anyone know at the time, this same caravan, led by Abu Sufyan on its return, would be the objective that would culminate in the Muslim victory at Badr just a few months later.

Somewhere around this time, either between the two raids launched in August or after, the Muslim community in Madinah was raided by an intrepid man named Kurz bin Jabir al-Fihri, of the Banu Fihr. He attacked the Prophet's sacred camels and apparently captured them all, though the actual number lost is not recorded.[18] Muhammad set off in hot pursuit, probably with the same force he used for the raid on al-'Ushayrah. They pursued them almost to Badr near the seacoast but failed to catch them. This same Kurz would later join the Muslim ranks and engage in several more raids on behalf of his former enemies before being one of the few killed during the conquest of Makkah.[19]

By this time, just one year after Muhammad's entry into Madinah and his establishment as the city's leading sayyid, he was faced with what can only be described as near total failure. His lieutenants had failed to plunder any of the caravans targeted, and even Muhammad had failed to achieve a victory. To add insult to injury, his own sacred camels had been carried off in a daring raid and he had failed to recover them. The only tangible result was that he had managed to wring a non-aggression alliance from at least one tribe near the coastal route. However, an intangible result that was not without merit was the invaluable experience some of his men were receiving in the basics of what is today called patrolling and movement to contact. Despite this, the overall result of his operations had certainly been a serious disappointment. It was critical for Muhammad, as a sayyid, to deliver on his promise to care for the families in his charge and to bring them success.

Among the difficulties he faced, one was the real problem of security in Madinah. It was apparent that somebody was relaying important information regarding the movements of Muhammad's men, for Qurayshi caravans had either managed to elude his forces or had maintained a significant force strength advantage. While the Prophet was receiving accurate intelligence assessments from Makkah, his enemies were gleaning actionable intelligence of similar importance from his own community. While it is possible that this intelligence came from the nonaligned Jewish tribes, it would seem that some of the information was taken from sources close to the nerve center of the *ummah*. Because it was extremely difficult and time-consuming to flush such moles from within the ranks, it was imperative for the Prophet to instead use tighter security measures for his operations. He had tried night movements and circuitous routes of march to affect this, but it was certainly not enough. Therefore, he decided to introduce the use of the *maktum*, or sealed letter of instruction.[20]

Secret letters of instruction were nothing new, and where or how Muhammad came upon the idea is unknown. However, he decided to use it for the next raid, and at the same time change the direction of the operation. He recruited 'Abdullah bin Jahsh to lead a small reconnaissance expedition near Makkah to test both the *maktum* and how an unexpected shift in objective would reveal Qurayshi deployments. In October 623, 'Abdullah departed Madinah with eight or twelve men and half as many camels, with the men riding the beasts in turn. He moved for two days, probably toward the seacoast as would have been habit, though this is uncertain, before opening the letter.[21] When he read it, 'Abdullah gasped in dismay. "We are God's and to Him do we return," he cried out, for the objective—the wadi of Nakhlah deep within Qurayshi territory—seemed like a suicide mission.[22] While there is some dispute over the exact contents, most sources indicate that 'Abdullah and his men were to merely observe the Quraysh along the short caravan route between Makkah and Al al-Ta'if, a resort town in the mountains to the east where Qurayshi nobles would travel to escape the oppressive heat of their city.[23] Therefore, it was designed to gain intelligence information to see how the Quraysh deployed and protected caravans in areas where they did not expect contact from the Muslims. The results would be astonishing.

'Abdullah was not only given his objective but was explicitly told not to force any of his men to go on such a dangerous mission. Nevertheless, all consented to go. As they moved south, possibly along the elevated plateau to the east of the Hijaz, two of 'Abdullah's men lost their camel and broke from the party to find it. With his force now reduced, one can imagine 'Abdullah's reaction when the party came upon a Qurayshi caravan guarded by only four men and bound for Makkah carrying wine, leather goods, and raisins. This was a far cry from the previous engagements where the Muslims had been outnumbered on nearly every occasion. Here was a Qurayshi caravan for the taking.

'Abdullah now exercised personal initiative and discussed the situation with his men. If they merely watched, the caravan would soon enter the *haram*, or forbidden area, of Makkah, where fighting was not allowed by tradition. Yet they had another problem if they decided to attack. Because they had departed Madinah during the month of Rajab, one of the four months considered sacred in which no fighting was to occur, they were not sure if the days of travel had taken them into the month of Sha'ban, in which fighting would be allowed. Any combat at this point could find them in violation of a sacred month. However, they collectively decided that such a lucrative target was too good to let slip by, and they decided to attack. Of interest in all of this discussion is that nowhere do we find the men discussing a possible violation of Muhammad's orders to merely perform reconnaissance, implying that it is possible, though not likely, that the Prophet left such a choice open to 'Abdullah as the commander on the spot. Instead, it would seem that 'Abdullah seized the initiative on his own accord.

They first resorted to a stratagem of deception, with at least one of 'Abdullah's men shaving his head to make it appear the group was on a pilgrimage. As such, they normally would not have been a threat, and the four guards relaxed their suspicions when they saw them.[24] The Muslim party then leaped upon them, killing one and capturing two others, along with seizing the entire caravan. One man managed to escape into the hills to bring the news of the attack to the Quraysh.

'Abdullah's men were ecstatic and returned to Madinah with the caravan in tow to represent the first operational success of the *ummah*. Before their arrival, 'Abdullah had divided up the loot, separating the share for each man in the raid while setting aside one-fifth for the Prophet. Their surprise at finding such a lightly guarded caravan was surpassed by the shock they received when Muhammad expressed his displeasure. It was immaterial that they were successful, for he indicated they had countermanded his orders not to engage in fighting. As a result, they had violated the sacred month of Rajab and had given the Quraysh a propaganda victory, for they were already spreading the word of this sordid deed.[25] 'Abdullah and his men were now classified as lawbreakers, and the Muslims in Madinah were dismayed. Some Muslims who had remained behind in Makkah attempted to blunt this criticism with propaganda of their own, but apparently with little success, for the Jews in the entire region considered it an omen against the Prophet.[26]

Even as this dispute raged, Muhammad received the *ayah*, or verse, of revelation about fighting in a sacred month:

They ask you concerning fighting in the Sacred Months. Say, Fighting therein is a great (transgression) but a greater (transgression) with Allah is to prevent mankind from following the way of Allah, to disbelieve in Him, to prevent access to Al-Masjid [the mosque] Al-Haram (at Makkah) (the sacred area), and to drive out its inhabitants, and Al-Fitnah [persecution] is worse than killing.[27]

What is fascinating about this recitation is that there is no evidence that at this time the Quraysh were prohibiting Muslims from engaging in a pilgrimage and going to the *ka'bah*.[28] Even when they were still in Makkah, most Muslims, unless they were a *mawla*, or servant, of another and thus prohibited from doing so, could circumambulate the shrine, and this arguably included Muhammad. Had the Muslims in Madinah not started their raids on the Qurayshi caravans, there is little evidence to suggest the two sides could not have coexisted. There is marginal evidence that the Quraysh were preparing operations against Madinah, but the evidence available is difficult to place in the timeline of events. Did the Qurayshi efforts come before or after Muhammad began his raids? Regardless of Qurayshi plans, some sources accept the notion that it was Muhammad who intended to take the offensive from the start.[29]

Moreover, the Muslims in Makkah were not actually driven out, save for perhaps Muhammad. Most preferred to migrate when Muhammad gave them permission while a number remained in Makkah until the conquest of the city by Muhammad's forces in 629. Thus, what Muhammad was engaging in after the raid at Nakhlah was a propaganda ploy to provide divine sanction for his men to break the traditional law of the area by fighting during sacred months. By doing so, he was initiating the *ummah* to the notion that legality outside of the Muslim community was unimportant. Laws that were not sanctioned and supported by Muhammad could be violated at will when it was necessary for the success of operations, or possibly even for more mundane tasks.

Such a declaration presented the Quraysh with a serious dilemma. They were more concerned about their genteel image among the outlying tribes of Arabia, so it would have been very difficult for them to also abrogate the sacred months in which to campaign, and there are only a few instances, all unsuccessful, when they did violate such months. The only one that could have led to success was when they organized the siege of Madinah during the sacred month of Dhu al-Qa'dah. While the Quraysh could still defend themselves if attacked, Muhammad's decision to fight in the sacred months gave the Muslims a four-month period of a one-sided truce. Muhammad, knowing the mind of his own people, surely must have understood that he was placing the Quraysh in an impossible position. He was forcing the Quraysh to live by their own book of rules while he could now violate such almost at will. Understanding this principle, he would take advantage of it on numerous occasions, and the Quraysh, hobbled by such false notions of legal niceties, paid the price. He even placed such pressure on Jewish tribes in Madinah by later engaging them during their Sabbath.[30]

Muhammad's resolution of the issue of the sacred months brought relief to 'Abdullah and his men, who up to this point were awaiting their fate with fear and trepidation. Now their raid had been sanctioned ex post facto. But was there more to this issue than merely a sacred month? Indeed, Muhammad had sent them out on their mission during the sacred month of Rajab, and surely he must have known that, even if merely a reconnaissance, there could have been fighting. Is it possible that Muhammad was concerned that the first successful raid was not led by himself but one of his lieutenants? Even though he had sent out initial raids under others, Muhammad had taken his hand to leading these operations when previous ones had been failures. Now, after having failed himself to engage and capture a Qurayshi caravan, one of Muhammad's lieutenants not only defeated the Quraysh but returned with plunder, and all of this against the Prophet's original instructions.

To make matters worse, 'Abdullah, before being told that the raid violated the law, had presumptuously divided up the loot, setting aside one-fifth for the prophet at a time when one-fourth was normally allotted a tribal chieftain.[31] By siding with the people that the raid was a violation, Muhammad did two things. First, he saved 'Abdullah's life, for what 'Abdullah did shortchanged the prophet, because only later would the recitation come about granting one-fifth of the loot to the prophet, rather than one-fourth. Second, it allowed Muhammad to await revelation then summarily change the law. In doing so, he declared the raid legal after the fact, but he also discarded the need to distribute this particular loot to the men. As a consequence, Muhammad was able to seize the entire caravan, using its wealth as seed money for future expeditions and providing his own household with badly needed finances.[32]

The consequences of the Nakhlah expedition were perceived as minor but were ultimately monumental. It clearly established a state of war between the Muslims and the Quraysh, and Muhammad was the one who declared it.[33] Although exegetes would argue centuries later that Qurayshi persecution started the war, it has already been noted that some of Muhammad's followers were the first to use physical violence to push their views while still in Makkah. Moreover, what the panegyrists for the Prophet fail to realize is that in their headlong pursuit to defend him, they open the door to the notion that any Muslim could wage war on an enemy simply for such things as verbal ridicule or a minor insult. Indeed, this could very well be the case; there is historical, hadith, and Qur'anic evidence to suggest this.[34] But foremost, with the success of one of his lieutenants, the pressure was now on Muhammad, as the sayyid of the *ummah*, to prove that he could lead a successful operation and not just dispatch it. He did not have long to wait for another opportunity.

Every year the Quraysh sent out two major caravans, one in the winter and the other in the summer, to biannually balance the lion's share of their wealth. Besides these two, there were always a number of smaller caravans to raid, but the two major ones, established by Hashim 'Abd Manef, Muhammad's great-grandfather, were the greatest prizes to seek. Muhammad, intimately familiar with the trading business, knew the general timings of these caravans. The specific intelligence he regularly received from Makkah gave him more details, thus providing him sufficient information to intercept them. He was informed that a major caravan escorted by seventy horsemen was coming south from Syria under the control of Abu Sufyan bin Harb, one of the important elders of the Quraysh.[35] He knew this in large measure because it was the very same caravan, then traveling north, that he had failed to intercept in the raid to al-'Ushayrah. By calculating the movement of the caravan, along with the time it took to offload and load goods, the Prophet was able to determine the most opportune time to send out scouts to herald the caravan's approach.

The caravan coming from Syria was loaded with wealth, having virtually every family among the Quraysh involved even if it offered but minimal profit. It was composed of one thousand camels, and at least one clan, the Makhzum, had upward of ten thousand *mithqals* of gold carried in the baggage. The total holdings of the caravan were upward of fifty thousand dinars, or five hundred thousand dirhams.[36] A mere threat to this caravan would incite the entire city of Makkah to action, and by plotting to take it, Muhammad was essentially threatening to bring down upon the people of Madinah, the very thing they feared: the full weight of Qurayshi might.

Yet to seize this prize would go beyond the monetary gain, for it would establish Muhammad as the principal leader in the Hijaz. Despite any risks involved, he began his preparations and in doing so realized that he would need more men to ensure success. Therefore, for the first time he tapped the manpower resources of the Ansar. Doing so was somewhat risky because the *zakat* and other charity of this group provided the base of wealth for the operations of the unemployed Muhajirun. Yet his need for immediate manpower was greater than the need for future tax revenue. It could even be said that he was taking a calculated risk, for if this force were to be destroyed, his days in Madinah would be numbered. Some of the people answered his summons eagerly, but others were very reluctant because they saw this move as an open invitation to all-out war with the Quraysh.[37] It was one thing to launch an occasional small raid on a caravan and quite another to unleash a full-scale operation that could entail serious casualties and invite a strong response from Makkah. Such was a daunting prospect indeed.

Muhammad dispatched a scout to locate the caravan, who was deceived as to the exact location of the caravan by false information given by a native of the area. When the scout returned to the Prophet, the two had a secret consultation in Muhammad's quarters, whereupon the Prophet came out and called on all who could procure an animal that was ready to ride to accompany him on the raid. Some, eager to now follow up the success of the Nakhlah expedition, asked if they could use their farm animals, but Muhammad refused due to the pressure of time, saying he only wanted "those who have their riding animals ready."[38]

Having quickly made preparations, Muhammad left Madinah on Saturday 9 December 623, with a force of approximately 83 Muhajirun and 231 Ansar, heading southwest toward the caravan watering location of Badr. He had 70 camels and only 2 horses in his force.[39] Before departing Muhammad personally inspected his men and sent home those he considered too young to fight; the range between 14 and 15 years of age was apparently the break-point.[40] As he looked his men over, the Muhajirun presented a mediocre lot, for they had recently been suffering from disease due to their recent change in venue and diet.[41] Nevertheless, if he was to intercept the caravan he would need every willing man available, regardless of physical condition. Realizing that his advance might be spotted by Qurayshi scouts, not to mention having a sudden premonition of evil regarding a mountain tribe in the area, Muhammad deviated off the main route from Madinah and followed obscure canyons and wadis until he debouched into the open plain of Badr.

Abu Sufyan was aware of the danger. He personally engaged in a reconnaissance of his own, riding well ahead of the slow-moving caravan to reach the wells of Badr just after two of Muhammad's scouts had left. When he arrived, he asked a local if he had seen anything unusual, and the man told him of two men who came earlier, took some water, and then left. Abu Sufyan went to the place where the men had rested. Spying camel droppings, he broke one open to find a date pit within. "By God, this is the fodder of Yathrib!"[42] His worst fears confirmed, he hastened back to the caravan and ordered it to quicken its pace and deviate to the coastal route, leaving Badr to the east. While this meant they would not get any water, he knew they could proceed without it if necessary, and now was certainly a time of extreme necessity. Concurrently, he ordered a rider to rush to Makkah and alert the town that the caravan was in jeopardy.

When this messenger arrived, having torn his shirt and cut the nose of his camel in grief, he cried "Oh, Quraysh, the transport camels, the transport camels! Muhammad and his companions are lying in wait for your property with Abu Sufyan. . . . Help! Help!"[43] With this warning ringing in their ears, the leaders of Makkah rapidly prepared a relief column of 1,000 men. About 100 were mounted and armored, with about 500 of the remaining infantry in chain mail as well. The clan of Makhzum, with so much to lose, contributed 180 men and one-third of the cavalry dispatched.[44] The Quraysh lightheartedly declared as they made their preparations that Muhammad would not find this caravan such an easy prey as the one at Nakhlah. With Abu Sufyan leading the caravan south, another of their key leaders, Amr bin Hisham, known to the Muslims as Abu Jahl, was in command of the relief effort.[45] Before leaving, the leaders in Makkah took hold of the curtains of the *ka'bah*, crying out "O Allah! Give victory to the exalted among the two armies, the most honored among the two groups, and the most righteous among the two tribes."[46] Twelve wealthy men of the Quraysh also determined to provide the necessary meat on the hoof for the journey, each supplying ten camels to be slaughtered for rations. Logistical lift was provided by seven hundred camels for this hastily organized force.[47]

Having prepared the relief force as speedily as possible, they marched hard to the north, soon meeting another messenger from Abu Sufyan declaring the caravan was now safely past the danger zone. But Abu Jahl was determined to press on ahead and thus changed the mission of protecting the caravan to one of engaging Muhammad's men. This caused Abu Sufyan to cry in anguish, "Woe to the people! This is the action of Amr bin Hisham," thereby exonerating himself of Abu Jahl's actions.[48] It was possible that Abu Jahl was determined to gain glory for himself at the expense of Abu Sufyan and thus gain power in Makkah, since the two were intense rivals.[49] However, it should also be noted that Abu Jahl probably had a far better appreciation of the danger presented by Muhammad's insurgency, and was thus willing to risk more in an effort to crush it.

Abu Jahl's rash decision to change the relief column's mission led to immediate complications. With a pending, though now seemingly unnecessary, battle in sight, a number of the Quraysh were not interested in either fighting their fellow clansmen or helping him establish primacy in Makkah due to a renowned victory. This was further exacerbated by the dream of one of the members of the al-Muttalib family, the very same from which Muhammad hailed, in which he foresaw the deaths of the principle nobles of the Quraysh in the coming battle. Abu Jahl could only lament with disdain that "this is yet another prophet from the clan of al-Muttalib," and urged his men to ignore the portent.[50] Relating such a dream could very well have been the action of a fifth columnist within the ranks of the Quraysh to instill fear and doubt, thus dampening their courage. Of the one thousand who started out, anywhere from two hundred to four hundred withdrew and headed back to Makkah, and those who did remain were still unsure about the situation.[51] With divided counsel and with overconfident leaders, the Qurayshi force pressed northward to the probable spot of Muhammad's force near Badr. They were so sure of victory that they even turned down offers of reinforcements from a nearby tribe.[52]

The area around Badr is essentially a bowl with mountains or ridges surrounding it on nearly every side. However, to the northwest and northeast there are passes, and to the south the terrain levels out to allow a caravan trail to pass through. It is about 1.6 miles wide from east to west and 2.5 miles long north to south. Those within the plain

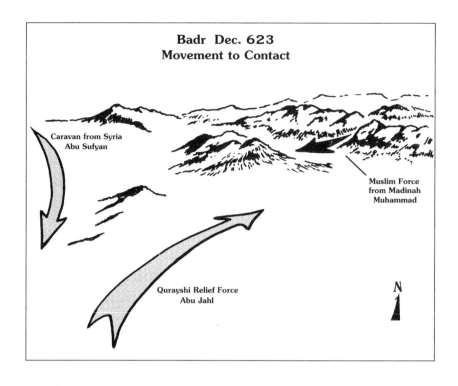

Badr Dec. 623
Movement to Contact

Caravan from Syria
Abu Sufyan

Muslim Force
from Madinah
Muhammad

Qurayshi Relief Force
Abu Jahl

N

would be hidden from view until a force moved over the ridges or up the caravan trail. Due to its wells, there was also a grove of trees on the south side of the plain that could make spotting an enemy force more difficult from the southern approach.

Having sent men to collect water at Badr, and those men not having returned, Abu Jahl realized where Muhammad's men probably were, though he would be unable to easily hear their movements because the Prophet had ordered the bells cut from the necks of his camels.[53] However, this mattered little as Abu Jahl's scouts confirmed his suspicions regarding the Muslims' location. Meanwhile, Muhammad was completely oblivious to the onrushing relief force until the day before contact, when his men captured the Qurayshi water bearers.[54] After trying to beat the truth out of them, and disbelieving it when they heard it, Muhammad admonished his men that these were indeed water bearers from a large relief force from Makkah. When the water bearers told the Prophet that the force killed nine to ten camels per day for food, Muhammad reckoned that the force was a thousand strong, which was an accurate assessment, though not taking into account those who had broken ranks and went back to Makkah. Muhammad, caught by surprise, now realized he was in serious trouble.[55] With his men on foot, faced with what he thought was a thousand men, many of them on horseback, he would be hard-pressed to withdraw into the mountains. With this in mind, and his need for some type of substantial victory, he was forced to make a stand, risking everything on one desperate engagement.

He now needed to inspire his men, for they had come out to raid a caravan, not to fight a pitched battle. He had pinned his hopes on the Ansar, and to them he turned for a declaration of loyalty. Securing this, he prepared for the first major fight of his life. Riding ahead of his men on his camel, he surveyed the plain to determine what to do. One of his officers, al-Hubib bin al-Mundhir, asked him if Allah had ordered them to fight a certain way or if this was just a matter of military tactics. When Muhammad said it was the latter, the officer advised that the wells of Badr to the west and south should be stopped up with rocks, and a cistern should be constructed to the east to hold plenty of water for the Muslims. Muhammad adopted the plan at once, and work teams quickly completed the projects.[56]

There is room for debate as to where Muhammad actually positioned his men. While tradition has determined that he positioned himself almost to the center of the Badr plain, the early documentation and common sense would indicate that he positioned the men further to the northeast, with their backs to the mountains and with his own headquarters on the slopes of the mountains overlooking the ground below. This placed his men close to their cistern and provided him a place to observe the action with a ready means to escape if the battle went poorly. In doing this, Muhammad placed his men on what Sun Tzu called "death ground."[57] With no room to maneuver they were compelled to fight and win, or die trying. However, Muhammad did have the foresight to position them in such a way that scattered survivors would be able to flee into the mountains if they fared badly in the fight, a concept reasonably well known to some military thinkers of that day.[58]

On the morning of 22 December 623, or 17 Ramadan AH 2, Abu Jahl's force stopped short of the slopes to the south of the Badr Plain and encamped. He sent a scout ahead to estimate the situation, and when he returned it was with grim news. He accurately reported the Muslim strength but then noted that they were prepared to fight to the death, and this would incur heavy casualties in the Qurayshi force. "I do not think a man of them will be slain till he slay one of you, and if they kill of you a number equal to their own, what is the good of living after that? Consider, then, what you will do."[59] With these words, dissension surfaced in the ranks of Abu Jahl's force, and he with difficulty put down the tide of division that could further weaken his force. As Abu Jahl struggled to control his wavering leaders and warriors, Muhammad moved about the ground near the Badr wells, placing his hand on the sand to declare that certain men of the Quraysh would die at such a point.[60] The differences between the two camps on the eve of battle were striking.

During the night, a light rain fell and the area where the Quraysh had encamped was in the wash of a wide wadi, thus becoming waterlogged. Meanwhile, the Muslims sheltered beneath their shields as Muhammad busied himself with prayer.[61] When the Friday morning of 23 December came, as the Muslims wearily gathered for prayer with the breaking dawn, the Quraysh found that their horsemen would have difficulty with the loose terrain, forcing many to dismount. Only the key leaders such as Abu Jahl remained mounted.[62] To make matters worse, there was further division within the Qurayshi camp. That night Abu Jahl had already rejected reinforcements offered by a neighboring tribe, apparently determined not to share in the glory of his anticipated victory, when he had an argument with fellow noble Utbah bin Rabi'ah. Utbah had been counseling the nobles that they should not engage in battle, and Abu Jahl chided him for his defeatism. "Your lungs are inflated with fear," he noted, to which Utbah retorted that his courage would be displayed on the field of battle. To emphasize his determination to attack Muhammad in the morning, Abu Jahl unsheathed his sword and slapped the back of his horse with the flat of the blade. Another, watching this exchange, left in bewilderment, noting that such discord among the leaders was a bad omen.[63]

As dawn broke, both sides began to make their preparations in what was to become an unusually hot day.[64] Even as the Quraysh were lining up, Utbah bin Rabi'ah rode on his red camel among the men, exhorting them not to fight against their family members, a fact very personal to him since one of his own sons had become a Muslim. "Do you not see them," referring to the Muslims, "how they crouch down on their mounts, keeping firmly in place, licking their lips like serpents?"[65] Utbah's openly displayed dissension put Abu Jahl into a fit of fury, declaring that if "it were anyone else saying this, I would bite him!"[66] Attempting to again rally his men, Abu Jahl cried out to Allah, asking him to destroy the army that was unrighteous in his sight.[67] With the advantage of their cavalry lost due to the soft ground, and lacking substantial water and already suffering from thirst, Abu Jahl moved his hesitant fighters over the ridge and onward to destiny in the Badr plain.

Even as he did so, Muhammad had completed arranging his men during the predawn hours with only a few clad in light chain mail for battle.[68] He personally used an arrow to align them by ranks into a straight line, even jabbing one of his men, Sawad bin Ghaziyyah, in the stomach with the arrow tip to get him in line. Sawad declared that the Prophet had injured him and demanded recompense on the spot. Muhammad uncovered his torso and told him to take it. Instead, the warrior leaned forward and kissed the Prophet on the stomach. When Muhammad asked him why he did this, Sawad said that he might very well be killed and wished that this be his last remembrance of his leader.[69] Having positioned his men, Muhammad returned to the small tent set up as his headquarters and demonstrated his confidence by taking a brief nap.[70] He placed Qays bin Abu Saʿsaʿa in command of the rear guard, composed of older men and probably armed with spears, while to the front Saʿd bin Khaythama was in command of the right and al-Miqdad bin al-Aswad in charge of the left. These two were leading the younger men, ardent and spoiling for the fight.[71] The latter commander was possibly the only Muslim actually on the battlefield mounted on horseback.[72] Several gusts of wind blew across the sand, and Muhammad cried out that the angels of Allah had arrived, so each man should mark his own hood and cap with a special symbol of identification to protect them from angelic wrath.[73]

As the Qurayshi force advanced slowly across the plain, several men stepped forward to initiate single combat. Two Muslims were killed in the first exchange, along with one of the Quraysh who had vowed to fight his way through to the Muslim water supply. He was met by Muhammad's uncle Hamzah, who slashed off part of one leg before the man managed to reach the water. Hamzah climbed into the pool and finished the Qurayshi warrior off with a single blow.[74] With these modest preliminaries complete, the champions came forward to do single combat. Honor and shame being a key virtue for such tribal cultures, three men from the princely class of the Quraysh, Utbah bin Rabiʿah along with one of his sons and Utbah's brother, demanded to have combat with men of equal social stature. Three dutifully stepped forward, including Muhammad's uncle Hamzah, his cousin 'Ali bin Abu Talib, and Ubaydah bin al-Harith. When the duel was over, the three Quraysh were dead and Ubaydah was mortally wounded when his leg was severed by the blow of a sword from Utbah's brother. As for Utbah bin Rabi'ah, he died displaying the very valor he had declared the night prior to Abu Jahl.

With the single combats essentially inconclusive, the moment for battle had arrived. Even as the sun began to cap the mountains to the southeast, Abu Jahl's men found the light blazing at an angle into their eyes, and they squinted to the northeast to see the Muslims remaining rock solid in their ranks.[75] The lines of the Quraysh now began to advance.

The Muslims remained stationary, the sound of mailed warriors steadily approaching their line. In the midst of the Qurayshi force they could see three battle flags of the 'Abd al-Dar, and several mounted men leading them on, their mail gleaming in the morning sun. Abu Jahl, on horseback, continued to urge his men forward, still sensing an unease and hesitance in their gait. "One should not kill the Muslims," he cried. "Instead, capture them so they can be chastised!"[76] Ahead he could see the four battle flags of the Muslims, with the larger one in the center and elevated to the rear—the green flag of Muhammad himself. Abu Jahl felt his ardor rise, and he cried out poetic verse about how his destiny was to wage war and conquer his foes.[77] Abu Jahl must have at this moment sensed that his desire for triumph was about to be fulfilled.

As for Muhammad, he had informed his men that anyone who killed any of the enemy would get that man's armor and weapons as plunder.[78] He watched the scene unfold below, a cloud of dust now rising from the ranks of the advancing enemy. Muhammad had ordered his men to keep the enemy at bay with missiles, only resorting to sword play at the last minute. Commands were now shouted out and several volleys of arrows were thrown from Muslim archers posted to the right and left of the main body. This was followed by a shower of stones from the main body of the Muslim force.[79] The arrows and stones, though mostly harmless against the armor and shields of the enemy, still served as a harbinger of the fight to come. The Muslims, being less armored, probably suffered more in the exchange, with at least one killed as far back as the cistern as he took a drink of water.[80] Following the missile skirmishing, the signal was given and the Muslims now began their own slow advance, marching in ranks toward their enemy. Then came the command to draw swords, and in unison the front rank unsheathed their curved Indian blades, a flash of brilliance like lightning dashing into the eyes of the Qurayshi soldiers, even as the rank behind leveled their spears.[81]

And then Muhammad gave the signal to charge. The Muslims suddenly cried out at the top of their lungs, shouting "One! One!" a sound like thunder echoing from the mountain sides as they broke ranks and bolted for the center of the Qurayshi lines.[82] As swords were wielded and spears thrust, the Qurayshi men began to feel the exhaustion already creeping over them as they cried out for the water they did not possess but now so desperately needed. In contrast, individual Muslims could fight for several minutes and then quickly pull from the ranks to refresh themselves in their trough before returning back to the fight, their gap filled by men in ranks behind them. One of them, ʿAwf bin al-Harith, while taking a respite from the fighting asked the Prophet what makes Allah laugh with joy. Muhammad replied that it was the man who charged "into the enemy without mail." On hearing this, ʿAwf stripped off his chain mail and tossed it aside. He then threw himself into the ranks of the Quraysh until he was killed.[83]

Because of their armor, few of the Quraysh fell in the first charge, but their morale was wavering even as Muhammad paced back and forth under his tent, declaring that the Quraysh would "be routed and will turn and flee. Nay, but the Hour (of doom) is their appointed tryst, and the Hour will be more wretched and more bitter (than this earthly failure)."[84] The Muslims purposely targeted the leaders of the enemy, and Abu Jahl's horse was quickly brought down. No longer seeing their leader hovering over them, the Qurayshi line shuddered and then broke in confusion as men, overcome by thirst, exhaustion, and doubt, turned to run. It was then that the real killing and maiming began, as the Muslims raced after them, swords flashing as they dismembered bodies and took heads. Even then, individual men, usually noblemen of the Quraysh, attempted to make a stand and rally their fleeing men until they were cut down.

Abu Jahl, finding himself cut off from his army along with his son Ikrimah, positioned himself with his back to a thicket of scrub, fighting until he was severely wounded. Muʿadh bin Amr cornered him, his sword severing a leg and sending the foot and calf flying. Ikrimah desperately fought to protect his father and brought his sword down on Mu'adh's shoulder, nearly severing the man's arm. Mu'adh staggered from the fight, and, with his father too injured to move, Ikrimah withdrew as well, leaving his father to his fate. Another Muslim passed by and gave Abu Jahl an additional blow, though still not fatal.[85] As for Mu'adh, he would rest and reenter the fight, soon after tearing off his mangled arm because he was dragging it around. Despite the severity of his wound, he would survive the battle and live into the days of the *khalifate* of 'Uthman.

With the Quraysh in full flight, Muhammad's men began to round up prisoners, a sight that angered one of the leading Ansar, Sa'd bin Mu'adh, who was now with the Prophet at his command tent. Muhammad could see the displeasure on the man's face and asked him why he disapproved taking prisoners. "This was the first defeat inflicted by God on the polytheists," Sa'd remarked. "Killing the prisoners would have been more pleasing to me than sparing them."[86] Despite Sa'd's attitude, the Muslims continued to assemble the prisoners, sorting through the dead and wounded to find friends or enemies and take stock of their incredible victory.

'Abdullah bin Mas'ud found Abu Jahl still alive and barely breathing from the wounds he had received. He placed his foot on his neck and asked, "Are you Abu Jahl?" Upon affirmation, he took hold of his beard and severed the dying man's head. He then took it and threw it at Muhammad's feet, who gave thanks to Allah for the great victory.[87] The dead Quraysh, a total of at least fifty and possibly as many as seventy, were thrown into one of the wells, with Muhammad reciting over them, "have you found what God threatened is true? For I have found that what my Lord promised me is true."[88] At least forty-three prisoners were taken, though some sources say as many as seventy were captured.[89] As for the Muslim dead, Ibn Ishaq states that only eight died at Badr, although other sources placed the number as high as fourteen.[90] Among the dead of the Quraysh were a disproportionately high number of nobles, and the loss of their core leaders had to be a serious blow to them. Many had stayed and died fighting, even as their servants and lower ranks fled. In addition, if the Quraysh had about seven hundred men on the field and suffered seventy dead, 10 percent were killed, a rate comparable or significantly higher in light of other battles not only ancient but even from the modern era.[91]

While it is tempting to attribute the Muslim victory at Badr to the power of Allah or to angelic intervention, just as Muslim writers would contend, there were conventional reasons why they won. The Quraysh were divided among themselves, uncertain as to the wisdom of their leader's actions and concerned about fighting their brethren from their clans. In contrast, the Muslims were actuated and motivated by one force: the will of their leader Muhammad. The weather also worked against the Quraysh, robbing them of the one element that could have proven decisive in battle, their cavalry. The Muslims were on the defensive, fully rested and provisioned, while the Quraysh lacked that vital necessity of water so crucial in the desert. This was accentuated by the fact that the Muslims were more lightly armored than the Quraysh, and thus more mobile and resilient in an infantry battle waged in the desert, which could still become sufficiently warm in December. Muhammad had also chosen the terrain carefully, following counsel and wisdom of those more experienced in the actual tactics of battle, while Abu Jahl scorned the advice brought to him by other noblemen of the Quraysh. The latter also allowed his army to be drawn into battle on ground not of his choosing. Finally, the Quraysh had underestimated Muhammad's capabilities while the prophet had overestimated theirs. The former approached the battle overconfident of an easy victory while the latter prepared to fight to the death, certain that he and his men would either immerge triumphant or his movement would be destroyed forever. Prepared to die, Muhammad's men triumphed, a factor that had brought victory to many combatants throughout history.

With the victory at Badr, Muhammad issued orders that the booty was not to be taken by anyone until the fighting was over so that it could be divided properly. Moreover, orders were given regarding the disposition of the prisoners. While most sources indicate they were to be ransomed, some also implied that they could be executed if the captors so desired because prisoners were the personal property of the ones who captured them.[92]

Among those captured was Muhammad's uncle al-Abbas bin ʿAbd al-Muttalib. Prior to the battle, Muhammad suspected that some of his immediate family would be in the fight and had given orders to spare them.[93] With al-Abbas now his prisoner, Muhammad may have understood why he received no word of the relief column, in that al-Abbas had been forced to go with them, and was thus unable to dispatch any messages to his nephew. Nevertheless, Muhammad had to be sure of his uncle and forced him to pay a ransom for his release, which additionally helped to maintain his cover. This also served as a convenient financial transfer mechanism, for while the amount stated in the sources is relatively small, it could have easily served as the conduit to funnel a much larger sum to the Prophet without the knowledge of other Qurayshi leaders.

Other prisoners were to be ransomed as well, but 'Abd al-Rahman bin Auf was deprived of his by the actions of Muhammad's *mu'adhdhin*, the man who called people to prayer. While in Makkah, Bilal had been treated cruelly by his master, Umayyah bin Khalaf. Now, Umayyah, his son, and a few others were prisoners of 'Abd al-Rahman. Bilal, recognizing his former master, began to cry out "the head of disbelief, Umayyah bin Khalaf! May I not be spared if they are spared."[94] He continued to cry out in like manner until a crowd began to circle 'Abd al-Rahman and his captives. 'Abd al-Rahman tried to protect them as best he could, especially in light of the significant ransom he would receive for them. But the crowd pressed in and murdered Umayyah and his son, hacking them to pieces. Afterward, 'Abd al-Rahman lamented what had transpired, bemoaning he had lost the monetary ransom he anticipated due to Bilal's rash behavior. But while Bilal's behavior was based on reckless emotion, the fate of two others was determined by cool calculation.

'Uqba bin Aub Mu'ayt and al-Nadr bin al-Harith had been both deeply involved in opposing the Prophet in Makkah. 'Uqba, in order to maintain the friendship of one who vehemently opposed Muhammad, went to the Prophet and spit in his face.[95] Al-Nadr had engaged in more aggressive tactics, insulting Muhammad and ridiculing his recitations, stating that he could "tell a better story than he," since he was intimately familiar with Persian legends.[96] On the way back to Madinah, 'Ali bin Abu Talib executed al-Nadr while 'Uqba was executed on express order of the Prophet. When 'Uqba asked Muhammad who would look after his children, the Prophet responded, "Hell." However, these executions were the exception, for Muhammad had ordered that the prisoners be cared for in anticipation of a hefty ransom.[97]

With the issue of the prisoners now settled, the Prophet prepared to pursue the caravan, which was the original object of his mission. At this point, having overheard much of the conversation and apparently having heard the Prophet recite that Allah was to grant to the Muslims either the relief army or the caravan, al-Abbas pointed out this fact to his nephew, telling him that it was not wise to pursue the caravan in contravention of what Allah had commanded.[98] Thus cautioned, Muhammad ordered his army to head for home, dispatching a messenger in advance to herald his triumph.

News of the victory reached Madinah quickly, with the Prophet himself returning soon after his messenger. The consequences of this startling victory were colossal, not only for the Muslims but for their opponents. The Quraysh were stunned to incomprehension as the news of the disaster came back to Makkah. At first those who remained behind refused to believe that their army had been defeated and their most important nobles killed. Stories of angelic beings fighting for the Muslims were convenient for both victor and vanquished; the former could claim divine support while the latter could explain away an incomprehensible defeat. One of Muhammad's uncles, Abu Lahab, was so enraged by the news that he beat the messenger who delivered it and then was struck with an illness, possibly a stroke, and died a week later.[99] Abu Sufyan, now the de facto senior leader of the Quraysh, had lost two sons in the battle, one killed and the other captured. Enraged, probably both by the defeat and Abu Jahl's recklessness, Abu Sufyan refused to ransom him. Instead, he arranged the later capture of a Muslim engaged in pilgrimage to Makkah and used him as a bargaining chip to retrieve his son.[100]

Yet the defeat of Abu Jahl's force was not as remarkable as some might think. The Quraysh made significant errors of judgment prior to the battle. While it could be attractive to say that the Qurayshi leaders underestimated the Muslims, it is more likely that they overestimated the commitment of their own junior leaders and forces. The exit of a significant number of troops prior to the battle should have been a warning of coming difficulties, but Abu Jahl was too stubborn to see it. The night before the battle, one of the nobles came to Abu Jahl expressing concern about the forthcoming battle. The Qurayshi leader reacted with a violent oath. "No, by God, we will not turn back until God decides between us and Muhammad," a confrontation that onlookers saw as being an evil premonition.[101] Moreover, despite hearing that the caravan was safe, Abu Jahl changed the nature of his mission. His initial goal was to save the caravan. With his mission accomplished, he arbitrarily altered it, embarking on one of high risk that would compel many of his men to fight members of their families. Both men and lesser nobles were thus confused and perplexed as they awaited the rising sun at the moment of battle. This was exacerbated by the lack of unity of command and the fact that the Quraysh did not choose the battleground. As a consequence, Abu Jahl's force may have been tactically on the offensive, but they were on the defensive operationally. This gave the Muslims a significant advantage.

Nevertheless, the Quraysh did perform well in certain areas. Had they exploited their abilities and lured Muhammad's force into an open fight on ground of their choosing, the results could have been dramatically different. For example, Abu Sufyan and Abu Jahl did a remarkable job of coordinating the movements of their two disparate forces while Abu Jahl maneuvered into an effective blocking position. Up until the morning of the battle, the Qurayshi operation had been a resounding success. Had they understood the moral factors faced by the Prophet and that he desperately needed a military triumph to confirm his position as the leading sayyid of Madinah, and had Abu Jahl been able to restrain his personal pride, the mere salvation of the caravan could have been sufficient to cause a revolution within the ranks of the people of Madinah.

But before one heaps condemnation upon Abu Jahl, it must be pointed out that of all of the Qurayshi leaders he probably had the clearest vision as to what needed to be done to snuff out Muhammad's insurgency. He saw that the only way to deal with such an insurgency was to totally destroy it. Short of the objective of total victory, the insurgency would continue to gnaw away at the Qurayshi will to resist until Makkah itself would fall. In this regard alone, Abu Jahl's death was a crippling blow to the Quraysh.

In contrast to the Quraysh, Muhammad and the Muslims had performed remarkably, if not with uniqueness. Their battle plan was simple and direct but was made more effective by the things they did correctly. Unlike the Quraysh, the Muslims were actuated by one spirit—the will of the Prophet, which he confirmed by taking an oath of support from the Ansar. This unity of command allowed Muhammad to take the initiative when he needed to, enabling him to capitalize upon the poor decisions of his opponent. He chose his ground carefully and took the time and effort to prepare it, giving himself every possible advantage in his circumstance. He also deployed his men on what could best be described as "death ground," placing his men with their backs to the mountains. To the uninitiated, this meant the inability to escape, but in reality it was probably the best location to allow his men, all of whom were on foot, to escape the enemy cavalry should they suffer defeat. However, all of these advantages were fraught with danger, for Muhammad was staking the entire future of his movement, and perhaps his very life, on a single card. His men, motivated and determined by the words of Allah carried by their Prophet, would almost certainly fight with ferocity, and on this Muhammad placed his hopes.

There was one other significant consequence to the Muslim victory, and this impacted the Jewish tribes in Madinah. To them the unthinkable had occurred, and now they were forced to face the Prophet of Allah, emboldened by victory and supported by acclamation, as he entered Madinah in triumph, his position as sayyid confirmed.

4

From Elation to Despair

One of the first things Muhammad did when he returned to Madinah after the astonishing Muslim victory at Badr was to sit down and relax in his mosque. Such was well deserved, for the Prophet had risked everything, staking the entire future on one moment to achieve his triumph. He was certainly aware that such a victory needed exploitation, and the most logical direction for this was regarding key opponents in Madinah. It is difficult to know exactly when the Prophet confronted the Jews, but it was certainly soon after the battle, for the nature of the confrontation clearly indicates he was playing off of the consternation created by his victory. There is also some confusion regarding what operations occurred next. Ibn Ishaq places two raids in advance of the siege of the Banu Qaynuqa, but a further analysis, including the timeline of Ibn Saʿd and al-Waqidi, suggests a different chronology. It is probably not critical which version is more accurate, but the following will adhere to the chronology laid out by Fazlur Rehman Shaikh, who strove to reconcile differences in the timeline.

Muhammad turned to his companions and said, "Let us proceed to the Jews." They then went to the Bait-al-Midras, which was a Jewish school in the central marketplace within the confines of the Banu Qaynuqa. He then called them to "surrender to Allah and you will be safe!" The Jews replied several times that Muhammad had indeed brought the declarations of Allah to them, but it was clear they were not going to embrace the Prophet's way. At this point Muhammad declared that "the earth is for Allah and I want to exile you from this land, so whoever among you has property should sell it, otherwise, know that the land is for Allah and His Apostle."[1] This precise exchange from al-Bukhari does not appear in the *sira* and *maghazi* literature, such as Ibn Ishaq, al-Tabari, Ibn Kathir, al-Waqidi, or Ibn Saʿd. Sources that do deal with this confrontation do so in a slightly different manner, but having similar import, and thus is probably the same incident. From the perspective of the *sira* literature, the Prophet assembled the Jews in the market and warned the Jews to "beware lest God bring upon you the vengeance that He brought upon Quraysh, and become Muslims. You know that I am the prophet who has been sent—you will find that in your scriptures."[2] While the version given by Ibn Ishaq and al-Tabari has some differences, both are a warning to the Jews. That preserved in al-Bukhari's hadith collection is clearly a direct threat. For the Prophet to go to the Jews forthwith and threaten them indicates to what level of confidence he had ascended. He now moved quickly to suppress key opponents within the city before engaging any of the Jewish tribes directly.

One of the first to be eliminated was Asma bint Marwan, a married woman with five children. There is some controversy among Muslim writers regarding this incident because Asma was a woman; some either deny the incident or ignore it completely, citing passages in Islamic writings that women are among those who are not to be attacked. Al-Tabari and Ibn Kathir do not mention it, but Ibn Ishaq, Ibn Hisham, al-Waqidi, and Ibn Saʿd do.[3] Moreover, a number of other Muslim writers, both classical and modern, accept the account as genuine, as do many western scholars.[4] However, this incident is not as controversial as some may think when one understands the conception of war within the Islamic worldview.

Warfare in early Islam is more than mere fighting; it also includes teaching, economics, politics, and propaganda. In the conception of this Islamic worldview, if one were to engage in disseminating propaganda, or in Asma's case, reciting poetry against the Prophet and his followers, then that individual, regardless of gender, has made himself or herself a target for retribution.[5] As such, Asma had engaged in warfare, having recited poetry to "revile Islam, offend the Prophet and instigate the (people) against him."[6] Part of the poetic verse she recited blamed the people of Madinah for accepting a stranger, placing the blame on the principal leaders of the two major tribes of the city, and hinting that somebody should assassinate the Prophet. Muhammad's personal

Table 4.1. Operations from the Battle of Badr to the Battle of Uhud

Date	Mission	Enemy	Muslims	Leader	Result
Dec 623	Assassination	Asma bint Marwan	1	'Umayr bin 'Adi	Success
Jan 624	Assassination	Abu 'Afak	1	Salim bin 'Umayr	Success
Jan 624	Al-Kudr; Sulaym/ Ghatafan	unknown	200	Muhammad	No Contact
Jan 624	Ghatafan	unknown	unknown	Ghalib bin 'Abdullah	Fighting
Jan 624	Madinah; Banu Qaynuqa	700	unknown	Muhammad	Victory
Mar 624	Al-Sawiq; Quraysh	unknown	200–400	Muhammad	No Contact
Jun 624	Dhu Amarr; Ghatafan/ Tha'labah/ Muharib	unknown	450	Muhammad	No Contact
Jul 624	Buhran; Sulaym	unknown	150–200	Muhammad	No Contact
Aug 624	Al-Qaradah; Quraysh		100	Zayd bin Harithah	Victory
Sep 624	Assassination	K'ab bin al-Ashraf	3–5	Muham- mad bin Maslamah	Success
Dec 624	Uhud; Quraysh	3,000	700	Muhammad	Defeat
Dec 624	Hamra al-Asad (Pursuit)	3,000	70	Muhammad	No Contact

court poet, Hassan bin Thabit, responded by issuing veiled threats that "death is coming" and that she would soon be drenched "in her blood."[7] Such bloodcurdling proclamations, followed by the predicted action, made a significant impact on friend and foe alike. Only a few days after the victory of Badr, one of Asma's relatives crept into her house in the deep of night, removed a nursing child from her breast, and "thrust his sword in her chest till it pierced up to her back."[8]

Asma's assassination was followed quickly by that of another promi-nent individual, Abu 'Afak, an elderly Jew of one of the lesser clans in

Madinah. Like Asma, Abu ʿAfak had recited poetic verse ridiculing the Qur'an and the Prophet. Muhammad asked for someone to eliminate him, and one of the members of the target's tribe infiltrated the man's home while he slept and plunged a sword through his liver until it reached his bed.[9] The assassination of these two public individuals, both known for reciting poetry that in Arabian culture was the equivalent of a journalistic and propagandistic activity, provided Muhammad with the gauge of his opponents' wherewithal. In both instances he saw no adverse reaction spring forth from the opposition, and he surely realized that he now had a good opportunity to deal with some of his Jewish tribal opposition without delay. It took only a few weeks for this to occur.

Even as the Prophet prepared to take on some of his Jewish opponents, he planned and conducted several other raids. One hit the Banu Sulaym, a neighboring tribe to the southeast of Madinah. This raid led to no fighting, but some animals were captured. Muhammad also commissioned another raid against the Banu Ghatafan, who resided northeast of Madinah. This raid led to a small amount of fighting and some loot taken.[10] However, this operation appears to have been more of a reconnaissance in preparation for a larger operation a few months later. At least one of these raids, that of al-Kudr against the Sulaym, was triggered by a report that reached the Prophet that they were mobilizing against him.[11] Yet once the Muslim force arrived in the area, the rumored raid was nowhere to be seen, and they contented themselves with seizing plunder.

The notion of rumors followed by the Prophet's response in the form of raids would be characteristic of his early operations, and this raises the question of how accurate these rumors were. While Muhammad's intelligence service within Makkah was phenomenal, it appears that either he had mediocre intelligence in the outlying areas or that he was possibly using such rumors to rally his hesitant men to provide justification for a series of raids against his neighbors. The mere threat of external attack would be sufficient to rally the faint at heart to engage in battle, regardless of the veracity of the reports and true reality of the situation. It is worth noting that Ibn Saʿd recounts one raid after another based on such rumors prior to the Muslim victory against the Quraysh at al-Khandaq in 627. But after withstanding the Qurayshi siege and destroying the Banu Qurayzah shortly thereafter, such rumors of possible attacks against the Muslims fade away, with Muhammad now ordering raids on neighboring tribes at will. As the confidence of his men grew, it apparently became unnecessary to resort to stratagems to encourage his men to fight.

But, before dealing any significant blows against neighboring opposition, the Prophet at last got his chance to deal with one of the major Jewish tribes in Madinah. As to the incident that gave Muhammad his casus belli, there is some divergence of views in the sources. Some say that the Jews merely displayed "jealousy" regarding the Muslim victory at Badr.[12] Another indicates that a Muslim woman was humiliated in the marketplace that was controlled by the Banu Qaynuqa. The former could merely be a general statement of the poetic verse that was being recited by the likes of Asma and Abu 'Afak. If it was the latter, then this incident offers an interesting glimpse into how Muhammad engaged in moral inversion, a classic technique of insurgency warfare. Moral inversion is where one takes their own actions and imputes them to an enemy, thereby placing blame on the other party instead of oneself. In this case, Ibn Hisham stated that

> An Arab woman took an ornament of hers and sold it in the market of Banu Qaynuqa. She sat there with one of their goldsmiths and the men present began pestering her to uncover her face. She refused, but the goldsmith managed to attach the hem of her dress to her back. When she got up, she was exposed, and they all laughed at her. She screamed and one of the Muslim men attacked and killed the goldsmith, who was a Jew. The Jews then seized the Muslim and killed him. The Muslim's family called for help from the other Muslims against the Jews. The Muslims were enraged, and so enmity arose between them and Banu Qaynuqa.[13]

There are several important items within this passage. The first involves the veil. The veil was adopted later by the rank and file Muslims, which thus implies that this incident is apocryphal. However, while this is generally the case, the veil predates the Prophet's time, and it is conceivable that this woman was wearing a veil.[14] While this might seem to be a trivial issue, it must be discussed, for if the passage is apocryphal then it could cast doubt upon the analysis of the more important elements, such as the response of the Muslims and the Jews and who does what first. When the woman screamed, a Muslim killed the Jew, striking first in an exponential manner, using force far beyond what the situation merited. In turn, a group of Jews, exercising the *lex talionis*, killed the Muslim.

At this juncture, save for the woman's embarrassment and some verbal recriminations, the incident should have been closed. Instead, the incident was quickly transformed into a cause célèbre, and Ibn Hisham indicates that the Muslims were angered but says nothing about the sensibilities of the Jews, even though one of their own suffered the ultimate consequence for his ill-advised prank. The lesson that could be derived from this account is that a Muslim in Madinah could inflict deadly harm on one who simply humiliated a Muslim woman, and that, should one arise and kill the Muslim in turn, it could lead to full-scale war. Moreover, the sources emphasize that it was the Muslims who were offended, even though they committed the first serious transgression. The incident, now turned on its head, became the catalyst the Prophet was seeking.

Coupled with this episode were passages of Surah 8 now revealed to the Prophet regarding the nonaggression treaty he had with the Qaynuqa. "And if thou fearest treachery from any folk, then throw back to them (their treaty) fairly. Lo! Allah loveth not the treacherous."[15] When Muhammad finished receiving this passage from Jibril, he looked at the angel and said, "I fear the Banu Qaynuqa."[16] While Ibn Kathir in his Tafsir places an emphasis on the need for both parties to be on an equal footing that war exists, what is missed is the crucial point that if Muhammad even suspected possible treachery he could immediately nullify a treaty.[17] While this did not imply that he could use the cover of a treaty to engage in offensive operations against an enemy, it does indicate that the slightest incident could be used as a rationale to abrogate an agreement and then immediately initiate hostilities.[18] By taking this initiative, and especially working counter to normal human behavior, which is risk aversive and would attempt to maintain or extend a treaty, Muhammad was able to gain a decisive edge over unprepared foes.

And the Qaynuqa were certainly unprepared. The siege was initiated on the Jewish Sabbath and lasted for about two weeks before the Jewish tribe, bereft of friends, realized that no help would be forthcoming and sought terms from Muhammad.[19] Being allied to the al-Khazraj tribe helped them in only one way—'Abdullah bin Ubayy, one of that tribe's key leaders, pleaded with Muhammad that their lives be spared, going so far as to seize the Prophet by the collar of his cloak, causing the Prophet to cry out, "Damn you! Let me go!"[20] 'Abdullah replied by telling the Prophet that seven hundred men at arms of the Qaynuqa had defended him in war and that he could not bear to see them cut down in a day, further emphasizing his point by saying, "I am a man who fears that circumstances may change."[21]

It is clear from this exchange that Muhammad planned to implement the extreme consequences of the victor in those days by executing the warriors and selling the women and children into slavery.[22] Instead, 'Abdullah's intervention highlights the real possibility that Muhammad may have been on the verge of overplaying his hand. Would the marginally committed and the uncommitted people of Madinah support the destruction of the Qaynuqa's men? Would 'Abdullah and other leaders instigate an insurrection against Muslim rule in the city, which at this time was tenuous at best? It is probable that Muhammad wanted to use the Banu Qaynuqa as an object lesson of what would happen to those who resisted the Prophet's will, but alas, his level of support was insufficient to sustain such a move. As a result, the Qaynuqa were spared.

The exile of the Banu Qaynuqa, though not as extreme as death and slavery, most assuredly placed a pall of defeat over many of Muhammad's opponents in the city. However, some possibly took secret delight in the Qaynuqa's defeat, and this included the two other Jewish tribes, the Banu al-Nadir and Qurayzah. These two tribes had sided with the smaller al-Aws tribe against the larger al-Khazraj. The latter, as a consequence, had received the support of the Qaynuqa. The latter's exile meant the lessening of the al-Khazraj's importance, thus elevating the al-Aws's, al-Nadir's, and Qurayzah's influence in Madinah. These tribes allowed their own petty jealousies and rivalries to blind them concerning the greater threat presented by Muhammad's movement to their own liberties, and even their lives.

Not long after the exile of the Banu Qaynuqa occurred a counterraid by the Quraysh that demonstrated their weakness of will. This raid, called in the sources al-Sawiq, or the raid of the barley gruel, was a pathetic attempt by Abu Sufyan to avenge himself of the Qurayshi defeat at Badr. Setting out in March 624 with possibly as many as two hundred men, he raided the outskirts of Madinah, killed one of the Ansar, and burned a few houses. He then turned his men about to make his escape, by this time being hotly pursued by the Prophet with two hundred of his own men. The Qurayshi troops discarded their provisions in the form of bags of *sawiq* to lighten their load so as to escape, an obvious indication of their lack of desire to get into a fight.[23] While the raid may have assuaged Abu Sufyan of his desire for revenge, its petty nature and their unwillingness to engage in mortal combat could only have raised the morale of the Muslims. Concurrently, it would have lessened his status in the eyes of those within the Quraysh who understood the true nature of the Muslim threat to their culture, and would have created more confusion and recriminations within the ranks of their leadership.

From the end of March until December 624, Muhammad worked to consolidate his position in Madinah while engaging in several raids against his neighbors. However, only one produced any significant material results while another had political ramifications. In August, Muhammad authorized his adopted son, Zayd bin Harithah, to raid a Qurayshi caravan moving along the trade route to al-Irak. The Quraysh had chosen to take this way because they were now concerned about the safety of the western caravan route, indicating in their council that the Prophet had blocked the coastal route and if they did not continue engaging in trade they would soon consume their current capital.[24] Zayd departed Madinah with one hundred mounted men, heading northeast. While Ibn Sa'd indicated these were horsemen, this appears improbable, for these same one hundred horsemen do not make their appearance at the battle of Uhud.[25] Moreover, neither Ibn Ishaq nor al-Tabari indicate they were on horseback, and al-Waqidi states that they were mounted on camels.[26] But even though mounted on camels, this force represented the most formidable mounted combat element yet fielded by the Muslims.

Muhammad must have had accurate intelligence about this caravan, for he otherwise would have continued patrolling the coastal route. Moreover, the Qurayshi traders were unfamiliar with the al-Irak route, for they needed to hire a special guide, Furat Ibn Hayyan, to lead them. Zayd managed to surprise the caravan near al-Qaradah, a watering waypoint in Najd. The Quraysh accompanying the caravan escaped, but the contents were captured along with their guide. The guide was brought to Muhammad who made a public display of asking him to embrace Islam, which Furat naturally did. However, the nature of this conversion, along with the ease in which Zayd was able to locate the caravan, raises the question as to whether Furat may have been an agent working for the Prophet from the beginning, with the public conversion done to hide this fact. If this was indeed correct, it would be essential for the Prophet to keep such information hidden, for he would not want the Quraysh to suspect such infiltration that was betraying their caravans. It is worth noting that Furat would be used in the capacity of a secret agent later on near the end of Muhammad's life and was even awarded an estate in al-Yamamah for his services.[27]

The spoil captured from Zayd's raid at al-Qaradah was possibly the most significant take to this point. Yet, although valued at one hundred thousand dirhams, this was still a small amount compared to the needs of the Muslim *ummah*.[28] Nevertheless, the take was sufficient to serve as a good reward for those who participated in such raids, helping to encourage future participation.

The raid at al-Qaradah dispelled all doubt for the Quraysh that their trading and security business was in serious jeopardy, a point highlighted by verses recited by Muhammad's court poet, Hassan bin Thabit: "You can say good-bye to the streams of Damascus, for in between are swords like the mouths of pregnant camels who feed on arak trees."[29] Both the primary coastal route and the secondary route to al-Irak were now seriously threatened, and because caravans typically moved on a routine schedule, it was difficult to adjust these schedules in an effort to avoid Muhammad's attacks. Moreover, there had to be some concern within their own ranks that the Prophet of Allah had spies in their midst, but exposing them was a different matter. It became apparent to some of the Qurayshi leaders that a more concerted effort needed to be made to stop the Muslims and their depredations. Important merchants and leaders approached Abu Sufyan and offered to raise the necessary money to recruit and equip a force necessary to avenge the previous losses.[30] They decided to use the profits from the caravan that had escaped the battle of Badr, the merchants managing to make 100 percent profit on the goods sold in the market, thereby raising as much as fifty thousand dinars for the operation.[31] It also seemed logical that the Quraysh made efforts to gain some support from within Madinah and may have found this in a nobleman who was part of the Banu al-Nadir named Ka'b bin al-Ashraf.

Ka'b was not only a wealthy individual but also a prominent reciter of poetry. As the former, he traveled to Makkah to eulogize those Quraysh killed at Badr, and possibly to rally support to drive Muhammad out of Madinah. As the latter, he used his poetic skills to ridicule Muhammad and the Muslims in an effort to make them a byword in the city. At one point, Ka'b called on the Madinans to "drive off that fool of yours that you may be safe,"[32] a mocking reference to Muhammad's own declaration that people should embrace Islam to be safe. He also ridiculed the wife of Muhammad's uncle Al-Abbas, his passages both sexually suggestive and derisive of the woman's physical features. While not a Jew himself, he had married into the Jewish al-Nadir tribe, and because of his status had taken on a leadership role among them.

Muhammad grasped the depth of this threat. Should Ka'b continue his propaganda campaign unabated, it could incite the uncommitted in Madinah against the Muslims, and so the Prophet asked if anyone would kill him. Muhammad bin Maslamah volunteered for the task, along with several others, including Abu Na'ilah who had been wet-nursed by the same woman as Ka'b, thus making them foster brothers. However, Muhammad bin Maslamah was well aware of Ka'b's reputation in combat and was nervous that, having now agreed to kill him, he might not be able to accomplish the deed. To this the Prophet said that he need only try.[33] Muhammad bin Maslamah then suggested that he use deception against Ka'b, to which the Prophet agreed. In September 624, Abu Na'ilah, whom Ka'b disliked immensely, approached Ka'b with a complaint.

"The advent of this man [i.e., the Prophet] is a calamity for us," bemoaned Abu Na'ilah. "The Arabs are fighting with us and they are shooting from one bow."

"Didn't I tell you Ibn Salama," Ka'b replied, "that things would turn out this way?"[34]

Feigning agreement, Abu Na'ilah related how some of the Muslims wished to buy food from Ka'b, asking what they could give him as a pledge. Ka'b suggested that they deliver either their women or children as surety, to which they refused with indignation. The would-be assassins then suggested that they mortgage their weapons to him, to which Ka'b agreed.

The three assassins arrived at Ka'b's home during the night and called for him. Ka'b got up to get dressed, although his wife urged him not to go. She noted that Ka'b was currently a man engaged in warfare, and it would thus be dangerous to go out at night. Moreover, she could "hear a voice as if blood is dropping from him."[35] Ka'b refused to heed her advice and put on his armor to greet the men at the entrance to his fortified home. They then asked if he would walk with them a ways, and to this he naïvely agreed. At this point, Ka'b was either blissfully ignorant or a fool. Or perhaps he believed he was invincible in combat and did not fear them. Regardless, he went walking with them in the dead of night until one of the men, pretending to smell the perfumed oil in his hair, grabbed Ka'b around his head and called on the others to strike him with their swords. As it was three against one, it would seem obvious that Ka'b would be killed quickly. Instead, the blows of the assassins rained down on him with no obvious effect, and Ka'b broke loose to respond in kind. Indeed, in the initial onslaught, the Muslims did more damage to themselves, with one of them striking a companion in the leg, severely wounding him.

This fracas continued sufficiently long enough for people in nearby homes to be awakened and to kindle lamps within. Aware that they were about to be discovered, Muhammad bin Maslamah remembered that he had a concealed dagger, and he used this to "thrust it into the lower part of his body; then I bore down upon it until I reached his genitals."[36] With this blow, Ka'b shrieked loudly and collapsed to the ground. The assassins then severed his head and brought it to the Prophet, dropping it at his feet.

There are some important points to gain from this incident besides the mere assassination of an enemy leader. The first is that the story told Ka'b had to have had a measure of truth within it. They related how the Prophet had brought them trouble that took them to the brink of starvation. This difficulty could come only in a few ways. Either the Muslims did not have any means of producing for themselves, or they were being boycotted by the non-Muslim elements in the city. The latter seems unlikely, considering Ka'b's willingness to sell them food for something of value. This would mean that the Muslims were having problems providing themselves with food, thus highlighting the logistical issues regarding insurgencies raised in a previous chapter. The need for sustenance had to be believable for Ka'b to succumb to the deception.

The second issue apparent here is the poor performance of the assassins. While the sources seem to indicate that they had trouble killing Ka'b because their own swords were obstructing one another, this still raises the issue as to the combat quality and effectiveness of the average Muslim warrior at this time.[37] Ka'b was wearing his chain mail, which would help to blunt the blows of his attackers. However, he was outnumbered at least three to one, and a few sources indicate there were as many as five attackers. Despite this advantage, they were not able to kill him quickly but had to at last rely upon a dagger thrust forced through his chain mail to finish the job. The assassination of Ka'b bin al-Ashraf demonstrates the inexperience of Muhammad's warriors in the early stages of the insurgency. Ka'b was apparently a better individual fighter and warrior, yet he fell victim to a deception operation.

The impact of this assassination was felt the very next day. In the morning, Muhammad issued a decree, calling on the faithful to "kill any Jew that falls into your power."[38] At this "the Jews were frightened, so none of them came out, nor did they speak. They were afraid that they would be suddenly attacked as Ibn al-Ashraf was attacked in the night."[39] Despite such caution, one Muslim did manage to kill a Jewish merchant with whom he had had profitable dealings. When the Muslim's brother, who was not part of the *ummah*, heard of this, he began to beat his brother, crying out that much of the fat on his body came from the man he killed. The Muslim then related that it was on Muhammad's orders, and that if the Prophet had ordered him to kill his brother he would do so. To this, the unbelieving sibling realized how serious the situation was. "By God, a religion that can bring one to this is astonishing!"[40] With that said, the unbelieving brother also became a Muslim.

Eventually, some of the al-Nadir's leaders came to the Prophet to complain of this state of affairs, noting that their leader had been killed treacherously. Muhammad replied by reminding them of Ka'b's actions and poetry, and how he had instigated others against the Muslims. In this fashion he implied that he was well aware who killed him, but instead of offering to pay bloodwit for the deed, he turned the incident on its head and wrested a nonaggression treaty from them.[41] This incident further highlights the fact that the major Jewish tribes were not part of the Covenant of Madinah. If they had been, they would have demanded bloodwit from the Prophet for the assassination per the covenant's conditions, and there would have been no need for an additional nonaggression treaty.

The assassination of Ka'b bin al-Ashraf may have been a decisive action. Had he lived, he may have been able to rally the al-Nadir, and perhaps even the Qurayzah, to fight against the Prophet when a Qurayshi army showed up outside of Madinah a few months later. Instead, the Jewish tribes, along with any other opposition within the city, were frozen into inaction, again forestalling any concerted effort against Muhammad's movement.

In the fall, the Qurayshi forces were mobilized in Makkah. This force would have included militias from each tribal element within the city along with any hired troops, or mercenaries, they could muster. One group, called the Ahabish, were a collection of men gathered from various subtribes and organized in what could best be described as a single combat unit.[42] While some scholars such as W. Montgomery Watt are probably accurate in describing the Ahabish as a confederation of Arabs, it would be an error to assume that the Quraysh did not also raise a body of foreign mercenaries to complement this force because there is evidence of two thousand Ethiopians hired for the battle.[43] Not only did the Quraysh raise their own militia, they also sent word to other tribes in order to raise mercenaries from them. In the meantime, al-Abbas watched these preparations carefully, sending Muhammad full details.[44] The Quraysh managed to raise a force of three thousand men, of which one hundred came from the al-Thaqif tribe near al-Ta'if. Of the total force, seven hundred were armored in chain mail while another two hundred were mounted on horseback. Three thousand camels provided the necessary transport for the logistical support.[45]

Organizing such a force would not have been beyond the skills of the Qurayshi leaders because they regularly plied the trade routes with caravans of several thousand camels. However, maintaining three thousand men in the field, along with an unknown number of camp followers, was another matter. If each man had at least one servant or wife accompanying them on the march, this would double the supplies needed for the operation. While some supplies could be obtained en route during the twelve days required to make the trip, especially forage for the animals, the vast majority of the provisions would have to be carried from Makkah. When calculating these statistics, fodder for the animals was halved, assuming that the other half could be obtained through foraging. The logistical transport and needs are listed in the table that follows.

As can be seen in table 4.2, a basic examination of the Qurayshi logistical requirements exceeded what they could carry. While they could still manage to conduct a field operation, they would have no means to engage in a lengthy siege. If Muhammad's uncle al-Abbas was providing fairly detailed information of the Qurayshi plans, the Prophet would probably have been at least reasonably aware that the Quraysh would be incapable of conducting a siege operation. This would naturally influence his plan of action. As the Qurayshi army, with Abu Sufyan in command, approached the city in December 624, Muhammad's original intent was to remain in Madinah, relying upon the city's fortifications and his enemy's own logistical difficulties to secure a victory. His

Table 4.2. Qurayshi Logistical Lift and Provisions for the Uhud Campaign

Category	Quantity	Pounds	Days	Total lbs
LOGISTICAL LIFT (POUNDS CARRIED)				
Men	3,000	20		60,000
Women/Servants	3,000	20		60,000
Camels	3,000	300		900,000
Horses	400	200		80,000
Total Lift				1,100,000
PROVISIONS (POUNDS REQUIRED)				
Food Needed	6,000	3	24	432,000
Camel Fodder	3,000	10	24	720,000
Horse Fodder	400	10	24	96,000
Total Provisions				1,248,000

Note: These statistics are derived from Engels, *Alexander the Great*, 14, and appendix. 5,144–45. The amount of load carried by each individual man was set as an approximation at 20 pounds. One ancient source indicates that disciplined soldiers in the field could each carry up to 80 pounds of flour. This load figure is clearly exceptional and the reason why the point was made. See Frontinus, *Stratagems*, book 4.i.6; Hashi, Kamoun, and Cianci, "Feed Requirements of the Camel," 73–75.

initial plan was to have the men fight in the streets while the women and children were secured in the castles and towers.[46]

'Abdullah bin Ubayy concurred with the Prophet's initial design, but some of the Muslims, especially those who were not present at Badr and thus were thirsting for a glorious victory on the field of battle, pestered the Prophet to sally forth and meet the enemy in open combat. 'Abdullah did his best to convince Muhammad to remain in Madinah, probably also aware of the Qurayshi supply difficulties, stating that "if they stay, they stay in an evil predicament, and if they come in, the men will fight them and the women and children will throw stones on them from the walls."[47] At last, Muhammad relented to the urging of his vocal supporters, despite the fact that even his closest companions urged him to remain in Madinah. He went to his home to put on his armor, choosing to don two sets of chain mail, with one being distinctly different from what he usually wore, implying his intent to disguise his presence on the battlefield.[48] The people now panicked, realizing that they had pressured the Prophet into a course of action contrary to his original purpose. However, Muhammad refused to change his mind. "When a prophet puts on his military dress," he said, "it does not behoove him to put it off before Allah decides between him and his enemies. So wait and do as I have commanded you. Go out in the name of Allah and you will receive (Divine) support as long as you exercise forbearance."[49]

Determined to now go into battle, Muhammad established three banners, one each for the al-Khazraj and al-Aws, and one for the Muhajirun. As he reviewed his men, he found that only one hundred had chain mail, the rest were for the most part without armor. He screened the men and purposely removed some who were too young, such as the son of ʿUmar bin al-Khattab.[50] Moreover, Muhammad refused the help of one group of well-equipped men because they were not Muslims but were allies of ʿAbdullah bin Ubayy.[51] His army, one thousand strong, was soon ready to depart the city.

The Quraysh, upon their arrival at Madinah, had only one primary approach route to attack the Muslim enclave on the northwest side of the city. The southern and eastern parts of Madinah were a chessboard of fortified houses, walled date palm groves, and wheat fields. To attack from these directions, especially from the south, would have required winding their way through narrow passages where they could be easily blocked and attacked from above by missiles. In addition, attacking from the south or west would involve moving through the sectors controlled by other tribes that were attempting to remain neutral. Such a move could enflame them and drive them to support the Muslims. On the western side was a wadi coupled with more fortified houses. Therefore, the only practical route for the Quraysh to directly attack the Muslims was from the northwest. Abu Sufyan's army approached from the west via Badr and then deployed to the northwest of the city, where he allowed his animals to graze in fields owned by the Muslims and prepared his men for the fight.

Rather than emerge directly from Madinah, Muhammad maneuvered his army to the east, circling round the north of the city until he arrived in the lee of Uhud, the large mountain to the north of Madinah that served as a dominating landmark. This maneuver required two days to accomplish and involved the Prophet using a local scout because he did not know the route. During the night they camped in the open on the northeast side of Madinah, with Muhammad appointing the trusty Muhammad bin Maslamah to use fifty men to patrol the perimeter of the camp. In the morning, the Muslims continued their movement, at this point passing through the land of a blind man, Mirbaʿ bin Qayzi, who was an open opponent of the Prophet. Mirbaʿ openly cursed the

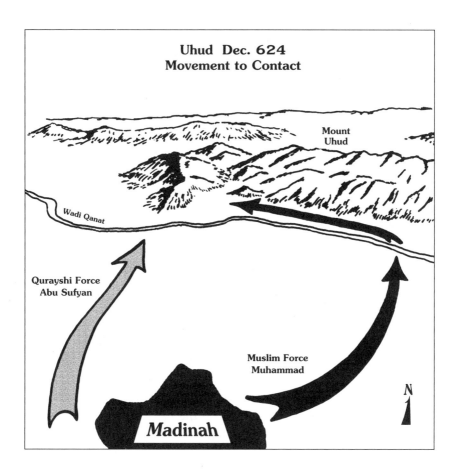

Uhud Dec. 624
Movement to Contact

Mount Uhud

Wadi Qanat

Qurayshi Force
Abu Sufyan

Muslim Force
Muhammad

Madinah

N

Prophet and the Muslims, and, although Muhammad gave orders to leave the man alone, some of the Muslims cracked his skull with blows from their bows.

Sometime during this deployment, ʿAbdullah bin Ubayy took three hundred men and returned to Madinah. While some sources indicate he did this because he thought Muhammad was foolish for fighting in the open, there is a possibility that Muhammad ordered him to go back to Madinah to protect the city.[52] If the latter is the case, it was because the Prophet realized that the victory at Badr was an anomaly, and that the coming battle would probably go badly for the Muslims. By dispatching ʿAbdullah back to Madinah, he could ensure that his base would still be protected if the main army was forced to flee into the mountains.[53] The later assertions of various Muslims that ʿAbdullah and his men deserted the Prophet would fit well with the need to maintain ʿAbdullah's cover if he was indeed operating as a true supporter of the Prophet but feigning to be disaffected to help control any malcontents in the city.

When the morning of 29 December 624 dawned, Muhammad's men were sheltered in a defile at the southern base of Uhud, and the Qurayshi camp was to their west. As at Badr, the Prophet chose to place a mountain to his rear, thus providing a means for his men to escape the Qurayshi cavalry if the battle went poorly. The Prophet's deployment was fairly simple. He organized his army in two ranks, possibly keeping those with armor in the second.[54] The first rank would initially skirmish while the second could be used to either reinforce the first or exploit any advantages gained. Because he had no cavalry, it was critical for the Prophet to protect his flanks from any sweeping movements of the two hundred cavalry in Abu Sufyan's army. To do this, he deployed a small contingent of fifty archers on his left under the command of ʿAbdullah bin Jubayr, giving them precise instructions that they were to remain at their posts regardless what became of the rest of the Muslim army during the battle.[55] It is the deployment and engagement of these archers that later invoked both recriminations and controversy.

The accepted tradition about the archers, and what has been retained to this day regarding the memorials on the battlefield, was that these men were stationed on a very small hillock located just north of the Wadi Qanat called ʿAynain. However, there are significant problems with this interpretation. The effective range of a typical archer was only about 150 yards, and while it could be up to 200 yards, the more likely effective engagement range was closer to 100 yards. Yet the distance from ʿAynain to the base of Uhud to the northeast is more than 900 yards.[56] This presents us with only three options. Perhaps the terrain had significantly changed since the battle, as contended by one author. But such a dramatic change would be coupled with a well-known geological event, and such an event was not recorded except for some erosion in the area.[57] If this is not the case, then we are left with only two options. Either Muhammad mistakenly placed his archers in a tactically exposed and untenable position, or he placed them somewhere else, most likely on the slopes of Mount Uhud proper on a place that at that time may have been called ʿAynain. For the purpose of describing the battle, the latter view will be accepted, but the former will be explored in due time.

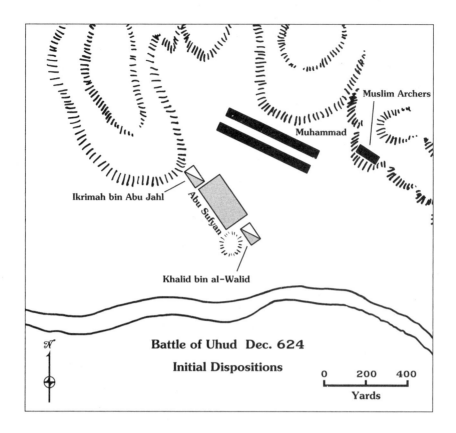

Muslim Archers

Muhammad

Ikrimah bin Abu Jahl

Abu Sufyan

Khalid bin al-Walid

Battle of Uhud Dec. 624

Initial Dispositions

0   200   400

Yards

If Muhammad did place his archers along the mountain's slopes, then his deployment would have been oriented almost due south facing Madinah. Such a deployment would have a few advantages. It would place him opposite the best approach route to the city, so if the Quraysh decided to ignore the Prophet's main army and strike at the city, they would not only be engaged by 'Abdullah bin Ubayy's three hundred men within but would also be attacked by Muhammad's men from behind. Concurrently, the Quraysh would be caught in the course of Wadi Qanat. While this dried riverbed is not impassable, any troops caught within could be attacked from the ridges with the advantage inherent in an elevated position, while the Qurayshi cavalry would find the rocky bed difficult for their horses to negotiate. Finally, such a deployment would be consistent with the Muslims' desire to engage in their prayer devotions. As they were already facing south toward Makkah, they stayed in their ranks while performing their prostrations. This deployment probably represents the most likely scenario and would be fairly consistent with the descriptions provided by al-Waqidi and Ibn Saʿd.[58] While Muhammad was still tactically inexperienced, he possessed a finely developed native shrewdness that carried him through many a crisis. Moreover, he was learning quickly from previous encounters. The green army of Muslims at the battle of Badr was now a thing of the past.

Abu Sufyan stood to his force and began to march east, probably deploying his men facing northeast and thus obliquely to the Muslims. In this manner he was oriented to land the hardest blow against the Muslim right. He took his small but still significant force of cavalry and divided it into two squadrons of about one hundred apiece, with Ikrimah bin Abu Jahl, the son of the slain Qurayshi leader at Badr, on the left flank, and Khalid bin al-Walid on the right.[59] Besides the cavalry, Abu Sufyan had a contingent of one hundred archers deployed under the command of ʿAbd Allah bin Abu Rabiʿah. The remainder of his men was a mix of swordsmen and spearmen rallied around their banner held by Talhah bin Abu Talhah. Behind the Qurayshi line was a group of women beating tambourines to encourage their men to fight, a common sight in many engagements among the Arabian people.

As the Prophet lined up his men, he held his sword aloft, crying out, "Who will take this sword with its right?" After several who wished to carry it were refused, Abu Dujanah, a conceited fighter festooned with a red turban, was granted the privilege, asking, "What is its right, O Apostle of God?" Muhammad answered, "That you should smite the enemy with it until it bends."[60] After having surrendered his sword, Muhammad asked which clan of the Quraysh was carrying their standard. When told it was the ʿAbd al-Dar, he said that "it befits us to be more faithful than them," then called for Musʿab bin ʿUmayr to carry the Prophet's standard.[61] Musʿab was of the ʿAbd al-Dar clan and one of Muhammad's most faithful converts, having been entrusted with the earliest teaching of the Qurʾan to the Muslims in Madinah after the First Pledge of al-ʿAqaba.[62]

Before the battle was joined, Abu Sufyan attempted to divide the al-Khazraj and al-Aws from the Prophet, but this effort failed.[63] Though understandable, this maneuver gave the impression that the Quraysh were hesitant and unwilling to fight. Such a diplomatic failure could easily boost the morale of the Muslims because it was ill-timed just before engaging in battle. But even as Abu Sufyan had opened such negotiations, some of those in his army were already preparing the battlefield. A contingent under Abu 'Amir, having seen the Muslims move into position in the shadow of Mount Uhud, ventured out the night prior to dig a series of camouflaged potholes in the ground.[64] The Quraysh had learned of the devastating effects of a Muslim charge at Badr, and it would appear that the potholes were intended to entrap them during their inevitable surge forward.

The morning of the battle was probably cool and clear for there is no indication in any of the sources of weather extremes that influenced the engagement. The Quraysh opened the action with a series of small skirmishes, the first led by the same Abu 'Amir whose men had laid their traps.[65] Abu 'Amir's men rushed forward, chanting taunts and hurling stones, only to quickly turn and retire with the hope that some of the Muslims would pursue and fall into the traps. Instead, Muhammad kept his men in check, and another group of Qurayshi skirmishers came forward, many on horseback, only to be driven back by a flight of missiles from the archers on the Muslim left and by skirmishers under al-Zubayr bin al-'Awwam throwing stones.[66] Then, as was common in such actions, the standard bearer of the Qurayshi force, Talhah bin Abu Talhah, stepped forward and announced a challenge for single combat. 'Ali bin Abu Talib, Talhah's cousin, responded and moved from the Muslim line, the two meeting in the no man's land between the battle lines. The men on both sides now watched enraptured as the two warriors clashed, with 'Ali quickly rushing forward and smashing the skull of the Qurayshi fighter.[67] As his body crumpled to the ground, Muhammad raised the cry of the *takbir*, shouting "Allahu Akbar," with the men responding in unison.

Abu Sufyan now called out "Al-Lat! Al-Uzza!" and sent his men forward. This was the moment that Muhammad had anticipated, and the lead rank of the Muslims pushed forward to meet their foe. As the typical range of an archer noted before was around 150 yards, it is probable that the battle lines were initially no more than 200 yards apart. Even then, the Muslim warriors would not charge full speed into the slowly moving Qurayshi ranks but instead would start at a lope and break into a sprint for the last 50 yards. In this way, about 350 Muslims on a front about 500 yards smashed into the Qurayshi ranks, avoiding the potholes because the advancing Quraysh had already passed them by.

As part of the Qurayshi cavalry attempted to reorganize behind their lines after being rebuffed by Muhammad's archers, the center of their infantry began to waver under the weight of the Muslim assault.

Abu Dujanah, carrying Muhammad's sword and wearing what others called his "death headband," thrashed his way rapidly through the Qurayshi ranks, far ahead of his companions.[68] Not far behind him was Muhammad's uncle, Hamzah, his sword flashing to and fro as he drove the enemy before him. However, unbeknownst to this great warrior, an Abyssinian slave and expert with the javelin named Wahshi was carefully stalking him, pledged to kill him in revenge for Hamzah having killed his master's uncle. Even as the battle seemed to be pitted against reasonably large, impersonal forces, the private nature of close-quarter combat continued to rear its head. Hamzah, the hero of Badr, was soon to become the prince of martyrs.

As the Qurayshi line began to crumble, a succession of men, each a son of the fallen Talhah, attempted to seize the standard and rally their side. Six of them were killed, one by one, either in hand-to-hand combat or by arrows. One of these was cut down by Hamzah. With the family wiped out, three others not related to Talhah took the standard only to die as well, the last a slave who attempted to hold up the standard after his hands had been hacked off. With so many bodies now strewn about the standard, the last to take it and hold it high was one of the women who were behind the warriors to urge them on.[69] Her efforts to keep the standard high were enough to help the Quraysh to rally. And in the midst of this confusion, Wahshi released his javelin, sending it through Hamzah's lower abdomen. He staggered toward his antagonist, only to collapse from the trauma and slowly expire.[70]

In the meantime, Muhammad's archers, now resting from their efforts after having driven off the Qurayshi cavalry, were watching the battle unfold in the plain below. They could see the center of the Qurayshi line giving way and the glint of sunlight flashing from the ankle bangles of the Qurayshi women as they lifted their robes to flee up the side of the western edge of Uhud to escape the spreading chaos.[71] With another incredible victory apparently in their grasp, many of the archers, in violation of the Prophet's orders, began to rush from their post intent on seizing any of the spoil left on the battlefield. 'Abdullah bin Jubayr, conspicuous in his gleaming white robe, cried out in vain to order them to hold their ground. While the sources imply that he stayed

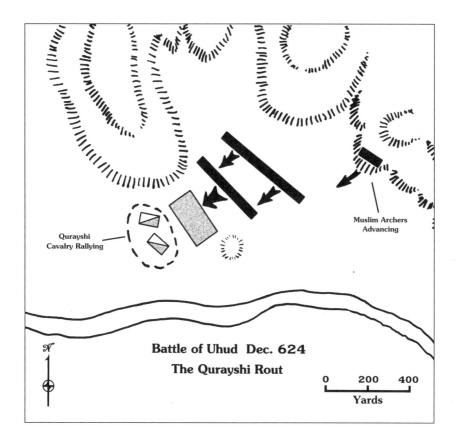

Qura: Qurayshi
Cavalry Rallying

Muslim Archers
Advancing

Battle of Uhud Dec. 624

The Qurayshi Rout

0   200   400

Yards

in position, it is probable that he decided to follow them as his only way to regain control of his command.

This movement of the archers, easily discernable along the slopes of the mountain, was detected by Khalid bin al-Walid and his men. He quickly rallied the cavalry, probably the entire force, to include what was once on the left flank, and spurred his men to swing wide to the Qurayshi right, possibly picking their way through the course of Wadi Qanat.[72] Had he done so, he would have emerged on the Muslim left flank undetected, a point reinforced by the surprise noted in contemporary accounts of the battle. Khalid's cavalry, though without armor, was an incredibly powerful force. A mounted warrior has significant advantages over a foot soldier, both in height as well as physical momentum. Even if Khalid's cavalry did not yet have the stirrup to stabilize them on their mounts, the dynamic of a cavalry charge by as many as

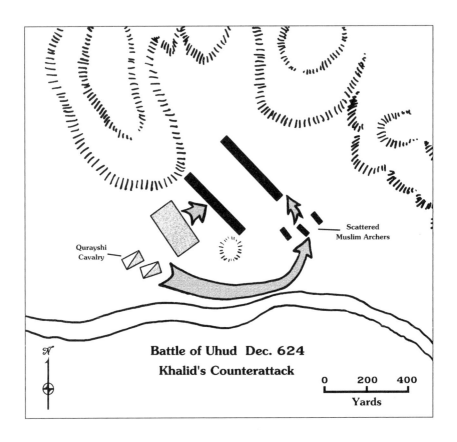

Battle of Uhud Dec. 624

Khalid's Counterattack

Quraishi Cavalry

Scattered Muslim Archers

N

0   200   400

Yards

three hundred or more men would still be well nigh irresistible on a disorganized formation of foot soldiers.[73]

The ground thundered and shook, a dust plume rising as Khalid's cavalry, the men shouting battle cries and the horses snorting and lathered from the strain, covered the six hundred yards into the Muslim left flank in fewer than forty-five seconds. 'Abdullah's archers, so jubilant when leaving their posts, barely knew what transpired as the Qurayshi horse rode through their midst, cutting them down almost to the man, to include their intrepid commander. With hardly any disruption to their momentum, Khalid aimed his force at the flank of the second rank of Muslims. As his cavalry crashed into this force with a tremendous clatter, there arose a cry of despair from the victorious first rank. "O Allah's Worshippers, beware of what is behind!"[74] The Muslim front line, entangled with Abu Sufyan's desperate infantry, now turned about to see the disaster unfolding in their rear. As the second rank was engulfed by Khalid's cavalry, one of the Prophet's men, at that point taking a rest and eating some dates to refresh himself, turned to Muhammad and asked, "Can you tell me where I will be if I should get martyred?" The Prophet's reply: "In Paradise," at which point the man tossed away the dates and plunged into the midst of the enemy until he was killed.[75] However, despite such individual acts of impulsive bravery, many of Muhammad's men were wavering, approaching the point of exhaustion and despair.[76]

One disaster was now compounded with a second, as somebody cried out that Muhammad had been slain.[77] Because the Prophet had exchanged his usual armor for that of one of his men, it was possible that his men mistook another who was cut down for Muhammad. However, the man with whom the Prophet did exchange armor, Ka'b bin Malik, survived the battle and was even the first to recognize that the Prophet was alive, since he was wearing Ka'b's armor. Nevertheless, with the false news now spreading of the Prophet's death, the Muslim army began to collapse in confusion, even to the point where the first rank was now fighting their men in the second.[78] Muhammad knew all too well that the battle was lost. The Prophet and his companions began to withdraw for the mountain, hushing Ka'b as he tried to draw overt attention to Muhammad's presence.[79] It was somewhere in the confusion of this moment that a hurled stone struck the Prophet in the face, shattering one of his teeth and slashing his lip, thus evoking a curse upon the Quraysh for having injured the Prophet of Allah.[80]

A few of Muhammad's companions now rallied to protect him. Abu Dujanah, having survived his excursion through the lines of the Quraysh, used his body to shield the Prophet from a flight of arrows, taking a number of the shafts in his back. Although wounded, he would survive the battle only to die during the battle of al-Yamamah, an action after the Prophet's death during the Apostates War.[81] Sa'd bin Abu Waqqas provided cover fire with a flurry of arrows while Talhah bin 'Ubaydullah, having already volunteered to die if need be, blocked a blow with his right arm that was meant for Muhammad, losing the use of a finger.[82]

During the ensuing confusion, one of Khalid's horsemen, Ubayy bin Khalaf, recognized Muhammad, perhaps because of the number of Muslims rallying about him. Ubayy charged at the Prophet, who took a spear from one of his men and thrust it into Ubayy's neck, forcing the Qurayshi warrior to be thrown from his horse. Although the wound appeared only superficial, he later died, declaring as his life slipped away that the Prophet had once told him he would be killed should they come face to face in battle.[83] Apparently, no other men of the Quraysh recognized Muhammad at this crucial moment, even though their cavalry was weaving to and fro through the chaotic throngs of the Muslims. The main body of the Muslims now began to flee for the safety of Uhud, working their way up the rocky slope that served as a bulwark against Khalid's cavalry. The triumphant Qurayshi infantry, rather than pursue up the mountain, contented themselves with gathering spoil and defacing the bodies of some of the dead Muslims left on the field.

The battle was over and Muhammad's army scattered. But could the Quraysh exploit the victory? There were two obstacles that prevented the Quraysh from turning this tactical victory into a decisive strategic one. The first involved the Muslims still in Madinah. While the Quraysh had a numerical advantage, the three hundred warriors in Madinah under 'Abdullah bin Ubayy would have been sufficient to delay any Qurayshi assault until the Muslims rallied their scattered field army. When considered in light of the previous discussion regarding the failure of the Quraysh to prepare for a lengthy siege, it can be determined that Abu Sufyan simply could not take the city, either by storm or starvation.

The other obstacle to a total Qurayshi victory was more subtle, yet far more fundamental than simply being able to conduct extended operations in the field. This involved the Qurayshi attitude toward war, an attitude that, while applicable to the raiding desert Bedouin, was not sufficient to stand up to Muhammad's radically different conception of war. Abu Sufyan found a rock to stand upon and called out to the Muslims ascending the side of Uhud. "Is Muhammad present amongst the people?" He received no answer as Muhammad told his companions to remain silent. Abu Sufyan then asked about Abu Bakr and 'Umar bin al-Khattab. When the Muslims at last responded to declare that all were alive and well, Abu Sufyan declared, "Our victory today is a counterbalance to yours in the battle of Badr, and in war (the victory) is always undecided and is shared in turns by the belligerents."[84] In this statement lay the seed of the ultimate Qurayshi defeat, for Abu Sufyan did not think in terms of victory. He was not alone in this regard, for another prominent man of the Quraysh, when he had overrun some of the Muslim leaders, merely slapped ʿUmar bin al-Khattab with the flat of his spear, telling him to save himself for he refused to kill him.[85] Such determination not to kill the enemy was in direct contrast to that of the Muslims, who typically used the words "Amit! Amit!" ("Kill! Kill!") when engaging in combat.

Many years after Muhammad's era, following the massive campaigns to defeat Napoleon in the early 1800s, a German staff officer named Carl von Clausewitz penned the draft of his now-famous *On War*. If one were to ask a reasonably educated military theorist or Western military officer about what they remember about Clausewitz, they would typically quote his famous dictum that "war is simply a continuation of political intercourse, with the addition of other means."[86] However, if one were to sum up Clausewitz's thinking in a single sentence, it would be found in his opening chapter: "War is thus an act of force to compel our enemy to do our will."[87] The statement is so simple as to be earth shattering yet is a concept largely neglected by many observers throughout history.

This same principle is echoed, either explicitly or implicitly, by the other great writers on war. Sun Tzu, writing around 500 BC tells us that "victory is the main object in war. If this is long delayed, weapons are blunted and morale depressed."[88] It is also implied by the likes of Antoine-Henri de Jomini and Helmuth von Moltke and was explicitly articulated by Mao Tse-Tung and Che Guevara.[89] The key theorists of war understood that the most fundamental aspect of war was to force an enemy to do one's will. In contrast, Abu Sufyan saw war as a game, a contest in which each side trades triumphs back and forth in the ebbing tides of martial sport. In essence, he saw no end to the war with Muhammad. In contrast, the Prophet's view of war was dramatically different; on countless occasions, he indicated that the final ultimate triumph would belong to Islam.[90] For Abu Sufyan, there was no such thing as victory. For Muhammad, there was no substitute for victory.

In most battles of the early and later medieval period, an army in flight typically suffered enormous casualties. It is uncertain how many of the Muslim dead were lost in the rout that ensued, and there is no evidence of the Quraysh taking any prisoners. There is some dispute as to the final tally sheet, but it is generally accepted that the Muslim loss in men was equivalent to the Qurayshi losses at Badr the previous year, with about sixty-five killed in action. The Quraysh lost about twenty-two men.[91] Among those Muslims killed was Hamzah, the Prophet's uncle, along with 'Abdullah bin Jahsh, the man who led the first victorious Muslim raid at Nakhlah. If these losses are reasonably accurate, then the Muslims suffered 10 percent of their engaged force in dead, a significant loss in light of the nature of battles of this era.[92] The wounded, including Muhammad, were cared for by the women. When the Prophet learned of Hamzah's mutilation, he vowed that he would mutilate thirty Quraysh the next time they engaged in battle. However, upon deeper reflection, he relented of this agenda and forbade his men to mutilate any enemy dead.[93]

At this point, it is necessary to explore one alternative angle of the battle based on the assumption that the location of the deployment of forces accepted by Islamic tradition is indeed accurate. For example, accepted tradition places Muhammad's archers on a very small hill today called 'Aynain. The problems presented by this deployment have already been noted, but what if this location is accurate? What would this mean? First, there is Hamidullah's supposition that the terrain had significantly changed since the time of the battle, and that the hill of 'Aynain was once part of a longer ridge. A key problem with that scenario is that, if much of the ridge was washed away by flooding or another geological event, could it be assumed that 'Aynain would remain as is without significant alteration? Furthermore, if 'Aynain was the end of a spur of the mountain, this would not fundamentally change the scenario already presented.

But if there was no significant geological event to change the landscape, and if 'Aynain, as located today, is correctly identified as the deployment spot of the archers, we are faced with another difficult interpretation. The archers would be unable to protect the Muslim army's flank and rear, which would thus allow for the Qurayshi cavalry to easily attack the Muslim rear and rout their army. In this context, the failure at Uhud would rest largely on Muhammad's faulty deployment of the archers. Consequently, this faulty deployment, in order not to jeopardize the Prophet's status as Allah's messenger, would need to be obfuscated. The story of the archers leaving their position and rushing for plunder would serve as a convenient scapegoat for the Muslim defeat, rather than Muhammad's failure to deploy his men properly. While such an explanation might be enticing to some, it has significant problems. The most critical is that there is absolutely no direct evidence in any of the hadith collections that such could have been the case. The hadith collectors were conscientious regarding their inclusion of material that is at times contradictory, as are the early *sira* collections. Had the battle been lost due to faulty deployment, there would have been some evidence within the hadith literature to this effect. Therefore, this interpretation would have to be considered highly unlikely. With this said, either the terrain had been significantly altered since the battle or Muhammad deployed his men differently than what is accepted as the official account today. The latter would seem to be the more likely occurrence.

Having been defeated at Uhud, Muhammad's immediate concern beyond the care of the wounded and burying the dead was to determine what the Quraysh would do next. As night fell, he decided to maintain contact with Abu Sufyan's forces to ensure they would not surprise him, while also demonstrating that the Muslims could quickly rally back to action. He organized a force of seventy mounted men, under ʿAli bin Abu Talib, to track down the Quraysh and determine their next course of action.[94] "If they are leading their horses and riding their camels, they are making for Mecca," Muhammad instructed ʿAli. "But if they are riding their horses and leading their camels, they are making for Medina."[95] When he moved out, he found that the Quraysh were riding their camels and leading the horses, thus indicating that they were heading home to Makkah. Nevertheless, Muhammad wanted to ensure that Abu Sufyan would maintain this course of action, resorting to a ruse by having this small party light more than five hundred campfires to convince the Qurayshi leader that he was being pursued by a force of considerable size.[96]

Muhammad remained at Hamra al-Asad, a place about eight miles south of Madinah, for three days to ensure that the Quraysh had departed. As for the Quraysh, they debated among themselves about going back in an effort to crush the Muslims once and for all, even telling a group of neutral riders on the way to Madinah to deliver a message that the Quraysh were returning to destroy them. However, Muhammad was amply provided with both information and support from the Banu Khuzaʿah, a tribe south of Makkah that was friendly to the Quraysh but had a secret agreement with the Prophet. One of the Khuzaʿah, Maʿbad al-Khuzaʿi, had been shadowing the Quraysh and, after meeting with

Muhammad, showed up among the Quraysh even as Abu Sufyan and the other nobles were debating their return to Madinah. At this crucial moment, Ma'bad, in his role as a double agent, deceived Abu Sufyan into believing that Muhammad was in pursuit with a huge army, "burning with anger" against the Quraysh over their loss.[97] He even went so far as to compose poetry about the earth shaking beneath the thundering hooves of Muhammad's riders who were in hot pursuit. Frightened by the imagery of this propaganda and the Prophet's disinformation operations in the field, Abu Sufyan turned his army away and marched back to Makkah. A golden opportunity for a decisive victory in the field had escaped his grasp.

5

From the Mountain to the Trench

The Muslim defeat at Uhud could have been decisive, but the Quraysh had failed to plan on following up any victory. Having withdrawn back to Makkah, they left Muhammad and the Muslims in position to recover from their loss and rebuild their movement. For the first six months after the defeat, from January to June 625, Muhammad concentrated on rebuilding, reorganizing, and preparing for his next encounter with the Quraysh. Nevertheless, during this period, and for almost the next eighteen months to follow, he avoided operations against his old adversary, instead preferring to attack or convert neighboring tribes and consolidate his hold on Madinah.

Operations to impose Islam on his neighbors bore little fruit during this time. Instead, some of these tribes, taking their cue from the Qurayshi victory at Uhud, took measures to deceive and entrap Muslim raiders and those engaged on missionary efforts. Only a few weeks after Uhud, Muhammad dispatched six Muslims to the subtribes of the ʿAdal and al-Qara, having been urged to do so by a delegation from these groups. These Muslims were then ambushed along the way near al-Raji, with five of them killed outright and the survivor traded to the Quraysh to be executed and hung on a cross.[1] Having suffered another setback, it was time for the Prophet to prepare his men to engage in a successful mission. Muhammad and his companions had to wait patiently for four months before they would be presented with a good opportunity. In the meantime, the Prophet decided to authorize an assassination mission

Table 5.1. Operations from the Battle of Uhud to the Destruction of the Banu Qurayzah

Date	Mission	Enemy	Muslims	Leader	Result
Jan 625	Al-Raji; Lihyan	unknown	7–10	Marthad al-Ghanwi	Defeat
Feb? 625	Assassination; Abu Sufyan	1	2	'Amr bin Umayyah	Failure
Apr 625	Qatan; Asad	unknown	150	Abu Salamah	Booty
May 625	Bi'r Ma'unah; Sulaym	unknown	40–70	Al-Mundhir bin 'Amr	Defeat
Jun 625	Qatan?; Asad	unknown	1?	Sufyan al-Lihyani	Booty?
Jun 625	Madinah; Banu Al-Nadir	unknown	unknown	Muhammad	Victory
Aug 625	Dhat al-Riqi; Anmar/ Tha'labah		400–800	Muhammad	No Contact
Nov 625	Badr al-Maw'id; Quraysh	unknown	1,500	Muhammad	No Contact
Jun 626	Dumat al-Jandal		1,000	Muhammad	Booty
Dec 626	Al-Khandaq; Quraysh/Allies	10,000	3,000+	Muhammad	Victory
Jan 627	Madinah; Banu Qurayzah	800	3,000+	Muhammad	Victory

against the Qurayshi leader, Abu Sufyan, apparently as a rejoinder for Abu Sufyan having commissioned one to kill Muhammad.[2]

Any mission to assassinate a leader is typically dangerous, but for some reason Muhammad chose to send an inexperienced team of two men led by 'Amr bin Umayyah to carry out his orders.[3] The reason for this was probably because 'Amr's conversion to Islam was not known among the Makkans, possibly to make it easier to catch his prey unawares. They had one camel between them, and because 'Amr's assistant was partially lame, he rode the camel most of the way. When they reached Makkah, they hobbled the camel in a hidden location outside the city and walked in. 'Amr's companion urged him to go to the *ka'bah* to circumambulate it and perform two prostrations in prayer.

'Amr demurred, indicating he was too well known as a troublemaker in Makkah to get away with something so careless. Nevertheless, his companion persisted and finally prevailed and, as 'Amr feared, he was recognized, the men shouting that he had obviously come to Makkah for no good purpose.[4]

The two rushed into the hills and hid in a cave while a Makkan search party combed the area for them. 'Amr was compelled to kill one of the pursuers before they were able to make their escape. The two became separated when 'Amr rashly decided to recover the still hanging body of the Muslim who had been crucified after the failed mission to the 'Adal and al-Qara. Having been spotted, 'Amr's companion fled on the camel while 'Amr escaped alone into the mountains on foot. The mission had been completely botched, largely because 'Amr allowed himself two serious indiscretions. As he worked his way northward toward Madinah, he encountered an elderly one-eyed shepherd at a cave. The two, apparently both from the same tribe, engaged in conversation, with the shepherd innocently raising his voice to declare, "I will not be a Muslim as long as I live, and will not believe in the faith of the Muslims." When the shepherd drifted off to sleep, 'Amr placed the tip of his bow against the man's good eye. He then leaned on it with all his weight, thrusting "it down until it came out the back of his neck." Having killed a man who was helpless and no threat, he then "rushed out like a wild beast and took to the highway like an eagle, fleeing for my life."[5]

But 'Amr's adventure was not yet complete. As he continued his flight he encountered two Qurayshi men who had been sent to spy on Madinah. He killed one with an arrow shot and captured the other, tying his thumbs together with his bowstring. When he finally reached Madinah, he presented his prisoner and gave his account to the Prophet, with Muhammad laughing so heartily that "his back teeth could be seen."[6] Muhammad praised him after receiving 'Amr's report, blessing him for his efforts. While 'Amr's mission had at least achieved something, he had failed to accomplish his goal, which was to kill Abu Sufyan. That Muhammad praised him for killing an elderly shepherd and capturing a spy indicates that the Prophet was probably anxious to receive any good news of success, no matter how obtuse it was. A few months later, the Prophet was able to organize the first successful operation in almost half a year.

Sparked by a rumor that two leaders of the Banu Asad Ibn Khuzaymah clan were planning a raid against the Muslims, Muhammad dispatched 150 men under Abu Salamah to preempt this operation. Abu Salamah's men surprised the enemy camp and scattered them without a fight, managing to seize an unspecified amount of booty in the process.[7] While offering little in the way of tangible success, the raid surely helped the shaken Muslims regain some measure of confidence in their conduct of operations. But while this accomplishment helped to bolster the spirits of the *ummah*, Muhammad was still leery of the tribes surrounding Madinah and the ability of the Muslims to hold their own against them. His fears were justified. A man of the Najd region, Abu Bara' 'Amir bin Malik bin Ja'far, came to the Prophet and offered him a gift of two horses and two camels, apparently as a means to open negotiations, but the Prophet refused to take them. "I do not accept presents from polytheists, so become a Muslim if you want me to accept it."[8]

Undeterred, Abu Bara' urged Muhammad to send a delegation to his people, pledging his own life as surety for the protection of the Muslims he sent. Approximately forty Muslims were sent under the leadership of al-Mundhir bin 'Amr, although some sources state the number was seventy. Among them was 'Amr bin Umayyah, now rested from his failed assassination operation against Abu Sufyan.[9] Like the group sent to the 'Adal and al-Qara, it too was ambushed. They attempted to send ahead one of their men carrying a letter to 'Amir bin Tufayl, but he was killed before he could deliver it. The rest of the Muslims were then attacked when they followed their messenger's trail, with the entire group fighting in desperation as their leader waded into the enemy "to embrace death."[10]

Only two survived, one found later among the pile of bodies, but 'Amr bin Umayyah, having been captured, was released as a repaid favor.[11] 'Amr would wander for four days trying to find his way back to Madinah. As he neared the city by the Wadi Qanat he met up with two men who, unbeknownst to him, had been part of a tribe that just concluded a peace treaty with Muhammad. 'Amr dispatched them both, taking them as possible enemies. He at last was able to report to the Prophet what had transpired. Unlike the previous mission, Muhammad was far from pleased, noting that he would have to pay the bloodwit for the two murdered men.[12] However, it should also be noted that there is no indication that the Prophet disliked 'Amr taking the personal initiative to wage an individualistic war on unbelievers. Little did 'Amr know, but his actions set in motion the coming expulsion of the Jewish Banu al-Nadir.

The two men killed by 'Amr bin Umayyah had been part of the Banu 'Amir, which had just concluded a nonaggression pact with Muhammad. This placed the Prophet in an interesting position. Under a typical agreement of this type, the leader of a tribe would pay the bloodwit for anyone of his tribe who wrongly killed a member of the other tribe. It is probable that at this point, Muhammad saw an opportunity to possibly remove one more element of opposition from Madinah. He would use the issue of the bloodwit for the Banu 'Amir to try and create a casus belli against the Banu al-Nadir.

Muhammad went to the Banu al-Nadir to ask them to assist in paying the bloodwit for the two men killed by 'Amr bin Umayyah. That he chose to do this is remarkable, for barring any other agreement to which we are not privy, the Covenant of Madinah clearly stipulated that the Muslims were to pay the bloodwit for any trespasses committed by one of their own.[13] Furthermore, since the al-Nadir were allies of the Banu 'Amir, they could have easily taken the position of one of the offended groups and justly demand that Muhammad pay his own bloodwit. They could have even used the incident as a casus belli to turn the tables on the Muslims, citing their recklessness as the rationale for waging war against them. After all, did not the Prophet refuse to pay bloodwit for the killing of K'ab bin al-Ashraf?[14]

That the Prophet went to the al-Nadir is either indicative of poverty on his part or of a hidden agenda. For their part, the al-Nadir made a grave mistake, if we are to take the source documents largely at face value. Cooler heads could have used this incident to generate a tremendous propaganda coup against the Prophet, declaring openly for all to hear that the mighty followers of Allah were bankrupt and had to turn to the despised Jews for financial aid. However, in such circumstances thoughtful minds rarely weigh in at the right moment, and instead some of the Jews planned to drop a rock on the Prophet when he neared their entrance, thus hopefully ridding them of his presence once and for all. Somehow the Prophet learned of their design, the sources typically attributing this to divine revelation, although one source indicates that one of the al-Nadir slipped out to bring this news to Muhammad.[15] He surprised his own companions by simply leaving the scene without explanation, ostensibly to retrieve something. His companions waited for him for some time and eventually departed to search for him. Upon finding the Prophet, he reported the treachery of the Jews and ordered his men to prepare for war.[16]

There is little doubt that Muhammad was seeking a casus belli, and with the treachery (either real or imagined) of the Banu al-Nadir, he had found it. What is interesting here is that had the al-Nadir been signatories of the Covenant of Madinah, they could have simply presented the offenders to make amends. But since they were not, as contended in a previous chapter, they had to fall back on any nonaggression pact they may have had with the Muslims with conditions unknown to us today. As for Muhammad, he still could have chosen to demand that they hand over the men who had plotted against him. That he did not is again a sure indication that he intended war, for he went to them and declared that they were to "go out from my land" and were given ten days to exile themselves.[17] This declaration made it clear that the Prophet already considered the whole of Madinah to be his personal property, as that belonging to the sayyid of the *ummah*.

As for the al-Nadir, they made two serious mistakes. They trusted in the word of 'Abdullah bin Ubayy, as well as some other leaders of the al-Khazraj, that, should the al-Nadir be attacked, 'Abdullah would rally two thousand fighters, both his own and men from the Banu Qurayzah and Ghatafan, to fight alongside them, and to even depart Madinah if the al-Nadir lost.[18] Such a promise could only have come from the mind of the Prophet, for had 'Abdullah made such an open declaration then his treachery would have been worse than that of the al-Nadir, marking him for certain death. Reportedly, Muhammad went to 'Abdullah and convinced him otherwise, but such conduct still raises the issue of why Muhammad tolerated such behavior within one individual in the *ummah*.[19] The sources, although mentioning this incident, provide no information as to what happened to 'Abdullah after the al-Nadir were defeated. That the al-Nadir relied upon this dubious source of support indicates that they probably misread the consequences of the Muslim defeat at Uhud, expecting a large portion of the Muslims to break ranks with the Prophet and join them. It also provides one more illustration of how 'Abdullah was probably working secretly with Muhammad while feigning opposition.

Their second error was in misjudging the nature of the terrain on which the fight would occur. While they were certainly well protected by the walls of their fortresses, they apparently failed to realize that the

Muslims, unlike any besieging army from outside of Madinah, had a ready source of local food and water. Concurrently, the livelihood of the Jewish tribe was in their extensive date palm groves. These were naturally outside the confines of their fortresses and thus subject to confiscation or destruction by the Muslims. Therefore, to retreat within their walls and allow themselves to be besieged courted disaster, though a circumstance not so obvious to the immediate observer. What was normally the bane of any besieging army—a lack of supplies—would not have a significant impact on Muhammad's men, who had over time infiltrated the city and established themselves within.

The siege was largely uneventful as there was little fighting on the part of the Muslims, although the al-Nadir did send a few volleys of arrows and stones from their walls.[20] During the midst of the siege, Muhammad turned on the Banu Qurayzah and besieged them as well, compelling them to relinquish any thought of helping the al-Nadir and compelling them to sign a new treaty with the Prophet.[21] The Prophet's men remained in their positions for two weeks before the al-Nadir decided to seek terms. What drove them to this point was when the Prophet ordered that their date palm groves be systematically destroyed. The al-Nadir complained, saying, "Muhammad, you have prohibited wanton destruction and blamed those guilty of it. Why then are you cutting down and burning our palm-trees?"[22] The al-Nadir was attempting to make the Prophet live up to his own book of rules, but their circumstances were far from favorable to push such a position. Instead, the Prophet issued a declaration regarding a revelation that he received from Allah, declaring that what trees they had destroyed was "by Allah's leave, in order that He might confound the evil-livers."[23]

The al-Nadir now agreed to go into exile, though their execution was originally decreed, having negotiated that they could depart with whatever they could load on camels, minus their armor and weapons.[24] They then proceeded to destroy their own homes, lest they give them over to the Muslims, and loaded the lintels of their doors, along with their women and children, onto six hundred camels they contracted for the job.[25] Many of them traveled either to Syria or Khaybar, where they attempted to rebuild their lives. Of the booty taken, the Muslims received 50 coats of mail, 50 helmets, and 340 swords.[26] Although useful, this did not amount to a significant haul in armaments. And while the land seized was arguably far more valuable, many of the date palm trees had been destroyed, and with no one of the skill needed to cultivate the fields, the land provided very little in the way of food resources for the Muslims.[27] As the al-Nadir had fallen with no serious fighting on the part of the Muslims, Muhammad declared that the booty seized was *fay*, or spoils taken without battle, and therefore belonged to him as his personal property to be distributed accordingly. He gave over the booty and land to the Muhajirun, with only two of the Ansar receiving a gift due to extreme poverty.[28]

While the siege of the al-Nadir had been a success, the only real consequences of the operation were the expulsion of a possible future enemy and any terror such expulsion inflicted on those that remained in Madinah. Little of value was taken in the spoils of war, and the land would now largely lay idle and untended, although there is some indication that other wealth was seized and used to purchase weapons in the future.[29] Furthermore, Surah 59, the recitation that was vocalized afterward regarding the al-Nadir, casts doubt on the actual origin of the conflict. This Surah says nothing about the alleged assassination attempt on Muhammad but simply states that war was waged on the al-Nadir "because they were opposed to Allah and His messenger."[30] Being opposed is far different from attempting to kill the Prophet of the Muslims.

With the al-Nadir out of the way, Muhammad spent an additional four to five months relatively inactive, choosing to prepare his men for their rematch scheduled with the Quraysh after their defeat at Uhud. He launched only one raid of four hundred men in August, directed north to the lands of the Banu Ghatafan. While they did encounter Ghatafan troops, neither side engaged in fighting, apparently because both combatants were approximately equal in strength. It was during this raid that Muhammad instituted the fear prayer, in which half the men remained positioned to fight while another half performed their prostrations.[31] Despite these raids, Muhammad's focus was still on the Quraysh, and arrangements were made to meet for battle near the end of the year.

In November 625, the Prophet departed Madinah with 1,500 men. Despite almost two years of war, only 10 of his men could be mounted on horseback, an indication of the financial struggles Muhammad continued to encounter. In contrast, Abu Sufyan organized a force of 2,000 men, with 50 on horseback, and began to move north toward the prearranged meeting place of Badr, site of the previous Qurayshi defeat. But what should have been a second Badr became stillborn, as Abu Sufyan realized that the harsh summer had depleted the forage along the way, making the transit northward difficult.[32] He turned his force around, leaving the Muslims to cool their heels at Badr for eight days. While Abu Sufyan's rationale was probably legitimate, the Muslims were able to turn the nonarrival of the Quraysh into a propaganda triumph, mocking the Qurayshi expedition as the "porridge army," for they had only come out to drink *sawiq*, a mixture of wheat or barley with water and butter that was often used as the principle ration during marches.[33] Muhammad's poets mocked them, with Hassan bin Thabit reciting that the Quraysh could say good-bye to the trade goods of Syria, as the Muslims were now blocking the way.[34]

While Muhammad waited, one of his key spies, Ma'bad al-Khuza'i of the Banu Khuza'ah, arrived, apparently to deliver news that Abu Sufyan was not coming. This same individual had been the one to dissuade Abu Sufyan from returning to Madinah after the Qurayshi victory at Uhud. In this case, it appears that he had been shadowing the Qurayshi force to keep the Prophet informed about his enemy's operations and location. Moreover, he had spoken to Qurayshi leaders and exaggerated the size of Muhammad's force so as to make them hesitant to march north to do battle.

Muhammad and his men returned from Badr disappointed and spent close to a half year reorganizing and preparing for future operations. That the Prophet at this time did not raid any Qurayshi caravans is probably indicative of his desire to regroup rather than engage in another major battle with his old foe. It could also be due to the possibility that the Quraysh simply did not dispatch a caravan during this time, afraid that it would be intercepted by the Muslims. Instead, Muhammad once more turned on his neighbors, leading one raid with one thousand men northward to Dumat al-Jandal. This raid was based on another rumor that he claimed to have received that a hostile tribe, possibly with Byzantine support, was organizing against the Muslims. But when they arrived in the area, they encountered no enemy forces.[35] Instead, they found some livestock that they could seize, even though the plunder taken was apparently so minimal that Ibn Ishaq did not find it worth mentioning.[36] It would seem more likely that Muhammad used the raid as a way to settle his restless men who were still reeling from their defeat at Uhud. The raid to Dumat al-Jandal, though a significant distance away, was an easy operation that allowed the Muslims a chance to recover their composure. However, while the Muslims were relatively inactive at this time, their most ardent enemies were not.

One advantage possessed by the Quraysh was their ability to organize coalitions in serious times of need.[37] After their victory at Uhud, the Qurayshi leaders were approached by the exiled leaders of the Banu al-Nadir to launch a full-fledged assault against the Muslims to defeat them in one decisive operation.[38] During the last months of 626, the Quraysh organized a massive coalition, the largest seen in Arabia in memory, with the intent of besieging the Muslims in Madinah and forcing their surrender. It would appear that the exiled al-Nadir offered money and supplies for this operation, for there is no evidence that they actually participated in the action. Providing financial support would be the only logical means by which they could entice the Quraysh to organize such a large expedition. Their allies included the Banu Sulaym and several smaller subtribes. In addition, a force of the Banu Ghatafan would arrive from the north and join the Qurayshi army, thus making this a coalition composed of three major tribal elements.[39] It would seem that some of the participants provided fighters while others supplied camels for transport. The Qurayshi and Sulaym force from the south was composed of 5,200 men and 300 cavalry, of which 4,000 foot and all the cavalry came from the Quraysh proper. In addition, they had at least 2,500 camels for transport.[40]

While the amount of transport was less than that used for the operation leading to the battle of Uhud, there is no indication that the Quraysh took a large contingent of women with them as support personnel. As such, Abu Sufyan, who served as the commander in chief, had obviously determined that the level of transport could not support such a luxury, and that the coalition army would have to take to the field using every camel possible to carry the supplies and equipment needed by the combatants. Nevertheless, the Qurayshi operation was embarking on this campaign with a very slender logistical tail, and it is possible that the needs of the force exceeded the logistical lift available. The Qurayshi supply problem would be exacerbated by the fact that the fields around Madinah had been harvested a month prior, which meant they would find little pasturage for their animals and grain for their personal use.[41] This would place the operation in serious jeopardy from the very beginning; thus, it would be necessary for the Quraysh to receive some type of commissary support once they reached Madinah. This could very well have been the role of the exiles of the Banu al-Nadir who were now residing in Khaybar. Regardless, the iron laws of supply could very well have doomed the enterprise from its inception.

Table 5.2. Qurayshi Logistical Lift and Provisions for the al-Khandaq Campaign

Category	Quantity	Pounds	Days	Total lbs
LOGISTICAL LIFT (POUNDS CARRIED)				
Men	5,500	20		110,000
Women/Servants	Negligible			
Camels	2,500	300		750,000
Horses	300	200		60,000
Total Lift				920,000
PROVISIONS (POUNDS REQUIRED)				
Food Needed	5,500	3	30	495,000
Camel Fodder	2,500	10	30	750,000
Horse Fodder	300	10	30	90,000
Total Provisions				1,335,000

Besides the Quraysh and Sulaym, the Ghatafan formed the third component of this grand coalition, called al-Ahzab, or the Confederates. We have few details regarding their army, but since the final count of the coalition force provided in the sources comes to 10,000 men, it would mean that the Ghatafan provided 4,500 of that total, with perhaps an additional 300 cavalry.[42] While the Quraysh were obviously at war with Muhammad, the Ghatafan were on shaky ground, as the leader of their expedition had previously made a treaty with the Prophet to pasture his flocks on Muslim land. However, the offer made by the Jewish leaders at Khaybar to give them one year of their date harvest was apparently far more valuable to them than access to some pastureland.[43] Having agreed upon a time to assemble near Madinah, the tribal leaders prepared their forces for what they anticipated to be the final campaign to eliminate the Muslim threat.

Muhammad was well aware of these preparations for he was alerted quickly through his very effective intelligence network operation with the Banu Khuzaʿah.[44] Unlike the Uhud campaign, there would be absolutely no doubt that the Muslims would remain within the confines of Madinah, this time relying upon their fortresses and stored supplies to hold off an anticipated siege. But there were those who believed that Madinah's defenses could be enhanced, and upon the advice of a Persian Muslim named Salman al-Farisi, Muhammad ordered a trench dug as an obstacle to block the most obvious assault lanes on the north and

northwest edges of the city. As the men worked to the chanting of poetic verse, Muhammad worked alongside them, prophesying that one
day they would eat of the riches of the Byzantines and Persians.[45]

While it is reasonably certain that some type of trench was dug,
there is little information as to its size and construction. Hamidullah's
assumption that the trench was 3-½ miles long, 30 feet wide, and 15 feet
deep would have required the movement of close to 5 million cubic feet
of earth.[46] Since it is believed that about three thousand people excavated the trench in six days, working during the day and taking breaks
at night, it would be impossible for them to move this quantity of soil.
Instead, they would only be able to excavate just over 1 million cubic
feet of earth during the time allotted.[47] With this in mind, it is more
likely that the trench was intermittent, being no more than a total of 2
miles in length, around 15 to 20 feet wide, and no more than 5 feet in
depth with a parapet of 3 to 4 additional feet to make the total depth
about 8 feet. There is also no clear evidence to indicate that the trench
was consistent in dimensions, or that it was shored up with brickwork,
despite an assertion of such later made by a claimant to the leadership
of the *ummah* during the *khalifate* of the Abbasid Mansur.[48]

While the sources provide no specifics as to the actual design of the
trench, it is most likely that the excavated soil would have been piled up
on the side of the Muslims. This would have enhanced the obstacle significantly, for any horseman from the Quraysh would need to leap not
only the trench itself, but somehow leap or claw up the parapet on the
far side. Any footman would have to descend into the trench and then
attempt to crawl up a seven- to nine-foot incline, all the while being
showered with missiles from the defenders above. Because wood was
extremely scarce in the region, the Quraysh would be unable to build
ladders or mobile bridges to breach the trench. And with the soil piled
up on the opposite side, they would be unable to push the soil of the
parapet back into the trench to fill it. The Quraysh were soon to learn
to their consternation that this new though simple artifice, unknown to
them at the time, was quite effective.

When the Quraysh and their allies arrived, they camped to the
northwest of Madinah while Muhammad and his three thousand fighters took up positions behind the trench. Determined to enhance their
chances, Abu Sufyan commissioned an attempt to befriend the last Jewish tribe in the city, the Banu Qurayzah, sending one of the leaders of
the exiled Banu al-Nadir for this purpose.[49] While the sources indicate

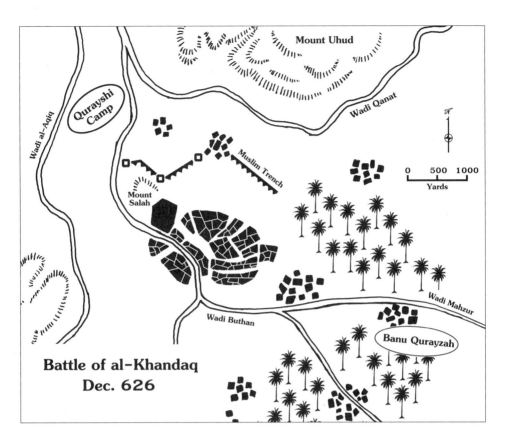

Battle of al-Khandaq
Dec. 626

that the Banu Qurayzah eventually agreed to join the Quraysh, there
are serious doubts as to the veracity of this. For their part, elements of
the Qurayzah provided shovels, picks, and baskets to help the Muslims
dig the trench, a point not consistent with ones intent on engaging in
hostilities.[50]

Regardless, Muhammad was certainly concerned about the status of
the Banu Qurayzah who were positioned within the city and behind the
Muslim defenses, and he sent a small reconnaissance team to secretly
ascertain their status in the upcoming battle. The statements made by
some of the Banu Qurayzah regarding how they had "no agreement
or undertaking with Muhammad" again demonstrates that they were
not part of the Covenant of Madinah, and at best had a nonaggression
pact with the Prophet.[51] Moreover, the statements as recorded in the
sources do not imply that the Qurayzah actually intended any offensive
action but that they simply planned to sit this one out. With the Banu

Qurayzah at best neutral and at worst possibly planning to join the coalition, Muhammad had no choice but to siphon off three hundred fighters to screen the Qurayzah's area to ensure that the Muslims would not be surprised. Despite his best efforts to keep this situation under wraps, the word apparently spread and fear gripped the Muslim warriors, shaking them to their core.

The siege went on for at least twenty days, and possibly longer, but with minimal fighting. When the Quraysh attempted to probe the Muslim position, they encountered the trench, which was an astonishing development to them. What little combat that occurred was largely the result of individual action. One of the Quraysh, 'Amr bin 'Abdu Wudd, led a group of elite Qurayshi horseman to search for a weakness in the trench. They discovered a point they could cross but soon found themselves hemmed in by the terrain and Muslim troops. 'Amr, a warrior of ninety years of age, called out a challenge to individual combat, and he was answered by the youthful 'Ali bin Abu Talib.[52] When confronted with 'Ali, 'Amr remonstrated, "O son of my brother, I do not want to kill you." 'Ali's response was both firm and unforgiving. "But I want to kill you."[53] 'Ali's answer was another indication of the sharp difference between the attitude of the Quraysh and the Muslims regarding warfare. While the Quraysh would prefer to seek a middle ground to compromise, the Muslims were committed to killing their enemies rather than negotiating some form of settlement.

The hand-to-hand fight that ensued did not last long. 'Amr's blade became wedged in 'Ali's shield, and the Muslim countered with a swift blow to his foe's neck. 'Amr crumpled to the ground as he quickly bled to death, and 'Ali then cried out, "Allah Akbar," which told the Muslims that 'Ali had been victorious.[54] With that, 'Amr's companions reined their horses and retreated. In addition to 'Amr, two other fighters of the Quraysh attempted to cross the trench and were killed. One was struck by arrows and mortally wounded, while another became trapped in the trench as he was pelted with stones. Crying out that a quick death was more honorable than being laid low by such humble missiles, 'Ali climbed into the trench and cut him down.[55] One major endeavor was made to force the trench, with Khalid bin al-Walid in command of the lion's share of Qurayshi forces to attempt this. Despite their efforts to force the obstacle, the Muslims were able to drive them back.[56]

The siege took its toll on both sides, and the Quraysh were very close to breaking the Muslim resistance. Despite the Qurayshi's logistical plight, similar problems plagued the Muslims, and at one point the crisis became sufficiently acute for Muhammad to send emissaries to the Ghatafan in an effort to buy them off. He offered them annually one-third of the dates of Madinah to have them withdraw, and they even went so far as to draft an agreement. However, the Ansar did not concur with these negotiations, contending that they had no intention of paying tribute to anyone.[57] With negotiations having come to naught, Muhammad decided to resort to a stratagem of deception to break the coalition.

The man chosen for this task was Nu'aym bin Mas'ud bin 'Amr of the Ghatafan tribe. He approached the Prophet and informed him that since becoming a Muslim he had not revealed this to any in his tribe, or to others in the Banu Qurayzah or Quraysh. Muhammad dispatched him to these tribes to sow distrust in the coalition, instructing Nu'aym that "war is deceit."[58] Nu'aym first went to the Banu Qurayzah. After allaying any fears and confirming his fealty, he noted that they alone would have to remain in Madinah if the coalition siege was a failure. To prevent the Quraysh and Ghatafan from simply breaking camp and departing, he convinced the Jews that they should ask for hostages to ensure that the others would carry the fight through. The Qurayzah agreed.

Nu'aym then went to the Quraysh and met with Abu Sufyan and his advisors. He convinced them that the Banu Qurayzah had contrived with Muhammad to try and seize some of the notable men of the Quraysh as hostages, only to hand them over to the Prophet to be beheaded. He convinced them not to hand over any hostages, and further convinced them to keep this matter a secret. He then went to the Ghatafan and convinced them to follow the same course of action as that of the Quraysh. The Quraysh soon sent negotiators to the Banu Qurayzah, indicating that their army was suffering from lack of supplies and therefore needed them to engage the Muslims at once and defeat them. They now asked the Jews to commit themselves, but the Qurayzah demurred, first demanding up to seventy hostages to ensure that the Quraysh and Ghatafan would carry through with their plans.[59] The trap was sprung, and the coalition became distrustful of the Jews, now afraid that they had made a secret alliance with Muhammad.[60]

The very next day, a harsh winter wind raced through the coalition camp, extinguishing their fires and blowing their tents apart. This, coupled with the dwindling supplies and the distrust growing among the coalition members, convinced Abu Sufyan to lift the siege. During the night, Muhammad sent a spy to infiltrate the Qurayshi camp to ascertain the effectiveness of his deception operation. As the man moved quietly between the men huddled in the cold darkness, he watched as Abu Sufyan, angry that the Banu Qurayzah had refused to join the coalition, mounted his hobbled camel to depart. "O people of the Quraysh! You are not in a position to stay. Hoofs (i.e., horses) and fat (i.e., camels) are destroyed, the plain became dry, Banu Qurayzah deserted us and the wind played havoc which you have seen, so you should ride (your camels) and I am also riding (mine)."[61] The Quraysh hurriedly broke camp, leaving a rearguard of two hundred cavalry under Khalid bin al-Walid to cover their withdrawal. When the Ghatafan heard the news, they broke camp as well and pulled out. The next morning, the Muslims awoke to find their enemies had gone. Wearily, they were sent by the Prophet to return to their homes and stand down. During the entire length of the siege, only six Muslims were killed and only three killed from the Quraysh.[62]

We now come to the anticlimactic destruction of the Jewish Banu Qurayzah, immediately following the battle of al-Khandaq. This event entails some controversy within Islamic history and is typically explained by noting that the Qurayzah, as the last Jewish tribe of substance in Madinah, broke their covenant with Muhammad, and thus deserved their fate.[63] However, internal evidence of the actual actions of the Prophet and his companions casts doubt on such assertions. Moreover, there is evidence that at best Muhammad had only a loose and nonbinding pact with the Banu Qurayzah, probably the one established with the Prophet when he exiled the Banu al-Nadir, thus calling in question whether a real agreement even existed.[64]

One piece of evidence that casts doubt on the notion that the Qurayzah had violated any nonaggression pact with the Muslims involves the conduct of Muhammad and his men when the coalition lifted their siege. Instead of turning directly on the treacherous Banu Qurayzah, the Prophet sent his men home and he returned to ʿAisha's single-room apartment to bathe.[65] While there, the angel Jibril came to chide him for laying down his arms. When Muhammad asked who he was to now fight, Jibril gestured toward the east and the Banu Qurayzah.[66] This line of conversation, repeated in nearly every early source, raises an important question. If the Banu Qurayzah's treachery had been so obvious, why was the Prophet so oblivious to it?

This is certainly an important point, for the Qurayzah's violation of any pact had not been apparent. Indeed, they may not have violated any agreement at all, this constituting another piece of evidence against the orthodox interpretation. If we are to take the sources at face value, the Jews of this tribe had only contemplated joining the coalition against the Muslims. Contemplating such action was no worse than what 'Abdullah bin 'Ubayy had openly planned to do in support of the Banu al-Nadir prior to the latter's exile. If the mere thought of joining an attacking army merited being besieged and destroyed, why was no action taken against 'Abdullah and some of the other leaders of the al-Khazraj? While it is tempting to accept the notion that the Qurayzah had committed treachery, it is probable that any explanation for Muhammad's determination to attack them must be found elsewhere, a feature even noted by one poet who lamented the Qurayzah's pointless destruction.[67]

So what was Muhammad's motivation? The seeds for this can be found in his earlier declaration after the battle of Badr that he intended to exile the Jews from the land. Such a declaration would have already set the Jews and Muslims at odds, which would explain much of the behavior on both sides. Muhammad had openly declared his intent, and as of December 626, he had implemented such intent with two of the three Jewish tribes in the city. It would only stand to reason that the Banu Qurayzah realized they were next, apparently believing that they could still succeed where others had failed. Therefore, even if the Qurayzah did violate some type of agreement, one must ask if anyone would blame them for doing so. Considering the Prophet's intent regarding the Jews of Madinah, the Qurayzah's leaders must have recognized that any agreement with Muhammad was only temporary at best. When the Muslim army arrived, approximately three thousand strong, the Qurayzah were outnumbered by three to one, although they had their fortifications to protect them. As Muhammad approached, they called out that the Prophet had "never been one to act impetuously," a point that clearly implied that the Prophet had preplanned such a move.[68]

Muhammad deployed his army near the Well of Ana, thus ensuring a ready supply of water. He then besieged the Qurayzah for twenty-five days, his men at times sending volleys of arrows arcing over the walls without knowing what damage they inflicted.[69] This technique was obviously more for harassment purposes than for actual effect, and the Muslims only did this occasionally to conserve their stock of arrows. The Jews responded in kind, sending volleys of both arrows and stones.[70] No serious effort was made by the Muslims to assault the walls and towers, partly because the men were already weary from the lengthy siege of al-Khandaq.[71]

As the condition of the besieged became desperate, one of the leaders of the Qurayzah, Ka'b bin Asad, presented three plans of action to them. The first was to become Muslims, but the people said they would not desert their old law. The second was to have the men kill their women and children so that they would fight without worrying about the fate of their loved ones. Should they win they would gain women and children as booty. This suggestion caused a howl of indignation to arise from the Jews. Barring this, he made one more suggestion. That very evening was the Sabbath. Ka'b suggested that they sally forth from their forts, possibly taking the Muslims by surprise as they would assume that the Jews would not fight on their holy day. This was also rejected, preferring to accept the stories that those before them who had desecrated the Sabbath had been transformed into apes and pigs.[72] At this point, Ka'b was exasperated, crying out that "not a single man among you from the day of your birth has ever passed a night resolved to do what he knows ought to be done."[73]

Ka'b's remark reminds one of Abu Sufyan's regarding the latter's view of warfare. Just as the Quraysh were unable to engage in combat to achieve a decisive victory, the Banu Qurayzah were unable to make a difficult decision at the decisive moment. Even when they asked for a negotiator by the name of Abu Luhaba, and he indicated to the Jews that Muhammad intended to slaughter their warriors, they still could not resolve themselves to take a resolute course of action.[74] Unlike the Qurayzah, Abu Luhaba understood the situation all too well, having realized that he had betrayed the Prophet's intent. When he left the fortresses of the Jews, he hurried to the Prophet's mosque and tied himself to one of the pillars, determined to remain there in contrition until Muhammad absolved him. But while Abu Luhaba found it necessary to act decisively to save his own life, the Qurayzah were unable to make a similar decision when faced with utter defeat.

One of the difficulties facing leaders in any combat situation is determining when there is a point of no return, and knowing that the only course of action is a complete and ruthless commitment to a particular decision. Hindsight makes such judgments appear simple, but they are not so easy to those facing them in the moment. It would appear that the Banu Qurayzah still believed they could somehow escape through negotiation, just as the Qaynuqa and al-Nadir had before them. With this in mind, they agreed to surrender on terms that would be established by a member of the al-Aws, one of their allies.

The man appointed by the Prophet to determine the fate of the Banu Qurayzah was Sa'd bin Mu'adh. He had been an early adherent to Islam, having been converted under the infiltration ministry of Mus'ab bin 'Umayr. Once converted, Sa'd had become a forceful advocate of Muhammad and Islam in Madinah, even advocating as noted previously the slaughter of Qurayshi prisoners at Badr. The Banu Qurayzah had misjudged Muhammad and their own situation, probably believing that one of their allies of the al-Aws would judge them leniently and allow them to go into exile. Even as Sa'd, who had been wounded during the battle of al-Khandaq and was recovering at the Prophet's mosque, approached, the rumor began to fly that he had already determined to have the warriors executed.[75]

Sa'd chose to apply a passage from the book of Deuteronomy to be the standard to judge the Jews, determining that the men were to be executed and the women and children taken as slaves. This decision was kept from the men, who were at that time sequestered in a building near the marketplace. The Prophet ordered a ditch dug in the center of the market and had the men brought out in groups of ten. Only as they approached the ditch did they realize their fate. One group after another had their heads removed by swift strokes of Indian blades as Muhammad watched. Some of the sequestered men began to comprehend what was happening when they noticed that groups were taken away but did not return.[76]

The judgment meted out to the Banu Qurayzah demonstrates the important aspect of insurgencies to make an enemy live up to their own rulebook. The passage Sa'd chose, from Deuteronomy 20:13–14, was taken out of context, for according to this section, peace terms were to be offered before a city was besieged. Muhammad offered no such terms to the Banu Qurayzah at this time, demanding instead virtual unconditional surrender to an arbiter of the Prophet's choosing. The very fact that they did not realize until the beheadings were being carried out that death was decreed for them indicates that they did not have the terms laid out before them. In addition, if one reads further into Deuteronomy 20 they will find that God had decreed that the Hebrews should completely destroy those people nearby within Canaan proper. If Saʿd had applied the passage within its context, the Banu Qurayzah would have been completely destroyed, including their women and children, along with all of their property and wealth. Nothing would have remained as plunder. Yet, by selectively applying this passage of the law to the Jews, Saʿd was placing the blame for their fate completely upon them, with the Muslims merely declaring the verdict. As for Saʿd, after he had passed judgment he returned to his hospital bed, only to have his wound to reopen. Before anyone realized what had happened, he had bled to death.

The number executed varies, but the total usually accepted is between six hundred and seven hundred men, along with one woman who became a combatant when she went to the walls and dropped a stone on a Muslim warrior's head. At least one man was spared when he converted to Islam.[77] The Jewish warriors were executed by members of every tribal element in the Muslim community, thus making all responsible for their deaths.[78] The women and children were sold as slaves, although the going price appears to have been ridiculously low. One Jewish merchant from a small subtribe in Madinah purchased two women and their three children for 150 dinars while another purchased three women and their children, the number of these not specified, for only 45 dinars.[79] These were bargain prices when a single slave could cost 40 to 80 dinars, even though a female slave could go for as little as 36 dinars.[80]

The loot, particularly in weapons and armor, collected was fair and probably the largest quantity collected up to this point in any one raid. In all, the Muslims collected 1,500 swords; 300 coats of chain mail; 1,000 spears; and 1,500 shields of differing quality.[81] Yet it should be noted that one cannot translate the quantities seized with any actual number of troops to be equipped. Because it would be necessary to maintain replacements for lost and damaged equipment, it could be estimated that the loot would be sufficient to equip men amounting to but one-half or, more likely, one-third of the weapons captured. Regardless, it was a significant gain in equipment for the modestly outfitted Muslims. Regarding the Banu Qurayzah, Hassan bin Thabit recited poetic verse extolling the Muslim triumph and the terrible humiliation that came upon the Jewish tribe, and that the Quraysh of Makkah should be forewarned that a "like punishment" was theirs in the future.[82]

The Muslim victory at al-Khandaq, along with the following triumph over the Banu Qurayzah, had significant consequences. For
the Makkans, their failure to conquer Madinah went far beyond the
battle itself. They had prided themselves on their ability to form coalitions to accomplish tremendous deeds, and now, at a critical juncture,
they failed to bring a coalition to victory. This failure discomfited their
friends and astonished those tribes still neutral. The al-Khandaq campaign was the high point of Qurayshi military power, a point not lost
on the Prophet, who predicted that the Muslims would now attack the
Quraysh at will.[83] This not only meant that the Quraysh could find the
safety of their caravans and of the others they escorted in serious jeopardy; it also meant that they could soon find themselves friendless.

However, the consequences of these two victories were even greater
for the Muslims and for Muhammad. The destruction of the Banu
Qurayzah made it clear to all in the region that the Prophet would
brook no opposition to his movement. Later he would state that he had
"been made victorious for a distance of one month journey with terror
(cast in the hearts of the enemy)."[84] The elimination of the last Jewish
tribe in Madinah was in large measure meant to create that sense of
terror, that sense of coming doom and destruction, to help push the
recalcitrant into openly supporting Muhammad's movement. Not long
after this he began to be called the king of the Hijaz by many in the
region.[85]

While the defeat of the Banu Qurayzah set an example for the region, the defeat of the Qurayshi coalition had more far reaching consequences. Some of these are obvious from the sources, such as the fact
that the Quraysh never again mounted an offensive against Madinah
and that Muhammad's movement was now growing in strength and
reputation. Yet there is another possible consequence that was far more
important. While there is little direct evidence, there is sufficient cir-
cumstantial material to imply that Muhammad began to receive some
type of material aid from the Sasanid, or Persian, Empire.

There are scant current-day observers who postulate that Muhammad received any outside aid, let alone from a specific empire.[86] When
examining the Muslim ascendancy, most recent scholarship tends to
merely speculate that the sources exaggerate the growth in Muhammad's army, particularly the number of horses deployed.[87] When analyzing the source data, it is common for many to cite the material as

unreliable regarding specific numbers and key facts, stating that such items are mere topoi, or terms used ex post facto to generically provide a detail in what was otherwise a vague historical narrative. Much of this skepticism derives partly from scholarly bewilderment at the use of such things as fantastical numbers in some ancient documents when describing campaigns and battles.[88] However, as has been demonstrated previously, a logistical analysis of the information in the early Islamic sources demonstrates that the numbers of men claimed deployed were possible, unless of course the compilers of the oral traditions later calculated the information out to ensure some kind of believability, a postulation that is unlikely. The analysis that will follow will include events that will be covered in more detail later. However, it is necessary to introduce such material here to explain the nature of the outside aid that Muhammad probably received after his victory at al-Khandaq.

An article of faith largely accepted in the historical community has been the notion that insurgencies, in particular guerrilla movements and revolutions, simply spring up from the ground, emerging from nowhere in a spontaneous fashion. It can be bluntly said that this is patent nonsense, for anyone who has ever carried out one of these operations knows full well the time, expense, and effort involved in organizing and conducting them. It is only in fantasy land that one would think that insurgent movements and revolutions simply rise up and throw off the shackles of an oppressive government or cast out an invading power solely on their own accord.

Any activity that one pursues is beset by what economists would call opportunity cost. This principle states that for everything one does, one must give up something else. In this process, people make choices every day based on what they are willing to give up compared to what they will gain if they pursue an alternate activity. Therefore, the key factor impacting opportunity cost is time, for it is a limited commodity for which there is no recompense. Since there are only twenty-four hours in a day, one must choose to not do certain things in order to do others. Moreover, the more primitive an environment, the more costly each activity becomes in terms of time expended, and therefore the more alternate activities that must be excluded in order to do any one given task. Machines of any type dramatically impact opportunity cost, for they become laborsaving devices that allow a person to do more in the same amount of time, regardless what that is. Therefore, when put simply, if one is to eat and live, one must work for the items needed, steal them, or receive them as gifts.[89]

When it comes to insurgency and its cousins, stealing is a poor substitute. In military parlance, one does not steal but instead gains plunder or loot through conquest and victory. While loot has always been a factor in warfare, one would be hard-pressed to find examples of armies that lived off the land and the enemy through such plunder. While there are some who might wish to think that Napoleon, for example, exercised such logistical methods, it is because he did often neglect the more important aspects of supply and support that his armies were defeated at the operational level. As Gunther Rothenberg so aptly noted, there was a "crucial shortcoming to Napoleon's system of war—his improvised and ramshackle logistics."[90] Another possible example would be Julius Caesar during his Gallic campaign. However, Caesar's legions were compelled to live on grain purchased from allied Gallic tribes, thus involving the need to be supported by a methodical system of planting, harvesting, and movement of these supplies to keep the legions fed, not to mention the need to have an adequate treasury to pay for it all. When the harvest was poor in a given year, he was forced to more widely distribute his men to not overtax a given region from which supply was drawn.[91]

In addition to Napoleon and Caesar, another favorite for the notion that an army can live off of the land and the enemy is Hannibal. However, it must be pointed out that Hannibal was unable to achieve victory in his invasion of Roman territory not as commonly supposed because he had no siege train but because he did not have the logistical network to remain stationary long enough to conduct a siege. He had to continue moving through Italy, plundering and sacking granaries in the hope of maintaining himself in the field while waiting for the rebellion against Rome that never materialized. Ultimately, lack of support, both logistical and political, that he failed to receive from his homeland led to his withdrawal from the Italian peninsula and his final defeat. While Hannibal had brilliantly conducted operations within the very heartland of Rome itself, he was unable to triumph, ultimately finding himself cut off and isolated in the toe of the Italian peninsula.[92]

While there will always be exceptions to the rule, and one could find examples of small forces that survive off of the land and their enemies, by and large any combatant force, regular or insurgent, needs organized logistical support. For the latter, this support becomes even more crucial when the insurgency begins to shift to more conventional operations to create a decision and secure the final victory. Early logistical support can be indigenous, such as local people offering food, fashioning clothing, and providing some equipment. But as the insurgency grows, it becomes necessary to move from the irregular construct of warfare to the more conventional. When this shift begins, it is essential for an insurgency to receive some outside support to provide necessities not created by the indigenous population.[93]

In recent times there are probably two individuals who have popularized the idea that an insurgency can simply live off the land and the enemy: Mao Tse-Tung and Che Guevara. Their writings helped to create the mythos that the noble insurgent and revolutionary, fighting for a higher cause that kings and princes could not comprehend, sacrifices all, including sustenance, comfort, and peace. He lives on scanty resources, moving swiftly and silently until he pounces upon his hapless foe, nibbling away at the combat forces of the established government and procuring his weapons from the fallen enemy. This sounds so good yet is complete drivel. While the revolutionary Marxist myth-makers may wish people to believe such, it is simply myth.

While Mao speaks of the need for supply in his military writings, he makes vague references to the need to receive food and equipment but provides little discussion as to how one actually achieves this, save for capture from the enemy. For example, at one point he states that "the Red Army has no sources from which to replenish its arms and especially its ammunition."[94] He speaks of the need to obtain food, clothing, and other equipment from the locals, but then contradicts himself by stating that the people have been excessively robbed by the government so that they "cry out in hunger and cold."[95] The question is never asked: if the established government is plundering its own citizens, how is there any surplus to supply a group of insurgent fighters who produce nothing of their own?

One place where Mao provides some details regarding supply is in his book *On Guerrilla Warfare*, written at the beginning of the Japanese invasion of China in 1937. However, while he again repeats the myth that his Marxist insurgents live off the enemy and have no rear areas, he goes on to say unequivocally that during the period of rapprochement with the Nationalist leadership it is necessary for the Nationalists to actively supply the Marxists guerrillas.[96] Thus, even Mao understood and admitted, though still in vague terms, that an insurgency needed outside support. While such statements from him that "you simply leave your farms and become soldiers" can have an element of romantic bluster, they fail to take into account who plants and harvests the crops when the farmers drop their tools to become soldiers.[97] The fact that Mao wrote so little about supply and logistics has led many observes to assume that insurgency warfare is about mobilizing the people, and about the various tactics used in operations.

Che Guevara was a serious student of Mao who came to believe this. When one examines Guevara's operations in Bolivia, it is amazing that anyone can consider him to be a genius of insurgency and guerrilla warfare. The same man that supposedly performed so brilliantly in Cuba failed miserably in the Congo and later in Bolivia. Guevara is best known for the concept of *foco*, the idea that a small group of insurgents can move into any area, particularly rural, and rally the exploited to their side, who then supply them with material needs and foot soldiers. As a true believer in Maoist ideals, Guevara in essence assumed that the revolution, initially supplied with some bare essentials, could just spring up from the ground as if by magic. Yet his Bolivian diary is replete with references to lack of food and supplies, along with a host of other problems that Clausewitz would describe as classic examples of friction, which made his insurgency a failure accentuated by sheer human misery.[98] Guevara's concept of *foco* has been discredited, but usually for the wrong reasons. Its true failure was born in the dreams of a wandering medical student from a well-to-do middle-class background who thought he could supply a combat force in the field in much the same way that he begged food off people while touring South America on a motorcycle.[99]

What Guevara apparently never learned was that even the most ardent Marxist insurgent was a well-paid operative who relied on somebody to carry his freight. A recent analysis of Bolshevik revolutionaries in Russia demonstrated that these individuals received competitive salaries necessary to maintain good talent in the movement, and this even before the failed 1905 revolution.[100] Being paid in modern times is much the same as somebody providing you a gift of food and equipment in archaic times. Since opportunity cost intrudes, even a Bedouin of the Arabian Desert has to choose between eating and conducting a raid. While the latter might help with the former, the best way to meet immediate needs and also do the yeoman's service of an insurgent warrior is for another to provide sufficient sustenance to allow him to engage in warfare on a somewhat regular basis.

An analysis of Muhammad's raids based on evidence presented by al-Waqidi and Ibn Saʿd demonstrates a poor return in regards to obtaining critical food supplies and even more desperately needed weapons. In the period of the year 627–28, 26 raids netted approximately 2,870 camels, 10,000 goats, and 200 slaves. Many of the raids recorded in the year 628 often provide no details of any of the loot seized, a probable indication that the amount was negligible.[101] While 10,000 goats might seem a large quantity taken, it should be noted that in Islamic legal calculations, a goat was considered one-tenth of a camel, indicative of its approximate sustenance level and value.[102] Because the standard camel meat ration for 100 men was one camel per day, one can see that 5,000 men could go through 10,000 goats in about 20 days, barring any other food source available at the time. And these 10,000 goats listed were seized in what was almost a two-year period of operations. In addition, there is the problem regarding the distribution of loot taken after battles. Muhammad did not have access to most of it, and even the fifth he kept was largely used for the benefit of the *ummah*. Only a small fraction, possibly as little as 4 percent, was available to the Prophet to expend on materials of war.[103]

The data available regarding the inability of Muhammad's men to live off the land tracks well with more recent sources on insurgency and guerrilla operations. Two of the most classic insurgency operations of the twentieth century in which we have an exclusive inside glimpse include Col. Paul von Lettow-Vorbeck's guerrilla operations in East Africa and T. E. Lawrence's raids in the Hijaz region so familiar to Muhammad's warriors. Both of these campaigns were conducted during World War I. In the former, Lettow-Vorbeck, for all his pluck and grit to put a good face on his impending defeat, spoke extensively of his supply problems and the mind-numbing exertions needed to provide food and munitions to his men. Initially, his force received some external support from Germany, but the British blockade on the homeland proved decisive, and Lettow-Vorbeck was left to his own devices, despite a late-war abortive effort by the German Imperial High Command to dispatch the L-59 Zeppelin with fifty tons of supplies for the beleaguered guerrilla commander.[104]

Starting with a field force of around twenty-five thousand men, Lettow-Vorbeck was compelled soon to demobilize more than 90 percent of his effectives simply because he could not feed them.[105] This is all the more telling because he was operating in one of the most fertile regions of eastern Africa, and a region largely friendly to his efforts. Time and time again he strove to mount a decisive operation against his enemies only to be bedeviled by severe logistical constraints compelling him to make operational decisions contrary to his own plans.[106] Even when he did capture significant supplies from his enemies, he typically had no means to move them and had to abandon or destroy such treasure troves.[107] Any success he ever had in living off the land came to a force of only about two thousand men, and this in an area the size of the states of Texas and New Mexico, or almost two times that of Imperial Germany. At times, the high fertility of the region proved to be a double-edged sword, providing sustenance to the enemy at such a rate as to force Lettow-Vorbeck to abandon a critical area or face total destruction against superior odds.[108] But even in his attempts to live off the land, Lettow-Vorbeck still found it necessary to establish rearward supply bases and engage load bearers to move the supplies forward to his half-starved men. Naturally, these bases became vulnerable to enemy attack on more than one occasion.

As for T. E. Lawrence, the demand for external supply was so acute that it drove the entire basis of his strategy—the need to capture Aqaba. Without this port he could not receive and coordinate the logistical support necessary to keep Prince Feisal's irregular Arab militia in the field. Aqaba so dominated his thinking that he engaged in a personal reconnaissance across the blazing Najd to test his theory that a land-directed assault was possible. He understood that the Arab revolt, at this time a mere nuisance to the Turks, would become a significant threat if they were bolstered by ready supplies of food, ammunition, water, money, and technical advisors.[109] Had the Turks properly analyzed their situation in Arabia, they would have taken greater care to protect Aqaba and ensure that the Arab revolt remained just that—a revolt of ill-equipped and poorly supplied raiders living daily hand-to-mouth in a wasteland. The fall of Aqaba to Feisal's men meant important outside support, and the Arab rebellion became an army.

Evidence for outside support to Muhammad's forces can be found in one area where we have some good statistics, the number of horses employed in various operations. While horses are often considered a significant asset of Arabia, in fact they were extremely rare during Muhammad's day. Among Muhammad's men, horses were so rare that they

Table 5.3. The Growth in Muhammad's Horse Cavalry Arm

Battle	Date	Horses	Source
Badr	Dec 623	2	Ibn Saʿd, *Kitab al-Tabaqat*, Vol. II, 10
Uhud	Dec 624	0	Ibn Kathir, *Al-Sira al-Nabawiyya*, Vol. III, 17
Badr II	Nov 625	10	Ibn Saʿd, *Kitab al-Tabaqat*, Vol. II, 72
Al-Khandaq	Dec 626	36	Al-Waqidi, *Kitab al-Maghazi*, 211; and Ibn Saʿd, *Kitab al-Tabaqat*, Vol. II, 92
Banu Lihyan	May 627	220	Ibn Saʿd, *Kitab al-Tabaqat*, Vol. II, 97
Al-Hudaybiyah	Jan 628	20+	Ibn Saʿd, *Kitab al-Tabaqat*, Vol. II, 118
Khaybar	Aug 628	200–300	Ibn Saʿd, *Kitab al-Tabaqat*, Vol. II, 134; and Hasan, *Sunan Abu Dawud*, Vol. II, #2730
Muʾtah	Jul 629	3–4?	Ibn Saʿd, *Kitab al-Tabaqat*, Vol. II, 160
Dhal al-Salasil	Oct 629	30	Ibn Saʿd, *Kitab al-Tabaqat*, Vol. II, 162.
Makkah	Nov 629	900	Al-Waqidi, *Kitab al-Maghazi*, 330
Hunayn	Dec 629	980	Al-Waqidi, *Kitab al-Maghazi*, 358
Tabuk	Jun 630	10,000	Ibn Saʿd, *Kitab al-Tabaqat*, Vol. II, 205

Sources: Ibn Saʿd, *Kitab al-Tabaqat*, Vol. 2; Ibn Kathir, *Al-Sira al-Nabawiyya*, Vol. 3; Al-Waqidi, *Kitab al-Maghazi*; and Hasan, *Sunan Abu Dawud.*

were considered a prized possession, never to be used for any common work.[110] None of the tribes in the Hijaz and the surrounding areas used horses to any serious extent save for perhaps the Banu Sulaym.[111] Even the Quraysh, with their access to considerable wealth, could only muster a cavalry force of two hundred to three hundred horsemen for any given operation. Mounted combat was thus a luxury reserved for the special few, for while camels were plentiful compared to horses, these were used mostly for transport and not for mounted fighting. Those who did ride a camel operated more like dragoons, riding to the battle and then dismounting to fight. The statistics we have show Muhammad gaining a marginal number of horses throughout his campaigns until we see a significant spike during the conquest of Makkah and the subsequent campaign of Tabuk.

The horses employed during the operation to take Makkah appear to have mostly come from the Banu Sulaym, but it would appear that none came from this tribe prior because the Muslims were still raiding them as late as April 629.[112] Despite the Sulaym's support during the conquest of Makkah, the massive spike to ten thousand horses for an operation eight months later is difficult to accept on the surface. Some modern observers simply accept the number without question, although a few imply that it is an exaggeration. However, what if the number, though obviously rounded off, is genuine? How could one account for the sudden spike in horse cavalry within Muhammad's ranks? There can be only one logical conclusion, that these horses were supplied by an outside power, one beyond Arabia and the immediate reach of the Muslims.

One may object by saying that the Muslims were breeding their horses. However, there is no evidence that such systematic breeding occurred among the Muslims in all of Arabia until the *khalifate* of ʿUmar.[113] Another argument would be that Muhammad purchased the horses. The usual price of a horse, even if discounted, would preclude this. In the Hijaz, the typical price of a horse was around four thousand dirhams, or four hundred dinars.[114] In one instance, when a leading Muslim traded a horse for a slave, he felt afterward that he had been cheated and wanted to annul the deal.[115] Since a typical male slave's value ranged from four hundred to ten thousand dirhams, with the average typically around eight hundred dirhams, this would imply that a horse, due to scarcity, was considered more valuable.[116]

An interesting comparison could give us an idea as to how much money or assets the Prophet would have needed to buy 9,000 horses. The value of a home in the region varied from 4,000 to 20,000 dirhams, depending of course on it size, condition, and location.[117] From this we can estimate the approximate value of property in Makkah around AD 630. If Makkah had around 7,500 people, and if this meant there were roughly 2,000 households, and if we establish 10,000 dirhams as the average price for a typical piece of property, we could estimate that the total value of private property in Makkah was around 20 million dirhams. To purchase 9,000 horses, even if discounted by 20 percent, would have cost Muhammad 28.8 million dirhams, a price at least equal to, and probably exceeding, the total property value of Makkah.[118]

Additional evidence can demonstrate that the Prophet probably did not purchase the horses. After the conquest of Makkah, Muhammad received deputations offering submission from most of the tribes in Arabia. During these meetings, Muhammad oftentimes offered the representatives a gift to finalize the agreements. Of those recorded by Ibn Sa'd, the total comes to 3,504 uqiyah, or 140,160 dirhams— sufficient to purchase but 35 horses.[119] As no Muslim of that era ever accused the Prophet of being stingy, the best conclusion that can come from this is that the Muslim treasury at that time did not have sufficient cash reserves to make any major purchase, especially something as valuable and rare as horses. If the statistic of 10,000 horses for the Tabuk campaign is accurate, it would seem logical that his only source for the lion's share of these was through some type of foreign assistance.

If the Muslims did receive a large quantity of horses as a form of foreign aid, the next obvious question is who provided them. We can eliminate the Byzantines forthwith, for they had already experienced some of the wrath of Muslim raids and had received the Prophet's ultimatum. Indeed, many of Muhammad's raids had been directed at disrupting trade along the western caravan route, a route that would have benefited the Byzantines. The Byzantines had also issued instructions to boycott sending military supplies and technologies to the Arabs south of their frontiers.[120] While it is possible that a local tribal chief, perhaps of the Banu Ghassan along the eastern Byzantine frontier, may have defied such an order and supplied the horses, there would be no obvious reason for doing so, nor could we imagine him sending close to ten thousand of them. We can also eliminate the Abyssinians. While the Negus was apparently friendly with Muhammad, there is no real evidence to suggest that he provided anything other than moral support to the Prophet's movement. Instead, the most logical source for a ready supply of horses, not to mention other material aid, would be from within the Persian Sasanid Empire.

In analyzing this concept, it must be understood that the Sasanid Empire was anything but monolithic. The emperor, Khusrau II (ca. 590–628), was far from a total autocrat, with the nobles exercising considerable sway locally.[121] Khusrau II's father had experienced the level of independence these nobles could demonstrate, and it would appear such self-determination had increased in his own reign as Khusrau II gained the throne by leading a group of nobles to depose rebels who had risen up against his father. When his armies were defeated by those of the Byzantine emperor Heraclius (610–641), Khusrau II demanded that the men who had broken ranks in battle be punished severely, provoking a rebellion among his leading generals, again demonstrating the level of autonomy shown by lesser nobles and leaders.[122] In this regard, a policy to support Muhammad may not have been his own but could have originated within the nobility. Whether from some of the nobles or from Khusrau II himself, the rationale for providing aid to the Muslims would have been to open a second front against the Byzantine forces of Heraclius.

The origination of a plan to do something in southern Arabia may have been sparked by the Byzantine military resurgence in 622. This could have been compounded by the fanciful, yet still partially factual, divination of the imminent collapse of the Sasanid Empire.[123] Khusrau II's father had invaded Yemen in the late 570s, but this invasion, being too distant and difficult to support, had fizzled, with many of the soldiers settling in Yemen and marrying the local women. It is conceivable that he, or some of his nobles, decided to revive contacts with these Persian soldiers, now known as the ʿAbna, to provide support for Muhammad in an effort to prevent the predicted collapse of the empire. The most logical item of support would be a shipment of horses, for the Persians had always excelled in developing effective horse cavalry.[124] There is some evidence that Khusrau II was well supplied with fine horses.[125] Possibly unable to find well-trained men for surplus mounts, these could have been used to bring enhanced mobility to the Muslim movement, thus improving their combat capability. In this way Muhammad's uprising could be used to attack the extended Byzantine flank from the south, even as Heraclius's army marched east, deeper into Persian lands. Such a threat could hopefully serve as a distraction to draw off Byzantine troops from the invasion. If this was the plan, it obviously came to fruition too late to save the Sasanids from defeat.

This explanation would not only account for the rapid growth in his horse supply, but it would also go a long way in rationalizing Muhammad's insistence on sending raids north toward Syria and the Byzantine frontier. For example, while one scholar postulates that Muhammad was incensed by the return of the True Cross to Jerusalem by the victorious Byzantine army as the rationale for the Tabuk campaign,[126] this raises the question why the Prophet would mobilize such a massive force for such a distant and difficult objective when he had at least three other individuals nearby claiming joint prophethood with Muhammad, claims that offered an even more potent challenge to his declaration of being the last prophet of Allah. He was facing three serious challenges to his leadership for Arabia, yet he organized several operations, one with fatal consequences to some of his closest companions, to fight a distant foe with which he had only marginal contact. Such focus on the Byzantine frontier almost borders on that of a strange fetish, unless it had some deeper driving force to compel him to make such commitments in that direction.

Furthermore, just prior to his death, Muhammad had organized a third expedition to move north. When the Prophet died, this force was still dispatched by the first *khalifa*, Abu Bakr, although much of Arabia was now in open rebellion to the nascent Muslim state. Even the urging of ʿUmar bin al-Khattab to use this army to quell the uprisings fell on deaf ears, with Abu Bakr insisting that the Prophet's orders, though he be dead, should be obeyed.[127] While such a contention sounds religiously pious, it rings hollow in light of Abu Bakr's later acquiescence to suggestions that the Qurʾan, originally intended to be recited orally by the Prophet and others, should be put down in writing for posterity.[128] Why were the Prophet's wishes so quickly discarded after the costly victory at al-Yamamah in 633 but followed blindly in the face of a rising flood of insurgent resistance one year prior? While there are often events in history that seem to have no basis in logic, such questions must be asked to ascertain what could have been occurring behind the scenes.

Further possibilities regarding Sasanid support for the Islamic movement can be found in both Muhammad's and Abu Bakr's behavior toward the ʿAbna. At one point after the conquest of Makkah, when Muhammad wanted Yemen to submit to his authority, he dispatched a messenger with instructions to "treat the people with ease and don't be hard on them," instructions that were unique.[129] Furthermore, before he died, Muhammad appointed a man named al-Aswad al-ʿAnsi as governor of Sanʾa in Yemen.[130] Al-Aswad was not the man he wished to support in the area, for he was a native Yemeni who advocated a form of nationalism that called for the ouster of the 'Abna, along with making a claim to prophethood that challenged Muhammad's. After establishing him as the local governor, the Prophet kept al-Aswad busy with diplomatic correspondence while concurrently dispatching an assassin to kill him. This man managed to infiltrate al-Aswad's inner circle and, with the support of members of the 'Abna, was able to complete the mission, though not performing the deed himself. Instead, the man who actually killed al-Aswad with his own hands was appointed governor of San'a, even though he had previously deserted Islam and declared allegiance to al-Aswad. It would appear that his only real qualification was that he was part of the 'Abna.[131] Thus, it can be seen that both Muhammad and Abu Bakr were willing to support the Sasanid remnants in Yemen, even if doing so compromised other Muslims in the process.

There are other more subtle aspects of possible Persian support. For example, there is the role of Salman al-Farisi, a Persian who had come to accept Islam, who not only counseled the Prophet to follow Persian practice to dig the trench north of Madinah to frustrate the Qurayshi siege of the city but also helped to assemble a *manjaniq*, or stone-throwing siege engine, to assist the Muslims in their assault on al-Ta'if, a machine apparently shipped in from Yemen.[132] Additionally, two men, Ghaylan bin Salama and 'Urwa bin Mas'ud, were dispatched to Jurash in Yemen to learn the use of war machines, possibly from engineers dispatched from Persia for this purpose.[133] In many ways, Salman operated as a foreign military advisor, although there is no direct evidence he was dispatched from Persia as such. Nevertheless, his military knowledge appears to have been extensive. It is often assumed that this account during the siege of al-Ta'if represents a topoi, for it is asserted that the Muslims did not encounter the *manjaniq* until their incursions into central Asia.[134] However, such a conclusion could very well be based on a false premise, assuming that the Muslims conducted their military operations in a vacuum, alone and without foreign assistance.

Salman's contribution to the Muslim cause was considered so significant that he received extensive treatment of his life in Ibn Sa'd's *al-Tabaqat*.[135] While some note that Muhammad also had Byzantine converts such as the emancipated slave Suhayb, Ibn Sa'd completely ignored this individual as providing nothing noteworthy, and al-Tabari does not mention him until after the Prophet's death during the end of 'Umar's *khalifate* where he was called upon to lead the people in prayer.[136]

The most serious objection to the thesis presented so far would be the argument that the Muslims threatened the Sasanid emperor and conquered them soon after Muhammad's death. Yet the very nature of Khusrau II's response to Muhammad's letter calling him to Islam sheds more light, and possibly support, for the thesis presented. While it is no secret that Muhammad did not like the Sasanids, this does not eliminate the prospect that the latter tried to use him to disrupt the Byzantine advance into their empire.[137] When Muhammad sent his deputation to Khusrau II just after the sealing of the Treaty of al-Hudaybiyah, he called on the Sasanid emperor to submit to Islam, and in doing so his empire would be safe. Khusrau II reportedly shredded the letter, declaring "How dare he write this to me when he is my slave!"[138] Perhaps this statement was more than just hyperbole in the emperor's eyes.

The Persian emperor then proceeded to instruct the 'Abna in Yemen to send two men to the Hijaz to seize the Prophet and deliver him to Persia for punishment. The behavior and attitude of the Sasanid emperor in this instance is that of a master to a servant. While Khusrau II, who considered himself the King of Kings, treated many including Heraclius, the Byzantine emperor, in similar fashion, it still demonstrates that he and Muhammad may have had some diplomatic relationship at this point.[139] His attitude that Muhammad was his slave could very well have its source in that he had just organized a large shipment of horses and other equipment to the Prophet to assist in his campaigns, an action that would have placed the Sasanid emperor in the position of a master to a servant. That Muhammad and the later Muslims turned on the Sasanids is not proof that there was no support at one time, for history is replete with examples of a stronger power being betrayed by a client state or entity bent on pursuing their own agendas.

All of these actions and the evidence presented—the sending of armies north to raid the Byzantines and their allies, especially with the massive operation of Tabuk after the conquest of Makkah; the efforts to support the 'Abna in Yemen, even at the expense of loyal Muslims; the surge in horses available for campaigning from sources directly unknown—indicate possible outside support. The reaction of the Sasanid emperor to Muhammad's letter calling him to Islam, along with military aid and advisors working through Yemen, provide evidence that this support most certainly came from sources within the Sasanid Empire. It is conceivable that they saw the rising Islamic movement as a way to open a new front against the resurgent Byzantines under Heraclius.

Muhammad's victory at al-Khandaq, followed by the destruction of the Banu Qurayzah, would have convinced the Sasanids that his movement had staying power, just as the American victory at Saratoga in 1777 convinced the French and Spanish that the colonists could defeat Britain during the American Revolution.

This conclusion in no way implies that Muhammad was a stooge to Khusrau II and his nobles, for his dislike for the Zoroastrians in Persia is well known.[140] Many leaders in history have taken advantage of a benefactor, first to consolidate their position and then to make themselves independent of the benefactor's largess and will. Muhammad's consolidation of power in Madinah now gave him the firm base he needed to extend his power well beyond Madinah, to encompass Makkah and perhaps all Arabia—or more. He could use Sasanid assistance to shift toward more conventional operations and bring about the ultimate triumph for which he longed. The arrival of promised military aid and support from the Sasanids may have even made him confident enough that he could take on the two major empires bordering Arabia, and could even defeat them.

6

The Surge

After the destruction of the Banu Qurayzah in January 627, Muhammad allowed his fighters to take a well-deserved break. It would seem that during this interlude he increased his horse-mounted force sixfold, organizing a cavalry force equal in size, if not yet in quality, to that of the Quraysh. This may have been the first installment of support offered from the Sasanids. His focus was now to consolidate his hold on the surrounding tribes to prepare for the grand invasion of Makkah. No longer do the sources regularly speak of Muhammad receiving rumors of pending attacks against the Muslims in Madinah, for it is apparent that Muhammad now realized he was strong enough to dispense with any pretenses and to directly strike any potential rivals. Moreover, for the first time he would engage in punitive operations against those tribes that would defeat any of the operations he dispatched.

Despite, or perhaps because of, the extensive success he enjoyed during this period, Muhammad seemingly overestimated the impact of the outside support he began to receive. Within one year he would make the second major mistake of his military career, an error in judgment that would have led to disaster had the Quraysh been more determined to triumph. Instead, the Prophet's forces would live to fight another day, and subsequent operations, coupled with the valuable experiences and allies gained, would culminate in the collapse of the Qurayshi state and Makkah's fall.

By April 627, Muhammad sent out the first expedition of that year led by Muhammad bin Maslamah, the Muslims having been now based at Madinah for just less than five years. This operation was possibly far more important than many historical analysts have noted, for it may have been the time when the Muslims captured a high-ranking individual from the important Banu Hanifah, which was to the east of Madinah. The Hanifa served as guardians of Persian caravans in that region and supplied a large quantity of grain to Makkah.[1] One of their key leaders, Thumamah bin al-Uthal, was transiting the region while engaged in a pilgrimage to Makkah and was swept up by a Muslim raid with a group of prisoners from the Banu Bakr.[2] His capture was a significant prize, for Thumamah had rejected Muhammad's earlier offer to become a Muslim and had even planned to send an assassin to have the Prophet killed. This made him a high-value target for the Muslims.[3] However, his captors did not know who he was until Muhammad made a positive identification of their prisoner when he was brought to Madinah.

Thumamah was tied securely to a pillar in the mosque, left exposed to the elements because the mosque had no roof for the main court. He was left there without food and water for at least three days, with the Prophet coming to him each day to ask him what he should do with him.[4] Thumamah gave a very political answer, stating that should the Prophet release him he would receive the thanks of a grateful man. On the third day the Prophet released him from his bonds, though not from captivity. Thumamah immediately converted to Islam and completed his pilgrimage to Makkah, declaring to the stunned Quraysh that he would now enforce a grain embargo against them.[5] This embargo would have started in the early summer of 627, though its more serious effects would take some time to settle in. Through what was initially a minor raid, Muhammad had secured a tremendous political triumph.

By May the Prophet was prepared to engage in a surge of operations, all aimed at neighboring tribes to pressure them to join his side. This strategy presents an interesting conundrum to modern counterinsurgency doctrine. Such doctrine typically claims that excessive force tends to push the local populace away from the counterinsurgent.[6] In contrast, insurgencies use tremendous force, even terror, to compel the same populace to join their cause. Yet the people do not largely join the counterinsurgency but instead "inexplicably" join the insurgency. The reason this remains a mystery to the modern counterinsurgent is because most simply do not understand human nature. In general, people

Table 6.1. Operations from the Siege of al-Khandaq to the Treaty of al-Hudaybiyah

Date	Mission	Enemy	Muslims	Leader	Result
Apr 627	Al-Qurada; Muharib?		30	Muhammad bin Maslamah	Booty
May 627	Lihyan		200–220	Muhammad	No Contact
June 627	Dhu Qarad; Ghatafan		500–700	Muhammad	Fighting
June 627	Al-Ghamr; Asad		40	'Ukkashah	Booty
June 627	Dhul al-Qas-sah; Tha'labah		10	Muhammad bin Maslamah	Defeat
June 627	Dhul al-Qas-sah; Tha'labah		40	Abu 'Ubaydah	No Contact
June 627	Al-Jamum; Sulaym		?	Zayd bin Harithah	Booty
July 627	Al-'Is; Quraysh	Caravan	170	Zayd bin Harithah	Victory
Aug 627	Al-Taraf; Tha'labah		15	Zayd bin Harithah	Booty
Aug 627	Hisma; Judham		500	Zayd bin Harithah	Booty
Sep 627	Wadi al-Qura; Badr bin Fazarah		?	Zayd bin Harithah	Defeat
Oct 627	Dumat al-Jandal; Kalb		700	'Abd al-Rahman bin 'Awf	Victory
Oct 627	Fadak; Sa'd		100	'Ali bin Abu Talib	Booty
Nov 627	Umm Qir-fah; Badr bin Fazarah			Zayd bin Harithah	Punitive
Nov 627	Muraysi Banu al-Mustaliq		?	Muhammad	Booty
Dec 627	Assassination	Abu Rafi	5	'Abdullah bin Unays	Success
Dec 627	Usayr bin Razim; Khaybar		30	'Abdullah bin Rawahah	Success
Dec 627	Al-Harrah; 'Uraynah		20	Kurz bin Jabir	Punitive
Jan 628	Makkah; al-Hudaybiyah		1,400	Muhammad	Treaty

desire to live in security and relative comfort within the context of their own cultural milieu. Any marginal amount of force presents itself more as a nuisance rather than a serious threat. An acceleration of force to significant levels changes this equation, with such violence becoming a serious menace to their desired security and comfort. Initially, local populations resist such force and seek ways to diminish or eliminate the threat. As the level of force continues to rise, a breaking point is eventually reached when the local population, facing either submission or near total destruction of their lifestyle, begins to realize that the best way out is to join the element imposing the pressure. There is no mathematical formula to determine this breaking point, and each culture handles the stress imposed upon it according to the character of its people and leaders, along with the norms and mores of their society.[7]

Such force is essentially imposed in two fashions. First, both the insurgent and counterinsurgent use force within their base camps. This force can include tight security measures to ensure that enemy elements do not infiltrate the camp and to protect any assets within. While it is tempting to acquiesce to the myth that insurgents do not hold terrain, this is simply myth.[8] Insurgents need base camps, and these must be protected. Without them the insurgents will grow weary and exhausted, and the movement will collapse for lack of support. Che Guevara learned this the hard way with fatal consequences in Bolivia in 1967. Protecting the base camp requires force, for government of any type is the application of compulsion. Muhammad solved this partly by instituting the death penalty for those who abandoned Islam.[9] The Prophet ensured that if anyone decided to leave they would face the ultimate consequence, both death in this life and eternity in the hellfire thereafter. Another way he handled this was to develop and nurture a first-rate intelligence service. Finally, he strove to co-opt his possible opponents in Madinah and get them to serve his interests.

The second way in which force is employed is in military operations outside the base camp. Muhammad sought to apply significant force including its consequences to his neighbors, both the Quraysh and the outlying tribes about Madinah, in an effort to compel them to join his cause. Such application of force is anathema to some involved in counterinsurgency, for they somehow believe that if one simply talks to an opponent they will see the logic of mutual toleration. This was by and large the approach of the Quraysh. While the Quraysh did try to impose a marginal, though largely ineffective, level of protective force to their base in Makkah, they failed miserably in applying such force to the Muslims and the outlying tribes. They were used to being able to negotiate their way to success and assumed they could continue to do the same in the new world of insurgency violence presented by Muhammad's uncompromising movement. In contrast, Muhammad employed terror, a word he used, to gradually impose his agenda on others, systematically breaking the will of any potential opponents.[10] Over time these tribes, seeing that they could receive no succor from the Quraysh to help in stopping the Muslim raids, turned to the Muslims and joined them. After all, the Prophet made it clear that Muslims could only raid non-Muslims, and thus the best way to stop the raiding was to join the raiders.[11]

As noted in a previous chapter, an analysis of Muhammad's raids demonstrated a poor return in loot that could be used to support his men. But while this loot was only marginally useful to the Muslims, its loss to its previous owners was significant. For any culture living at the level of basic subsistence, the loss of only 1 percent of their assets can prove to be serious. Losses greater can be devastating. However, that 1 percent gained by the insurgents in captured loot largely proves to be of minimal use to the raiders. In this manner, the impact of raiding is exponential on the victimized culture compared to the assets gained by the aggressor. With this in mind, the insurgent leader must always focus on the consequences of the raids upon his enemy and not on the loot gained by his own forces. In this manner, Muhammad's surge in operations in the summer of 627 would have tremendous impact on neighboring tribes. The Prophet gauged this impact correctly but failed to appreciate its lack of ready influence on the Quraysh. When he launched his pilgrimage raid on Makkah in January 628, it was before the impact of his raids on the region, along with the grain boycott of the Banu Hanifah, could bring the Quraysh to their knees.

The first major operation of this surge was led by the Prophet, who organized 200–220 horse-mounted men to raid the Banu Lihyan, a tribe that resided northeast of Makkah.[12] The choice of this raid revealed the essentials of Muhammad's strategy, for he actively sought to pull away any tribes friendly to Makkah that were close to the city. He already had the Banu Khuza'ah tribe in his pocket, these lying to the south of Makkah. Should he gain the support of the Banu Lihyan, he could effectively isolate his prize. Moreover, this represented his first horse cavalry operation, apparently intent on testing out the effect of his newfound mobility. However, in this operation, Muhammad encountered one of the most effective counterinsurgency doctrines employed, the use of fortified localities.

The Banu Lihyan apparently had their own modest intelligence network, and they were watching the Prophet's moves. Although Muhammad feigned that he was marching north toward Syria, the Lihyan were apprised of his true objective. The tribal leaders took the people and any other moveable assets and ensconced them in fortified posts in the mountains. For up to two days Muhammad's men occupied the area and scoured the countryside in search of anything to loot but found nothing of value.[13] Instead the Prophet ordered his men to march further south toward Makkah in the hope of alarming the Makkans that he was about to raid them. Muhammad had been effectively checked, leaving his poets to lambaste the "weasels" who hid from battle in the rocks.[14] But while the mission was largely a failure, it did give the Prophet the opportunity to provide practical exercise in highly mobile operations to a select group of his men.

Muhammad launched his first major wave of operations in June, but these began only after the Banu Ghatafan, with a small band of cavalry, raided the Prophet's sacred camels, riding off with twenty. The Muslims rallied and sent a force to pursue. Its composition was interesting because it appears to have contained only one or two horsemen. One of the riders managed to catch up to the raiders, but he was killed in the fight. The rest of the Muslims pursued on foot, planning to rally with Muhammad at Dhu Qarad. Why Muhammad chose not to use his newly formed cavalry force is hard to say, but it would seem that the most likely explanation was that his cavalry had just returned from the operation against the Banu Lihyan and the horses were insufficiently rested and prepared to engage in a hot pursuit. Indeed, it is very possible that the Ghatafan raid was organized to take advantage of Muhammad's absence from Madinah, and it was only by chance that he had just returned prior to the attack.

One of the men in pursuit, Salama bin ʿAmr bin al-Akwa, recited poetic verse against the raiders, stating that "today, mean crowd, you die!"[15] It is an interesting perspective connected to insurgencies that when the insurgents attack, it is justified and noble, but when an enemy returns the favor, those who did so are reprehensible and despicable.[16]

This represents the tactic of moral inversion, where the insurgent takes on the character of nobleness and justice while the target culture is branded as oppressive and evil. In recent times such moral inversion is taken as granted to the insurgent, but in the world of Muhammad, moral inversion served more to bolster one's own side rather than convince outside observers that one's cause was just. As it was, Salama, though on foot, managed to catch the raiders. Even though they were mounted, he used the terrain to avoid their attacks and in turn engaged them effectively with his bow. One by one the raiders fell, and Salama marked each body to indicate he had the rights to the spoils of war. When it was over, half of the stolen camels had been recovered.

Another interesting aspect about this recovery operation was that while Salama was moving out rapidly in advance, Muhammad was following up with anywhere from five hundred to seven hundred men. Salama and Muhammad's men finally met up at the rally point of Dhu Qarad, near Khaybar and close to Ghatafan territory. Salama wanted to push on with one hundred men as a punitive operation to recover the remainder of the herd and sever the heads of the raiders. However, Muhammad cautioned him to "be gentle," apparently intent on not using too much force that would arouse the entire tribe against his small expedition.[17] Moreover, he quite possibly based this on the ad hoc nature of his logistics for this operation. Muhammad's men had been traveling light and fast, and the ration rate was indicative of the hasty planning for the mission, as the Prophet issued only meat on the hoof for his men.[18] Overextended and without sufficient rations for a far-reaching operation, the last thing he wanted to do was get into a pitched battle with a well-fed and rested Ghatafan force on their own territory.

The raid of Dhu Qarad against the Ghatafan demonstrates an interesting lack of readiness by the Muslims to respond against a raid on their own base. This is revelatory in that while raiding others, Muhammad was not overly concerned about being attacked in turn. No band of men had been prepared as part of a ready reaction force, even though the Prophet had departed for the Banu Lihyan with what was probably only 10 percent of his effective combat force. To not have the administrator of Madinah, Ibn Umm Maktum, prepared to face a possible raid was either caused by lack of foresight and planning or was indicative that the Muslims were rarely raided. It would seem more probable that the latter was the case, implying that, save for Qurayshi attacks against Madinah, Muhammad's base was largely secure against all others. Having a secure base was essential for his operations, allowing him to range extensively over an area the size of modern-day Indiana. Had the Quraysh more aggressively used their abilities to develop coalitions, and had they demonstrated the wherewithal to take the war to Muhammad, they may have been able to organize outlying tribes to hound and harry Muhammad's base of operations, thus significantly reducing his ability to raid others.

At this point there is some dispute as to which raids followed, for at least one source places the attack against the Banu al-Mustaliq after the raid on the Ghatafan. Al-Waqidi and Ibn Saʿd accept an earlier date while Ibn Ishaq and al-Tabari accept a date about one year later. For the purposes of this study, the later date is accepted, although there is no need to be contentious on the matter. This raid, with some interesting aspects regarding insurgency warfare, will be discussed later on.

With Muhammad and his men back in Madinah, he put the finishing touches on his operations for June. The focus of these attacks was to punish the Ghatafan for their previous attack on Madinah and to raid recalcitrant neighbors to compel them to join him. Several raids were dispatched to attack the Banu Thaʿlabah, a subtribe of the Ghatafan, but these ended in either defeat or no contact. The first raid is of interest because only ten Muslims under Muhammad bin Maslamah engaged one hundred of the enemy in a night operation. As noted earlier, night operations were largely avoided by the Bedouin tribes for superstitious reasons, making this action a novelty.[19] The battle began with an hour-long exchange of arrows followed by an attack of the Thaʿlabah with spears. The Muslim force was wiped out save for the commander, who was left on the battlefield severely wounded, ostensibly to die of exposure in the desert. He was found by a Muslim scout, who brought him back to Madinah for recovery. The Prophet dispatched a punitive force but it made no contact, simply seizing some livestock for their trouble.[20]

Following these actions, Muhammad used his adopted son, Zayd bin Harithah, to lead a succession of raids. Allowing the same man to lead a string of raids was very unique, and there must have been a compelling reason why the Prophet trusted Zayd with such operations. It is possible that such trust had little to do with Zayd's combat abilities and more to do with his status, or perhaps more likely his lack of status within the *ummah*. To understand this, it is necessary to examine some background as well as enter into one of the controversial episodes that surround the Prophet's life.

Zayd bin Harithah had been Muhammad's slave in the early days of Islam and was also one of his earliest converts. Later, Zayd was manumitted and became the Prophet's adopted son, in large measure because of the inability of Muhammad's wife Khadijah to have sons that lived beyond infancy. In many cultures, including Arabia, sons are desired as the basis for the continuity of a family's lineage, and without them one is considered to be less than a full man, as "sons are the wealth of the house."[21] Many men in Arabia received their *kunyah*, or nicknames, based on the name of their firstborn son. Therefore, Muhammad was often called "Abu al-Qasim," or "Father of al-Qasim," this being his firstborn son who subsequently died in infancy. While *kunyahs* were normally used as a term of respect, it is very possible that some among the Prophet's enemies used it as a not-so-subtle jab at his manhood and place in society.[22] It is probably due to this desire to have a natural-born son that Muhammad sought out numerous wives, though some were married for the purpose of creating tribal alliances or providing protection to the widows of close companions killed in action.

During the early years in Madinah, Zayd enjoyed the rights of an adopted son, as the principle heir of Muhammad's estate. In due course he was married to the stunningly beautiful Zaynab bint Jahsh, but the marriage was apparently not a happy one. Around February 627, the Prophet arranged to have Zayd divorce his wife, and he in turn married her. This caused a measure of scandal, not only among the Arabs but even among the Prophet's own household, with ʿAisha being arguably the most offended.[23] In Arab culture of that time, it was simply unacceptable for a man to marry the divorced wife of his adopted son, but Muhammad soon produced a recitation contained in Surah 37 that dispensed with such cultural restrictions. Included in this was the negation of the principle of granting inheritance rights to an adopted son. Thus Zayd not only lost his wife but was disinherited as well.[24]

But while the early sources focus on the conflicts created by this situation in Muhammad's domestic affairs, they neglect to ask a simple question: what did this mean for Zayd? By the Prophet's declaration, Zayd was no longer his adopted son, and thus no longer heir to his estate and possible heir-apparent to the leadership of the *ummah*. So why would Muhammad now allow Zayd the honor of leading a succession of raids, an honor he never granted to anyone before or after? There could be two possibilities here, and the evidence available can support either position.

The first is that Muhammad still trusted Zayd to be a faithful Muslim. Zayd had led one of the early raids against a Qurayshi caravan and captured significant loot. This indicated that he had a measure of talent and ability in conducting such operations, and this merited future responsibility in such matters, even if a few of the raids were minor. But there are problems with this interpretation. Muhammad had other lieutenants that had achieved much in raiding, yet these men rarely if ever again received an independent command. If simply being a faithful Muslim was the criteria, the Prophet could have found a number of men to lead raids on a rotational basis, especially some of his closest companions such as Abu Bakr, 'Umar bin al-Khattab, and 'Uthman bin 'Affan.

The evidence regarding this situation can also support a more controversial interpretation, that is, the Prophet saw in Zayd the danger of competition for the leadership of the infantile *ummah*. Just as 'Abdullah bin Jahsh had succeeded at the raid of Nakhlah and thus demonstrated that he was a latent threat to Muhammad's claim to leadership, so too could this be the case for Zayd. Of additional interest is that prior to the divorce, Zayd had been married to 'Abdullah bin Jahsh's sister, thus placing him close to a man that the Prophet may have seen as a possible challenge to his authority.[25] To take Zaynab for himself would be to push Zayd aside, and thus remove any possible challenge by lineage, even via adoption. Allowing Zayd the honor of leading a series of expeditions not only kept him busy and often out of Madinah, but it could very well lead to his death in battle.[26] It is unlikely that the latter was the Prophet's desire, but it does offer an intriguing interpretation to an otherwise puzzling series of events. Beyond this, there appears to be no logical rationale as to why Zayd was allowed to lead a series of repetitive raids.

Each of these raids led by Zayd was relatively minor, save for one. The first was an action against the Banu Sulaym, seizing a few captives and a small amount of booty. The second, which occurred in July, was an attempt to intercept a Qurayshi caravan from Syria, and the Prophet mounted 170 men on camelback for the operation.[27] This raid was successful, seizing both captives and a large quantity of silver, although the sources do not say precisely how much. Returning with the booty, Zayd was sent on two more raids in August. The first involved only 15 men and was directed at one of the subtribes of the Banu Ghatafan. Its success was minimal. The next raid was launched as a punitive operation to punish the Banu Judham, who lay to the north Madinah. The Judham had intercepted one of the Prophet's ambassadors, having just left the court of Heraclius, the Byzantine emperor. The ambassador was ambushed and robbed, but another subtribe intercepted the raiders and restored his lost property. The ambassador returned to Madinah and reported this to the Prophet.

Muhammad decided to punish the Judham and organized a party of five hundred men under Zayd to do the task. They traveled by night and remained hidden by day, led by a local guide. They came upon the Judham and launched a furious attack, killing the tribe's chief and his son, and seizing one thousand camels, five thousand sheep and goats, and one hundred women and children.[28] The remaining leaders of the Judham now appealed to Muhammad directly, stating that they had just recently become Muslims and should be protected from his raids. Muhammad relented and agreed to return the booty seized, though no compensation was offered for those killed. While the raid had netted nothing in loot, it did bring another tribe into the fold of Islam.

While there is some evidence that Zayd engaged in an operation against the Banu Fazarah, a small branch of the Banu Badr, little is known of this operation. However, it did set in motion a desire by the Banu Fazarah to seek revenge, an opportunity that would come soon enough. In the meantime, the Prophet sent out two more raids, one under 'Abd al-Rahman bin 'Awf and the other under Muhammad's cousin 'Ali. The first involved seven hundred men and was directed against the Banu Kalb at Dumat al-Jandal, a tribe of Christian Arabs in northern Arabia.[29] 'Abd al-Rahman, through a show of force, convinced the Christian leader to embrace Islam while those who remained Christians were required to pay the *jizyah* protection tax. The Muslim leader also married the daughter of the tribal chieftain to cement the alliance. The second raid involved one hundred men under 'Ali directed against the small tribe of the Banu Sa'd at Fadak, a tribe that was apparently intent on allying with the Jews at Khaybar to attack Madinah.[30] 'Ali's men maintained the now-standard traveling tactic of moving by night and remaining concealed during the day, the mission requiring six days before reaching their objective. They seized a local who indicated he would provide information if they would not kill him, and this man led the Muslims who then attacked the tribe and took five hundred camels and two thousand sheep and goats while also forcing the people of the Banu Sa'd to flee.

During the period of these raids, Muhammad felt strong enough that he could organize a caravan to carry the goods of his companions, probably some of the plunder taken in recent raids, to be traded in Syria. Zayd bin Harithah was entrusted with the security of this operation. While they were heading north, they passed the area of the Banu Fazarah, whom Zayd had previously raided. The men of the Banu Fazarah, with an obvious bent for revenge, descended on the caravan, overwhelmed the guards, and looted it. Zayd was among the wounded, and when he returned to Madinah the Prophet decided that a punitive expedition was necessary. He mobilized the expedition, although the sources do not tell us how many men were involved, and he placed Zayd in command, who had taken an oath not to engage in sexual intercourse until he avenged himself.[31] They marched north, traveling only at night. Although they were spotted, they still managed to ambush a significant element of the Banu Fazarah, capturing their legendary matriarch, the elderly Umm Qirfah.[32] To punish the Fazarah, Zayd ordered one of his men, Qays bin al-Musahhar, to execute her, and he did so by tying each of her legs to separate ropes that were then tied to two camels. The camels were made to run in opposite directions, tearing the elderly woman apart.[33]

Zayd's execution of this matriarch would have a lasting impact that would outlive the Prophet. The Banu Fazarah would later surrender to Islam, but resentment would remain rife in the tribe.[34] When Muhammad died in 632, most of the Arabian tribes would leave Islam, including the Fazarah. One of their women, Umm Ziml Salma, would serve as the matriarchal rallying point for resistance because she was the daughter of Umm Qirfah. The latter's execution had developed a burning hatred for Islam in Umm Ziml Salma's heart, and this hatred was only vanquished when she, along with more than one hundred of her warriors, were left as a heap of broken and torn bodies at the end of the battle of Zafar in 633.[35]

These operations were sufficient to convince a subtribe of the Banu Khuza'ah, the Banu Mustaliq, to prepare for operations against the Muslims. This was even more critical for the Khuza'ah, who were secret allies of the Prophet. To have one of their clans break away could lead to greater disaffection. Certainly based on intelligence he received from the Khuza'ah, Muhammad first sent a spy to ascertain the situation and upon confirmation organized an expedition to preempt any raid against him. The number of men who participated is unknown, but the sources indicate that the Muslims took thirty horses with them, ten of them ridden by some Muhajirun, and the balance ridden by a group of Ansars. We are also told that many of the *munafiqun*, or hypocrites, joined in as their first expedition.[36] There is some dispute regarding this operation, and as noted prior, some such as al-Waqidi and Ibn Sa'd place it much earlier while Ibn Ishaq and al-Tabari set it at a later date.[37] The exact timing of this operation is not overly crucial here, nor is analyzing several well-known incidents that occurred in connection with it.

The Muslim force marched south and engaged the Banu Mustaliq at one of their watering spots called al-Muraysi. Muhammad organized the Muhajirun under Abu Bakr and placed the Ansar under Sa'd bin 'Ubadah. The leader of the Mustaliq, al-Harith bin Abu Dirar, watched in dismay as a number of his men fled in fear before the battle even began. The fighting opened with a flurry of arrows followed by a Muslim charge. The Mustaliq broke at once and scattered, leaving behind two thousand camels, five hundred sheep and goats, and two hundred prisoners. Among those captured was the daughter of al-Harith bin Abu Dirar, Juwayriyah bint al-Harith. She was considered extremely attractive and immediately raised the ire of 'Aisha, who saw her as a serious competitor to the Prophet's affections when Muhammad declared that he would manumit and marry her.[38] But while the attack against the Mustaliq shattered any possible resistance that might grow within the Khuza'ah, the aftermath offered some revelatory aspects as to the conduct of insurgency warfare.

During the march back, several men, one each from the Muhajirun and Ansars, had a dispute over watering rights at a spring. In the process a hue and cry arose between the two groups to the point that they seized their weapons and came to blows.[39] At this juncture, 'Abdullah bin Ubayy, possibly upset over his subordinate role in supporting the Prophet, cried out to the people from Madinah around him:

They dispute our priority, they outnumber us in our own country, and nothing so fits us and the vagabonds of Quraysh as the ancient saying, "Feed a dog and it will devour you." By Allah when we return to Medina the stronger will drive out the weaker. . . . This is what you have done to yourselves. You have let them occupy your country, and you have divided yourselves. You have let them occupy your country, and you have divided your property among them. Had you but kept your property from them they would have gone elsewhere.[40]

This lament by 'Abdullah provides a fascinating glimpse into the nature of insurgencies, for while he may have been cooperating with Muhammad, it would appear that at one juncture he had serious misgivings about the Muslim presence in Madinah. What this statement demonstrates is the important nature of the support base for an insurgency. Put simply, if an insurgency can find little or no logistical support, it will collapse under its own weight, for the fighters in an insurgency are typically adverse to the day-to-day grind of productive work necessary to provide the essentials of life. Had the al-Khazraj and al-Aws refused to accept the Muslim presence, Muhammad's movement, barring any other base from which to operate, would have evaporated.

'Abdullah's statement was certainly a sign of possible revolution in the midst of the *ummah*, at least on the surface, and his own son recognized it as such. Approaching the Prophet, 'Abdullah bin 'Abdullah bin Ubayy asked permission of Muhammad to kill his own father. Being of cooler judgment and possibly realizing that 'Abdullah bin Ubayy had simply uttered this in frustration, Muhammad urged patience on the young man. "Let us deal kindly with him and make much of his companionship while he is with us."[41] In addition, the Prophet was concerned for the political effect on the *ummah* and neighboring tribes if had he given the order to have 'Abdullah bin Ubayy put to death at this time.[42] To prevent the men from dwelling too much on the conflicts sparked by tribal jealousy, Muhammad ordered his men to begin marching at once, even though it was the heat of the day. They marched nonstop for almost two days until the men were so exhausted that they collapsed to the ground and fell asleep when the Prophet ordered a halt.

Muhammad's raids to the north of Madinah had by this point stirred up some determined resistance. However, this resistance was disjointed and uncoordinated, so any call by a prominent individual in the region to rally and organize resistance would certainly be an important threat to Muhammad's movement. Several men were involved in doing this, among them a Jew who lived at Khaybar named Sallam bin Abu'l-Huqayq, better known in the sources as Abu Rafi. The al-Aws had been the ones who killed Ka'b bin al-Ashraf, and now the al-Khazraj asked permission of the Prophet to go and eliminate the Jew from Khaybar. Muhammad granted their request, and in early December 627, five men set out on the mission, one of them, 'Abdullah bin 'Atik, because he was conversant in the "language of the Jews" and familiar with the area.[43] Abu Rafi lived in a fortified house or castle, and it was necessary for the men to penetrate the basic security provided.

The men first penetrated one of the Khaybar settlements where Abu Rafi had located his home just before the gates were closed for the night. The group then waited in the dark while 'Abdullah went on ahead to the castle to see if he could gain admittance. He followed some of Abu Rafi's servants to the main gate and then pretended to be relieving himself. The gatekeeper, assuming him to be one of Abu Rafi's retainers, grew impatient and implored him to enter before the gate was barred. 'Abdullah went in and then veered off into hiding, waiting for the gatekeeper to leave. Once alone, he recovered the gate keys that were hanging on a peg and opened the gate to allow the other four to enter. They then had to endure a lengthy period of tense waiting because Abu Rafi was in an upper room entertaining guests. At long last the guests went to other rooms for the night and the people of the castle settled down. 'Abdullah led his companions through the lower rooms of the house, closing each door behind them one by one to ensure no night watchman would suspect their presence. At last they reached a spiral staircase to the upper room.[44]

Ascending this, they came to a locked door. 'Abdullah knocked and Abu Rafi's wife opened the door, inquiring what he needed. The men then pushed their way in, holding a blade over the terrified woman's head to ensure her silence. They could not find their target in the pitch darkness, so they called out his name. Unaware of his pending doom, Abu Rafi responded and 'Abdullah charged at him, now able to see the whiteness of the man's form. However, in the darkened room he was unable to bring his blade effectively to bear. 'Abdullah had to repeat the attack before finally thrusting his blade through Abu Rafi's abdomen, hearing a bone shatter as the blade went home. The men then struggled to make good their escape, with 'Abdullah the last man out stumbling down the spiral staircase and dislocating his leg.[45] The attack and escape attempt made sufficient noise to rouse others in the castle, and the men barely managed to exit the gate before the alarm was sounded. They quickly hid themselves as men with lit torches began to search the area for the attackers. Failing in this, they returned to attend to Abu Rafi, who was now dead. The Muslims, wanting to guarantee the success of their mission, sent one of their men to mingle with the crowd. Not only did he receive confirmation, he also heard Abu Rafi's wife remark that she had heard the voice of ʿAbdullah bin ʿAtik but then said that this was impossible, for to her knowledge ʿAbdullah was nowhere in the area.[46]

The raid on Abu Rafi provides some interesting aspects of special operations conducted by the Prophet's men. We see that security at Abu Rafi's castle was far from adequate because there was apparently no method devised to ascertain the identity of those who came and went from the main gate, save for perhaps facial recognition during daylight hours. In this case, the Muslims were fortunate to have come upon the castle when some men came out in the dark to search for a stray animal, thus providing ʿAbdullah bin ʿAtik his chance to slip inside. The Muslims were assisted in this regard by their prior planning to assign to the mission ʿAbdullah, who could speak the local dialect of Hebrew-Aramaic and was sufficiently familiar with the area. The mission also demonstrates that despite the Muslims now having some reputation for special assassination operations, Abu Rafi did not ascertain that the threat was sufficiently serious enough to warrant better security.[47]

Another item that stands out was the lack of martial ability in at least one of the assassins. We have already seen how this was an issue with those who deceived and ambushed Kaʿb bin al-Ashraf, and it would appear their personal training and ability had not improved much. ʿAbdullah bin ʿAtik had to attack an unarmed elderly man several times before he could finally bring his blade to bear with sufficient skill to kill his victim. When wielding a sword, cutting is more familiar to the hand of the user than thrusting, although thrusting is considered by some to be the sign of proper discipline and training.[48] Nevertheless, ʿAbdullah should have been able to give Abu Rafi a sufficiently powerful slashing blow to at least severely wound, if not kill, him. Instead, the testimony of the sources indicated that he only gave the elderly man a glancing blow and had to hide in the room until the commotion settled sufficiently for him to attack again. Thus, while there could be little doubt regarding the courage of Muhammad's men, the examples we have of them engaging in specialized individual combat often demonstrated a singular lack of skill in handling their personal weapons.

The assassination of Abu Rafi was followed soon after by the Prophet's effort to ensure that confusion continued to reign in Khaybar. Abu Rafi was one of Khaybar's key leaders, and with his death the people of the city appointed Usayr bin Razim as their military leader, or amir.[49] In this capacity he began to organize not only the Jews in Khaybar but also the neighboring tribes such as the Banu Ghatafan. Once more, Muhammad chose a special operation to disrupt this organization before it could come to fruition. Initially, the Prophet sent 'Abdullah bin Rawahah and three other men to collect intelligence and determine the extent of Usayr's preparations. Once the situation was sufficiently clear, the Prophet called for volunteers to go to Khaybar and attempt to bring Usayr to Madinah on the pretext of engaging in a diplomatic mission. Thirty responded and were dispatched as an embassy under 'Abdullah bin Rawahah sometime in late December 627 or early January 628.

Upon their arrival in Khaybar, they met with Usayr and announced the reason for their visit, indicating that Muhammad wished that the leader of Khaybar would come to Madinah to receive special recognition by the Prophet, to include confirmation of his appointment as amir. Why Usayr, who had already received such an honor from the people of Khaybar, would accede to such a request is difficult to ascertain. Usayr with thirty other Jews rode toward Madinah with the Muslims, each Muslim paired with a Jew on their camel. Usayr was riding with 'Abdullah bin Unays, who, unbeknownst to Usayr, had participated in the attack on Abu Rafi. The Muslim later stated that when they were only a few miles out from Khaybar, Usayr had second thoughts. The Jewish leader, riding behind the Muslim, now reached for the man's sword. 'Abdullah bin Unays turned his camel off the route and waited until they were alone. He then struck the man down. The other Muslims, upon learning of this, turned on the other Jews and killed all but one, who managed to escape.

Typically the accounts focus on Usayr as being treacherous, turning on his Muslim escort before reaching Madinah. However, what stands out in this account is that Usayr, and probably the remaining Jews, were unarmed. Usayr had with him only a *shawhat*, a stick from which bows are made.[50] While implying a weapon, there is no indication the stick was strung but was instead used as a staff, which was common in Arabia.[51] Since Usayr and his men were almost assuredly unarmed, this raises the question why he would attempt to resist once they had left Khaybar. Either he realized something was seriously amiss, and was thus very brave, or he lost his mind and was very foolish. The former would seem more likely, and he had decided to resist in one last-ditch effort, believing he had been deceived into going with the Muslims to Madinah.

About the time of these special operations, a group of eight men from the Banu 'Uraynah, a subtribe of the Hawazin located to the northeast of Madinah, arrived to embrace Islam.[52] During their visit they complained to the Prophet that the climate of the city was not agreeable to them, and Muhammad instructed them to go and drink the milk and urine of his sacred camels that were pastured near Quba, just south of the city. Instead, the men decided to steal the camels, killing the herdsmen in the process and taking off with the herd. Several Muslims discovered what had happened the next morning, and one raced on horseback to report to the Prophet while the other stood on a rise and shouted out "ya sabahah!" to announce that a raid had taken place.[53]

Upon receiving the report of the incident, the Prophet dispatched a former enemy now turned Muslim, Kurz bin Jabir al-Fihri, along with twenty men to pursue them and retrieve the beasts. After all, who better to track down insurgents than a former insurgent? The raiders were captured and brought back to the Prophet, who ordered that their eyes be gouged out and their hands and feet amputated. They were then left to the elements to die of exposure, even being refused water when they cried out for it.[54] The punishment meted out to the 'Uraynah raiders was decreed to be that issued to any who had become Muslims and committed *hirabah*, that is, highway robbery or causing mischief in the land.[55] A disputed element in the account involves the method of execution. Most sources simply say that the herdsman was killed by the raiders, but Ibn Sa'd, in his *al-Tabaqat*, states that the raiders actually pierced his tongue, cut out his eyes, and cut off his hands and feet.[56] Nevertheless, the Prophet chose to use a very brutal and public form of execution to provide an example regarding two issues: leaving Islam and raiding a Muslim, especially the Prophet. As a form of counterinsurgency, it was extremely effective, for Madinah was never again raided during the Prophet's lifetime.

By the end of 627, Muhammad apparently believed that his movement had gained sufficient strength to press the Quraysh openly, a fact that would have obtained significant bolstering had he received some type of pledge of support from groups within the Sasanid Empire.

To this end he quickly organized an *umrah*, or lesser pilgrimage, to Makkah, calling on not only his companions but also any Bedouin of the area to accompany him because he assumed the Quraysh would oppose this move. Nevertheless, many Bedouin tribes, though invited to go with the Muslims, remained aloof and waited to see how events would play out.[57] The *umrah*, unlike the hajj, could be conducted at any time during the year, with the Prophet choosing to set out during the sacred month of Dhu'l Qadah, a month in which no fighting was to occur. The date corresponded to 14 January 628. The number of men who accompanied the Prophet on this *umrah* vary according to the source, ranging anywhere between 700 to 1,900 men, though 1,400 is the more common number provided. Of particular interest is that the Prophet appears to have only taken 20 horsemen, though it was possible he brought more with him.[58]

Several points are revealing about the nature of this operation, such as how the Muslims viewed this *umrah* as being a *ghazwah*, or expedition, and that only four women accompanied the army.[59] Moreover, while many reports indicate superficially that the Muslims traveled in a state of self-defense, bearing sheathed swords only, apparently Muhammad heeded the advice of 'Umar bin al-Khattab that he should take his arms and horses with him. The evidence suggests that they not only had swords but also spears and bowmen, with some clad in chain mail.[60] In addition, the attitude of Muhammad and Abu Bakr that they should fight their way through to the *ka'bah* should they be barred entry, even if they were to destroy the Quraysh, indicates that this operation was more than a simple pilgrimage.[61] Finally, it is important to note that prior to this campaign there was no peace treaty with the Quraysh. If a peaceful procession to Makkah was the true intent, this would be logically quite difficult in light of the fact that the Muslims were engaged in open warfare with the Quraysh, and that Muhammad had violated sacred months on a number of occasions prior.[62] For Muhammad to expect to simply walk into Makkah unmolested was the height of real audacity. The evidence clearly indicates that this was a military expedition disguised as an *umrah*, a point not lost on the Quraysh.[63]

As Muhammad's force neared the city, the Quraysh were alerted and mobilized their militia, along with their professional force, the Ahabish. A force of five hundred men under Ikrimah bin Abu Jahl, the son of the slain Qurayshi leader at the battle of Badr, sallied forth to block the Muslim advance while Khalid bin al-Walid led two hundred cavalry to serve as a mobile reserve. Muhammad, having sent spies ahead from the Banu Khuza'ah to discover the intent and movements of the Quraysh, now resorted to maneuvering through narrow passes north of the city in an effort to circumvent the enemy's blocking force.[64] Concurrently, he used his small force of cavalry to screen his flanks and provide security against Khalid's horsemen.[65] However, Qurayshi troops mirrored these movements and still managed to block Muhammad's advance. This compelled the Prophet to call a halt and set up camp at al-Hudaybiyah, a well located about five miles east of Makkah on the edge of the sacred zone that surrounded the city. Sometime during this action, a detachment of forty to fifty Qurayshi men attempted to surround the Muslim force so as to take some prisoners. However, they quickly learned that these Muslim pilgrims were sufficiently well armed to fight back and the detachment was quickly captured. Muhammad decided to release them, probably as a goodwill gesture.[66]

While the Quraysh appeared to be in a strong position, they encountered division within their own ranks that had bedeviled each and every operation against the Muslims. Having sent out several men to determine what Muhammad planned, one of their own leaders who led the troops of the Ahabish, al-Hulays bin Zabban, threatened that if they did not allow the Muslims a chance to complete a pilgrimage he would withdraw the Ahabish and leave the Quraysh to their fate. Pleading for patience, the Qurayshi leaders indicated they intended to secure acceptable terms with Muhammad.[67] To make matters worse, there is some evidence, presented by the historian al-Tabari, to suggest that Khalid bin al-Walid, the key leader of the Qurayshi cavalry, may have already secretly embraced Islam. In this guise, he still retained his position among the Quraysh and was apparently being used by Muhammad to discreetly leverage back Ikrimah's blocking force.[68] If the information provided by al-Tabari is even partially correct, this would have had a chilling effect on the decision making of the Qurayshi leaders, who would have been staring at the possible defection of the most valuable portion of their army.

One of the Qurayshi negotiators, 'Urwa bin Mas'ud al-Thaqafi, convinced the Quraysh that he could gain a true knowledge of what Muhammad was up to and they consented to let him travel to the Muslim camp. After speaking closely to Muhammad, he returned to inform the Quraysh that the Muslims were wholly devoted to their prophet and willing to die for him. "I have been to Chosroes [Khusrau II] in his kingdom, and Caesar in his kingdom and the Negus [of Abyssinia] in his kingdom, but never have I seen a king among a people like Muhammad among his companions."[69]

This report would have sent ice water rushing through the veins of the Qurayshi leaders, and they were now more determined than ever to formulate some type of treaty with the Muslims. In doing this, they wanted to believe that they were negotiating from strength, but a key principle of insurgency warfare is that one should only negotiate when one is losing unless it is designed to deceive an enemy. By initiating negotiations with Muhammad, the Quraysh were clearly signaling that they believed themselves to be weak, even though they almost certainly had the military edge on the Prophet at that moment. Resolute action by the Qurayshi leaders could have crushed the Muslim movement on that day if they had been united. Instead, the Quraysh were more concerned about their reputation with the Bedouin tribes, fearful that Muhammad would push into Makkah by force.

But why then would Muhammad strike a deal with the Quraysh? The reason for this can be found in his statement that "war has exhausted and harmed Quraysh. If they wish, we will grant them a delay, and they can leave me to deal with the people," that is, the Bedouin tribes.[70] In essence, Muhammad was possibly facing the fact that he had overestimated his own capabilities and was too weak to push the situation. Prior to embarking on this operation, he had solicited support from the Bedouin tribes but virtually all remained aloof. Had he fought it out with the Quraysh, there still was the real possibility he would be defeated. Instead, by establishing a treaty with the Quraysh, the Prophet would have his hands freed to attack the outlying Arabian tribes at will, forcing them into his movement and thus building a greater coalition than the Quraysh could have ever imagined. In this fashion, he could dramatically increase the odds of future success in his favor, completing the isolation and ultimate fall of Makkah.

Before the treaty was negotiated, Muhammad sent 'Uthman bin 'Affan to the Quraysh to set up negotiations only to receive a distressing report that his friend had been seized and killed. This would later prove to be in error, but at that point Muhammad must have realized how delicate his situation was. He now pulled his men together to extract a crucial oath from them, the Bay'ah al-Ridwan, or oath of divine pleasure. The men gathered around the Prophet by a small tree and pledged themselves to defend him to the death if need be.[71] However, such desperation was unnecessary, as the Quraysh sent another emissary, Suhayl bin 'Amr, to negotiate the terms of a truce. When the Prophet saw this particular man coming, he knew he had the upper hand in negotiations, certain that the Quraysh now wanted to strike some kind of deal.[72]

When the negotiations began, Suhayl refused to acknowledge Muhammad as the Prophet of Allah, instead demanding that the document state that Muhammad bin 'Abdullah was the signatory for the Muslims, thus forcing the Prophet to use his family lineage for his name. The treaty was drafted by 'Ali bin Abu Talib and had six key provisions. The first was that there would be a ten-year truce between the Muslims and Quraysh. The second stated that, should anyone come to Muhammad from Makkah to declare himself a Muslim, he was to be returned immediately to Makkah and not be allowed to stay in Madinah unless permission was granted by one in authority over him. In contrast, the third provision stated that if any Muslim in Madinah wished to return to Makkah and leave Islam, they should be allowed to do so without hindrance. The fourth provision stated that there should be no surreptitious raids or betrayal of the treaty's terms. The fifth provision stated that the Muslims and Quraysh could develop any tribal alliances they wished. And last, the treaty stated that the Muslims could return a year later to engage in the *umrah*, remaining there for three nights, armed with sheathed swords but no other weapons.[73] In addition to the provisions, it was determined that "there are to be no secret agreements, bad faith, or antagonism between us."[74]

There is no doubt that the companions of the Prophet clearly saw this treaty as a humiliating defeat. This was even more apparent when Muhammad was forced at the very moment the treaty was ratified to return a Muslim back to his pagan family after he had fled from Makkah. 'Umar bin al-Khattab went to Abu Bakr, crying out, "Is he not God's apostle, and are we not Muslims, and are they not polytheists?" Abu Bakr agreed to all of these. "Then why," 'Umar continued, "should we agree to what is demeaning to our religion?" 'Umar then went to Muhammad and asked the same questions, to which the Prophet replied that he would not dare go against the commandment of Allah.[75] Even as the Muslims disputed the nature of the treaty, a representative of the Banu Khuza'ah who was present, having been secret allies of the Muslims all this time, now stepped forward to declare the tribe as openly for Muhammad. The Banu Bakr then responded in kind, siding with the Quraysh. This did little to enliven the spirits of the Muslims.

The men were so dejected that Muhammad had to order them repeatedly to prepare for the sacrifice of the sacred camels brought along for the *umrah*, even though they had failed to reach Makkah. The Prophet led by example, first shaving his head before ordering the sacrifices to begin. One of the first camels slaughtered, in plain view of the Qurayshi negotiators, was the one that had belonged to Abu Jahl, the fallen commander of the Quraysh at the battle of Badr. The camel was clearly identifiable by such things as its silver nose ring, and its slaughter cut the Qurayshi men deeply.[76] In this fashion, Muhammad attempted to incite his enemies to violate the treaty, thus granting him a casus belli. However, the Quraysh were too cautious for this, instead departing the scene in silent rage.

As the Muslims trekked homeward, Muhammad began to recite verses that became the heart of Sura 48, indicating that the Muslims had been given a "signal victory."[77] Despite facing defeat, the Prophet quickly developed an information posture to transform it into triumph, with the emphasis being that he had received the "willing pledge" of death from his men.[78] The *sira* and Tafsir literature also typically interprets this as a victory because it established peace and made the Muslims a recognized equal partner with the Quraysh. This opened the way for Muslims, especially those outside of Madinah, to now openly declare their beliefs and spread them to the Bedouin tribes. However, there is an even more important aspect of this event that usually goes unnoticed. The critical success here for the Muslims was the failure of the Quraysh to win the war. At this decisive moment, had they been reasonably unified and resolute, they could have smashed the Muslim force in the field, possibly killed the Prophet, and then issued their own propaganda poetry to declare that the Muslims were intent on once again violating a sacred month to engage in a raid. In this manner they could have justified their actions and emerged as the dominant force in the Hijaz. Instead, the Quraysh prematurely rushed to negotiate away their advantage, largely because of their indecision and the fractures within their own leadership.

But the Treaty of al-Hudaybiyah had another interesting consequence as well. A young Muslim named Abu Basir ʿUtba bin Asid was languishing in captivity in Makkah as the Prophet and his men were returning to Madinah. He managed to engineer his escape, and he naturally rushed to Madinah—with two bounty hunters of the Quraysh hot on his trail—arriving three days after the Muslims had returned. Abu Basir gained an audience with the Prophet even as the bounty hunters arrived, demanding that Muhammad turn Abu Basir over to them per the terms of the treaty. Muhammad complied, stating that perhaps Allah would provide a way to escape, along with others held in captivity in Makkah. As the bounty hunters led Abu Basir back toward Makkah, they foolishly dropped their guard, and the Muslim managed to kill one of them, the other fleeing for his life back to Madinah to tell Muhammad what had happened. Not long after came Abu Basir, certain that his ingenuity in escaping would be praised by the Prophet.

It is at this point that a few of the early sources seem to twist the situation, for they imply that Muhammad, rather than praising the intrepid Muslim escapee, decided to send Abu Basir back to the Quraysh in compliance to the treaty.[79] However, others such as Ibn Ishaq do not imply this at all, and al-Waqidi directly states that Muhammad allowed Abu Basir to go free where he wished.[80] Having heard Muhammad say, "Woe is his mother, he would have kindled a war had there been others with him," Abu Basir needed little additional encouragement to flee to the coast and become the rallying point for seventy men who fled Makkah and who joined him in raiding Qurayshi caravans along the western caravan route.[81]

Abu Basir and his "Band of Seventy" became a Muslim proxy raiding party, at least implicitly supported by Muhammad if not directly supplied by him, to wage war upon the Quraysh during the life of the Treaty of al-Hudaybiyah. The situation became so serious that the Quraysh sent dispatches to the Prophet begging him to take in Abu Basir and his companions and thus stop the raids, thereby highlighting their own willingness to overlook the treaty violation. The only reason why they would have done that is if they were convinced that Abu Basir was operating as a proxy for the Prophet, knowing that he had operational control over this ostensibly renegade force.[82]

Not only did Muhammad subtly abrogate the treaty with his support of Abu Basir, he soon openly violated it as he realized that the Quraysh were unable or unwilling to force him to stick to its provisions. A few Muslim women in Makkah wanted to migrate to Madinah, and they managed to slip away and travel there seeking asylum. Muhammad now recited Sura 60:10, stating that believing Muslim women could not be held back in Makkah against their will. Thus, he openly declared that Allah had commanded him to violate a key treaty provision. He further cited passages that commanded the Muslims to pay back any dowries for women that fled to Madinah, and that the Quraysh should pay back any dowries of women that had left Islam and fled back to Makkah, the latter implying that some women, as per the treaty, had actually left Madinah for Makkah.[83]

What is of interest here is that if Muhammad paid out any dowries, this wealth would have come from plunder captured from the Quraysh and others. However, if the Quraysh paid back any dowries, this wealth would come from their trading operations. Thus, the latter circumstance would hurt the Quraysh far more because the wealth came directly from their business enterprises. In this manner, Muhammad not only openly abrogated part of the treaty, thus putting the Quraysh in the position of either demanding enforcement or neglecting it, but he also brilliantly turned the tables on them by creating a situation where he could essentially plunder them once again, even if only in small measure. In two separate circumstances, the Prophet placed the Quraysh in the unenviable position of being unable to enforce the very treaty they so willingly rushed into. If the Qurayshi leaders believed that Muhammad would now relent and scale back his operations, they were woefully mistaken.

Triumph

The Treaty of al-Hudaybiyah had been a "signal victory" for the Prophet. For the Quraysh, the immediate success of having stopped Muhammad's raids was offset by the ongoing trade boycotts against them, the rising tide of famine in the city of Makkah, and the unexpected onslaught of Abu Basir's "Band of Seventy" along the western caravan route to Syria. Beset by external pressures and facing fractious political problems within, the Qurayshi leadership had to realize at this point that it was only a matter of time before they would have to come to new terms with Muhammad's movement. Indeed, several key leaders did see the handwriting on the wall and determined that it was time to seek out greener pastures.

It has been noted in an earlier chapter that Khalid bin al-Walid may have already covertly sided with the Muslims at al-Hudaybiyah. He now determined to make his allegiance open and final, and to that end proceeded to head north to the city of the Prophet. Along the way he encountered 'Amr bin al-As, who, along with Khalid, was an important cavalry leader for the Quraysh. 'Amr had already decided to join the Muslim cause not long after the Qurayshi failure at the battle of al-Khandaq, although he had kept his Islam secret from his closest companions. Later, he realized it was better to serve as a Muslim in Madinah than go hungry in Makkah. It was on his trip north to Madinah that he met up with Khalid. The latter was adamant. "The way has become clear. The man is certainly a prophet, and by Allah I'm going to be a

Muslim. How much longer should I delay?" Both arrived in Madinah to give the Prophet their allegiance, with 'Amr asking if he would be forgiven past actions. "Give allegiance, 'Amr, for Islam does away with all that preceded it."[1]

It is difficult to say exactly when Khalid and 'Amr made this trip to Madinah. Ibn Ishaq places it around the time of the conquest of the Banu Qurayzah, in early 627, while al-Tabari places it around the time of the conquest of Khaybar, or late 628. One source places the date as late as the spring of 629.[2] It is possible that all are partially correct, in that the early date may have been Khalid's initial acceptance of Islam, with the Prophet having him return to Makkah to provide intelligence and disrupt the councils of the Quraysh. The later dates may have been when Khalid and 'Amr both decided to at last migrate to Madinah, with one source simply confusing the exact time it occurred. The fact that Khalid is mentioned as being with the Quraysh at al-Hudaybiyah, although he may have met up with the Prophet to coordinate action with him, could support this view. Moreover, Khalid and 'Amr do not show up as leaders of Muslim forces until near the conquest of Makkah. If they had migrated earlier to Madinah, it would indicate that either the Prophet did not trust them to lead any raids or they did not remain and went back to Makkah for a period of time.

Regardless of exactly when Khalid and 'Amr surrendered to Islam, the fact remains that their defection was a significant blow to the Quraysh. Both had served as cavalry commanders, and Khalid in particular had demonstrated noteworthy talent. It was he who rallied the Qurayshi cavalry at the battle of Uhud that turned the tide and led to their victory over the Muslims. The psychological blow was probably as serious as the loss of their military talents, and with the deaths of a number of important Qurayshi nobles in battle, the people of Makkah would surely have had difficulty finding qualified leaders to take their place.

The Treaty of al-Hudaybiyah had been ratified in January 628. Throughout the spring and summer, Muhammad strengthened his position at home and prepared his forces for future engagements even as he allowed Abu Basir to freely engage the Quraysh as his proxy.[3] The Prophet probably had his sights already set on the agricultural settlement of Khaybar to the north, for many of the displaced Jews from Madinah had settled there. These had a personal score to settle with the Muslims, and there is certainly evidence of some agitation coming from that quarter.

Table 7.1. Operations from the Treaty of al-Hudaybiyah to the Conquest of Makkah

Date	Mission	Enemy	Muslims	Leader	Result
Aug 628	Khaybar; Jews		1,400+	Muhammad	Victory
??	Najd			Aban bin Sa'id	??
Nov 628	Turbah; Hawazin		30	'Umar bin al-Khattab	No Contact
Nov 628	Najd; Hawazin			Abu Bakr	Booty
Nov 628	Fadak; Murrah		30	Bashir bin Sa'd	Defeat
Nov 628	Fadak; Murrah		200	Ghalib bin 'Abdullah	Punitive
Dec 628	Mayfa'ah; Tha'labah		130	Ghalib bin 'Abdullah	Booty
Jan 629	Jinab/Yumn; Ghatafan		300	Bashir bin Sa'd	Booty
Feb 629	Makkah; umrah		2,000	Muhammad	Pilgrimage
Apr 629	Sulaym		50	Ibn Abi al-'Awja	Defeat
Apr 629	Al-Kadid; Mulawwih (Layth)		10	Ghalib bin 'Abdullah	Booty
May 629	Dhat Atlah; Quda'ah		15	Ka'b al-Ghifari	Defeat
May 629	Siy; Hawazin		24	Shuja	Booty
Jul 629	Mu'tah; Byzantine allies		3,000	Zayd bin Harithah	Defeat
Oct 629	Dhal al-Salasil; Bali/Quda'ah		500	'Amr bin al-'As	Punitive; No Contact
Sep 629	Sif al-Bahr		300	Abu 'Ubaydah	No Contact
Oct 629	Khadirah; Ghatafan		16		
Nov 629	Batn Idam; feint		8	Abu Qatadah	No Contact
Nov 629	Makkah; Quraysh		10,000	Muhammad	Victory

Muhammad organized a force of about 1,400 to 1,600 men, accompanied by 200-horse cavalry.[4] While the cavalry would be largely useless in a siege operation, he obviously took them as a security precaution in case the nearby Banu Ghatafan decided to assist the Jews in Khaybar. There is no mention as to the number of camels they took for transport, though it is probable they would have used every beast they could muster. The only food taken was *sawiq*, dried barley mixed with water later to moisten it before it was eaten.[5] Muhammad probably could have mustered more men for the campaign, but it is apparent that his supply situation dictated a smaller force. His reasoning was obvious; it was far better to effectively supply a small operational force than to attempt to push a poorly supplied larger force into harm's way. The lessons learned from this operation, as well as the much larger campaign of Tabuk later, would serve Muhammad's companions well in the years ahead. During the Riddah, or Apostates War, after the Prophet's death in 632, Abu Bakr adopted the same strategy of using smaller forces to overcome larger, though isolated, enemy armies.

The distance to Khaybar was about eight *barids*, or ninety-six miles, and would typically take a camel-mounted force four days to reach.[6] We are not told exactly how long the entire operation lasted, but the evidence suggests that it was completed in about one month.[7] Beyond this, the Muslim force would have encountered serious logistical difficulties, and indeed the sources tell us that they began to feel the effects of this late in the campaign, mitigated only by the capture of some local supplies. The sources provide no evidence of any effort made by Muhammad to organize a supply convoy from Madinah to maintain his forces in the field, and thus the men were left to what they carried or could secure through plunder. Moreover, there is evidence that they were already running low on supplies when they arrived.[8]

Khaybar was uniquely organized and situated, the city positioned on a series of bluffs overlooking a valley below where they had planted their date palms. The city was laid out much in the same fashion as Madinah, with small subsections individually fortified, presenting any attacker with a chessboard maze of winding narrow streets and walled off residences that created nests of resistance. In addition, the more wealthy men of Khaybar had built themselves fortified homes, or castles. Some, like that of the Jew Marhab, were positioned on small buttes in the middle of the valley while others were interspersed with the rest of the town. There is some dispute in the sources regarding the

Table 7.2. Muslim Logistic Lift and Provisions for the Khaybar Campaign

Category	Quantity	Pounds	Days	Total lbs
LOGISTICAL LIFT (POUNDS CARRIED)				
Men	1,600	20		32,000
Women/Servants	Negligible			
Camels	1,500	300		450,000
Horses	200	200		40,000
Total Lift				522,000
PROVISIONS (POUNDS REQUIRED)				
Food Needed	1,600	3	30	144,000
Camel Fodder	1,500	10	30	450,000
Horse Fodder	200	10	30	60,000
Total Provisions				654,000

number of fortifications, with one source indicating only seven. However, observations by Hamidullah, as well as photographic evidence, indicate that there were far more than that, and this would substantiate the argument of Ibn Sa'd and others that the forts were numerous.[9] It was also reported that the people of Khaybar could muster a force of close to ten thousand fighters, though this would seem to be an exaggeration unless the number includes any allies they were attempting to organize.[10]

The Muslim army traveled by night to maintain the secrecy of their operational objective, and the Prophet assembled his men on the high ground to the south of the city to await the dawn. As the sun began to rise and the people of the city emerged from their fortified enclaves to harvest their dates, they saw the Muslim army approaching. "Allahu Akbar!" The Prophet shouted. "Khaibar is destroyed, for whenever we approach the land of a people—then what an evil morning for those who have been warned."[11] Terrified, they cried out that Muhammad's army had arrived, even as they fled for the relative safety of their walls. Their reaction clearly indicated that they had not been scouting the area for the possibility of a Muslim attack and were thus unprepared for the siege that followed.[12] Naturally, their surprise at Muhammad's arrival raises the question of how they could be caught unawares if they were planning operations against the Muslims.

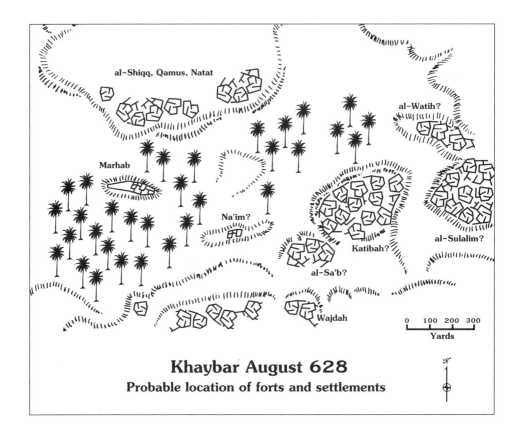

Khaybar August 628

Probable location of forts and settlements

al-Shiqq, Qamus, Natat

al-Watih?

Marhab

Na'im?

al-Sulalim?

Katibah?

al-Sa'b?

Wajdah

0   100   200   300

Yards

N

Although Muhammad probably kept his camp farther to the east of the city, he moved his army down into the valley so as to dominate the maze of fortresses from within.[13] In this way he could severely limit if not prevent any direct communications between the fortified sections. As a consequence, each portion of the city became effectively isolated, allowing the Prophet to concentrate his smaller force on each in turn. When the Banu Ghatafan heard that the Muslims had encamped at Khaybar, they assembled a force and began to march westward but turned back when they heard a rumor of a raid against their settlements.[14] While nowhere stated in the sources, it is very possible that Muhammad had sent his cavalry to launch a feint against the Ghatafan, convincing them that a move toward Khaybar was too dangerous. Without adequate intelligence and with no coordinating communications with the Jews, the leaders of the Ghatafan were operationally blind. Unable to ascertain the true nature of the situation, they decided to defend their own ground and leave Khaybar to its fate.

The first fort to be attacked was Na'im, probably situated on a small hill in the valley. The Muslims moved forward, protected by a wall of shields as the Jews scrambled along the tops of their walls and hurled flights of arrows to try to drive them off. Some of the Muslims were wounded with their standard bearer, Sa'd bin 'Ubadah, among them. Nevertheless, they pressed the attack and the fortress fell, but not after Mahmud bin Maslamah was killed when a millstone was tossed from above, crushing his skull.[15] The next fortress to fall was that of Qamus, the property owned by the late Abu Rafi, who had just recently been assassinated. It was possibly situated on the north side of the valley, and its surrender yielded a significant number of women and children as captives.

Muhammad suffered frequently from severe migraines, and it was at this critical moment that he was incapacitated. Abu Bakr and 'Umar bin al-Khattab were in turn delegated the authority to attack the next fortress, that of Marhab, situated on a prominent height in the middle of the valley. Both of their assaults failed, although they probably weakened the defenders' resolve. Muhammad, having recovered some from his malady, then gave the banner to his cousin 'Ali bin Abu Talib, who launched the third attack on the fort. As the Muslims closed in, Marhab personally rode from his fort to challenge any Muslim to individual combat. Muhammad looked to his men and asked, "Who will deal with this fellow?"[16] Muhammad bin Maslamah, the brother of the slain Mahmud, came forward to volunteer, anxious to avenge his brother. The two met with a small tree between them, and gradually they slashed away at its branches until it was whittled down to a stump. Marhab now lunged forward at Muhammad bin Maslamah, his sword striking the Muslim's shield and piercing it. However, Marhab was unable to withdraw the blade, allowing the Muslim to respond in kind, striking him down.[17] With Marhab dead, his brother Yasir came forward to engage in individual combat, and he too fell, having been killed by al-Zubayr bin al-'Awwam.

About ten days into the siege the Muslims' supplies began to grow thin, and some of the men came to Muhammad begging for sustenance, material help he simply could not offer.[18] Keenly aware that his operation could become a disastrous rout, he prayed that Allah would provide supplies from one of the forts, as those already taken had offered very little in the way of provisions. The Muslims doubled their efforts against the fortress of Sa'b bin Mu'adh, who was defending his walls with five hundred men. At last it fell, and within its walls the men found a significant hoard of provisions they desperately needed, along with stocks of cloth, finished clothing, and loads of cut timber.[19] Among the items seized were twenty to thirty donkeys, which the Muslims in their ravenous hunger promptly slaughtered and prepared to eat. Upon seeing this, Muhammad prohibited them from eating donkey meat because he considered the meat to be unclean and thus unfit for consumption. However, he did consent to have them eat some of their horses, and two were quickly consumed, a curious dispensation in light of their scarcity.[20]

At one point during the operation the Muslims allegedly captured several throwing machines, possibly *manjaniqs*. Demonstrating initiative and ingenuity, they turned these devices on other forts not yet fallen, using them to assist in their reduction. Concurrently, Muslim warriors engaged in fierce hand-to-hand fighting at the entrances of each castle, possibly using battering rams on a few of these gates. While Muhammad did not personally engage in the fight, he was often quite close to the action, where one Muslim protected the Prophet with his shield even as he fired arrows at the Jews on the walls. For encouragement, the Prophet smiled at him.[21] The last two fortresses to fall were al-Watih and al-Sulalim, and with their surrender the resistance in Khaybar collapsed and the Muslims emerged victorious. Despite the intensity of the fighting, only fifteen to seventeen Muslims were killed in action while ninety-three Jews died.[22]

As the action in Khaybar was winding down, Muhammad had brought before him a very important prisoner. This was Kinanah bin al-Rabi bin Abu al-Huqayq, a relation of the previously assassinated Abu Rafi and a leader of Khaybar and treasurer of the Banu al-Nadir, exiled from Madinah by the Prophet three years prior. When questioned about the al-Nadir's wealth, Kinanah denied having any knowledge of where it was. Even when someone pointed out that he had a habit of visiting a certain ruin every morning, he still denied its existence. "Do you know," the Prophet asked him, "that if we find you have it I shall kill you?" Kinanah gave his assent. Muhammad dispatched a team to dig in the area and some of the treasure was found. When confronted as to where the rest was, Kinanah still refused to divulge its whereabouts, and the Prophet ordered him to be tortured. Al-Zubayr bin al-'Awwam used flint and steel to slowly burn a hole into Kinanah's chest until he was almost dead, yet the stubborn man refused to talk. At that point,

Kinanah was too far gone to provide any information, and Muhammad handed him over to Muhammad bin Maslamah who beheaded him in revenge for his brother who was killed at the Na'im fort.[23]

The Muslim victory at Khaybar was a close-run thing, far more operationally risky than the sources would intimate. There is ample evidence that in this battle, the first offensive siege in which the Muslims engaged, they ran a serious risk of exhausting their supplies and being forced to withdraw, just as the Quraysh had during the earlier siege of Madinah. There is no direct evidence to indicate that Muhammad had learned from the failure of others in previous actions, but it is plausible to believe that he did. As a combatant commander, the Prophet was resourceful enough to analyze the reason for failure in others and to reverse the situation to learn from them. It is also interesting to contrast Muhammad's operations at Khaybar with that of the Quraysh during the siege of Madinah. During the siege of Khaybar Muhammad doggedly pushed his lieutenants and men to engage in high-risk combat operations to achieve a rapid victory; in contrast, the Qurayshi warriors almost went out of their way to avoid serious combat during the siege of Madinah.

Concurrently, it could be argued that the Jews of Khaybar failed miserably, but such an assessment would be made only through hindsight. One could hardly blame the various Jewish clans and families for hunkering down behind their walls and waiting for the besieging Muslims to encounter their own supply problems. After all, had not Muhammad done the same to the Quraysh at Madinah? Nevertheless, to simply rely upon fortifications in any circumstance is a shortsighted operational plan, and the failure of the Jewish leaders was their apparent lack of foresight to develop contingency plans should things not turn out as they had hoped. As some of their forts began to fall, it was incumbent upon them to seize the initiative and sally from their sanctuaries and take on the Muslims in direct combat. Lack of direct communication between the various fortified zones, the bane of the way in which many towns were arranged in Arabia at that time meant that it was next to impossible to coordinate any action between themselves. This allowed each fort to be reduced piecemeal by a force that was smaller than the opposition's whole but sufficient against the disparate parts.

The fall of Khaybar came as a stunning shock to the Quraysh, especially since Muhammad had authorized one of his men to travel to Makkah and spread disinformation while attempting to secure his property there. As the last fort fell, the Prophet allowed al-Hajjaj bin 'Ilat al-Sulami to go to Makkah and collect money that he had distributed in various projects to Makkan merchants. Before departing, he even secured permission from the Prophet to tell lies to aide in the retrieval of his wealth. When he arrived in Makkah, al-Hajjaj told the Quraysh that the Jews had defeated the Muslims and captured Muhammad, news they received with much joy and jubilation. This false report actually helped to facilitate the recovery of al-Hajjaj's money.[24] Another angle he played was to ask the Makkans to help him collect his money because he wished to travel north and purchase some of the captured Muslims before the merchants beat him to it. Al-Hajjaj even went so far as to deceive his wife by telling her this same story, for she was still residing in Makkah and had no clue that he had become a Muslim.

When Muhammad's uncle, al-Abbas, heard the news he went to al-Hajjaj to clarify the facts. The two met secretly after al-Hajjaj had collected his money. He told al-Abbas the truth, stating that the town had been captured and plundered by the Muslims, and that Muhammad was now married to the daughter of Khaybar's leader. When al-Abbas expressed surprise, al-Hajjaj revealed that he had become a secret Muslim, and he asked al-Abbas to keep this hidden for three nights, long enough for al-Hajjaj to make his escape. After the three nights al-Abbas scented himself and put on his robe to circumambulate the ka'bah. When the Quraysh saw him they were astonished by his calm demeanor after receiving such bad news about his nephew. When confronted, al-Abbas told them what really happened, and even who told him. The Quraysh were infuriated, declaring that an enemy had been in their midst and yet escaped.[25] But more than that, the Quraysh had just been through a psychological wringer, having first heard news of the Muslim defeat only to have their hopes dashed by the terrible reality that Muhammad had just conquered one of the great cities of the Hijaz.

The Jews of Khaybar, having now been defeated and subjugated by the Muslims, approached Muhammad with a suggestion. Because the Muslims had neither the skill nor the manpower to work the date palm groves, perhaps they should remain and work as tenant farmers, providing the Muslims half of the produce annually. Muhammad approved of their suggestion on the one condition that he could expel them for any reason.[26] While he left them to work the land, he made sure that they surrendered any gold or silver to him, even executing those who refused to divulge any treasure troves.[27]

Muhammad took the time to relax and enjoy the well-earned victory by sitting down to eat a meal of lamb with some of his companions. His favorite piece was the shoulder, but, unknown to them, the Jewish woman who had prepared the meal had poisoned the meat. As the Prophet put the meat in his mouth, he realized something was wrong with it and spat it out. Unfortunately, a companion swallowed a piece and died. When the woman was confronted why she took such a risk, she cleverly declared that if Muhammad was indeed a prophet, he would have survived the attempt to poison him. By doing so she now realized he was the true prophet of Allah. Some sources indicate that Muhammad forgave her, though Ibn Sa'd states that she was put to death, this being the "approved version" of the incident.[28]

The booty was divided up, including the land holdings of the city, with each foot soldier receiving a single share and each horseman receiving a double share. Enough foodstuffs were seized as to allow the Prophet to establish extensive annual food allotments to his wives that came to approximately twenty-four thousand pounds of dates and twenty-four thousand pounds of barley.[29] Moreover, his wives and men received immediate gifts of dates and barley. Al-Abbas alone received twenty-eight thousand pounds of dates, and this while still residing in Makkah ostensibly as a loyal Qurayshi. 'Ali bin Abu Talib and his wife Fatima received fourteen thousand pounds of dates and twenty-eight thousand pounds barley.[30] The evidence available mentions very little regarding gold or silver seized, which was not surprising since the people of Khaybar had apparently expended considerable sums of money to prepare for war with Muhammad. As for Muhammad, he selected the beautiful Safiyah, the wife of the late tortured treasurer Kinanah, for himself.[31]

Khaybar became an example to other towns in the region that had far less ability to defend against the Muslim expansion. Fadak, located just to the south of Khaybar, decided to reach terms with the Prophet at once, pledging to support the same deal granted to the Jewish survivors at Khaybar while also agreeing to pay the special protection tax, the *jizyah*, to maintain their own religious identity. Fadak became *fay*, or the Prophet's private property, from which he could draw ongoing sustenance for his own family as well as the needy of his clan, the Banu Hashim.[32] In addition, as the Prophet marched back to Madinah, settlements in the Wadi al-Qura and the people of Taima surrendered as well. This, along with the property of the Banu al-Nadir and his portion of Khaybar, provided the Prophet his first significant foundation of wealth to support his movement, giving him the means to grant ongoing largess to select individuals who offered the greatest allegiance.

With Khaybar subdued, Muhammad turned his attention against a branch of the Banu Hawazin, situated to the southeast of Madinah, sending a raiding party of thirty men under 'Umar bin al-Khattab, who at last was assigned to lead a raid.[33] However, no contact was made when the intended victims vacated the area. This operation was in conjunction with a raid led by Abu Bakr against another branch of the Hawazin to the east of Madinah. He managed to capture some of the people of the tribe and brought them back to the Prophet, including a very beautiful woman that Muhammad used to pay a ransom to receive back some Muslim prisoners held in Makkah.[34]

Despite Muhammad's success, some of the branches of tribes that had made agreements with the Muslims attempted to break away and pursue their own independent policy. One of these was the Banu Murrah located near Fadak. Having heard the rumblings of such, Muhammad sent Bashir bin Sa'd al-Ansari, along with thirty men, to investigate the situation. Apparently, the men of the Murrah, having some understanding of the Muslim method of warfare, used their livestock as bait. The Muslims fell for it, driving the camels and goats off in ostensible triumph. Instead, the Muslims were tracked and ambushed during the night, with most of them killed and the animals recovered by the tribe. As a consequence, the Prophet commissioned an immediate punitive action against the Murrah. Sending out two hundred men under Ghalib bin 'Abdullah al-Laythi, they departed having heard Muhammad's instructions that if victorious "do not show leniency to them."[35] The raid was reasonably successful as they seized camels and killed some of the tribesmen.

From the end of 628 to the middle of 629, Muhammad focused his raids on some of the key tribes nearby that had so far remained recalcitrant to his agenda. As the word calling these tribes to Islam had already gone forth, the Prophet had no qualms about issuing orders to take some of them by surprise. Each of these raids was designed to despoil these stubborn tribes—particularly the Ghatafan, Hawazin, and Sulaym—sufficiently to drive them into acquiescence. By February 629, the Prophet had to be sufficiently pleased with the performance of his men, as most of the operations had enjoyed reasonable success. It had now been a year since the signing of the Treaty of al-Hudaybiyah, so the Prophet gave orders for his men to prepare to embark on another *umrah* to Makkah. Up to two thousand men mobilized for this event, along with a host of sacred camels and other beasts for the sacrifice. Early sources indicate that camels were scarce at this time, thus the Prophet allowed his men to sacrifice oxen.[36] However, what the sources do not indicate is that the Prophet probably had sufficient camels but that he wanted to maintain them as transport for future operations and not expend them as a sacrifice.

Besides having sacrificial beasts, the Prophet ensured that his men went fully armed with swords, coats of mail, and spears loaded on camels, along with at least one hundred horsemen.[37] By doing this, the Prophet was in violation of the treaty's provision that he would return for the *umrah* one year later with but sheathed swords alone for self-defense. However, Muhammad had prepared to maintain the spirit of the treaty, even if he violated its letter.

As the force approached Makkah, the Quraysh were terrified, for they interpreted this as an invading army armed to the teeth. Yet they were too afraid to move on the Prophet to demand that he abide by the treaty. They did not have to bother, for outside the sacred area, the Prophet's column met up with the supply column carrying some of the weapons, and there he ordered the latter to remain behind under a guard of two hundred men while the remainder proceeded unarmed into the city. As they entered, one of the Prophet's companions was holding the halter of the Prophet's camel while reciting poetic verse:

> Get out of his way, you unbelievers, make way.
> Every good thing goes with His apostle.
> O Lord I believe in his word.
> I know God's truth in accepting it.
> We will fight you about its interpretation.
> As we have fought you about its revelation.
> With strokes that will remove heads from shoulders.
> And make friend unmindful of friend.[38]

Such words were clearly a taunt against the Quraysh that was so offensive that even 'Umar bin al-Khattab protested, convincing Muhammad to urge his companion to instead recite "there is no god but Allah alone. He supported His servant, honoured his army, defeated his enemies alone."[39] The Quraysh evacuated the city for the mountains to the northwest, and for three days they were subjected to the repeated sound of the *adhan* coming from the roof of the *ka'bah* as the Muslims engaged in the rituals of sacrifice and fellowship. When they first arrived, Muhammad knew that his men were physically weak from previous deprivations and illness, so he ordered them to sprint about the *ka'bah* when they were visible to the Quraysh while on the opposite side they could slow to a walk. In this way he strove to give his enemies the impression that his men were physically strong.[40]

Muhammad and his men remained in the city three full days, and while there, assisted by his uncle al-Abbas, he married Maymunah bint al-Harith from the Banu Hilal.[41] Because of this marriage, established before entering the city, the Prophet determined to stay longer than the prescribed three days stipulated by the Treaty of al-Hudaybiyah. Indeed, this could have been his very intention, which would have again put the Quraysh in the position of having once more allowed the treaty to be violated. During the late morning of the fourth day, Qurayshi representatives came to the Prophet and told him that his time was up. Muhammad then proffered his offer of a marriage feast, but the Quraysh were adamant. "We don't need your food, so get out."[42] Leaving his new wife in the care of a companion, the Prophet and his men departed for Madinah.

The "fulfilled *umrah*" was a propaganda triumph for Muhammad. The Quraysh, unable or unwilling to enforce the terms of the Treaty of al-Hudaybiyah, now had to undergo the humiliation of the Muslims arriving fully armed on the frontier of the sacred area. They had to listen to the din and cry of the Muslims as they engaged in the festivities of the occasion, while concurrently they received no visible financial gain for their pilgrimage.[43] When the Prophet returned to Madinah, he at once decided to increase pressure on his neighbors to compel their submission. During the months of April and May he launched four operations, one against the Banu Sulaym, the next against the Banu al-Mulawwih, a probe to the frontier of Syria at Dhat Atlah, and a raid against the Banu Hawazin.[44] Two of the raids met defeat, while the other two managed to collect some plunder. These raids were minor affairs, and one in particular, the one toward Syria, may have been more for reconnaissance purposes. As it was, the Prophet was already planning a much larger raid to advance north.

Why Muhammad would choose to send another raid of three thousand men to the Syrian frontier seems inexplicable on the surface. There was really nothing to gain for him to antagonize the Christian

Arab allies of the Byzantine Emperor Heraclius, especially since he had still not subdued Makkah. Ostensibly, the cause for this raid was punitive since members of the Banu Ghassan, Christianized Arabs and allies to the Byzantine emperor, had ambushed one of Muhammad's emissaries.[45] Yet to make such a move with such a large force, in essence the core of his army was to stake much on a mission with little return. The best explanation for this move can be found in what was postulated in a previous chapter—that Muhammad was now beginning to receive tangible support from Sasanid sources, and this support demanded that he launch some type of operation northward to relieve the pressure of Byzantine forces that had already driven deeply into Persian territory. That the operation as launched was already too late to help the beleaguered Sasanids does not negate this theory, for the slowness of communications as well as the desire of many Sasanids to rise from the ashes of their shattered empire can be ample reason why they would demand that Muhammad engage in such a hazardous operation and open another front against their long-time foe.[46]

The Prophet was certainly worried about the risky nature of this mission, for he placed Zayd bin Harithah, his former adopted son, in command with two men as assistants below him. If one was killed, the others in turn would automatically be hailed as the new commander of the force. This was the first recorded time Muhammad established such a procedure. While the three thousand men who went on the mission were not the maximum that Muhammad could muster, they did represent the lion's share of his fighting force. Thus, if he was engaging in a punitive raid simply to avenge an envoy, he was risking a sizeable force on a lengthy mission for very limited results. The logistical lift for the campaign would have had to have been twice that of Khaybar, and because the trip would take close to twenty-five days, the men would also need a way station in between to resupply or would need to scrounge whatever they could find nearby.[47] Thus, this operation to Mu'tah in Syria represented the most ambitious campaign Muhammad had launched yet, but with benefits that simply did not match the risk. The one thing that mitigated this risk was the fact that some on the raid knew the western caravan route quite well and could therefore find places to pick up additional supplies.

The men departed in late July or early August, moving north during one of the hottest months of the year.[48] Nevertheless, they managed to reach the area of Mu'tah just east of the Dead Sea only to encounter the largest force they had ever seen. The sources might be exaggerating the size of the enemy army, for they indicate that the Muslim force engaged at least one hundred thousand Byzantines and their Ghassan allies.[49] It is difficult to say how many Byzantine troops were really in the area at the time. Heraclius had just finished his conquest of Sasanid lands, and his army was in the process of transitioning homeward, as well as reoccupying lands now vacated by the Sasanid troops. It may have been that the Byzantine camp, near Karak in modern day Jordan, was a waypoint for soldiers to assemble. The local commander was the *vicarius* Theodore, the deputy of the Praetorian Prefect, who received aid from a Qurayshi spy to understand Muslim tactics and behaviors as he assembled forces to deal with this new threat.

When Zayd realized how seriously he was outnumbered, he and his men sheltered on a reverse slope for several days and out of sight of the enemy scouts, debating what they should do. A few suggested that they dispatch a rider to Madinah to ask Muhammad for reinforcements. However, it would take the messenger almost a week to get there, and then it would take time for the army to assemble and march north, thus necessitating a delay of up to a month before they arrived. This suggestion was clearly impractical. The other obvious suggestion, not openly mentioned in the sources, was simply to withdraw; few in counsel would have believed that a retreat would be seen as unseemly in light of the seriousness of the situation. But it was 'Abdullah bin Rawahah's advice that carried the day. He boldly suggested that they came there either for victory or martyrdom, that either was fine with him, and that they should attack. The others at length concurred. The next morning they deployed and began to advance when they encountered a large force of Byzantine and Arab troops moving swiftly toward them. During their vacillation, Theodore had seized the initiative to launch his own attack.[50]

The Muslim force fell back to the village of Mu'tah, establishing a center under Zayd and two wings, the right under Qutbah bin Qatadah and the left under 'Abayah bin Malik.[51] The battle opened with hurled javelins and other missiles, and Zayd, apparently standing alone at the front of the men, fell beneath a hail of missiles, wounded and bleeding to death. The second in command, Ja'far bin Abu Talib, Muhammad's cousin and the older brother of 'Ali, advanced to take the banner while still mounted on his horse. As the battle closed in around him, he dismounted and hamstrung his beast, indicating he had no intent on retreat. He fell in the first skirmishes, with anywhere from fifty to ninety wounds on his body, the fatal one literally slicing him in half.[52] At last, nervous and hesitant, 'Abdullah threw himself into the fray after discarding a piece of meat offered by his cousin, crying out, "And you are [still] in this world!"[53] After shedding his armor he charged forward with a spear and was quickly overwhelmed by the mass of enemy spears and blades.

With their three commanders dead and the enemy closing in, the Muslim army began to waver. On the right flank, Qutbah managed to launch a sharp counterattack that claimed the life of the commander of the Byzantine Arab auxiliary troops, but this was simply too little against the greater mass before them.[54] The Muslim army collapsed and broke, scattering in all directions to flee their pursuing foe. Khalid bin al-Walid, now openly working with the Muslims, had accompanied the army but without being given any responsibility. The command of the army now fell to him by desperate acclamation, and he fought a fierce rearguard action, shattering nine swords in his hands in the process.[55] Part of the army managed to remain on the field through the night, and the next morning he planned to meet the enemy once more with an altered order of battle. The enemy forces, now probably just Byzantine Arab auxiliaries, believed that the Muslims had been reinforced and thus withdrew.[56]

The psychologically shattered Muslim army now abandoned the field rather than attempting a suicidal pursuit. During this fight it is hard to imagine that only a few were killed in action, but a Muslim source indicates only eight died, although one Christian source claims that they had destroyed most of the Muslim army.[57] The truth may be somewhere in between. Despondent, they slowly slogged their way back to Madinah only to be met by the women of the town who scorned them for having fled the battle and not being martyred. Muhammad rebuked them, well aware that he could ill-afford to lose some of his best men in such a futile venture. Within, he had his own turmoil to face, as messengers had already brought him news of the death of Zayd and Ja'far even before the return of the army. Mu'tah represented Muhammad's first serious offensive effort outside of the immediate sphere of Madinah. It had been a failure, but that did not mean the Prophet did not learn from it. For one, he had learned that Khalid bin al-Walid was a real asset to his movement, even though he was a relatively new Muslim. It would only make sense to place more responsibility on the former Qurayshi cavalry commander. Additional reflection also convinced the Prophet to give Khalid's comrade in arms, 'Amr bin al-'As, a chance to prove himself in an operation. Another learning point surely had something to do with supply. The sheer dynamic of moving three thousand men close to six hundred miles, while similar in some respects to moving a trading caravan to Syria, represented a significantly greater problem that involved maintaining a large force in the field. These lessons would not go unheeded, although it would take at least one major operation later for the lessons to bear fruit.

Muhammad allowed his men to rest for several months and he worked to integrate newcomers to his movement. The Banu Sulaym had at last decided to embrace Islam and declare their allegiance to the Prophet, and as this tribe had a significant element of horsemen to their credit, such an alliance gave the Prophet a very strong mobile combat element when mixed with the two hundred or more horsemen he already had. As October came, Muhammad received a report that a distant tribe to the north, the Banu Quda'ah, had planned to attack Madinah. He summoned 'Amr bin al-'As and appointed him the commander of a force of five hundred men with thirty horse cavalry. This operation was unique in several ways. First, 'Amr had only recently converted to Islam and to this date had not demonstrated anything significant regarding his sacrifice for his new-found religion. The next item that was unique was that Muhammad granted him a force of horse cavalry, for prior to this the use of cavalry had only been during operations led directly by the Prophet.

These dispositions had to raise questions within the ranks of some of his more faithful companions. Why would the Prophet so quickly promote a newcomer who once opposed Islam? Why would he grant him a special privilege for his field command that others had not received? There is no doubt that 'Amr was a talented field officer, a point he amply demonstrated when he fought for the Quraysh. That Muhammad would grant such significant responsibility to a new convert indicates a high level of trust, something that must have been developed or gained through either special insight or a deep understanding of the personality of the man in question. With this in mind, the Prophet was not willing to give 'Amr a loose rein, assigning Abu Bakr and 'Umar bin al-Khattab to accompany the operation.[58] Since these men were not in command, it is apparent that they served the capacity of the modern-day political officer in some armies. Muhammad longed to use 'Amr's military abilities but wanted to ensure his loyalty by assigning key political leaders to watch him. The operation was partially punitive and managed to disperse the enemy forces assembling in the north.

Even at this late date and after a number of years of conducting raids, the Muslims still had much to learn about logistics. Indeed, logistical matters still represented their weakest link when conducting operations. This was amply illustrated by a raid, composed of three hundred men under Abu ʿUbaydah bin al-Jarrah, to punish a tribe along the sea coast while also attempting to ambush a Qurayshi caravan.[59] The men were issued scanty rations and at one point were down to only one date per day. They failed to make contact with their intended targets even as they were reduced to eating the leaves from trees and a few camels that one of their men managed to purchase. The raid was to the point of logistical disaster when a large fish, possibly a whale, was found washed up on the beach. The famished warriors gorged themselves on its flesh for a number of days until they recovered their strength sufficiently to trek back to Madinah.[60]

By the time Abu ʿUbaydah's raid returned to Madinah, Muhammad was ready to make his second attempt at Makkah. He now had several allies to rely upon, although many of the neighboring tribes remained aloof.[61] With his plans complete, he now only needed a casus belli to launch his attack. He was provided this by the ill-advised conduct of some of the Quraysh, with the flames fanned by Muhammad's special agents in Makkah who would strive to ensure that the Prophet would have his chance. To understand how this developed, it is necessary to begin with some background.

The Treaty of al-Hudaybiyah, ratified almost two years earlier, had openly exposed the Banu Khuzaʿah as the supporters of Muhammad. At the same time, the Banu Bakr had sided with the Quraysh. While the Khuzaʿah resided outside of Makkah, they had agents within the city. One of these was Budayl bin Warqa, who had become a clandestine supporter of Muhammad and had moved into Makkah to run his business and watch the Quraysh. Budayl, as an operative representing the Muslim cause, would now play a pivotal role in a brewing war by proxy that would open up Makkah to being attacked by the Muslims.

With the treaty established, one of the branches of the Banu Bakr decided to use the period of peace to attempt to take revenge for the previous killing of one of their men by the Banu Khuzaʿah. They attacked some of the men at one of their wells, killing one and thus sparking a small war. In preparing for this attack, the Bakr had secretly received logistical support from elements of the Quraysh in the form of weapons, and some Quraysh had even fought with their ally undercover. As this fight intensified, the men of the Bakr-Quraysh coalition drove some of the Khuza'ah into the sacred area surrounding Makkah. Some in the coalition now attempted to temper the moment by reminding everyone that they were in the area of Makkah where no fighting was allowed. However, the leader of the Bakr party cried out that since "you used to steal in the sacred area, won't you take vengeance in it?"[62] Obviously, precedents established by both the Quraysh and Muhammad had influenced the decision making at this point. If the Prophet could raid in the sacred area and violate the sacred months, then why could not the Banu Bakr? With such steel-trap logic, the Bakr drove the Khuza'ah to fall back for safety on their prepositioned secret agents residing in Makkah, particularly Budayl. The Khuza'ah then appealed to Muhammad for help.

The first to arrive in Madinah was 'Amr bin Salim al-Khuza'i of one of the tribe's branches to ask Muhammad to maintain their old alliance and come to Makkah with his army. Muhammad was surely aware of the grievances of the Banu Bakr during the development of the Treaty of al-Hudaybiyah, yet he did nothing to resolve the issue. Instead, he allowed it to simmer, relying upon hotheads within the tribes to create conflict that he could exploit. Even as Muhammad was promising support, Budayl showed up with a number of other men from the Khuza'ah, providing the Prophet a full report, naturally from the Khuza'ah's perspective, on what had transpired. Having completed what amounted to a propaganda mission, they left for Makkah, and in the process stumbled upon Abu Sufyan, the key leader of the Quraysh, who was traveling to Madinah to negotiate with Muhammad regarding the growing conflict. He asked Budayl from whence he came, and Budayl denied that he had traveled to Madinah. Instead, he claimed he had come from the seacoast on a matter of business. As they separated, Abu Sufyan knew that if Budayl and his companions had been to Madinah, they would have fed their camels on dates, the pits showing up within the droppings. Breaking open one of the pieces of dung, Abu Sufyan saw the date stone within. "By God, I swear Budayl has come from Muhammad."[63] At last, but all too late, the light of understanding was dawning on the Qurayshi leader. He now hastened to Madinah.

When Abu Sufyan arrived after three days of traveling, he first went to visit his daughter who was one of the wives of the Prophet. She treated him coldly. He then attempted to meet with Muhammad, but he would not negotiate. Abu Sufyan pleaded with him, stating that he had not been present at the signing of the Treaty of al-Hudaybiyah, but was now calling on the Prophet to renew the terms and maintain the peace. Muhammad then asked him cryptically what had caused the need to make any changes, stating that he was willing to abide by the original agreement and warning Abu Sufyan about making alterations.[64] In this manner, Muhammad used moral inversion to place the blame for the abrogation of the treaty on the Quraysh while completely ignoring his own previous violations. Having never challenged these, Abu Sufyan was in no position to object.

Desperate, Abu Sufyan turned to Abu Bakr to intervene, but he too refused to speak to him. With growing panic, he next went to 'Umar bin al-Khattab and then to 'Ali bin Abu Talib, all in vain. Only the latter spoke to him, simply saying that if Muhammad had made his decision on something, it was impossible to change his mind. He then advised Abu Sufyan to declare himself a protector of men, meaning that he would be the guarantor of safety for any who wished to remain neutral. The Qurayshi leader asked if this would suffice, and 'Ali could only reply that there was nothing else he could do. With that said, Abu Sufyan went to the Prophet's mosque and loudly declared that he was now the protector between men; he then hurried back to Makkah, arriving five days later.

The leaders of Makkah had to have been astonished when they heard the news Abu Sufyan brought. When he told the others on the *mala'* what he had done, even though Muhammad had not even endorsed his actions, the elders cried out that 'Ali bin Abu Talib had simply made a fool of him and that his declaration had no value. "We know none more foolish than [you]," they jeered. "[You] . . . bring us neither war that we may be warned, nor peace that we may feel safe."[65] In essence, what Abu Sufyan had done was to declare a unilateral peace—that the Quraysh would in effect offer no resistance if Muhammad attacked. This was an open invitation, and Muhammad was not slow in taking advantage of it. While he was already determined to attack Makkah, Abu Sufyan's declaration only threw the door open wide. Muhammad moved quickly to organize his men for the attack and sent messages to the surrounding tribes calling on them to join him. The Prophet did not even wait for some of his allies to reach him at Madinah but instead began marching south with some joining him on the way.[66]

Despite his intent, Muhammad was determined to keep the Quraysh in the dark as to his true objective. After all, he had conducted other raids prior where the Quraysh thought Makkah was the objective but it was not. As the preparations were nearing completion, his intelligence service picked up information that one of the veterans of the battle of Badr, Hatib bin Abu Balta, had sent a dispatch to some people he knew in Makkah asking them to watch after his property and protect it from being plundered when the Muslims attacked.[67] The letter was carried by a woman who concealed it in her hair. Muhammad sent ʿAli bin Abu Talib with a team of men to track her down and demand the letter. When found outside Madinah, she initially denied the accusation. ʿAli threatened first to strip her bodily and then to even kill her if she did not produce the letter. Under this kind of pressure she pulled it from her hair and handed it over.[68] ʿUmar bin al-Khattab was furious when he learned of this breach in security and demanded the right to cut off Hatib's head. Muhammad interceded on behalf of the frightened Muslim, stating that as a veteran of Badr, Allah may have already forgiven him any future indiscretions. As for Hatib, his defense was simple and irrefutable—he was not connected to the Quraysh and had no relatives there. Thus, he had no one there to watch over and protect his property as the other Muslims had.

Hatib's statement provides insight into an aspect of Muhammad's insurgency operations against Makkah that is largely overlooked. Many of the Muhajirun, including the Prophet, had family still residing in Makkah. These family members, acting on the basis of loyalty first to family before clan and tribe, typically took steps to watch out for their seemingly wayward family members who had flocked to Madinah to be with the Prophet. Essentially, these family members became part of a loosely organized fifth column within Makkah, and at minimum supported the property claims of their relatives now living in Madinah. Some were almost certainly more active in supporting Muhammad's cause, possibly sending intelligence and other resources to the Prophet and his men, some of that based on the generated wealth of that very property in Makkah.[69] The former would indirectly undermine the efforts of Qurayshi leaders who attempted to stave off Muhammad's claims on the city, while the latter were active agents focused on bringing the downfall of the current regime. The Qurayshi failure had not only been one of defeating Muhammad in the field or destroying his base in Madinah, but also in failing to suppress or eliminate the fifth column within their own city.

In addition to suppressing information leaks from Madinah, Muhammad took an additional step to deceive the Quraysh of his intentions. He dispatched an eight-man raiding team under Abu Qatadah bin Rib'i to launch a feint to the east. After this team departed, the Prophet took his growing army and began to march south, although it was already ten days into the month of Ramadan and the men were fasting. To raise the necessary manpower, he emptied Madinah, leaving behind only a very small detachment to handle security and administration.[70] By the time he was near Makkah, he had mustered a force of ten thousand men and one thousand horsemen.[71] Makkah, the long-sought for prize, was now within his grasp.

As a city Makkah was extremely vulnerable to an attack. Like almost every city in the Hijaz, it had no ring wall, but unlike others it lacked the basic character of the fortified communities one would find in places such as Khaybar or Madinah. This was in large measure due to the fact that Makkah was populated mostly by the Quraysh, and therefore had little tribal competition within its environs. In addition, it would appear that for too many years the Quraysh had relied upon their ability to organize a sufficient defensive force, along with a network of active coalitions, to keep Makah protected from attack. Therefore, any type of strategy that would have emphasized fortifications had been neglected. However, boycotts engineered by Muhammad, coupled with the strangulation of trade along the western caravan route, had significantly damaged their ability to raise the support they now so desperately needed. Had Makkah been fortified as Madinah was, it is unlikely Muhammad could have conquered the city for he probably would not have had the means to maintain his men in the field, encountering the same logistical problems, or worse, as at Khaybar. Instead, the Quraysh were isolated and alone as Muhammad's army closed in.

The Qurayshi leadership was paralyzed and unable to act, even to the point that they failed to post patrols to the north. As Muhammad's army neared, they were completely ignorant of his true whereabouts, and it was at this point that Budayl bin Warqa took Abu Sufyan and a companion traveling in an attempt to locate Muhammad's army and ascertain what was going on. Abu Sufyan certainly realized by this time that Budayl was the Prophet's agent, and he may have been relying upon this in an effort to meet with Muhammad for one last chance at a negotiated settlement. Traveling in the dark along a well-traveled route, they came upon the Muslim army. Muhammad had ordered every man to build an individual fire, thus giving the impression to any Qurayshi scout that the Muslim army was four or five times its actual strength.[72] When Abu Sufyan saw the thousands of fires in the distance he gasped in surprise. Taking his cue, Budayl said that "these, by God, are (the fires of) Khuza'a which war has kindled."[73] Abu Sufyan protested, saying that the Banu Khuza'ah could not muster such a force.

As if by prearrangement, al-Abbas just happened to ride up in the dark, saddled on Muhammad's mule. He had gone out to meet the Prophet and had been sent back to Makkah to demand the Qurayshi surrender.[74] Al-Abbas told Abu Sufyan that what he saw was Muhammad's army, and that he was concerned the Quraysh would be slaughtered if Makkah was conquered. Moreover, he informed the Qurayshi leader that if Muhammad captured him, he would be beheaded.[75] Al-Abbas then proposed that Abu Sufyan ride with him into the Muslim camp to meet with Muhammad. Abu Sufyan agreed, taking one of his sons with him while Budayl, his mission complete, returned to Makkah. Abu Sufyan was held in al-Abbas's protection until the morning, when he had an audience with the Prophet. When Abu Sufyan demurred as to Muhammad's status as Allah's prophet, al-Abbas told him bluntly that he better recite the *shahadah*, the statement of Islamic faith, or he would lose his head. At this, he relented and embraced Islam.[76]

Muhammad now tasked Abu Sufyan to provide protection for the people of Makkah. He was to go there and declare that anyone who fled to the *ka'bah*, stayed with Abu Sufyan, or even simply locked themselves in their homes would be safe. Before he was allowed to go, Abu Sufyan was required to watch awestruck as Muhammad's army marched past. He then departed in haste, rushing to Makkah to warn the people. When he arrived and made his declaration, Abu Sufyan's wife emerged from their home, grabbed him by his facial hair, and cried out, "Kill this fat greasy bladder of lard! What a rotten protector of the people!"[77] Her argument had a point. Up until that time, most of the people of Makkah were looking to the *mala'* and men like Abu Sufyan to protect them from attack. Now, as the critical moment had arrived, all they heard was that they were to flee to their dwellings and cower in fear, awaiting their fate.

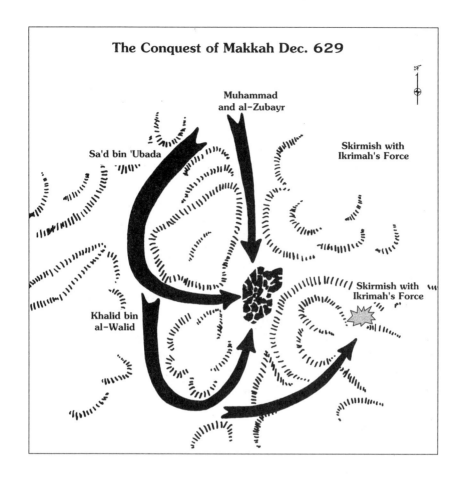

The Conquest of Makkah Dec. 629

Muhammad and al-Zubayr

Sa'd bin 'Ubada

Skirmish with Ikrimah's Force

Khalid bin al-Walid

Skirmish with Ikrimah's Force

Muhammad's army had been prepared for the worst, fully intent on slaughtering the Quraysh once they entered Makkah, a fact openly announced by the verbal taunts of the Prophet's standard bearer.[78] But now that Muhammad had Abu Sufyan to disarm most opposition, he could fall back on what was clearly his original intent, to dominate the Quraysh and to rule much of Arabia through them, having already intimated to Abu Bakr that the Quraysh could now be "milked."[79] The army was now just outside the northern edge of the city and had broken their Ramadan fast in order to strengthen themselves for the coming attack.[80] The Prophet then divided his force into three contingents. The first, led by Sa'd bin 'Ubadah, was composed of the light infantry and was to swing around the western side of Makkah and enter by the Kada Pass.[81] The second, led by Khalid bin al-Walid and apparently composed of cavalry, was to initially accompany Sa'd's force and then continue further south, entering Makkah from the Yemen road.[82] The third, under al-Zubayr bin al-'Awwam, was to enter Makkah from the north while the Prophet and his mounted closest companions, clad in their greenish-black iron armor, would parallel his route.[83]

Before dispatching them, he gave orders that six men and four women were to be proscribed and shown no mercy. Among them were Ikrimah bin Abu Jahl, the son of the fallen Qurayshi leader at Badr, 'Abdullah bin Sa'd bin Abu Sarh, a former scribe who had apostatized, Hind bint 'Utbah, the wife of Abu Sufyan who had cut out Hamzah's liver after he was killed at Uhud, and 'Abdullah bin Hilal bin Khatal al-Adrami, who had employed two singing girls, also on the proscribed list, to mock the Prophet when he was in Makkah prior to his *hijrah*.[84] Otherwise, the people were to be left unmolested unless they offered any resistance or were found in the streets.

The advance was reasonably well timed and coordinated, with Abu Bakr's father and sister watching on the mountain of Abu Qubays to the east of Makkah. The cavalry under Khalid were purposely held back until a specific moment, then unleashed to advance into the city. When Abu Bakr's father, who was blind, had this described to him by his daughter, he asked her to take him quickly back to the city before they were caught up in the attack. However, they were too late, and the cavalry overtook them, with one of the horsemen, not knowing her identity in the confusion, plundering Abu Bakr's sister of a silver necklace.[85]

Khalid's force was the only one to encounter any resistance. Ikrimah, realizing that his life was forfeit, organized a small cavalry detachment with part of the Ahabish near the mountain of Khandamah, located east of Makkah.[86] They engaged Khalid's men with a flight of arrows, and the Muslims charged, quickly entangling them in close quarter combat. They shattered Ikrimah's force, killing twenty-four of his men and putting the rest to flight. Ikrimah managed to escape and later surrendered and embraced Islam when his wife went to the Prophet to plead for his life. Two Muslims fell during Khalid's attack, one of them the intrepid Kurz bin Jabir al-Fihri, who had years earlier led one of the few successful raids against the Muslims in Madinah. The two had gotten separated from the main body of Khalid's cavalry and were ambushed and killed in the narrow mountain defiles.

As the army poured into Makkah, the men began to search for the proscribed individuals. Only three of the ten were found and killed. Of these, one was the singing girl Qaribah, who was found in the streets and cut down.[87] Another was Ibn Khatal al-Adrami, who had employed the singing girls. He had fled to the *ka'bah*, clinging to its curtains for safety. But when the Prophet was informed of this, he ordered him killed regardless, and Abu Barzah took his sword and slashed open the man's abdomen.[88] The remainder of those who were proscribed, one by one, managed to arrange some form of absolution for their previous acts, and all were allowed to enter the fold of Islam.

One of those who managed to escape execution was 'Abdullah bin Sa'd bin Abu Sarh. Previously as a Muslim he had migrated to Madinah and because he could read and write had become one of the Prophet's scribes, taking down by dictation some of the recitations Muhammad articulated. During the process he occasionally altered the nature of the dictation, making literary and grammatical changes to Qur'anic passages that went unnoticed by the Prophet. As a consequence, 'Abdullah became disillusioned with Muhammad's claims to divine inspiration, apostatizing and fleeing back to Makkah.[89] When the city was conquered he went into hiding, but because he was a foster brother to 'Uthman bin 'Affan, he managed to come to the Prophet to seek forgiveness. This was granted begrudgingly, with 'Abdullah going on to become a senior administrative official in the post-Muhammad Islamic state.[90]

Muhammad at last went to the *ka'bah*, where he had it purged of the idols that represented all other religious philosophies in the city. There would no longer be a multitude of ideologies but only one, the worship of Allah and submission to his decrees. With the city under his administrative and military control, the Prophet first confirmed some of the official offices held by members of the Qusay clan while at the same time centralizing control of the *siqayah* and *rifadah*, the right to water and feed pilgrims, to himself.[91] These two offices, coupled with the new provisions of Islamic taxation such as the *zakat*, were the basis for real power in the city. This gave the Prophet and those agents he appointed direct control of all finances, while the other offices were merely ceremonial.

Regarding Makkah, the revolution was now complete, but this still left outlying areas around the city that could oppose the new regime. The best way to combat this was to launch an aggressive offensive campaign to smash the remaining idols in the area and to bring the tribes under the dominion of the new Makkah. Muhammad swiftly organized a series of raids through the rest of November and into December 629 to accomplish this. These operations, numbering from two hundred to three hundred men each, were entrusted to men such as 'Ali bin Abu Talib, Khalid bin al-Walid, and 'Amr bin al-As, and they destroyed the various idols and killed the priestesses who officiated at them, though apparently finding little of value in the storehouses.[92] In one operation against the Banu Jadhimah conducted by Khalid in December, the goal of the mission was to bring the tribe to Islam. Khalid clearly exceeded his instructions, for when he arrived in their territory and they indicated they were already Muslims, he disarmed them nonetheless and made them captives. He then ordered them to be executed, though many under his command refused to obey it.[93] When the Prophet received the report of what Khalid had done, he ordered the payment of bloodwit for the dead and raised his hands declaring, "O Allah! I am free from what Khalid has done."[94] Nevertheless, Muhammad did nothing to discipline his headstrong general, either indicating political weakness or tacit approval.[95]

But to truly mop up any opposition in the area, the Prophet was going to have to deal with two formidable foes, the Banu Hawazin and Banu Thaqif. The former coalesced in the area of central Arabia to the northeast of Makkah and had yet to declare their submission to the Prophet. Moreover, Muhammad had received reports that their tribal chief, Malik bin 'Auf al-Nasri, was assembling their fighters along with elements of several other allied tribes to resist the Muslim ascendancy.[96] Malik decided to organize not only the men but also the women, children, and all of their livestock. His rationale was that the men would fight more fiercely if they knew that their loved ones were at stake, and he disregarded the advice of Durayd bin al-Simmah, an elderly war leader from the allied Banu Jusham who saw this as a serious error in judgment.[97] "You sheep-tender," he snapped, while making a clicking sound with his fingers to demonstrate his disapproval. "Do you suppose that anything will turn back a man that runs away? If all goes well nothing will help you but sword and lance; if it goes ill you will be disgraced with your family and property."[98] It was obvious that this elder, experienced as he was in desert fighting, found Malik, then only thirty years old, to be nothing more than a neophyte, although Malik did choose his ground wisely, using a valley that was excellent for cavalry. Even though Durayd commended him for his selection of the battlefield, he admonished him regarding his deployment, advice that Malik chose to ignore.[99]

Table 7.3. Operations from the Conquest of Makkah to the Death of Muhammad

Date	Mission	Enemy	Muslims	Leader	Result
Nov 629	Yalamlam		200		
Nov 629	'Uranah		300	Khalid bin Sa'id	
Dec 629	Jadhimah		350	Khalid bin al-Walid	Victory
Dec 629	Various; destroy shrines				Victory
Dec 629	Hunayn; Hawazin		12,000	Muhammad	Victory
Dec 629	Al-Ta'if; Thaqif		12,000	Muhammad	Defeat
Mar 630	Al-'Arj; Tamim		50	'Uyaynah bin Hisn	Victory
Apr 630	Mashab; Khath'am		20	Qutbah bin 'Amir	Booty
May 630	Zujj; al-Qurta			Al-Dahhak bin Sufyan	Booty
Jun 630	Shu'aybah; Abyssinians		300	'Alqamah bin Mujazzaz	Fighting
Jun 630	Al-Fuls; Tayyi		150	'Ali bin Abu Talib	Success
Jun 630	Al-Hubab; 'Udhrah			'Ukkashah	Success
July 630	Tabuk; Byzantine allies		30,000	Muhammad	No Contact
Aug 630	Dumat al-Jandal		420	Khalid bin al-Walid	Victory
Sept 630	Al-Yaman; al-Harith bin Ka'b		400	Khalid bin al-Walid	Victory
Dec 631	Al-Yaman; Madhhij		300	'Ali bin Abu Talib	Victory
Apr 632	Dhu al-Khalasah; shrine		150	Jarir bin 'Abdullah	Victory
Feb 632	Makkah; farewell pilgrimage			Muhammad	Pilgrimage
Jun 632	Mutah?		3,000	Usamah bin Zayd	Booty
8 Jun 632	Death of Muhammad				

Muhammad organized his army to depart Makkah and press northeast to engage this threat, adding two thousand Quraysh to the ten thousand men he already had. The Quraysh were so depleted economically and militarily from the lengthy war with the Prophet that Muhammad had to arrange to borrow armor and weapons from a polytheist to help equip some of them. As they departed Makkah, Abu Bakr looked over the company of men and declared, "Today we will not be overpowered because of our small number."[100] He was soon to receive a serious shock to his notions of superiority.

When they made contact with the Hawazin, Malik sent three spies to penetrate Muhammad's camp, but they returned out of fear without garnering any information, possibly an indication that Muhammad's camp security was improving. In turn, Muhammad sent 'Abdullah bin Abu Hadrad al-Aslami into the Hawazin camp, there to overhear Malik tell his lieutenants that "until now, Muhammad has not led men who fight with understanding. Tomorrow morning, with your kin and livestock behind you, and your rows of men before, you will break their legs with the attack of 20,000 swordsmen."[101] When 'Abdullah returned with this information, 'Umar bin al-Khattab declared he was a liar, but Muhammad knew better. This fight would possibly be the most difficult of their lives.

The morning of 3 January 630 arrived and Muhammad arrayed his forces in ranks, handing out flags and banners to key men in the formations. Of the Muhajirun, there were seven hundred men and three hundred horses; of the Ansar, there were four thousand men and five hundred horses while the remainder belonged to various allied tribes and the Quraysh.[102] When examining the numbers, even though obviously rounded off, it is apparent that the Muhajirun, as the closest companions of the Prophet, formed an elite corps, with close to 50 percent of the men mounted on horseback. These men would provide the most committed fighters available to the Prophet and thus were to him what Alexander's Companion Cavalry was to the great Macedonian.

The Muslim army now moved out, slowly winding its way into the Wadi Hunayn located about thirty miles northeast of Makkah. The Hawazin had already positioned themselves in the crevasses along the slopes of the wadi, and when most of the Muslim army was in the trap, they sprang their ambush. A hail of arrows came down upon the Muslim columns and, coupled with the shouts of thousands of the enemy, its effect was almost immediate. The cavalry of the Banu Sulaym were in the lead, and turned at once to retreat from the enemy missiles. While normally a legitimate maneuver in such combat, its impact was to panic the Muslim infantry that was trailing them.[103] Nevertheless, in the midst of this chaos, some of the Muslim infantry mounted a counterattack effective enough to drive some of the enemy archers off and even collect some spoils.[104] But such success was fleeting, and these too were promptly swept up in the retreat. This quickly became a rout, and Muhammad was suddenly faced with pending disaster much like the day of Uhud.

The Prophet now stood fast, mounted on his mule, Duldul, with his Companion Cavalry and some infantry standing as a rock in the raging torrent about them. Among them were Muhammad's former enemies, such as Abu Sufyan who was holding the reigns of the Prophet's mount. Also with the Prophet were Abu Bakr, 'Umar bin al-Khattab, 'Ali bin Abu Talib, and the Prophet's uncle al-Abbas. As they stood their ground, they called out to the retreating men to rally even as Hawazin cavalry strove to overrun them. Abu Sufyan gasped at the sight, exclaiming that "their flight will not stop before they get to the sea!"[105] Abu Qatadah turned to 'Umar and moaned, "What is wrong with the people?" 'Umar could only sigh fatalistically that "it is the order of Allah."[106] Muhammad tried to rally the men, but in vain. He quickly turned to al-Abbas, who was known to have a loud voice, and asked him to do his best. Al-Abbas called them out by tribe and affiliation, and many of the men began to now rally, even dropping from their camels when the beasts refused to turn about. With the men reassembling, some having fled as far back as the Muslim camp, the Muslims began to gradually counterattack.

The Hawazin began to give ground and Muhammad now called on his men to kill the enemy at will. In their fury, the Muslims waded into their loosely organized ranks, driving them back so far as to push them to their camp. Once there, the Muslims even turned on the children, cutting a number of them down mercilessly until the Prophet arrived to stop them.[107] Anywhere from seventy to one hundred of the Banu Malik, a branch of the Banu Thaqif and allies of the Hawazin, alone were cut down that day, a significant number lost in battle at a time when forces in the field in Arabia tended to avoid a fight to the finish.[108] Among the slain was Durayd bin al-Simmah, who, being elderly and unable to fight, was caught in the collapse and slain while sitting in the *howdah* on his camel.[109] Most of the Hawazin's women and children were overtaken in the rout and captured. Meanwhile, the men scattered, a large number of them making for al-Ta'if, the home city of the Banu Thaqif, with Malik bin 'Auf al-Nasri among them. Along the road he attempted to rally his shattered army and collect what women and children escaped the debacle.

Despite the fierceness of the fighting described in the early sources, Ibn Ishaq and al-Tabari record only four Muslim deaths while Ibn Sa'd lists only three.[110] This could possibly be explained in that only the more prominent Muslims killed in the battle were listed, though such would seem to be inconsistent with the records of previous battles. Nevertheless, there is some evidence of others being killed whose names are not listed, especially since at least one of these the Prophet considered to be destined for the hellfire.[111] Consequently, the number of dead among the Muslims may have been higher.

Muhammad ordered that all of the plunder, along with the women and children, be collected together and escorted to the town of al-Ji'ranah for safekeeping, as he now had his sights set on besieging the stronghold of the Banu Thaqif, the city of al-Ta'if. The loot was extensive, with close to 6,000 women and children taken, along with 24,000 camels, more than 40,000 goats, and 160,000 dirhams in silver.[112] The disposition of these items would have to wait until Muhammad had finished his campaign.

The Muslim army now moved south to al-Ta'if, a city situated in the mountains east of Makkah, which was not only the center of the Banu Thaqif but also served as the location of summer homes for many of the well-to-do among the Quraysh due to its cooler climate. Thus, many within Muhammad's army were familiar with this city and its inhabitants and had some knowledge as to what to expect. Al-Ta'if, unlike other cities and towns in Arabia, had a ring wall which encompassed most of the dwellings, a fact due to the homogenous nature of the population. In fact, the name itself is derived from an ancient adjective that means "to have a wall around it."[113] The Prophet besieged the city for eighteen to twenty days, using siege machines in an attempt to make a breech while also employing a prickly hedge to block communications from the outside to the defenders.[114] When they initially set up their camp, the Muslims were too close to the wall, and the Thaqif showered them with a "locust swarm" of arrows, causing some casualties that compelled the Muslims to pull back to a safer location.[115]

When one pictures this siege, one should not think of an intense battle but rather a low-intensity almost leisurely affair where the work was methodical but slow and the men often pulled back to consult among themselves as to how best to proceed with each assault. Although the glory of martyrdom is often discussed in early Islamic literature, there was clearly no hurry on the part of most to die uselessly in this action; thus, efforts were made to avoid losses. Salman al-Farisi, the same Persian Muslim who had advised the Prophet to dig the ditch before the siege of Madinah, set up a *manjaniq* and used it to hurl stones at the gate and wall, but apparently with little effect. Several other men organized the construction of two covered rams in an attempt to undermine the wall, but the defenders threw their plows into a furnace, tossing the red-hot iron pieces down on the roofs of the rams to set them alight.[116]

Frustrated by this stubborn resistance, Muhammad ordered the burning of the Thaqif's vineyards to compel their surrender, much like he had with the Banu al-Nadir. This probably caused some consternation among the Quraysh in his army, as some owned land in the area. If they were irritated, there is no record of it. However, the Thaqif were driven almost to the point of despair by the Prophet's order, and even as the smoke drifted across their city from their burning vineyards they asked Muhammad to show mercy and desist. He did, but the Thaqif still refused to surrender. He then attempted to promote servile insurrection by promising freedom to any slave that surrendered to the Muslims. While thirteen did emerge from the city, this was far too few to have an impact on the defenders.[117]

Even negotiations were attempted at times. During one of the many lulls in the fighting, Abu Sufyan and al-Mughira bin Shu'ba attempted to arrange the surrender of some of the women and children who were relatives of the Quraysh and concerned that they would be caught up in any disaster that might encompass a city taken by storm. Yet despite such entreaties, even they refused to come out, and while certainly tempted, the Thaqif did not force them to depart in order to save their rations.[118] This latter point may have convinced Muhammad that the Thaqif were well prepared to face a long siege and thus outlast his own supplies. Indeed, this may have been a stratagem to portray this very thing.[119]

Confronted with such stiff opposition, and possibly facing severe lo-gistical problems, Muhammad decided to break off the siege. His men were flabbergasted, for as the chosen of Allah, they could not under-stand how a pagan stronghold could resist their will, particularly after such triumphs as Khaybar and Makkah. They demanded to have one more attempt at the wall, and Muhammad relented, their attack being driven back with some losses. Now they too agreed it was time to leave, and the army dismantled their camp and withdrew.[120] While the Mus-lims fell back to al-Ji'ranah to dispose of the plunder from the battle of Hunayn, Muhammad already began to arrange for political pressure to be placed on the Banu Thaqif to force their submission. Their losses had not been too heavy, with Ibn Ishaq listing only twelve killed in ac-tion. However, as noted before, these may have only been the more prominent who were listed, for among those listed was Abu Bakr's son 'Abdullah.[121] Moreover, those wounded were not listed, even if among the elite such as Abu Sufyan, who lost an eye during the fighting.[122]

The Banu Thaqif did not remain independent much longer. At first one of their tribesmen, 'Urwah bin Mas'ud, attempted to call them to Islam but was killed while shouting the *adhan* over their city. His son then came to the Prophet and said that he would organize a band to rob and terrorize the Thaqif until they submitted to Muhammad's authority. The Prophet commissioned him to do so, and just as Abu Basir had previously raided Qurayshi caravans as Muhammad's proxy, so too did the son of 'Urwah bin Mas'ud raid the Thaqif.[123] Thus, when Muhammad's conventional military efforts failed, he returned to the more subtle methods of indirect warfare that had brought the Quraysh to their knees. It did not take the tribe long to realize that their best option was to join the fold of Islam.

The surrender of the Banu Thaqif to Islam seemed to have been a signal for the other tribes in Arabia to embrace Muhammad as not only the Prophet of Allah but as the titular head of the Arabian people. In late March 630, Muhammad sent out his first tax collectors to receive the *zakat* from the tribes while these tribes also sent delegations to es-tablish peace under the moniker of Islam. However, there were several holdouts, and the Prophet began to organize asymmetric insurgencies to undermine those who refused submission. Among these was the Banu Hanifah to the east, led by their own declared prophet, Musay-limah bin Habib; the Banu 'Ans bin Malik to the south in Yemen, led by their prophet, al-Aswad al-'Ansi; and the Banu Tamim under Tulayhah bin Khuwaylid al-Asadi. In the case of the first two, Muhammad dispatched men to infiltrate the leadership of these tribes to disrupt and confuse them as he planned more conventional combat actions against them for a later date. However, his mind was certainly preoccupied by the largest operation he had planned to date, an expedition north to Syria.

The origins of the Tabuk campaign, much like that to Mu'tah, are puzzling and have already been explored in a previous chapter. However, for the Prophet to organize such a risky operation for such a distant objective would be out of character for him unless some other driving force demanded his compliance. If he was indeed receiving aid from the Sasanids, then their insistence that he again attack northward to the Christian lands of the Byzantines would make logical sense. In essence, to keep the support coming he would have to placate his paymaster, even if with just symbolic gestures, while striving to make himself independent of their help. While a massive operation, Tabuk was indeed largely symbolic since the Muslims never engaged Byzantine forces or that of their Arab allies who were said to be concentrating forces in Syria.[124] However, in line with the possibility of supporting Sasanid objectives, he did manage to impose a treaty on the local governor of the major port of Ayla, later known as al-'Aqabah, in which the locals paid the *jizyah* protection tax.[125] Whether this treaty would have compelled the merchants of Ayla to restrict Byzantine trade is difficult to say.

Muhammad announced the operation during a period of extreme heat and drought in July 630. Needless to say, his men were reluctant to embark, especially since the Prophet broke with his usual secrecy and announced the objective so as to give the men an idea as to the extent of the provisions they had to prepare.[126] For other raids, the Prophet had the Muslims list their availability in a register maintained in the mosque. However, the number needed for this operation was so extensive that the register was dispensed with.[127] Instead, the men focused primarily on preparing supplies and searching for camels to ride, as the prospect of a long walk north was far from appealing. Men with means provided mounts for riding while others contributed cash to help fund the expedition. 'Uthman bin 'Affan is said to have funded one-third of the army, which of course raises the question of how he managed to lay hold of such wealth.[128] Besides cash, he ensured that he would fully equip at least one hundred transport camels, and this contribution of wealth elicited a remark from the Prophet that 'Uthman would no longer bear the consequences of sin the remainder of his life.[129]

Some men refused to go, and they received public shaming as *munafiqun*, which included 'Abdullah bin Ubayy, who accompanied the Prophet initially only to return to Madinah with a portion of the army.[130] As for some who remained behind, such humiliation had its effect, with a few deciding to join the expedition later.[131] When Muhammad realized that he once more had to empty the city, he decided to leave 'Ali bin Abu Talib behind to care for his family. This prompted the *munafiqun* to spread rumors that 'Ali was a burden to the Prophet, which was why he was not taken on the campaign. 'Ali would later join the campaign simply as a way to quell such dissension, but Muhammad sent him back, knowing that having someone trustworthy to watch over his family was as critical as campaigning. Furthermore, it allowed the Prophet to have an additional set of eyes and ears to watch over the man he had established to administer the city in his absence.

As the largest operation Muhammad ever mounted, the logistical needs for the Tabuk campaign were massive. The force was composed of thirty thousand men, ten thousand horses, and twelve thousand to fifteen thousand camels.[132] Travel to the northern waypoint of Tabuk would take about seventeen days with the army moving approximately two miles per hour and marching for ten hours per day. Calculating a seventeen-day, one-way trip, we can see that the Prophet could manage to muster the necessary lift to supply his army on the move, though it would be necessary to completely resupply once they reached Tabuk. Some forage for the animals could be found along the route, which probably followed the same general path later taken by the Hijaz railway built prior to World War I. Besides food, the men also needed to carry the various other items needed by an army in the field, such as tents, pioneer tools, cooking materials, extra clothing and armor, as well as spare swords and spears and ammunition for missile weapons. This would consume any spare logistical lift. As can be seen, a Muslim army this size could make the trek, but it would encounter severe logistical constraints along the way, which is why they called it *ghazwa al-usra*, or the expedition of great difficulty.[133]

While the need to carry food and other equipment was an issue, an additional and very serious problem for the army was their need for potable water. Water sources in the Hijaz are difficult to find to begin with, and the sources indicate that water shortages and thirst were deadly

Table 7.4. Muslim Logistical Lift and Provisions for the Tabuk Campaign

Category	Quantity	Pounds	Days	Total lbs
LOGISTICAL LIFT (POUNDS CARRIED)				
Men	30,000	20		600,000
Camels	12,000	300		3,600,000
Horses	10,000	200		2,000,000
Total Lift				6,200,000
PROVISIONS (POUNDS REQUIRED)				
Food Needed	30,000	3	17	1,530,000
Camel Fodder	12,000	10	17	2,040,000
Horse Fodder	10,000	10	17	1,700,000
Total Provisions				5,270,000

obstacles. The Prophet deployed scouts in advance of the army, leading the army to known or little-known water sources along the way, but even then they were confronted by two problems.[134] The first was the time it took to draw water for all of the men and animals, and the second was that the wells could be temporarily drawn dry, needing time to recharge. Drawing the water could take an army of this size all night to accomplish.[135] Thus, it would require significant field discipline within the ranks to cycle formations of men and beasts in turns to accomplish this feat. And since well water is drawn from permeable subsoil, such wells would often run dry, requiring a waiting period before the water would recharge them.

During the march, either there or on the way back, the men became so thirsty that some killed camels and cut open their stomachs to drink whatever fluid they could find.[136] A brief rain shower also brought welcome respite just as the army was becoming especially desperate for water.[137] Even the need for extra rations was felt, for the men debated if they should kill camels for food, which the Prophet finally endorsed as they were preparing to return to Madinah.[138] As the column advanced it would have stretched out behind anywhere from seven to eight miles, and after a number of days the number of stragglers was significant. Had the army been ambushed in the passes along the way, a momentous disaster could have engulfed the Muslim army, possibly with long-range consequences. As it was, the Prophet's army managed to reach Tabuk where they remained for ten to twenty days, depending on the source. This rest period may have been necessary for the army to recover sufficiently for the return trek.[139]

While remaining at Tabuk, Muhammad was able to compel the local chief to submit to his authority and pay *jizyah*, and he also authorized Khalid bin al-Walid to launch a raid against a Christian enclave at Dumat al-Jandal. In essence, Tabuk became a forward base camp for the Muslims to launch a raid against a location that had eluded them before. Khalid left Tabuk almost as soon as the army settled into their camp, taking 420 horse cavalry for the operation.[140] Khalid's men found the leader of Dumat al-Jandal, Ukaydir bin ʿAbduʾl-Malik, along with his brother looking for some lost cattle in the dark. Khalid's men ambushed them and Ukaydir's brother was killed in the short fight that ensued while Ukaydir was captured. Dragged to the Prophet, Muhammad forced Ukaydir, who refused to convert to Islam, to pay *jizyah* as a condition to being allowed to live.[141] Khalid also brought back some badly needed plunder, including two thousand camels and eight hundred head of cattle.[142] With Khalid's return, the Muslim army made its way back to Madinah, stopping briefly outside Madinah to destroy a rival mosque that Abu ʿAmir, who had fought the Prophet at the battle of Uhud, had set up to promote the worship of other gods along with Allah.[143]

Tabuk was Muhammad's last major campaign, although he had failed to engage the Byzantines. That does not mean it was without value, for many of the closest companions of the Prophet learned much regarding the movement of a large army through the desert. Such experience would prove invaluable to Abu Bakr, who as first *khalifa*, had to suppress the apostates after the Prophet's death. Although Muhammad authorized several raids to the south against Christians in Yemen, the Prophet returned to Madinah and settled into administering what was becoming a rapidly growing confederation. He finally was able to participate in the hajj, his only major pilgrimage since he had migrated to Madinah. In late May 632, the Prophet fell seriously ill, even though he had sufficient strength to authorize another raid north against the Christian allies of the Byzantines. However, before this raid could depart, Muhammad bin ʿAbdullah bin ʿAbd al-Muttalib, of the Banu Quraysh, the last Prophet of Allah, rested his head on the lap of his beloved ʿAisha and breathed his last. It was 8 June 632.

The Generalship of Muhammad, the Prophet of Allah

It had been twenty-three years from the time Muhammad took on the task to be the Prophet of Allah to the pinnacle of his triumph and death. He had gone from keeping his followers a closely guarded secret to being the de facto king of most of Arabia, although there were still some pockets of resistance to his movement that his first successor, Abu Bakr, would need to suppress during the Riddah, or Apostates War. When evaluating the Prophet's generalship during the two decades that he conducted operations, one is confronted by the possible danger of misinterpretation regarding what Muhammad knew as a man versus what he recited from Allah. Early Islamic tradition is clear that the Prophet, while being without error regarding his recitations, was still human like anyone else, and as noted previously it was necessary for him to learn and grow in human knowledge.[1] Therefore, like any other person, Muhammad gained knowledge and experience over time, and his operations reflect such growth. Moreover, like any other general, Muhammad had both strengths and weaknesses.

As the prophet of Allah, Muhammad operated in three specific planes of military endeavor, symmetric insurgency, asymmetric insurgency, and asymmetric conventional warfare. These three aspects in large measure established the norm of how many Muslim warriors would wage war in the future, and as a consequence his operations can be divided into three distinct stages.[2] The first stage, where he emphasized tolerance and freedom of religion, was while he was still in Makkah and his following was very small. This phase was in large measure a symmetric insurgency, for he was using the same concepts and techniques within the worldview of the Quraysh. The Quraysh, who had started out under Qusay 150 years prior as a movement that focused on their way as the final truth, had devolved to the point that all religious ideas were to be accepted within a swirl of pluralistic tolerance. The only aspect that they had trouble with was if another claimed that their religious worldview was the only way or truth. Therefore, when Muhammad began to preach against the religious diversity of Makkah, the Quraysh began to turn on him.

When several prominent Qurayshi men, such as Hamzah bin 'Abd al-Muttalib and 'Umar bin al-Khattab, came to Islam, Muhammad began to alter his techniques. He not only had personal protection from his uncle Abu Talib but now had two powerful men who could act as bodyguards for other members of the infantile *ummah*. These two allowed the Prophet to begin the transformation to stage two, which emphasized personal and collective self-defense against ridicule and persecution. By this point he also began to move toward asymmetric insurgency, for now his tactics focused on an exponential response to insults, where Hamzah and others used physical force and even threatened death to those who opposed Islam.[3] The migration to Madinah accentuated this asymmetry when Muhammad began employing propaganda, assassinations, and kidnappings, the latter two in particular being fairly unique to the region.

Once in Madinah, Muhammad utilized raids that went beyond the norm of what was expected in Arabia, and when men were killed during these operations, he refused to pay the bloodwit. In doing this, he openly incited other tribes to engage in blood feuds against the Muslims, but these failed to organize in large measure because those leaders who attempted to do so, such as Ka'b bin al-Ashraf, were assassinated by men who had hidden their Islam to their families and the general public. These men moved about their former tribes and clans at will, not only collecting intelligence but engaging in more active operations when called upon.[4] This had a chilling effect on any who thought of organizing some type of resistance, allowing the Prophet to take on each tribe individually rather than as a collective whole. Had the tribes of the Hijaz managed to organize with the Quraysh, Muhammad's movement would have been crushed. In conjunction with his raids, the Prophet organized alliances, embargoes, and even waged war on the Quraysh during a time of peace by secretly supporting a proxy in Abu Basir.

It took only a half year for Muhammad to move from stage two to stage three, emphasizing offensive action to bring the tribes, particularly the Quraysh, to Islam.[5] This stage lasted almost ten years and culminated in the fall of Makkah and the submission of almost every tribe in Arabia to Muhammad's movement. Once he moved to stage three, the Prophet used a mix of insurgency and conventional techniques, relying on the former in the first half and gradually shifting to the latter during the second. But even when he shifted to more conventional operations, Muhammad strove to maintain an asymmetric angle. His siege operations, such as at Khaybar and al-Ta'if, demonstrated significant techniques that were unfamiliar to his foes. At Khaybar he not only was able to maintain himself in the field long enough to complete the siege, but he also moved his men into the very center of the complex of fortifications, denying the Jews the means to intercommunicate while reducing each fort in turn. At al-Ta'if he employed siege engines which, while unsuccessful, were new to the region. At the battle of al-Khandaq he employed a trench to block the Qurayshi cavalry, a technique that was a noteworthy surprise to them. He also on two occasions, with the siege of the Banu al-Nadir and al-Ta'if, used wholesale scorched-earth tactics, another novelty to the area, to flush out besieged opponents.

One aspect of Muhammad's methodology that was asymmetric to his opponents was his emphasis on total victory.[6] This demand for victory, that is, actually compelling opponents to do his will, was foreign to the Quraysh and the Arabian tribes. By demanding total surrender to the ways of Islam, Muhammad stressed an aspect of warfare that pushed others beyond their current understanding. To the Arab tribes, warfare was about sport and play, a pastime to break the boredom and monotony of desert life in which men could show courage and honor. To the Quraysh, warfare was only engaged in as a last resort in an effort to develop some type of negotiated settlement to support their mercantile ventures. Muhammad wanted neither sport nor compromise. The final, absolute victory of Islam was his only objective, and it remained his focus regardless what methodology of warfare he used.

Had Saul Alinsky, the writer of radical political warfare literature in the twentieth century, lived during Muhammad's day, he would have been impressed with how the Prophet applied his rules for conflict to his fight with the Quraysh and the Arab tribes.[7] The Prophet forced his will upon his enemies by using many of the techniques Alinsky highlighted centuries later. He demonstrated that power was not just what he possessed but more importantly what his enemies believed he had. The Quraysh never clearly understood what capabilities, or lack thereof, the Prophet had. They repeatedly underestimated his abilities but concurrently overestimated the risk of confrontation. Awed by rumors that spread through the region when the Muslims engaged in raids, the Quraysh tended to believe such rumors and never confronted the Muslims with the intent of destroying them.

Muhammad also strove to stay within the experience of his men. At the battle of Badr, his men engaged the Quraysh with skirmishing that probably lasted for several hours. When Muhammad believed that a decisive moment came, he resorted to the simple but age-old expedient to win a battle—they charged. While not inventive, it certainly allowed the Muslims to maximize their religious ardor while minimizing their lack of combat experience. It was not until the battle of Uhud that the Prophet used some form of field maneuvering, demonstrating that his men had learned much in the year since Badr.[8] Regarding the raids, Muhammad was careful to assign men on the basis of experience to particular operations. For example, when he assigned 'Amr bin Umayyah to assassinate Abu Sufyan, he apparently considered the mission so risky that he sent a man with little experience to conduct it, probably thinking that if he were killed, the loss to the Muslims would be minimal. Conversely, when he sent assassins to kill the likes of Asma bint Marwan and Abu Rafi, he sent men who had connections with either the family or the region so that they could negotiate hazards to bring the operation to successful fruition.

In contrast, Muhammad worked to go outside the experience of his opponents. Simply demanding total submission to Islam was new to the region, but his use of assassinations, kidnappings, movement at night, and violation of sacred months when no combat was to occur certainly pushed his enemies to the edge of their experience level. In essence, he turned their superstitions against them, a concept already well understood in an ancient world replete with such.[9] His creation of a new "super tribe," the *ummah*, composed of people from every group in the Hijaz and even beyond, certainly went against every notion of tribal, clan, and family solidarity that is a hallmark of Arabian culture still prevalent today. But while he was able to negate tribal loyalty through the power of his personality, Muhammad was unable in many ways to dissolve these permanently, and his death saw the Arabs descend periodically back to those local loyalties they knew and understood best.

While building loyalty to himself and the ways of Allah, the Prophet looked for the means to force the Quraysh to live up to their own book of rules and thus constrain their operations. He understood intimately how the Qurayshi leadership thought and acted, and made his plans accordingly. This detailed understanding, and the fact that he abandoned such concepts regarding his own life, meant that he had an inside look at his key opponents, while the latter were blind regarding the Prophet. Typically, the Qurayshi response to Muhammad's actions was in line with how they viewed the world but not in line with Muhammad's new vision. Time and again, the Quraysh expected Muhammad to respond the way a Qurayshi would, only to be surprised or disappointed. Muhammad's subtle violations of the Treaty of al-Hudaybiyah offers a prime example where he continued to demand that the Quraysh abide by the terms even as he allowed Muslim women to migrate to Madinah, and he secretly supported a proxy war against Qurayshi caravans, both in contravention of the treaty.[10] That the Quraysh did not even demand that Muhammad stick to the treaty highlights their weakness of will as well as their political and military vulnerabilities.

Muhammad used ridicule with élan and demonstrated that he and his court poets were masters of the technique. He engaged in a relentless campaign of propaganda, with the lion's share directed at the Quraysh. In contrast, the people who did try to engage in such ridicule were assassinated, and by the time we reach the midterm period of the campaign, we see no evidence of a concerted propaganda assault against Muhammad and the Muslims. The Quraysh did attempt to create such information operations, but their efforts were feeble and disjointed, as attested by their poetry. In fact, most of their poetry focused on their personal prowess in battle, something that any outside observer would already begin to question after their defeat at Badr. To be effective, propaganda must have some type of viable fact and force behind it, and while Muhammad's did, the Quraysh showed serious weaknesses in this area.[11] In a land where oral testimony and poetic verse served as the conduit for history and culture, the Muslims reigned supreme over their enemies.

While poetry and propaganda served to bolster his own side and confuse his enemies, Muhammad had to ensure that his men were engaged in activities they enjoyed. This point is simple: *razzias*, or raiding, is far more easy and fun than being involved in the back-breaking work of agriculture or even business. Raiding allowed his men to enjoy the thrill of a risky activity that required little focused, long-term effort. The very character of insurgency involves the avoidance of serious labor unless some element of the population is pushed into that work by a measure of force. The *Ansar* did most of the hard work in Madinah, tending date palms and harvesting fields, with a portion of the surplus going to Muhammad to support his men. Meanwhile, the Muhajirun largely failed to help the *Ansar* in these efforts. It was apparently much more enjoyable to hang out in the *suffah* of the Prophet's mosque and recite Qur'anic passages while placing one's name on a register, waiting for the Prophet to announce a raid. Muhammad understood the character of his closest associates and realized that he had a ready-made element for the purposes of combat in a small wars environment.

Since he had such personnel on hand, this allowed the Prophet to keep the pressure on his enemies. Because many of the Muhajirun did wait on Muhammad to announce a combat action, the Prophet could pick and choose when he planned to engage his enemies. This meant the initiative was his, and during the entire period when at Madinah, the initiative was almost exclusively with the Muslims. This forced the Quraysh to operate in a reactive rather than proactive mode, and even when they launched a counteroffensive that led to such actions as Uhud and al-Khandaq, these were done as reactions to Muhammad's moves rather than part of a concerted strategy to destroy the Muslim insurgency.

As Muhammad kept the pressure on, he also used the technique that the threat is worse than the actual event itself. This appeal to the sword of Damocles proved to be very effective, for the Quraysh cowered at the very notion that the Muslims might invade Makkah. During the eight years prior to the fall of the city, the Qurayshi leaders and populace were arguably consumed by this one thought, and one can imagine that every day and virtually every conscious minute, the Quraysh had resting in the back of their minds that nagging terror that one day Muhammad's men would come flooding into their defenseless city. Moreover, Muhammad could use this technique effectively with anyone, and the sources record countless events in which he could be brutal with punishments on the one hand but very magnanimous and forgiving with those who came in defeat to profess Islam on the other. One learned quickly that the Prophet's anger was not something to trifle with, but if one surrendered to Islam and begged forgiveness, they would be assured of receiving absolution.

The entire effect of such tactics was magnified by the fact that Muhammad placed his entire focus on the Quraysh. This focus personalized and polarized the opposition for the *ummah*, making his men more willing to kill even their family members. Almost all of his operations, save for the few that were directed northward against the Byzantine frontier, were directed at the Quraysh. Even raids sent out against neighboring tribes were done primarily to bring them to the fold of Islam so as to shatter the Qurayshi coalition system and to isolate Makkah from any allies. By the time Muhammad organized his march on Makkah, the Quraysh stood almost alone, stark naked in their helplessness before the might of the prophet of Allah.

To engage and defeat the Quraysh found Muhammad maximizing his strengths and avoiding his weaknesses. Fortunately for him, his strengths proved to be asymmetric to the weaknesses of his opponents, thus granting him key advantages. He remained focused on his final victory and steadfast to this even during what appeared to be some of the darkest hours of the movement.[12] His statesmanship, coupled with his effective use of cunning, deception, and a phenomenal intelligence service, allowed him to maintain control of Madinah even while deployed for weeks and months at a time on campaigns.[13] He maintained superb control of the moral factors regarding his men and the *ummah* as a whole to develop this.[14] He demonstrated that he was a quick learner, adapting rapidly to new ideas that he believed would benefit his operations and give him the advantage of surprise.[15] Through all of this, his inward eye grasped the ultimate victory, a point he never relinquished, while this same inward eye allowed him to understand ever-changing situations and take advantage of them. In this regard he possessed the critical feature of coup d'oeil, the "quick recognition of a truth that the mind would ordinarily miss or would perceive only after long study and reflection," a feature of his life that only became better with experience.[16]

His small wars demonstrated that he could develop superiority at the crucial point of action, made effective by his decisiveness and audacity, and his use of superior operational speed, even though his men were often moving on foot.[17] This is all the more remarkable when it is noted that he and his men did this without maps or compasses, and often at night.[18] Even more crucial, Muhammad managed to control the rhythm of operations, getting the Quraysh to mimic his pace rather than intensify the operational tempo based on their own competitive strategy. A key aspect of insurgency operations is for the insurgent to control such tempo. Should the counterinsurgent increase this dramatically, he can effectively smash the insurgency by sheer force of effort. The Prophet's use of gradualism allowed him to pressure his opponents without becoming an obvious significant threat, building to his triumph with many hardly understanding the threat before them.[19] Muhammad intuitively mastered the ability to regulate this tempo, a point that the Quraysh apparently never understood. In this manner he also strove to overcome the constant friction of war, although this was only partially pursued by his efforts.[20]

Despite these points, possibly the most important aspect of Muhammad's success was contained in his own dynamic personality. Even claiming to be the prophet of Allah would have been insufficient without the charisma he emanated, which was a key factor in his being able to control and influence events. While the impact of personality in warfare is largely overlooked in today's world of automated armies, in the ancient world the influence of a dominant personality was probably multiplied significantly. It was the person of Muhammad who kept the *ummah* coherent and focused on the objectives that he, as their leader, determined.[21]

To most effectively influence this, the Prophet's *ummah* was a nation at arms in which there was essentially no such thing as a noncombatant in the group, save for perhaps the smallest children. Everyone in the *ummah* was directed toward supporting the goals set forth by Muhammad, although of course there were those who dissented, these individuals at times receiving censure for their lack of cooperation. In this way Muhammad's men maintained their martial spirit in a far more comprehensive manner than their enemies. Each man, even woman, was expected to either engage in campaigning or be prepared to support the men who actively participated in operations, with men more oriented toward fighting and women toward logistical and administrative support. Moreover, every person was under a form of discipline similar to what was found in armies of the ancient world, thus making the *ummah* oriented first and foremost toward warfare.[22]

Typically, any analysis by others of Muhammad's generalship has focused on his strengths, with most sources taking a pious approach to the subject.[23] Even those attempting a more balanced approach fail to discuss the Prophet's weaknesses in military matters.[24] But the Prophet did have military weaknesses and these were revealed during his campaigning.

Muhammad was administratively weak in his dispositions, relying more upon his status as prophet and rarely delegating any real authority to a subordinate. In this regard his forceful personality became a detriment. This weakness was demonstrated by whom he selected to lead raids and to administer Madinah in his absence when he personally campaigned. In both cases, he rarely gave a lieutenant such responsibility in more than one instance, instead offering leadership to numerous individuals who may or may not have been adequately capable to perform the task. While Muhammad later gave repeated field commands to his adopted son Zayd bin Harithah, it can be argued that he may have done this with the hidden desire that Zayd should fall in combat, particularly when leading the Mu'tah operation, in light of the controversy over Zayd's wife, Zaynab bint Jahsh. In contrast, it is of interest that even though he claimed that Abu Bakr was his closest friend, there is no record Muhammad ever gave control of Madinah over to him in his absence.[25] Instead, the Prophet's dispositions regarding leadership, both military and political, demonstrated a decided lack of trust in any subordinate, indicating that he feared possible mutiny or rebellion within his own ranks if he allowed another individual to have a sustained position of leadership within the *ummah*. Compounding this problem was his lack of staff to assist him in operational planning. Not only did Muhammad operate as the commander in chief, he also served as his own chief of staff, logistician, and intelligence chief. Sensory and information overload can weigh down the best, and Muhammad was no exception.

The case of 'Abdullah bin Jahsh is an excellent example of this lack of trust. Although he conducted the first successful action for the Muslims, Muhammad ensured that 'Abdullah never again led an operation. This would be contradictory to the development of an effective military force to not reward outstanding field leadership, unless of course one was concerned that this individual would possibly rise up to take control of the movement. 'Abdullah's success was his own undoing, for he did what the Prophet had failed to do to that point: bring battlefield success to the *ummah*. Concurrently, it can be argued that Muhammad never experienced an open mutiny as even some of the great captains did, such as Julius Caesar, although he came close to this after the raid on the Banu Mustaliq. In this light, one could say that the results of his leadership selections justified his decisions.

Coupled with these administrative problems was his significant lack of understanding regarding logistics. While he did have sources of money and material items, he had little knowledge about the employment of proper logistical factors in the field. Instead, he relied upon the time-honored technique of letting individuals organize their own supply, concepts that were ancient but by then outmoded.[26] While using such supply techniques may have allowed him to muster the maximum number of men for an operation, it severely constrained the sustainability of these forces in the field. The Prophet did not learn or understand the evolving logistical principles as delineated and used by such forces as the Byzantines and Sasanid Persians, particularly those laid out by the Byzantine emperor Maurice. For example, Muhammad had no conception of developing a supply line from his base to maintain his forces in the field, in developing supply depots from which to draw previously stocked resources, or even in operating an organized commissary, preferring to either carry with him what he needed or forage for it.[27] Had his opponents a better grasp of logistical constraints and the problems faced by the Muslims, the latter of which Muhammad at least understood, they may have been able to hand him significant defeats due to this weakness.

When Muhammad shifted to conventional operations, this weakness in logistics began to have a telling effect as he placed his army in peril due to supply problems during the Tabuk campaign. Had he met any serious opposition during that operation, he would have assuredly been handed a significant and possibly decisive defeat. Nevertheless, the Tabuk campaign did teach some of Muhammad's companions the problems inherent in lack of supply, lessons that were attested to by Abu Bakr's more effective administrative procedures during the Riddah following the Prophet's death.[28] The second *khalifa*, 'Umar bin al-Khattab, developed even more sophisticated logistical support for his armies invading Syria and al-Irak.[29] This weakness in logistical understanding was partly offset by the financial and material assets made available through such wealthy men as al-Abbas and possible Sasanid support. This support gave Muhammad a significant material advantage over most of his enemies, who probably had even less understanding of logistical matters than Muhammad had.

Another area where Muhammad demonstrated some weakness was in developing estimates of enemy capabilities, for he tended to underestimate what his enemies usually could do and to overestimate his own capabilities. While his intelligence service did excellent work, and while he had a sound psychological grasp of his principle opponent, the Quraysh, Muhammad often assumed that many would simply submit when faced with but minimal force. This was particularly true when he engaged in smaller operations against neighboring tribes, where a number of his patrols were ambushed and severely handled. His attempt to embark on the *umrah*, or lesser pilgrimage that culminated in the Treaty of al-Hudaybiyah, almost resulted in disaster. Had the Quraysh been committed as a unified group to destroy the Muslim movement, they could have done so within sight of the mountains of Makkah. Instead, Muhammad was allowed to slip away to reorganize and try again later with a larger force. In effect, Muhammad's enemies allowed him to learn from his mistakes and over time he became a more effective campaigner.

Connected to a weakness in making estimates was the fact that Muhammad was vulnerable to surprise. On more than one occasion, he or his forces were ambushed effectively, and some of these could have been ruinous. His failure to identify the relief column under Abu Jahl that led to the battle of Badr was possibly his most telling mistake, and it could have easily destroyed the young Islamic movement and cost him his life. Even had he survived the defeat, his position in Madinah would have been tenuous at best, and he and his closest followers may have been expelled by his many opponents who were only looking for a sufficient excuse to do so.

Muhammad also allowed his base in Madinah to be successfully raided, a fact that illustrated not only his deficient security preparations but also his lack of delegation to the administrative governor of the city while he was gone. The fact that he later convinced the raider to join his ranks is testimony to the strong appeal of his movement but does not eliminate the fact that he was caught off guard by an intrepid opponent. He was also surprised by the strength of resistance he encountered from the Quraysh when he traveled on the *umrah*, as well as the forces of the Hawazin and their allies that ambushed the Muslims successfully at the battle of Hunayn. In the latter, it was probably the lack of exploitation by the Hawazin that prevented Muhammad's army from being shattered, which allowed Muhammad and his companions to rally their fleeing men to return to the fight and win. The fact that he could be ambushed so easily is underscored by the general lack of security in the Muslim camp, demonstrated by one spy who infiltrated and drew Muhammad's own sword, holding it over the dozing prophet who saved himself largely by his own forceful personality.[30] On another occasion, the Prophet and his companions overslept after the Khaybar campaign and missed the *Fajr*, or dawn prayer, because the entire camp was asleep.[31] Other armies in early history were surprised by such a failure with dire results.[32]

As a prophet who appealed to mass support, Muhammad was also vulnerable to popular opinion and local superstitions. His march to Badr was based largely on his need to achieve a significant victory to counter that of ʿAbdullah bin Jahsh, and at one point he deviated his route because he felt that moving a certain direction was laced with bad omens simply based on the names of the people living there, which were the Arabic for "fire" and "burning."[33] Regarding these names, he could have easily turned the words in his favor by redirecting their meaning to the fate to be endured by those who rejected Islam. Instead, he took a devious route that may have wasted precious time, costing him his true objective.[34] He allowed popular opinion to control his operational decisions prior to the battle of Uhud, yielding to the clamor of the people instead of staying the course with his original—and correctly assessed—plan to defend within the city. He even had a chance to adhere to his original plan when the people realized what they had done and relented, but he decided to take to the field nonetheless. The result was an operational defeat that could have been nothing less than disastrous had the Quraysh been prepared to exploit it. However, it should be noted that this weakness became less of a problem as the Prophet gained more political and military success over time.

Lastly, Muhammad never demonstrated any real tactical combat ability. He was strategically strong and operationally capable, but when it came to engaging in tactical operations, he never showed real success against a determined opponent in a symmetric fight. This was amply demonstrated at the battle of Hunayn, where the Muslim force was routed and could have easily been completely driven from the field or even destroyed. Had his small command group with his closest companions been overrun, his defeat would have been ensured and with fatal results. Moreover, he never developed stratagems to defeat tribes that had fled to the mountains for protection, such as the Banu Lihyan.

While Muhammad could move decisively on such potential foes, he sometimes failed to achieve the surprise he desired. Failing this, he was at a loss as to how to entrap his elusive quarry, preferring to withdraw and try again later.

In other areas of tactical ability, the Prophet never demonstrated any acumen. He never conducted a successful ambush, nor did he ever find a way to effectively counter enemy cavalry in an open engagement, such as with the use of caltrops or similar devices. He never countermarched rapidly from one location to another to deceive an opponent and gain a decisive advantage in the field, or never had to relieve a besieged garrison. Although ready and willing to expropriate ideas from others, such as the ditch at the siege of Madinah or the use of engines at al-Ta'if, he never exhibited any ability to develop new techniques or technologies of his own in the field. For example, despite operating in a desert environment, he never conceived of the idea to have his men create a dust cloud to screen his movements or to deceive his enemies as to his true intent and strength, though he did deploy at Badr in such a way as to put the rising sun to his back.[35] Indeed, in large measure his combat operations were quite predictable if his enemies had used any form of operational intelligence to analyze his field craft. Even his asymmetric insurgency operations began to show a decided mark of predictability.

In comparing Muhammad with some of the great generals preceding him, we find numerous times where he intuitively used the methods of such skillful commanders. On a number of occasions he used his enemies' religious superstitions against them, such as attacking the Jews on their Sabbath, and he naturally declared divine sanction in his favor, such as declaring the wind at Badr to be angelic beings fighting on the Muslims' behalf.[36] He hid his operational intentions even from his closest associates, which at least helped him maintain some security in a crafty and devious world.[37] He created rumors of enemy attacks to stir the ardor of his men for raiding, and he usually developed his operations to take advantage of favorable weather, with the notable exception being the campaign of Tabuk.[38] He generally ate like the rest of the *ummah* and maintained a very Spartan lifestyle with simple habits that could only serve to enhance the bond he had with his men.[39] While he could judge them strictly according to the light of Allah that he recited, he could also be very magnanimous, offering ready absolution to the contrite.[40] He used the Treaty of al-Hudaybiyah to effectively lower the guard of the Quraysh, thereby making them vulnerable to other asymmetric techniques that continued to wear down their opposition.[41] The Prophet also effectively transformed the treaty into a Muslim victory to hearten his men and maintain commitment to the cause.[42]

Muhammad demonstrated many sound operational techniques as well. He strove to use feints and misdirection where at all possible, using additional fires to deceive Abu Sufyan of his true strength when marching on Makkah, employing deception to ward off the Banu Ghatafan from intervening when he besieged Khaybar, and using sealed instructions to maintain operational security.[43] He even engaged in a most novel activity of night movement, despite its difficulties and dangers, to conceal the direction of his raids and to help his men conserve their strength.[44] Muhammad used Islam to ensure that he had a committed combat force, refusing to accept those outside of the *ummah* to assist him in operations.[45] He took steps to ensure that his men had confidence in his field decisions, such as the order to lift the siege of al-Ta'if, and on the one occasion after the raid on the Banu Mustaliq when his men appeared to be close to rioting or mutiny, he used a forced march to occupy their minds and exhaust their bodies.[46] When caught off guard, such as prior to the battle of Badr, Muhammad hid his anxiety from his men, and when one of his dispatched armies fled the field of battle after the encounter at Mu'tah, the Prophet interceded on their behalf and protected his men from the taunts of the people.[47] Yet on another occasion, he extracted an oath from his men at al-Hudaybiyah that they would not flee the field if attacked, thus securing their pledge to protect the Muslim movement at a critically weak moment. And of course, he called for his warriors to fight to a martyr's end for the sake of Allah, a position not much different from other cultures that called for such sacrifice for the protection of the state.[48]

When engaging his enemies, the Prophet effectively used a fortified base to wear down the Quraysh and sap their will to resist. Moreover, he curried favor with them and other tribes by ordering his men not to mutilate the dead, a practice often engaged in by other cultures throughout history.[49] When marching on Makkah, he chose to offer the Quraysh sanctuaries that allowed them a means to escape the terrors of defeat by a conquering force, thus shattering their will to oppose his invasion.[50] When defeating an enemy, such as at Hunayn, he could show generosity to them in an effort to bind them to him, even at times intermarrying into their tribes. When distributing the plunder from that battle, he ensured that the most important leaders of the Quraysh received extra gifts, binding them to himself and the Islamic movement.[51]

In contrast, Muhammad could use techniques and contrivances that appear harsh or cynical on the surface to the modern eye. He used 'Abdullah bin Ubayy, either with or without his knowledge, to keep the opposition in Madinah divided and hesitant.[52] He apparently planned to kidnap the leaders of Khaybar and hold them for ransom or convince them to surrender their city to him, a technique used on occasion by others.[53] The Prophet's employment of assassination pushed his enemies far outside their own level of experience, particularly when he used men who were part of the target's tribe and were familiar with the geography and language of the area.[54] He used torture, a technique familiar to other cultures of the era, to attempt to extract important information or secure key alliances.[55] He also engaged in shocking techniques to cow his enemies into submission, such as executing the warriors of the Banu Qurayzah and selling the surviving women and children into slavery. The extinction of this tribal group, a serious departure from the accepted norms of fighting in Arabia, sent a chilling message to the Hijaz region and beyond that the Prophet would brook no opposition to the ascendancy of Islam.[56]

In assessing the Prophet's military career, it must be understood that he engaged in only four major battles (Badr, Uhud, Makkah, and Hunayn) and six sieges (Banu Qaynuqa, Banu al-Nadir, al-Khandaq, Banu Qurayzah, Khaybar, and al-Ta'if). Of the battles, he won at Badr by a concerted charge and won at Makkah due to lack of opposition. At Hunayn he nearly lost, and in the one set piece engagement he fought, the battle of Uhud, he was defeated. Regarding the sieges, he won all but al-Ta'if, but sieges are not the same as engaging in open combat where it is necessary to maneuver and control forces in the field. It is almost certain that Muhammad understood his weakness in this area, which would explain why he avoided set-piece battles and focused on what he and his men knew best, asymmetric insurgency.[57] His shift to conventional operations only came when he had to conduct them, and even then he tried to approach these asymmetrically to avoid the strengths of his enemies. It would be difficult to place Muhammad in the ranks of Hannibal, Alexander, or Julius Caesar. It would even be hard to declare him an equal of such men as Alcibiades, Iphicrates, Epaminondas, or Scipio Africanus. Nevertheless, Muhammad sufficiently used many of the stratagems and techniques of great field commanders as well as statesmen, organizing a campaign sufficient to defeat his foes and dominate the Arabian Peninsula. In itself this represents a remarkable achievement.

Yet Muhammad's campaigns came with a hefty price tag, much greater than many would assess today. It is common to relate how few casualties there were during his campaigns, with the numbers ranging from 1,400 to 1,800 dead.[58] These numbers appear to be a bargain on the surface, especially in light of the devastation wrought by modern conflicts. However, when analyzing war dead, one must look beyond the raw numbers and examine them in light of the population base of the region in which the conflict was fought. Making a population estimate of the Hijaz is difficult at best, but some extrapolations can be made. Considering the populations of Makkah, Madinah, Khaybar, and the immediate tribes around these cities, it could be estimated that the total population base of the region was no more than 50,000 souls. However, we could use a higher number of 80,000 for the purpose of comparison.[59] With this in mind, we can make our comparison with combat losses in World War I and World War II.

The analysis indicates that Muhammad's ten years of combat with the Quraysh and surrounding tribes in the Hijaz had casualty percentages that can rival those of some of the chief belligerents in the two major wars of the twentieth century. Of course, Muhammad's campaigns were not nearly as destructive, for the devastating nature of modern combat weapons is fearsome. Nor do the raw numbers during his campaigns reach the mind-boggling totals of modern wars. Yet the flip side to this tells us that Muhammad's campaigns were still devastating in human life, especially more so because the weapons used were of such limited capability. At the same time, it should be noted that some of the regions and cities he conquered soon became deserted fields of ruins, the most obvious example being Khaybar when ʿUmar bin al-Khattab, as the second *khalifa*, followed the Prophet's instructions to expel all non-Muslims from Arabia.[60] While all warfare is devastating in its own right, Muhammad's campaigns were clearly devastating for western Arabia, and such an ordeal had the effect of driving most of the remaining tribes of the peninsula into submission. Had his campaigns been less traumatic, it is unlikely that these tribes, fiercely independent in their own right, would have surrendered their sovereignty.

When examining Muhammad's strengths and weaknesses, we must also ask what there was about the Quraysh that made them vulnerable

Table 8.1. Comparative Analysis of Populations and War Dead

Nation/Region	Population	War Dead	Percentage
MUHAMMAD'S CAMPAIGN			
Hijaz est. 1	50,000	1,400–1,800	2.8–3.6
Hijaz est. 2	80,000	1,400–1,800	1.8–2.3
WORLD WAR I			
Germany	65,000,000	1,659,000	2.6
Britain	46,000,000	658,704	1.4
WORLD WAR II			
Germany	78,000,000	3,250,000	4.2
Britain	47,500,000	305,800	0.7

Sources: For World War I, see Gleichen, *Chronology of the Great War*, part 3, 196–97; and Burg and Purcell, *Almanac of World War I*, 12, 239. For World War II, see Ellis, *World War II*, 253–54.

to the Prophet's insurgency. After all, is there not a proverb that says for a perfect battle like Cannae to occur, you need not only a Hannibal but also a Terentius Varro?[61] While the Quraysh had their share of strengths, it was their vulnerabilities placed in contrast to Muhammad's capabilities that made them ideal victims for the insurgency that finally subdued them.

Through their emphasis on trade and business, the Quraysh quickly learned to build negotiated coalitions to accomplish their ends. Coalitions have advantages, but oftentimes the weaknesses outweigh these. In many cases, each coalition partner is more concerned about their own agenda, leading to self-interested fragmentation as the coalition is placed under stress. As one German analyst many years later noted, a key problem in coalition warfare is that "each power is inclined to leave the heaviest burden to the others."[62] While the Quraysh styled themselves as leaders in Arabia, they did not have the sufficient resources to carry the burden of campaigning, and as they engaged in their struggle with the Prophet, many of the tribes in the area, though having some type of commercial contract with Makkah, remained aloof from the contest waiting to see who would triumph. The Qurayshi efforts to create a grand coalition did lead to the siege of Madinah, offering them a real opportunity to bring victory to their cause. When they failed to induce the Muslims to surrender the awe in which others held the Quraysh was forever shattered, and they were by and large left alone to their fate.

Qurayshi leadership was also incredibly indecisive. Only on a few occasions did they shake themselves from their stupor in an effort to thwart Muhammad's purposes. Faced with Muhammad's challenge, they simply could not develop an effective counterstrategy that would have won the day for them. They bickered among themselves, this in large measure a result of their own philosophical worldview but one that was also encouraged by the machinations of the Prophet's agents within their midst. Coupled with this was their lack of audacity and boldness. Their cultural milieu created within them a risk aversion that was detrimental to effective military operations. A few of their leaders, such as Abu Jahl and Khalid bin al-Walid, demonstrated firm and capable generalship in the field, backed by personal courage. Abu Jahl and some of the nobles with him fought to the death at Badr, while Khalid demonstrated both boldness and coup d'oeil at the battle of Uhud.[63] Had the Quraysh been unified around such men, they could have inflicted serious defeats on the Muslims and possibly destroyed the insurgency in its infancy. Indeed, even when the Quraysh had a chance to kill Muhammad when still in Makkah, they were so distraught over the possibility of creating a blood feud that they simply could not execute the plan with vigor.

This lack of decisiveness was systemic, growing from the inability to seize the moment and grasp victory when it was theirs for the taking. Because this weakness was an outgrowth of their worldview, it is quite probable that they no longer understood what true victory even was. They were used to negotiating deals where each side, both buyer and seller, came out with an advantage. With the world of business and finance as their backdrop, they had difficulty seeing beyond the notion of mutual advantages gained in business deals to understand that the key concept in counterinsurgency operations is the necessity to crush the enemy and force them to do their will. Any negotiation that involved the surrender of critical issues would be a victory for the insurgency and could easily lead to more compromises and the eventual downfall of the established state. In some measure these compromises actually occurred, such as with their failure to enforce the Treaty of al-Hudaybiyah, and therefore the Quraysh slowly crumbled.

But of all the problems that the Quraysh displayed, none was as decisive and telling as their reliance on the notion of diversity and toleration. They had formally believed in an absolutist worldview that demanded others to acknowledge and abide by this, but it took only a few generations for this to slip away.[64] It was replaced by a worldview based on their acceptance of polytheism that acceded to multiple interpretations of the legal foundations of their community. Fueled by their rising affluence, it took little time for the leaders of Makkah to succumb to the notion that the only things really important in life were their growing wealth and being left alone to spend it as they saw fit. As long as others were allowed to do much of what they wanted without harming others, their traditional rights and status went unquestioned. Muhammad's initial challenge regarding their neglect of the poor and pilgrims was not too serious, but when he decried the polytheism of the city, he was laying an axe at the very root of the system of toleration the Quraysh had created.

The challenge faced by the Quraysh is actually a problem faced by all of mankind. Throughout history a core conflict has involved the contrast of the one versus the many, or put another way, unity versus diversity. The Quraysh had a diverse culture, one of which they were proud. However, such diversity failed to provide answers to the crucial questions of life they faced. When Muhammad recited the Qur'an and called them to obedience to the simple unity of Allah, they were dumbfounded as to how to respond. The Quraysh had no foundation, fundamental focus, or law in which to unify their culture. It was a society of fragmented families and clans, and the surrounding Arab tribes were not much better off.

Toleration sounds so genteel on the surface, but when faced with an absolutist threat, it has no fundamental principles on which to rally opposition. Muhammad's small core of believers, focused on his prophethood and the recitations uttered from Allah, served as a foundational law that could invigorate followers to sacrifice everything, including their lives, for the sake of this higher cause. The Quraysh had no such ideals. Because they had no principles to die for, they ultimately had nothing to fight for, a point clearly demonstrated at the battle of Badr.[65] Drained of their ability to resist, it was simply a matter of time until the crumbling edifice of their diverse culture was overwhelmed by a philosophy demanding total obedience to the One. In this way, despite any weaknesses exhibited, Muhammad fulfilled the most critical dictum of warfare: he compelled his enemies to do his will.

Glossary of Terms

'**Abna**: A group of Persians who settled in Yemen.

adhan: The Islamic call to prayer, uttered vocally. See *mu'adhdhin*.

Ahabish: A group of professional soldiers believed to have come from various tribes and hired to fight for the Quraysh.

Allah Akbar: Known as the *takbir*, the cry that "Allah is Great" or "the Greatest."

amir: A military leader.

Ansar: The Muslim "helpers" in Madinah who supported the Muhajirun, or Muslim emigrants from Makkah. See **Muhajirun**.

barid: A distance equivalent to approximately twelve miles.

bay'ah: The oath of allegiance given to a nobleman.

Bay'ah al-Ridwan: Oath of divine pleasure, which was the oath to fight to the death given to the Prophet Muhammad prior to the signing of the Treaty of al-Hudaybiyah.

dinar: A weight of currency typically equivalent in value to ten times a dirham. Typically a gold coin 4.4 grams in weight.

dirham: A weight of currency, typically a silver coin 3.08 grams in weight.

diya: The financial compensation, or bloodwit, provided for murder or injury.

fay: Plunder seized without fighting, and thus the personal property of the Prophet Muhammad.

al-fitnah: A severe trial.

ghazwah: A military expedition led specifically by the Prophet Muhammad.

ghazwa al-usra: The expedition of great difficulty, that is, the campaign to Tabuk.

hadith: The recorded sayings of the Prophet Muhammad that highlights and explains many Qur'anic passages. Initially recited orally until taken down in writing in various collections. See *sunnah*.

hajaru al-aswad: The black stone embedded in the eastern corner of the *ka'bah*. Islamic tradition states that this stone fell from heaven at Adam's feet and was once white but has since turned black due to the sins of mankind.

hajj: The annual major pilgrimage to Makkah conducted during the month of Ramadan.

haram: Something that is forbidden.

hijrah: The migration of the Prophet Muhammad from Makkah to Madinah.

hirabah: Engaging in brigandage or highway robbery against Muslims.

howdah: An enclosed cupola mounted on a camel to allow the rider, usually a woman, privacy and protection from the elements during travel.

ihram: The state of consecration prior to making the sacrifices during a pilgrimage.

jahiliyah: The period of ignorance prior to the coming of the Prophet Muhammad.

jihad: To engage in a form of struggle, often equated with physical combat in early Islamic sources. Some weak hadith and later sources also cite an inner struggle against evil.

jizyah: The protection tax levied on non-Muslims, typically Jews and Christians, who refused to convert to Islam but who wished to remain within Islamic territory.

ka'bah: Literally "cube." It is the cube-like structure in Makkah that serves as the focal point of Islamic worship and practice. Islamic tradition states that it predated the Noahic flood and was rebuilt by Abraham and his son Ishmael. The *hajaru al-aswad* is embedded in its eastern corner.

khalifa: A successor, in this case, to the Prophet Muhammad.

khalifate: A developed empire under the leadership of a Khalifa.

kunyah: The nickname of people in Arabia, typically established on the basis of one's firstborn son, although some highlighted a significant characteristic of a person.

lex talionis: The law of retribution that allowed tribal leaders to deter criminal activity.

liwa': A strip of cloth typically attached to the pole arm of an Arab warrior signifying that he had been delegated a position of battlefield command.

maghazi: A term denoting military expeditions or campaigns. The term is typically used in Islamic literature that deals mostly with military actions.

maktum: Something sealed or hidden, such as a secret letter or philosophical concept.

mala': The council in Makkah that handled the day-to-day governance of the city.

manjaniq: A small throwing machine similar to a catapult.

al-Masjid: A mosque. Mosques predated Muhammad's arrival as the Prophet of Allah and thus were not exclusively a Muslim place of worship.

mawla: A client or servant of another.

mithqal: A weight of currency similar to a dinar but possibly of slightly lesser value.

mu'adhdhin: The one who calls faithful Muslims to prayer. See *adhan*.

Muhajirun: The Muslims of Makkah who migrated to Madinah. They formed the initial core of Muhammad's fighters. See **Ansar**.

munafiqun: The hypocrites; Muslims who claimed fidelity but were not truly committed to the cause. 'Abdullah bin Ubayy was considered to be the chief leader of the hypocrites.

qiblah: The direction of prayer for the Muslim. When Muhammad migrated to Madinah, the direction of prayer was initially toward Jerusalem. A later recitation would change this direction to Makkah.

razzia: A desert raid.

Riddah: Apostasy, particularly applied to the Apostates War immediately after the Prophet Muhammad's death.

rifadah: A special tax levied on property holders in Makkah to provide pilgrims to the city with sustenance.

sadaqah: Charitable giving in the cause of Allah, often considered similar to the *zakat* in early Islamic texts.

sariyah: A raid led by a lieutenant of the Prophet Muhammad.

sawiq: Powdered barley, dates, or wheat mixed with water to create an edible paste. *Sawiq* was often the principle ration for Arab warriors conducting a raid. It was carried dry, only hydrated prior to consumption.

sayyid: A nobleman or master. Typically distinct from a *shaykh*. It was a term sometimes used later on to denote a descendant of the Prophet Muhammad.

shahadah: The Islamic statement of faith, the first utterance when one converts to Islam. It says that there is no god but Allah, and that Muhammad is Allah's prophet.

shawhat: A hard stick used for both a staff and bow.

shaykh: A title of respect given to a leader of a tribe or important family.

siqayah: The right to provide water to pilgrims coming to Makkah.

sira: Early historical literature regarding the life of the Prophet Muhammad.

suffah: A raised platform or veranda as part of the Prophet's mosque where the poor Muhajirun would stay. It was from here that many of the early raids were prepared. This was possibly the origin for the term *Sufi*.

Sufi: The deep inner way or path to Allah. The early companions of the Prophet were considered to be perfect Sufis, thus the term was seen by later Sufis as unnecessary at that time.

sunnah: The ways of Muhammad, initially transmitted orally but later preserved in writing. The *sunnah* is often intermingled with hadith, or sayings of the Prophet.

Surah: A chapter of the Qur'an.

Tafsir: A commentary of the Qur'an that uses hadith literature and historical examples to explain the passages.

takbir: The cry that "Allah is Great."

ummah: The community of Muslim believers.

umrah: The lesser pilgrimage, distinct from the hajj because an *umrah* could be conducted anytime during the year.

vicarius: A Latin term; a substitute or deputy, typically used of a person in a military capacity.

wadi: A water wash that is typically dry but becomes a raging torrent after a storm.

ya sabahah: Literally, "Oh, the morning!" A phrase uttered when a raid or some other disaster strikes a people.

zakat: The annual payment by a Muslim of 2.5 percent of their accumulated wealth for the purposes of supporting the Islamic cause. *Zakat* could be used for anything from relieving the distress of poverty to supporting fighters in the way of Allah. Also see *sadaqah*.

Notes

Introduction

1. I am well aware that the German term often translated as "politics" actually refers more to social discourse or engagement. However, the word "politics" suffices here for my discussion on insurgencies.

2. Qadi 'Iyad, *Ash-Shifa*, part 3, ch. 1, sec. 1, 279–89; sec. 3, 293–95.

3. Donner, *Narratives of Islamic Origins*, 5–25. It is important to note here that I am aware of Donner's more recent research, first penned in an essay and then compiled into a book, where he contends that much of what we may know from the hadith literature cannot be trusted, and that only material from the Qur'an can provide us with what the early Islamic community was like. In that context, he asserts among other things that the words "Islam" and "Muslim" were later constructs, and that the early followers of Muhammad were simply called "believers," and were thus largely like Christians and Jews of the region. It is not the place here to deal with these issues in detail, but suffice it to say I believe his most recent approach has problems in methodology, and specifically in assumptions. See Donner, *Muhammad and the Believers*.

4. Donner, *Narratives of Islamic Origins*, 7.

5. Ibid., 13.

6. Ibid., 14.

7. Ibid., 19.

8. Ibid., 22–23.

9. Ibid., 25–31.

10. Noth and Conrad, *Early Arabic Historical Tradition*, 72.

11. Ibid., 27.

12. Donner, *Narratives of Islamic Origins*, 137–38.

13. When examining many of the contentions of certain scholars regarding the information in the early Islamic sources and their overt dismissal of them out of hand,

it should be noted that interpretations can sometimes be colored by the extent an individual participates in endeavors outside the normal realm of academia. Being too secluded can possibly have a narrowing effect on one's analysis.

14. Noth and Conrad, *Early Arabic Historical Tradition*, 87.

15. D'Este, *Patton*, 4, 48.

16. Fraser, *Knights Cross*, 99.

17. For a discussion of topoi, see Donner, *Narratives of Islamic Origins*, 266–71.

18. Noth and Conrad, *Early Arabic Historical Tradition*, 114, 116, 131.

19. For an excessive example of this, see Noth's discussion (134–35) of the Arabic usage for the phrase to "cross over." In this case he explains away a Muslim soldier's rest period by some water so that he could ultimately "cross over" and engage an enemy force. To simply say that a common turn of phrase becomes a topos is to seriously abuse the historical record from one's own personal bias, whatever that may be.

20. For examples see Frontinus, *Stratagems*, book 2, ch. 2; Polyaenus, *Stratagems of War*, excerpts 46.9, 47.1, 49.1, 49.2.; and Vegetius, "Military Institutions," 153.

21. Noth and Conrad, *Early Arabic Historical Tradition*, 142.

22. Ibid., 173.

23. Ibid., 177.

24. To my knowledge, Noth does not attempt to evaluate the movements of Alexander's army in space and time. But herein lies the point. When he dismisses the ability of a Muslim army to do this, he apparently does so simply on the basis that it is a Muslim army, not on the basis of making an adequate comparison to the campaigns of someone like Alexander.

25. Udet, *Mein Fliegerleben*, 57–60.

26. McCudden, *Flying Fury*, 185–87; Rickenbacker, *Fighting the Flying Circus*, 317–18.

27. Donner, *Narratives of Islamic Origins*, 209–10.

28. Ibid., n17.

29. Strange, *Recollections of an Airman*, 112–15.

30. Von Mises, *Theory and History*, 211.

31. Donner, *Narratives of Islamic Origins*, 29.

32. Tacitus, Histories, vol. 2, xiv.

33. Julius Caesar, *Gallic War*, xvii.

34. For examples, see Ibn Khallikan, who collected a massive biographical dictionary that he completed around AD 1256 (*Wafayat al-A'Yan Wa Anba' Abna' Al-Zaman*, vol. 1, vii). Specifics regarding the dates for key traditionalists are as follows: al-Bukhari, ca. 860, or 230 years after the Prophet's death (entry #543); Imam Muslim, ca. 880, or 250 years after (entry #690); Imam Malik, ca. 785, or 155 years after (entry #524); Ibn Ishaq, ca. 750, or 120 years after (entry #586); al-Waqidi, ca. 815, or 185 years after (entry #618); and al-Tabari, ca. 910, or 280 years after (entry #165).

35. Regarding the capabilities of the Pony Express, see www.ponyexpress.org, the website for the Pony Express Museum in St. Joseph, Missouri. Regarding Noth's discussion of the *barid*, see Noth and Conrad, *Early Arabic Historical Tradition*, 78–79.

36. For a good example, see Noth and Conrad, *Early Arabic Historical Tradition*, 135–37.

37. Donner notes that this was Wansbrough's conclusion, indicating that it was

impossible to piece together Islamic origins from the source material and that it is "futile to try" (*Narratives of Islamic Origins*, 25n65). This, of course, raises the question why Wansbrough devoted his entire life to the study of Islam and the Orient, and even continued to do so after publishing his conclusions.

38. A Shi'ite tradition draws a clear distinction between a prophet and apostle. The usage here is in accord with Sunni tradition. See Kulayni, "*Al-Kafi* Selections," book 4, #299, #300. It should be noted, however, that Sunni tradition also draws a distinction between a prophet and a messenger, with the former much more numerous than the latter. Unlike previous prophets or messengers, Muhammad had the unique title of Messenger of God. See Hughes, *Dictionary of Islam*, 475.

39. Lane, *Arabic-English Lexicon*, part 1, 83; and Omar, *Dictionary of the Holy Qur'an*, 28–29.

Chapter 1. Revolution

1. Watt, *Muhammad at Mecca*, 32–33.

2. Ibn Ishaq, *Sirat Rasul Allah*, 81.

3. Ibid., 227.

4. Ibid., 195; and Ibn Kathir, *Al-Sira al-Nabawiyya*, 1:101, 106.

5. Watt, *Muhammad at Mecca*, 2–3, 11–14.

6. For example, see Crone, *Meccan Trade and the Rise of Islam*, 133–48.

7. Ibid., 144, 156.

8. Ibn Kathir, *Al-Sira al-Nabawiyya*, 2:109.

9. Theophanes the Confessor, *Chronicle of Theophanes Confessor*, 362; and John of Nikiu, *Chronicle of John*, 72.

10. Theophanes, *Chronicle of Theophanes*, 362.

11. Al-Tabari, *Ta'rikh al-rusul wa'l-muluk*, I.I, 965.

12. Theophanes, *Chronicles of Theophanes*, 389; and Ostrogorsky, *History of the Byzantine State*, 73. Khusrau is also called Chosroes in some sources.

13. Surah 30:1–3; Ibn Kathir, *Tafsir Al-Qur'an Al-'Azim*, 7:517–24; and Kaegi, *Heraclius Emperor of Byzantium*, 78.

14. Al-Baladhuri, *Kitab Futuh al-Buldan*, 1.105–7: 160–62.

15. Watt, *Muhammad at Mecca*, 8.

16. The contention of one scholar that Arabs did not build walls for lack of technical ability would seem to be incorrect, considering their abilities to build walled hamlets within their cities. Instead, the most logical reason why Arab cities in the Hijaz had no outer wall, excepting al-Ta'if, is because the polity of the people precluded the unifying conception of a community needing a single defensive system. See King and Cameron, *Byzantine and Early Islamic Near East*, 189.

17. Muhammad would later change the traditional Arabian concepts of inheritance, a clear indication of his problems with it. See Kahn, *Sahih al-Bukhari*, 9.10; and Hasan, *Sunan Abu Dawud*, 2.2880. Also see Surah 4:11–12, 176–77; and Ibn Kathir, *Tafsir Al-Qur'an Al-'Azim*, 2:389–98.

18. Much like the issue of inheritance, Muhammad would alter the distribution formula regarding plunder taken in battle. In changing the formula, he would reduce his take from one-quarter to one-fifth of the total.

19. Watt, *Muhammad at Mecca*, 71.

20. Ibn Ishaq, *Sirat Rasul Allah*, 118.

21. Hughes, *Dictionary of Islam*, 257.

22. King and Cameron, *Byzantine and Early Islamic Near East*, 204; and Ibn Ishaq, *Sirat Rasul Allah*, 21–22.

23. Ibn Ishaq, *Sirat Rasul Allah*, 53; Ibn Kathir, *Al-Sira al-Nabawiyya*, 1:68–69; and Haykal, *Life of Muhammad*, 35.

24. Ibn Ishaq, *Sirat Rasul Allah*, 55.

25. Watt, *Muhammad at Mecca*, 7.

26. Ibn Ishaq, *Sirat Rasul Allah*, 56.

27. Bashear, *Arabs and Others in Early Islam*, 7. As for the status of *mawla*, the al-Aws and al-Khazraj were *mawla* to the Jewish tribes from an early date in Madinah. See Ibn Ishaq, *Sirat Rasul Allah*, 197; and Al-Tabari, *Kitab al-Jihad*, I.I: 1209. Julius Wellhausen's contention that the Jews were the clients of these two tribes is mistaken. See Lecker, "Constitution of Medina," 48–50. It will be demonstrated later that it makes no sense if the al-Khazraj had Jewish tribes as their clients, for their declaration of support for Muhammad indicated they would have to break their treaties with the Jews. This would only be necessary if they were an equal or subordinate position.

28. Bashear, *Arabs and Others in Early Islam*, 27.

29. Watt, *Muhammad at Mecca*, 20–21.

30. Ibid., 17.

31. The *lex talionis* mirrors the ancient dictum of Exodus 21:22–25.

32. It is important to note the difference between *diya* and *diyâ*, as the latter with the diacritical mark references a landed estate.

33. For an example of this position, see Firestone, *Jihad, The Origin of Holy War*, 24–25.

34. Ibn Saʿd, *Kitab al-Tabaqat al-Kabir*, 2:8.

35. There are exceptions regarding the reach of a *shaykh*'s influence, with wealth being the key criteria. See Lancaster and Lancaster, "Concepts of Leadership in Bedouin Society," 41. Regarding their claim to influence, see ibid., 45.

36. For a medieval, though comprehensive, overview of Muhammad's call to prophethood, see Ibn Taymiyyah, *Al-Jawab al-Sahih*, 146–73. Unfortunately, this English translation is a heavily edited single volume of a much more massive multivolume work done by the preeminent Shaykh al-Islam.

37. Ibn Ishaq, *Sirat Rasul Allah*, 121, 133. The view of some contemporaries was that if Muhammad's mission was successful, it would mean a ruling position for the Quraysh. Also see Watt, *Muhammad at Mecca*, 144.

38. Ibn Ishaq, *Sirat Rasul Allah*, 94.

39. Rehman Shaikh, *Chronology of Prophetic Events*, 50. Rehman Shaikh's chronological analysis contradicts traditionally accepted dates among Orientalists, but his research is far more comprehensive regarding the calendars and their correlation.

40. Ibn Ishaq, *Sirat Rasul Allah*, 82; Ibn Kathir *Al-Sira al-Nabawiyya*, 1:189–93; Khan, *Sahih al-Bukhari*, vol. 5, #166, #168; Siddiqi, *Sahih Imam Muslim*, vol. 7, #2430, #2437; Khaliyl, *Jamiʿ al-Tirmidhi*, vol. 6, #3877; and Ibn Saʿd, *Kitab al-Tabaqat al-Kabir*, 8:9–12. One exception to these can be found in *al-Tabaqat* 1:147–48. Compare the descriptions of Khadijah with those of Safiyah bint Huyayy, Juwayriyah bint al-Harith, Zaynab bint Jahsh, and Rayhana bint Zayd in Khan, *Sahih al-Bukhari*, vol.

5, #522; Ibn Sa'd, *al-Tabaqat* 8:83, 87, 92; Ibn Ishaq, *Sirat Rasul Allah*, 493; and Al-Tabari, *Kitab al-Jihad*, I.I, 1460–62.

41. Some of Muhammad's opponents used his *kunyah* almost in ridicule. See Ibn Ishaq, *Sirat Rasul Allah*, 461; see Al-Tabari, *Kitab al-Jihad*, I.I, 1486, for a different, and possibly more revealing, translation of the event discussed in Ibn Ishaq's *Sira Rasul Allah*. Also note the curse uttered on Muhammad by his enemies as recorded in Ibn Ishaq, 180; see Ibn Kathir, *Al-Sira al-Nabawiyya*, 1:56, 239. Regarding the importance of children and sons, see Hughes, "Children," in *Dictionary of Islam*, 50–53. Finally see Ibn Kathir, *Al-Sira al-Nabawiyya*, 2:89, indicating that 'Aisha was very jealous of Khadijah because she bore Muhammad two sons.

42. Ibn Kathir, *Al-Sira al-Nabawiyya*, 1:321, 325.

43. Ibid., 2:111.

44. Ibn Ishaq, *Sirat Rasul Allah*, 144, 225.

45. Khan, *Sahih al-Bukhari*, vol. 5, #6; vol. 1, #455.

46. Ibn Ishaq, *Sirat Rasul Allah*, 57.

47. A Shi'ite tradition states that al-Abbas apparently exhausted his wealth. While it does not state that he did so supporting Muhammad's insurgency, the implications would be there. See Kulayni, "*Al-Kafi* Selections," book 4, #377.

48. Abu Zahra, *Four Imams*, 25–30; 142–55; 265–70; 407–10; also see Horovitz, *Earliest Biographies*, 79–80, on Ibn Ishaq and the possibility of Abbasid bias.

49. For example, see Ibn Kathir's comment about Muhammad's dinner with Qurayshi leaders that highlighted 'Ali bin Abu Talib's role as Muhammad's *khalifa*, or successor; Ibn Kathir, *Al-Sira al-Nabawiyya*, 1:333. Compare this to Al-Tabari, *Kitab al-Jihad*, I.I, 1172–73; and Ibn Ishaq, *Sirat Rasul Allah*, 118, regarding this same incident.

50. Ibn Sa'd, *Kitab al-Tabaqat al-Kabir*, 1:230.

51. The comment by one of Muhammad's warriors after the Muslim victory at Badr is telling. Upon receiving congratulations for the victory he said, "By God, we only met some bald old women like the sacrificial camels who are hobbled, and we slaughtered them!" (Ibn Ishaq, *Sirat Rasul Allah*, 308).

52. Ibid., 35–36.

53. Muhammad's uncle Abu Lahab offered initial support, only to withdraw it when the Prophet told him that his parents were in the hellfire due to their idol worship. See Ibn Kathir, *Al-Sira al-Nabawiyya*, 2:98–99.

54. Ibn Ishaq, *Sirat Rasul Allah*, 62, 63, 67.

55. Ibid., 133.

56. For example, compare Ibn Ishaq, *Sirat Rasul Allah*, 141–42, 143–45, and 146, with 130–31, 136, 162, 179–80, 187, and 191.

57. Regarding Bilal, see Ibn Ishaq, *Sirat Rasul Allah*, 143–44; regarding the killing of any early Muslims, see Ibn Ishaq, *Sirat Rasul Allah*, 145; and Ibn Sa'd, *Kitab al-Tabaqat al-Kabir*, 8:185–86. There are significant problems with the claim that Abu Jahl actually thrust his spear into the belly of an elderly woman to kill her. The particular problem involves guilt and the bloodwit, for the clan of the woman's family could have demanded the bloodwit from Abu Jahl. Furthermore, if Abu Jahl could be so flippant as to casually murder a woman, why was he so squeamish about having Muhammad killed? Finally, Ibn Kathir notes that the account regarding this murdered

woman lacks a chain of early authorities, thereby making it suspect. See Ibn Kathir, *Al-Sira al-Nabawiyya*, 1:358.

58. The principle of protection and allegiance is very ancient and cross-cultural. An early example can be seen in the Bible, Genesis 12 and 15. It was also present in many medieval European documents and was articulated as a key aspect of English law in Calvin's Case, (1608) Trinity Term, 6 James I. See Sheppard, *Selected Writings of Sir Edward Coke*, 1:175–76. Medieval Islamic writings discuss this issue as well. See Qadi 'Iyad, *Ash-Shifa*, Part 2, ch. 1, sec. 3, 217–18.

59. Haykal, *Life of Muhammad*, 92.

60. Ibn Ishaq, *Sirat Rasul Allah*, 53. When Qusay seized control of the *ka'bah*, he fought several small wars with neighboring tribes to secure it. The Quraysh joined him in this effort, and this was the origin of their name, for Quraysh was from the ancient Arabic *al-taqarrush*, which means to join together. See Ibn Sa'd, *Kitab al-Tabaqat al-Kabir*, 1:68. Qusay was the first to be called "Qurayshi" and was considered the *sharif*, or chief, of Makkah because "there was none to dispute his claim." Nearly every facet of life, from sending caravans and commissioning raids to circumcising boys and declaring when a girl had reached puberty and was of marriageable age, were controlled by Qusay. See Ibn Sa'd, *Kitab al-Tabaqat al-Kabir*, 1:69, 71.

61. Ibn Ishaq, *Sirat Rasul Allah*, 132; and Ibn Kathir, *Al-Sira al-Nabawiyya*, 1:323.

62. Ibn Ishaq, *Sirat Rasul Allah*, 172–73.

63. Ibid., 152.

64. Ibn Kathir, *Tafsir Al-Qur'an Al-'Azim*, 7:256–57, 312–16. Regarding the development of Trinitarian doctrine in Ethiopia, see Schaff and Wace, *Nicene and Post-Nicene Fathers*, vol. 2, *Ecclesiastical History of Socrates*, Bk I, XIX; and vol. 4 Athanasius, *Apolgia ad Constantium*, 31.

65. Ibn Khaldun, *Muqaddimah*, 1:256–57; Al-Mubarakpuri, *Ar-Raheeq al-Makhtum*, 98; and Haykal, *Life of Muhammad*, 155.

66. Ibn Ishaq, *Sirat Rasul Allah*, 194; Al-Tabari, *Ta'rikh al-rusul wa'l-muluk*, VI, 118–19n193. Apparently, al-Mut'im bin 'Adiy offered only limited protection, as Muhammad continued to seek something more comprehensive. See Ibn Ishaq, *Sirat Rasul Allah*, 194.

67. Ibn Ishaq, *Sirat Rasul Allah*, 135. Abu Jahl's opposition to Islam is also demonstrated in a story that entered Sufi legend. This story relates how Abu Jahl had some pebbles in his hand and he asked Muhammad if he could declare what was hidden within his fist. Muhammad instead got the pebbles to cry out the *shahadah*, the Muslim profession of faith, which angered Abu Jahl so much that he dashed the pebbles to the ground. See Nicholson, *Mathnawi of Jalalu'ddin Rumi*, Bk I, 117.

68. Ibn Ishaq, *Sirat Rasul Allah*, 192–93, 195–96; and Al-Tabari, *Ta'rikh al-rusul wa'l-muluk*, I.I, 1207.

69. Al-Tabari, *Ta'rikh al-rusul wa'l-muluk*, I.I, 1204.

70. Ibn Ishaq, *Sirat Rasul Allah*, 191.

71. Ibid., 195. It is interesting to compare this answer given by the Prophet in contrast to the way a Sufi legend recounts how he was challenged by a group of Arab *shaykhs* to share the kingdom of Allah with them. In the latter, Muhammad told them clearly that "God hath given the Amirate to me." Once the Amirate was established

under the Prophet, recounted stories had no ambiguity; the kingdom was to go to the Prophet. See Nicholson, *Mathnawi of Jalalu'ddin Rumi*, Bk IV, 425–27.

72. Ibn Ishaq, *Sirat Rasul Allah*, 198.

73. Ibid., 198–99. Ibn Sa'd, *Kitab al-Tabaqat al-Kabir*, 1:254–55. While it is often assumed that Sufism as a philosophy refrains from warfare and fighting, the great Sufi Rumi understood that physical fighting was for men, and that to refrain from war was the path of women. See Nicholson, *Mathnawi of Jalalu'ddin Rumi*, Bk VI, 227–28.

74. Ibn Ishaq, *Sirat Rasul Allah*, 200.

75. Ibid.; and Al-Tabari, *Ta'rikh al-rusul wa'l-muluk*, I.I, 1215.

76. Al-Tabari, *Ta'rikh al-rusul wa'l-muluk*, I.I, 1222.

77. Watt rejects this as later invention to hide persecutions of the Hashim clan, which simply makes no sense. See Watt, *Muhammad at Mecca*, 147. It is important to note that a Shi'ite history accepts this account as accurate, only omitting al-Abbas's speech, despite the fact that it places the Prophet's uncle in a positive light in contrast to Shi'ite leanings. See Hosain, *Early History of Islam*, 1:74. A Qadiani source also accepts the account as legitimate and includes al-Abbas's speech. See Ali, *Muhammad the Prophet*, 66.

78. Ibn Sa'd, *Kitab al-Tabaqat al-Kabir*, 1:257.

79. This is obvious from the timeline of Muhammad's efforts to reach out to various tribes around Makkah. See Ibn Ishaq, *Sirat Rasul Allah*, 192–97. Also note the comment made by Ibn Kathir, *Al-Sira al-Nabawiyya*, 2:131: "But he found no one to shelter or aid him."

80. Ibn Ishaq, *Sirat Rasul Allah*, 203–4.

81. Watt, *Muhammad at Mecca*, 145–49; Ali, *Muhammad the Prophet*, 66. Hosain; *Early History of Islam*, 1:74–75; Glubb, *Life and Times of Muhammad*, 144; Gabriel, *Muhammad*, 61; Ramadan, *Messenger*, 76; Rogerson, *Prophet Muhammad, a Biography*, 117; and Armstrong, *Muhammad*, 150–51. Armstrong mentions the event but not that the Jews were the object. The same occurs in Ibn Abdul Wahab, *Biography of the Prophet*, 1:313. Ibn Abdul Wahab (or Wahhab) was the son of the famous founder of the Wahhabi movement that controlled much of Arabia in the mid-eighteenth century. There are several key Muslim authors who do mention the incident and that the Jews were the object. See Siddiqui, *Life of Muhammad*, 125; Haykal, *Life of Muhammad*, 157; Al-Mubarakpuri, *Sealed Nectar*, 159; and Ibn Kathir, *Al-Sira al-Nabawiyya*, 2:134.

82. Ibn Ishaq, *Sirat Rasul Allah*, 204.

83. Ibid., 208, 212.

84. Ibid., 205.

85. Ibn Kathir, *Tafsir Al-Qur'an Al-'Azim*, 6:5886. Ibid., 582.

87. Ibid.

88. Ibn Ishaq, *Sirat Rasul Allah*, 307; and Ibn Kathir, *Al-Sira al-Nabawiyya*, 2:304–5.

89. Surah 2:193. Ibn Ishaq, *Sirat Rasul Allah*, 213fn states it is verse 198, the incongruence due to differences in editions of the Qur'an.

Chapter 2. The Insurgency Grows

1. Ibn Kathir, *Al-Sira al-Nabawiyya*, 2:194.
2. Ibn Ishaq, *Sirat Rasul Allah*, 221.
3. Ibid., 222, 224.
4. Watt, *Muhammad at Mecca*, 141.
5. Al-Tabari, *Ta'rikh al-rusul wa'l-muluk*, I.I, 1221.
6. This would be based on internal evidence regarding the number of fighters. See the table 2.2 regarding the population of Madinah. For example, the Qaynuqa were allied with al-Khazraj while al-Nadir and Qurayzah allied with al-Aws, thus creating an uneasy balance in the city. See Watt, *Muhammad at Mecca*, 141.
7. Ibid., 142.
8. Lecker, *Constitution of Medina*.
9. Qureshi, *Letters of the Holy Prophet Muhammad*, 34–42.
10. Ibid., #46, 42.
11. Ibid., #12, 36.
12. Lecker, *Constitution of Medina*, 97.
13. Ibn Sa'd, *Kitab al-Tabaqat al-Kabir*, 2:95; and Al-Waqidi, *Kitab al-Maghazi*, 196. Regarding al-Waqidi's veracity, for which there has been doubts expressed by some historians, early Islamic commentators have indicated that while he was sound in historical work he was weak regarding judicial judgments. See Ibn Khallikan, *Wafayat al-A'Yan Wa Anba' Abna' Al-Zaman*, 4:326. One author noted that there were many who transmitted hadith material that reject al-Waqidi's work, but still found that "he is held a sound authority of the *sira*, the *maghazi*, the conquest and *fiqh*." See Horovitz, *Earliest Biographies of the Prophet*, 116.
14. Lecker, *Constitution of Medina*, 50.
15. Quoted in ibid., 53.
16. Ibn Ishaq, *Sirat Rasul Allah*, 204.
17. Cited in Glubb, *Life and Times of Muhammad*, 170.
18. Ibn Ishaq, *Sirat Rasul Allah*, 218.
19. Ibid., 363, 464.
20. Ibn Sa'd, *Kitab al-Tabaqat al-Kabir*, 2:69.
21. Watt, *Muhammad at Medina*, 157, 195.
22. The statistics offered here correlate with both Hamidullah's estimates and the contention of Lecker that the Jews formed about half the population of the city. See *Constitution of Medina*, 53.
23. Ibn Ishaq, *Sirat Rasul Allah*, 336. There are minor contentions regarding the exact numbers, but those provided by Ibn Ishaq suffice for this analysis.
24. Khan, *Sahih al-Bukhari*, vol. 4, #293.
25. Ibn Sa'd, *Kitab al-Tabaqat al-Kabir*, 1:279–80.
26. Al-Tabari, *Ta'rikh al-rusul wa'l-muluk*, I.I, 1261. Muhammad formally connected himself to the clan of al-Najjar in Madinah, of which his maternal relatives were part of a subclan, becoming their chief when their leader died. However, this was more a formalism than a practicality. See Ibn Ishaq, *Sirat Rasul Allah*, 235. An interesting Sufi account regarding the joining of the Muhajirun and Ansar compared their linkage to a collection of mature grapes in a garden. As true believers, their

former allegiances and identity were dissolved, having become one juice when the grapes were squeezed. In contrast, the immature grapes were noted for being stone-hard and thus equated to unbelievers and heretics fit for damnation. See Nicholson, *Mathnawi of Jalalu'ddin Rumi*, book 2, 414–17.

27. In light of many modern tendencies to equate Sufism with pacifism, it is applicable to note that one ancient Persian Sufi source considers the men of the *suffah* to be the best of the early Muslims and ideal Sufis because they renounced a regular livelihood. Of course, the source does not directly connect this to the fact that they subsisted largely on armed raiding, but the implications are obvious. See al-Hujwiri, *Kashf al-Mahjub*, 81–82. On another note, it is puzzling that Richard Gabriel could consider the *suffah* to be Muhammad's secret police, for the sources clearly indicate that the *suffah* was a place, not an organization. See Gabriel, *Muhammad*, xxv, 75. Gabriel also misidentifies those who stayed in the *suffah*, indicating they were of the Ansar, but they were almost exclusively of the Muhajirun. For a brief overview of the *suffah*, see Hamidullah, *Battlefields of the Prophet Muhammad*, 136. Of those who resided in the *suffah*, see Ibn Sa'd, *Kitab al-Tabaqat al-Kabir*, 1:300–302.

28. Khan, *Sahih al-Bukhari*, vol. 1, #431; vol. 4, #250; vol. 5, #702; vol. 8, #459; and Siddiqi, *Sahih Imam Muslim*, vol. 2, #803; vol. 8, #2769R3.

29. Omar, *Dictionary of the Holy Qur'an*, 565–66; and Steingass, *English-Arabic Translator Dictionary*, 408.

30. Ibn Taymiyyah, *Al-Hisba fi al-Islam*, 51.

31. Ibn Ishaq, *Sirat Rasul Allah*, 234.

32. Siddiqi, *Sahih Imam Muslim*, vol. 5, #1771.

33. Ibn Ishaq, *Sirat Rasul Allah*, 235; al-Qayrawani, *A Madinan View on the Sunnah*, 33; and al-Qardawi, *Fiqh az-Zakat*, 15–16, 23.

34. For a good classical examination of *zakat*, see Ibn Naqib al-Misri, *'Umdat al-Salik*, book H, 246–76. It is important to note that while the Prophet strove to be fair in his handling of *zakat*, it is clear that the rules ensure that anything paid is of the proper amount and quality. For example, when *zakat* was paid on grain, it was to be paid after it was winnowed to ensure that no chaff was included in the amount. See ibid., h3.4, 255.

35. Kahn, *Sahih al-Bukhari*, vol. 2, #537.

36. Examples are as follows: from the hadith, Kahn, *Sahih al-Bukhari*, vol. 3, #485, #486, #489, #516; Siddiqi, *Sahih Imam Muslim*, vol. 3, #990; Khaliyl, *Jami' al-Tirmidhi*, vol. 2, #618, #637, #664; Al-Khattab, *Sunan an-Nasa'i*, vol. 3, #2440, #2444, 2446; and Karim, *Al-Hadith, Mishkat-ul-Masabih, al-Tabrizi*, vol. 2, ch. 8, sec. 1, #247w, #248, Sec 2, #252, #254w, #256w. Additional examples can be found in Ibn Kathir, *Tafsir Al-Qur'an Al-'Azim*, 1:684–85, 4:415–18, and 10:237–38.

37. Ibn Sallam, *Kitab al-Amwal*, 554.

38. Ibn Kathir, *Tafsir Al-Qur'an Al-'Azim*, 4:458–59.

39. Ibid., 1:596–97; and Surah 2:216.

40. Kahn, *Sahih al-Bukhari*, vol. 1, #445; and Al-Khattab, *Sunan an-Nasa'i*, vol. 2, #447. While some ancient armies conducted unit-level exercises, there is a decided lack of evidence that they ever engaged in large-scale, army-level training. Even though some professional armies, such as Greek or Roman, did conduct unit training, most armies rarely ever went beyond individual skill-level training. This was the

case even up to the beginning of the modern era, when we began to see some type of formation training. See Luvaas, *Frederick the Great on the Art of War*, 66. Regarding the ancient world, some early authorities speak of small-unit-formation drill and individual weapons training. See Vegetius, *Military Institutions of the Romans*, 89, 94; and Polyaenus, *Stratagems of War*, VIII.16.8. However, the concept of large-scale, army-level training was virtually unknown, save for only a few possible instances or references. Polyaenus, *Stratagems of War*, III.9.10 and III.9.31; and Onasander, *General*, x (1). The medieval European world was possibly more stultified in this regard, with little to no unit training at all. See Boutell, *Arms and Armour*, 98. In most cases, men were typically busied with camp duties, engineering tasks, or foraging. Polyaenus, *Stratagems of War*, III.9.35. For an overview of training in the ancient world, see Delbrück; *History of the Art of War*, 149–50, 180–81, and 283–84.

41. Machiavelli, *The Prince*, 46–47 and 106–7. The technique of actually developing one's own opposition is also used in politics, when a politician, facing a hard-charging opponent, actually recruits another candidate of the same opposition group to get the two to split their constituency, thereby ensuring the politician's victory. Within the United States, some states have laws to try and stop what are called "straw candidates" from running. However, enforcing such laws is naturally very difficult. An excellent classic historical account of creating an enemy who is really a friend involves Camillo Cavour and Vittorio Emanuele of Sardinia, and the incendiary Giuseppe Garibaldi. Garibaldi received the secret financial and moral support of Emanuele, who was bent on uniting Italy under his House of Savoy, while probably also receiving some support from Cavour, though the latter is still debated in history. While many in Garibaldi's band of Red Shirts who invaded Sicily in 1860 wanted a republican government, Garibaldi staunchly supported a monarchy under Emanuele, a point made to his men but not to outsiders. His invasion was portrayed as a disaster to the kingdoms of the Two Sicilies and Naples, who openly welcomed Sardinian troops in an effort to stop it. As such, what looked like a menace turned to the advantage of the House of Savoy, culminating in the crowning of Vittorio Emanuele as the first king of Italy. See Martin, *Red Shirt and the Cross of Savoy*, 532–40, for an overview of the relationship of Garibaldi with the House of Savoy. For some additional thoughts on forming an enemy when one is lacking, see Greene, *48 Laws of Power*, 12–14. In some ways, this concept follows the ancient Chinese stratagem of "befriending an enemy to attack one nearby."

42. Watt, *Muhammad at Medina*, 156–57.

43. Kahn, *Sahih al-Bukhari*, vol. 8, #271; and Ibn Ishaq, *Sirat Rasul Allah*, 491.

44. Hasan, *Sunan Abu Dawud*, vol. 2, #2998.

45. This contention even appears in some of the early accounts. See Ibn Ishaq, *Sirat Rasul Allah*, 372; and Ibn Saʻd, *Kitab al-Tabaqat al-Kabir*, 2:46. However, Ibn Saʻd implies that this may have been a fictitious front. He cites one hadith tradition where "Ibn Ubayyi deserted with a contingent as if he was an oppressed person going in front of them."

46. Al-Waqidi, *Kitab al-Maghazi*, 138; and Watt, *Muhammad at Medina*, 22.

47. Ibn Kathir, *Al-Sira al-Nabawiyya*, 3:119.

48. Ibn Ishaq, *Sirat Rasul Allah*, 437.

49. Kahn, *Sahih al-Bukhari*, vol. 6, #274. The phrase transliterated is *"inna lillahi wa inna ilaihi raji'un."* See Khaliyl, *Jami' al-Tirmidhi*, vol. 6, #3511, for further explanation on this phrase.

50. Ibn Ishaq, *Sirat Rasul Allah*, 496; and Al-Tabari, *Ta'rikh al-rusul wa'l-muluk*, I.I, 1523. 'Ali's suggestion is part of the reason why 'Aisha hated him so intensely.

51. Ibn Ishaq, *Sirat Rasul Allah*, 495.

52. Ibn Kathir, *Al-Sira al-Nabawiyya*, 4:7.

53. Kahn, *Sahih al-Bukhari*, vol. 2, #359, #360, #433, #447; vol. 6, #192, #193, #194; vol. 7, #687; Ansari, *Sunan Ibn-e-Majah*, vol. 2, #1521; and Ibn Ishaq, *Sirat Rasul Allah*, 623.

54. Kahn, *Sahih al-Bukhari*, vol. 6, #192; Ibn Kathir, *Tafsir Al-Qur'an Al-'Azim*, 4:484–85, 524–25; and Surah 9:80.

55. Ibn Kathir, *Al-Sira al-Nabawiyya*, 3:260. Muhammad used his shirt to dress a martyred man before burial.

56. Siddiqi, *Sahih Imam Muslim*, 8, #3029; and Surah 24:33.

57. Ibn Kathir, *Tafsir Al-Qur'an Al-'Azim*, 7:80–82.

58. Ibn Ishaq, *Sirat Rasul Allah*, 492.

59. Ibid., 491; and Kahn, *Sahih al-Bukhari*, vol. 8, #655.

60. Ibn Kathir, *Tafsir Al-Qur'an Al-'Azim*, 9:653–55; and Surah 63:7.

61. Ibn Ishaq, *Sirat Rasul Allah*, 492.

62. Kahn, *Sahih al-Bukhari*, vol. 4, #758; Ibn Sa'd, *Kitab al-Tabaqat al-Kabir*, 1:508–9; and Kahn, *Sahih al-Bukhari*, vol. 9, #357.

63. Ibn Ishaq, *Sirat Rasul Allah*, 239.

64. For example, compare Surah 12:21–35 with Genesis 39:1–23. In explaining these differences, Muhammad and the early Muslims indicated that the Hebrew and Christian scriptures had been adulterated with additions and deletions. For a reasonably thorough discussion of this adulteration, see Ibn Taymiyyah *Al-Jawab al-Sahih*, 210–54.

65. Ibn Kathir, *Al-Sira al-Nabawiyya*, 2:184.

66. This is apparently based on their later agreement with Muhammad to pay him 50 percent of their production so they would be allowed to remain in Khaybar and work their land after they were conquered by the Muslims. The conquest of Khaybar is dealt with in a later chapter.

67. Barreveld, Introduction, Sec. 4.1; and Hashi, Kamoun, and Cianci, 73–75.

68. Ibn Sa'd, *Kitab al-Tabaqat al-Kabir*, 1:483.

69. Hamidullah, *Battlefields of the Prophet Muhammad*, #212, 109.

70. Ibn Sa'd, *Kitab al-Tabaqat al-Kabir*, 2:36.

71. For example, on one raid the men were down to one date per day for their ration. See Kahn, *Sahih al-Bukhari*, vol. 4, #226.

72. Ibn Sa'd, *Kitab al-Tabaqat al-Kabir*, 1:296, cites that only one carpenter plied his trade in Madinah. Ibn Taymiyyah noted that the city imported clothing, an obvious indicator that there were few if any skilled craftsmen available to produce clothes. See Ibn Taymiyyah, *Al-Hisba fi al-Islam*, 37.

73. Gies and Gies, *Cathedral, Forge, and Waterwheel*, 58; and Ashdown, *European Arms & Armour*, 86–87.

74. Norman and Pottinger, *English Weapons and Warfare*, 14.

75. Gies and Gies, *Cathedral, Forge, and Waterwheel*, 64; and Ibn Saʿd, *Kitab al-Tabaqat al-Kabir*, 1:576–77.

76. France, *Western Warfare in the Age of the Crusades*, 32.

77. Kahn, *Sahih al-Bukhari*, vol. 4, ch. 120, 137–38. Slaves would typically cost 800 dirhams but could go for as little as 400 or as high as 3,000 or 10,000 dirhams, depending on their quality. One reference even has a female slave as low as 360 dirhams, with nine *uqiyyah* equal to this amount. See Al-Khattab, *Sunan an-Nasaʾi*, vol. 5, #4660. The cost ratio of horses to slaves in Arabia was far better than in medieval Gaul, but this is indicative of the plentitude of slaves in the former. For variations in the price of slaves, see Khaliyl, *Jamiʿ al-Tirmidhi*, vol. 3, #1260; Kahn, *Sahih al-Bukhari*, vol. 3, #693, and vol. 9, #80, #296; and Hasan, *Sunan Abu Dawud*, vol. 3, #3605. Slave contracts could be as much as 3,000 dirhams as per Al-Khattab, *Sunan an-Nasaʾi*, 4:506–7, ch. 48. For a discussion of the cost ratio of slaves to horses in Gaul, see Boissonnade, *Life and Work in Medieval Europe*, 74.

78. Ibn Saʿd, *Kitab al-Tabaqat al-Kabir*, 1:585; and Khattab, *Sunan an-Nasaʾi*, vol. 5, #4643.

79. This is a point noted by T. E. Lawrence during his operations in the Hijaz during World War I. See Lawrence, *Seven Pillars of Wisdom*, 147.

80. Hill, "Role of the Camel," 34; and Callwell, *Small Wars*, 425. Yet, despite detractors, there are instances in which camels have engaged in cavalry-type charges. For an excellent, albeit humorous, modern example, see Lawrence, *Seven Pillars*, 303–5.

81. Ibn Ishaq, *Sirat Rasul Allah*, 246–47.

Chapter 3. The Road to Badr

1. Al-Tabari, *Taʾrikh al-rusul waʾl-muluk*, I.I, 1265.

2. Hill, "Role of the Camel," 35.

3. Watt, *Muhammad at Medina*, 339–40.

4. Al-Waqidi, *Kitab al-Maghazi*, 33. Al-Tabari indicates these were horsemen, but it is probable his information was mistaken or there was an error in transmission from another source. See al-Tabari, *Taʾrikh al-rusul waʾl-muluk*, I.I, 1267.

5. Bashier, *War and Peace*, 1–2; Qureshi, *Foreign Policy of Hadrat Muhammad*, 185; Rahman, *Muhammad as a Military Leader*, 15–16; Haykal, *Life of Muhammad*, 202–3; and Al-Mubarakpuri, *Sealed Nectar*, 199–200. Interestingly enough, the work done by Ibn Abdul Wahab, the son of the leader of the Wahabi uprising in Arabia, is more forthright about this, indicating that they had the right to fight simply because they had been previously "wronged" while in Makkah. See Ibn Abdul Wahab, *Biography of the Prophet*, 1:367–70.

6. The tables of battles presented were developed from Watt, *Muhammad at Medina*, excursus B, 339–43; Rehman Shaikh, *Chronology of Prophetic Events*, and cross referenced to Ibn Saʿd's *al-Tabaqat* and Ibn Ishaq's *Sirat Rasul Allah*.

7. al-Duyati, "Ibn Nuhaas," 174.

8. Ibn Taymiyyah, *Al-Furqan bayna Awliya*, 144.

9. Nicholson, *Mathnawi of Jalaluʾddin Rumi*, book 1, 76. Sufism is typically misunderstood, for the movement is often interpreted as a mystical ideal that negates the literal interpretation and application of the Qurʾan and hadith literature. Instead,

Sufism accepts the literal interpretation first, and then adds mystical applications beyond the literal meaning. For example, one early Sufi writer states clearly that the Law is to be followed in all of its requirements. See Al-Qushayri, *Al-Risala al-qushayriyya*, 105. Imam al-Ghazali, considered one of the most famous of Sufi masters, stated clearly that philosophers who taught doctrines contrary to the teachings of the Prophet Muhammad were to be classified as infidels and put to death. Al-Ghazali, *Incoherence of the Philosophers*, 226–27. Even one Sufi who is considered to be broadly tolerant in his views accepted the literal interpretation and even application of commands to engage in warfare. Ibn al-Arabi, *Futuhat al-Makkiyah*, sec. 4.24, #327. Regarding the origin of Sufism, see Sedgwick, *Sufism, the Essentials*, 5. Sedgwick also provides an excellent brief overview of the issue of jihad, or physical combat, and how Sufis engage in such fighting, 70–75.

10. Al-Waqidi, *Kitab al-Maghazi*, 33. Al-Waqidi indicates that three hundred were under Abu Jahl countering Hamzah's raid, and then states that two hundred men under Abu Sufyan countered 'Ubaydah's raid. It is possible that both men were escorting the caravan and divided forces, since it is unlikely they were conducting two separate caravans at the same time.

11. Ibn Ishaq, *Sirat Rasul Allah*, 281, 283–84; and Ibn Sa'd, *Kitab al-Tabaqat al-Kabir*, 2:4.

12. Polyaenus, *Stratagems of War*, 3.9.47, points out that night movement in desert areas is critical for conserving water. The obvious reason for noting this was that while Greek forces may have operated in arid climates, they were not prone to conduct operations in deserts and thus needed some type of advice regarding operations in arid wastelands.

13. Onasander, *General*, ch. 39, 1.

14. Jandora, *March from Medina*, 19.

15. Al-Waqidi, *Kitab al-Maghazi*, 34; and Ibn Sa'd, *Kitab al-Tabaqat al-Kabir*, 2:5–6.

16. Ibn Ishaq, *Sirat Rasul Allah*, 281; and Ibn Sa'd, *Kitab al-Tabaqat al-Kabir*, 2:5.

17. Ibn Sa'd, *Kitab al-Tabaqat al-Kabir*, 2:7.

18. Ibid., 6; and Al-Tabari, *Ta'rikh al-rusul wa'l-muluk*, I.I, 1271.

19. Al-Tabari, *Ta'rikh al-rusul wa'l-muluk*, I.I, 1638.

20. Qureshi, *Foreign Policy of Hadrat Muhammad*, 186.

21. Al-Tabari, *Ta'rikh al-rusul wa'l-muluk*, I.I, 1277, implies movement toward the seacoast when he relates another hadith account of the raid that confused another wadi of similar name near Yanbu.

22. Ibn Kathir, *Al-Sira al-Nabawiyya*, 2:245.

23. Compare the account provided by Qureshi, *Foreign Policy of Hadrat Muhammad*, 190, with Ibn Ishaq, *Sirat Rasul Allah*, 287; Ibn Kathir, *Al-Sira al-Nabawiyya*, 2:242; and al-Tabari, *Ta'rikh al-rusul wa'l-muluk*, I.I, 1274.

24. Ibn Ishaq, *Sirat Rasul Allah*, 287.

25. It is worth noting that there may have been a previous raid launched during a sacred month. If so, then the controversy over the violation of the sacred month by 'Abdullah bin Jahsh would appear to be a smoke screen to hide some other issue. See Ibn Kathir, *Al-Sira al-Nabawiyya*, 2:241.

26. Al-Tabari, *Ta'rikh al-rusul wa'l-muluk*, I.I, 1276; and Ibn Kathir, *Al-Sira al-Nabawiyya*, 2:243.

27. Surah 2:217, as quoted in Ibn Kathir, *Tafsir Al-Qur'an Al-'Azim*, 1:598.

28. Ibn Ishaq, *Sirat Rasul Allah*, 313.

29. Ibid., 221. Watt concurs with this assessment. See Watt, *Muhammad at Medina*, 2. A modern-era equivalent is the English Puritans who fled their homeland to settle in colonies in North America during the Great English Migration of the 1630s. While many left during a period of hostility between Puritans and the Crown, there is no evidence to suggest that they could not have returned to England for visitations. What Muhammad and his small group of disciples did was the equivalent to a group of Puritans fleeing to North America and then almost immediately engaging in high seas raids on English shipping.

30. Ibn Sa'd, *Kitab al-Tabaqat al-Kabir*, 2:32, 34, 59, 60, 71, 79, 91, 96, 109, 117, 163, 198, 203. One operation during a sacred month was the armed *umrah* to Makkah that led to the treaty of al-Hudaybiyah. Considering the Prophet's previous track record, it is understandable why the Quraysh opposed his *umrah* at that time. In contrast, the record shows that the Quraysh violated the sacred months just three times, the first a dismal failure, and another leading to the abortive siege of Madinah. See ibid., 33, 71, and 80.

31. See al-Tabari, *Ta'rikh al-rusul wa'l-muluk*, 7:20n46, for an explanation of the development of the division of plunder in days prior to Islam. Naturally, the point could be raised that the one-fifth was a construct after the fact to fit the Islamic legal precept regarding division of spoil that was established later. While this is possible, the record still raises the issue that 'Abdullah may have possibly been trying to divert additional plunder to his small raiding team at the Prophet's expense. To have done that would have been a grave insult to a sayyid or *shaykh*.

32. Ibn Ishaq, *Sirat Rasul Allah*, 288; and Al-Tabari, *Ta'rikh al-rusul wa'l-muluk*, I.I, 1276.

33. Al-Tabari, *Ta'rikh al-rusul wa'l-muluk*, I.I, 1285. Although the Quraysh had discussed the possibility that Muhammad would attack them after his migration to Madinah, there is no clear indication that a state of war existed between the Quraysh and Muslims until the successful raid at Nakhlah. See Ibn Kathir, *Al-Sira al-Nabawiyya*, 2:152.

34. Ibn Ishaq, *Sirat Rasul Allah*, 118, 131. An interesting example of such private warfare involves 'Umar bin al-Khattab while still in Makkah. When pressed by a group ridiculing his Islamic faith, he would grab an elderly chief as a hostage to afford himself protection. In one case a group of polytheists "charged at him and he attacked 'Utba, getting him down and beating him. He poked his fingers into the eye of 'Utba, who began to scream." What does not make sense in this account is the notion that polytheists were physically attacking 'Umar, for even if he was a considerably strong man, it would take only a few to return the beating while he was on the ground pummeling 'Utba. Instead, the sense of the passage and the ones around it was that 'Umar was being ridiculed and responded with physical force to assert himself. See Ibn Kathir, *Al-Sira al-Nabawiyya*, 1:321. In addition to 'Umar, see Muhammad's threat against his uncle Abu Lahab in Surah 111. See Ibn Kathir, *Tafsir Al-Qur'an Al-'Azim*, vol. 10, 622–27. On another occasion, a man mocked Muhammad, and he

later prayed openly that the man would lose the use of his fingers. See Ibn Kathir, *Al-Sira al-Nabawiyya*, 2:30. On another occasion, Muhammad stated that the angel Jibril had cursed the Prophet's persecutors with a death sentence. See Ibn Kathir, *Al-Sira al-Nabawiyya*, 2:56. Regarding the command to now allow the Muslims to fight, see Ibn Ishaq, *Sirat Rasul Allah*, 213; and Ibn Kathir, *Tafsir Al-Qur'an Al-'Azim*, 1:531–34.

35. Al-Tabari, *Ta'rikh al-rusul wa'l-muluk*, I.I, 1285.

36. Al-Waqidi, *Kitab al-Maghazi*, 39. A *mithqal* was the equivalent weight of one dinar, but the shipment was worth much more because it was composed of gold rather than silver.

37. Ibn Ishaq, *Sirat Rasul Allah*, 289.

38. Siddiqi, *Sahih Imam Muslim*, vol. 5, #1901.

39. Ibn Ishaq, *Sirat Rasul Allah*, 336. There is some minor dispute as to the exact numbers. For example, Kahn, *Sahih al-Bukhari*, vol. 5, #292 says there were 60 Muhajirun and 249 Ansar, while the *al-Tabaqat* (2:10) says there were 74 Muhajirun, of 305 total. Other sources vary, with the total ranging from about 300 to 319.

40. Kahn, *Sahih al-Bukhari*, vol. 3, #832.

41. Ibn Kathir, *Al-Sira al-Nabawiyya*, 2:280.

42. Ibn Ishaq, *Sirat Rasul Allah*, 295. Yathrib was of course the pre-Islamic name for Madinah, which was still used by the Quraysh and others in the Hijaz.

43. Ibid., 291.

44. Al-Waqidi, *Kitab al-Maghazi*, 44; and Ibn Sa'd, *Kitab al-Tabaqat al-Kabir*, 2:14. At least one source indicates only sixty horsemen were available for the relief mission while another claims that as many as two hundred cavalry were used. See Ibn Kathir, *Al-Sira al-Nabawiyya*, 2:257.

45. The case of Abu Jahl is a clear example of how victors write the histories. The pejorative name Abu Jahl means "Father of Folly, or Ignorance," an obvious reference to his very vocal opposition to Muhammad and the Muslims. This term will be used throughout this book, but in contrast it should be noted that the Quraysh had nicknamed Muhammad "Mudhammam," which means "reprobate." The use of such nicknames, and that Abu Jahl's became enshrined in history while Muhammad's has been forgotten is a good example of the use of moral inversion. See Ibn Ishaq, *Sirat Rasul Allah*, 162.

46. Ibn Kathir, *Tafsir Al-Qur'an Al-'Azim*, 4:282.

47. Ibn Kathir, *Al-Sira al-Nabawiyya*, 2:257; An-Naisaburi, *Reasons and Occasions of Revelation*, #481; and Al-Waqidi, *Kitab al-Maghazi*, 44.

48. Ibn Sa'd, *Kitab al-Tabaqat al-Kabir*, 2:12.

49. Watt, *Muhammad at Medina*, 11.

50. Al-Tabari, *Ta'rikh al-rusul wa'l-muluk*, I.I, 1306.

51. Recent Muslim writers typically mention how Muhammad's force defeated 1,000 Quraysh on the battlefield. However, there is no doubt that at least several hundred left Abu Jahl's force prior, significantly cutting into the Qurayshi numbers available. See al-Tabari, *Ta'rikh al-rusul wa'l-muluk*, I.I, 1307; and Watt, *Muhammad at Medina*, 11. Examples of recent writings that indicate the Quraysh were one thousand include Qureshi, *Foreign Policy of Hadrat Muhammad*, 195; Bashier, *War and Peace*, 43; and al-Mubarakpuri, *Sealed Nectar*, 211–12. The first two hardly mention that any troops left at all, while the last inflates the initial number leaving Makkah to

1,300, thus explaining how the Quraysh could still have 1,000 at the battle. In reality, it is more likely that they only had about 700 on hand once the fighting started.

52. Al-Tabari, *Ta'rikh al-rusul wa'l-muluk*, I.I, 1311.

53. Ibn Kathir, *Al-Sira al-Nabawiyya*, 2:258.

54. It is the contention of one recent writer that it is a "fable" of Orientalists that Muhammad came out only for the caravan and was unaware of the onrushing Qurayshi relief force. This is patently absurd and does violence to all of the accepted early sources regarding the battle. This writer states that had the Muslims really wanted to attack the caravan they would have marched northwest, a remark that indicts the author's lack of knowledge of the terrain in the area and how such a movement would be extremely difficult if not impossible for a fast-moving army. The trade road to Badr, going southwest, was the most direct and rapid way to reach the caravan route, a point that completely escapes this writer. That the caravan was the initial objective is even alluded to in the Qur'an (Surah 8:7), and is supported by such imminent authorities as Ibn Kathir (*Tafsir Al-Qur'an Al-'Azim*, 4:261). One can only surmise that this was done in a headlong and wholly unnecessary attempt to claim that the Prophet never made an error on the battlefield. See Rizvi, *Battles of the Prophet*, 9.

55. Kahn, *Sahih al-Bukhari*, vol. 5, #287; and Ibn Ishaq, *Sirat Rasul Allah*, 340.

56. Ibn Ishaq, *Sirat Rasul Allah*, 297.

57. Sun Tzu, *Art of War*, ch. 11, 10, 131.

58. Vegetius, *Military Institutions*, 170.

59. Ibn Ishaq, *Sirat Rasul Allah*, 298.

60. Ibn Kathir, *Al-Sira al-Nabawiyya*, 2:262.

61. Ibid., 266.

62. Ibn Sa'd, *Kitab al-Tabaqat al-Kabir*, 2:14; Ibn Ishaq, *Sirat Rasul Allah*, 353; and Al-Tabari, *Ta'rikh al-rusul wa'l-muluk*, I.I, 1289.

63. Al-Tabari, *Ta'rikh al-rusul wa'l-muluk*, I.I, 1314–15.

64. Ibn Sa'd, *Kitab al-Tabaqat al-Kabir*, 2:24.

65. Ibn Ishaq, *Sirat Rasul Allah*, 298; and Ibn Kathir, *Al-Sira al-Nabawiyya*, 2:282.

66. Al-Tabari, *Ta'rikh al-rusul wa'l-muluk*, I.I, 1290.

67. Ibn Kathir, *Tafsir Al-Qur'an Al-'Azim*, 4:281.

68. Ibn Ishaq, *Sirat Rasul Allah*, 347; and Khaliyl *Jami' Al-Tirmidhi*, vol. 3, #1677.

69. Al-Tabari, *Ta'rikh al-rusul wa'l-muluk*, I.I, 1319.

70. Ibn Sa'd, *Kitab al-Tabaqat al-Kabir*, 2:14–15; and Ibn Ishaq, *Sirat Rasul Allah*, 300.

71. An-Naisaburi, *Reasons and Occasions of Revelation*, #469.

72. Ibn Kathir, *Al-Sira al-Nabawiyya*, 2:257–58. There was one other man with a horse, but evidence suggests that this was reserved for Muhammad should he need to escape to Madinah. See ibid., 2:272.

73. Ibn Sa'd, *Kitab al-Tabaqat al-Kabir*, 2:15. The precise nature of this symbol is unknown.

74. Al-Tabari, *Ta'rikh al-rusul wa'l-muluk*, I.I, 1317.

75. Al-Waqidi, *Kitab al-Maghazi*, 49. Al-Waqidi's description implies that the two forces were facing each other almost precisely on an east–west axis.

76. Ibid., 54.

77. Ibn Kathir, *Al-Sira al-Nabawiyya*, 2:288.

78. Al-Waqidi, *Kitab al-Maghazi*, 65.

79. Hamidullah, *Battlefields of the Prophet*, #58, 36; and An-Naisaburi, *Reasons and Occasions of Revelation*, #478.

80. Ibn Ishaq, *Sirat Rasul Allah*, 300.

81. The use of drawn swords to flash light at an enemy was apparently well known to other cultures in the ancient world. See Onasander, *General*, ch. 29, 2. It is also possible they were exposing the blades to the sun to warm them and make them flexible before combat. See al-Tabari, *Ta'rikh al-rusul wa'l-muluk*, I.I, 1941.

82. Ibn Kathir, *Al-Sira al-Nabawiyya*, 2:276.

83. Ibn Ishaq, *Sirat Rasul Allah*, 300; and al-Tabari, *Ta'rikh al-rusul wa'l-muluk*, I.I, 1322.

84. Al-Tabari, *Ta'rikh al-rusul wa'l-muluk*, I.I, 1320.

85. Ibn Ishaq, *Sirat Rasul Allah*, 304.

86. Al-Tabari, *Ta'rikh al-rusul wa'l-muluk*, I.I, 1323.

87. Kahn, *Sahih al-Bukhari*, vol. 5, #300; and Ibn Ishaq, *Sirat Rasul Allah*, 304.

88. Ibn Ishaq, *Sirat Rasul Allah*, 305.

89. The statistics vary regarding the Qurayshi casualties. The numbers provided appear to be the most readily accepted. See Ibn Ishaq, *Sirat Rasul Allah*, 338–39; Al-Waqidi, *Kitab al-Maghazi*, 71; and Ibn Kathir, *Al-Sira al-Nabawiyya*, 2:306. Other deviations on the statistics can be found in *Ibn Sa'd, Kitab al-Tabaqat al-Kabir*, 2:23. Other figures can be found in Siddiqi, *Sahih Imam Muslim*, vol. 5, #1763. Also see Watt, *Muhammad at Medina*, 12.

90. Ibn Ishaq, *Sirat Rasul Allah*, 337.

91. Dodge, *Hannibal*, Appendix A, 669; and Dodge, *Gustavus Adolphus*, Appendix B, 850–51. Unfortunately, we have no statistics regarding the wounded in early Muslim battles and thus cannot make a comparison to overall casualty rates. However, the number of killed in action can be assessed and compared.

92. Ibn Sa'd, *Kitab al-Tabaqat al-Kabir*, 2:23.

93. Ibn Ishaq, *Sirat Rasul Allah*, 301. This order to spare Muhammad's family members upset some of the Muslims. One, Abu Hudhayfah, was forward enough to openly complain, saying that the other Muslims were to kill their brothers and other family members and yet were expected to protect Muhammad's family. This comment reached Muhammad, and Abu Hudhayfah feared for his life afterward, hoping that one day martyrdom in combat would cleanse him of such an affront. His wish was granted when he was killed in action while rallying his command to launch a counterattack at the battle of al-Yamamah in 633.

94. Al-Tabari, *Ta'rikh al-rusul wa'l-muluk*, I.I, 1327; and Ibn Ishaq, *Sirat Rasul Allah*, 303.

95. Ibn Ishaq, *Sirat Rasul Allah*, 164.

96. Ibid., 136.

97. Ibid., 308–9.

98. Ibn Sa'd, *Kitab al-Tabaqat al-Kabir*, 2:24.

99. Ibn Ishaq, *Sirat Rasul Allah*, 310.

100. Ibid., 313.

101. Ibid., 298.

Chapter 4. From Elation to Despair

1. Kahn, *Sahih al-Bukhari*, vol. 9, #447, #77; vol. 4, #392.

2. Ibn Ishaq, *Sirat Rasul Allah*, 363; and al-Tabari, *Ta'rikh al-rusul wa'l-muluk*, I.I, 1359–60.

3. Ibn Ishaq, *Sirat Rasul Allah*, 675–76; al-Waqidi, *Kitab al-Maghazi*, 90; Ibn Sa'd, *Kitab al-Tabaqat al-Kabir*, 2:30–31; and Watt, *Muhammad at Medina*, 178, citing Ibn Hisham.

4. Qadi 'Iyad, *Ash-Shifa*, part 4, ch. 1, sec. 2, 378–79; Ibn Sallam, *Kitab al-Amwal*, 197–81; Haykal, *Life of Muhammad*, 243; Qureshi, *Foreign Policy of Hadrat Muhammad*, 312; Rehman Shaikh, *Chronology of Prophetic Events*, 99; Abu Khalil, *Atlas on the Prophet's Biography*, 123; and Glubb, *Life and Times of Muhammad*, 195.

5. Hasan, *Sunan Abu Dawud*, vol. 3, #4348, #4349; Ibn Naqib al-Misri, *'Umdat al-Salik*, 45, 50, w52.1(26); Ibn Sallam, *Kitab al-Amwal*, 179–81; and Qadi 'Iyad, *Ash-Shifa*, part 4, ch. 1, sec. 2, 376–80.

6. Ibn Sa'd, *Kitab al-Tabaqat al-Kabir*, 2:30.

7. Ibn Ishaq, *Sirat Rasul Allah* 676.

8. Ibn Sa'd, *Kitab al-Tabaqat al-Kabir*, 2:31.

9. Ibid. While Ibn Sa'd indicated that the weather was hot at the time, this appears to be inconsistent with the date of the incident, or that it was possible the region had experienced a brief heat wave during the period in question.

10. Al-Tabari, *Ta'rikh al-rusul wa'l-muluk*, I.I, 1364.

11. Ibn Sa'd, *Kitab al-Tabaqat al-Kabir*, 2:34.

12. Ibid., 32.

13. Quoted in Ibn Kathir, *Al-Sira al-Nabawiyya*, 3:3.

14. Esposito, *Oxford Dictionary of Islam*, 112; and Guindi, *Veil*, 13–22. While the veil did predate Islam, the evidence suggests that Muhammad's later use of the veil for his wives was patterned after the Persian model. See Guindi, *Veil*, 14–16. The evidence also suggests that the purpose of the veil was not so much about modesty as it was about protecting the rights, privileges, and perhaps even the safety of the sayyid or nobleman to whom the woman belonged. Ibid., 92–95. Also see Ibn al-Arabi, *Futuhat al-Makkiyah*, sec. 4.75, #800. There is also some early evidence that the veil was used to culturally divide married women from single women, especially if the latter were behaving much like prostitutes, with some of those even wearing the veil. See an-Naisaburi, *Reasons and Occasions of Revelation*, #718, #719; and Ibn Kathir, *Tafsir Al-Qur'an Al-'Azim*, 8:45–46. Indeed, murdering a tribal leader for his wife was not unknown in the Middle Eastern world, as attested to by the accusations leveled against Khalid bin al-Walid, who had a man judicially killed to seize his wife during the Riddah. See Al-Tabari, *Ta'rikh al-rusul wa'l-muluk*, I.I, 1924–27. Muhammad had cause to be concerned because he survived a number of assassination attempts. In one instance, a group of men wearing the *aakal*, or male version of the veil used to protect oneself from the elements, infiltrated Muhammad's entourage with the express purpose of pushing him from his mount and over a cliff. See an-Naisaburi, *Reasons and Occasions of Revelation*, #516.

15. Surah 8:58.

16. Al-Tabari, *Ta'rikh al-rusul wa'l-muluk*, I.I, 1360.

17. Ibn Kathir, *Tafsir Al-Qur'an Al-'Azim*, 4:341–42.

18. A treaty could, or at least should, not be used to cover aggressive action by a Muslim army. During the *khalifate* of Mu'awiyah, the *khalifa* attempted to attack the Byzantines during an active treaty, and even advanced his army to the frontier before he was admonished that he should not do this, at which point Mu'awiyah desisted. See Khaliyl, *Jami' al-Tirmidhi*, vol. 3, #1580.

19. Ibn Sa'd, *Kitab al-Tabaqat al-Kabir*, 2:32.

20. Al-Tabari, *Ta'rikh al-rusul wa'l-muluk*, I.I, 1361. Guillaume's translation of Ibn Ishaq appears to be too genteel here. It is apparent that Muhammad was cursing 'Abdullah for interfering.

21. Ibn Ishaq, *Sirat Rasul Allah*, 363.

22. The wholesale slaughter of prisoners of war was by and large an innovation in ancient warfare, for most would be typically sold as slaves. To actually put to death a group of able-bodied men would have normally been considered a waste of resources, done in the extreme only to make a very harsh example. However, the vanquished were always at the mercy of the victor. After all, one of Julius Caesar's Gallic opponents is quoted as saying, "It was the right of war that conquerors dictated as they pleased to the conquered," and there is no record that Julius Caesar disagreed. See Caesar, *Gallic War*, book I, 36. Yet some examples of the slaughter of prisoners can be found in various ancient records, as can examples where they were spared. Regarding examples where they are put to death, see Garsoian, *Buzandaran Patmut'iwnk'*, book 4, ch. 23, 156; book 4, ch. 58, 178. For examples where prisoners are spared, see ibid., book 4, ch. 55, 175–76; Mango, *Nikephoros Patriarch of Constantinople*, #10, 53; and John of Nikiu, *Chronicle of John*, CVII, 37, 38. Onasander states that prisoners should by and large be spared. See Onasander, *General*, ch. 35(1), 1–2.

23. Ibn Sa'd, *Kitab al-Tabaqat al-Kabir*, 2:34.

24. Al-Waqidi, *Kitab al-Maghazi*, 100; and Ibn Ishaq, *Sirat Rasul Allah*, 364.

25. Ibn Sa'd, *Kitab al-Tabaqat al-Kabir*, 2:40.

26. Al-Waqidi, *Kitab al-Maghazi*, 101.

27. Al-Tabari, *Ta'rikh al-rusul wa'l-muluk*, I.I, 1798; Al-Baladhuri, *Kitab Futuh al-Buldan*, part 1, 93, 141. Al-Tabari, *Ta'rikh al-rusul wa'l-muluk*, vol. 11, n137. There are some sources that indicate Furat became a Muslim at the battle of al-Khandaq, having been captured as a Makkan spy. Regardless of the accounts, it is of interest that he is seen operating as an undercover agent in his early years and only later commanded troops during the wars of conquest. Perhaps spying and being a secret agent is truly a young man's game.

28. Ibn Sa'd, *Kitab al-Tabaqat al-Kabir*, vol. 2. 41–42. Both Ibn Sa'd and al-Waqidi indicate that Muhammad's share of one-fifth came to twenty thousand dirhams, of which only four thousand dirhams would belong to him for his personal use. This implies that the total amount was equal to one hundred thousand dirhams or more.

29. Ibn Ishaq, *Sirat Rasul Allah*, 364.

30. Ibid., 370.

31. Ibn Sa'd, *Kitab al-Tabaqat al-Kabir*, 2:42.

32. Ibn Ishaq, *Sirat Rasul Allah*, 366.

33. Al-Tabari, *Ta'rikh al-rusul wa'l-muluk*, I.I, 1370.

34. Ibn Sa'd, *Kitab al-Tabaqat al-Kabir*, 2:36; and Ibn Kathir, *Al-Sira al-Nabawi-yya*, 3:8.

35. Kahn, *Sahih al-Bukhari*, vol. 5, #369.

36. Ibn Ishaq, *Sirat Rasul Allah*, 368.

37. Ibn Sa'd, *Kitab al-Tabaqat al-Kabir*, 2:37.

38. Ibn Ishaq, *Sirat Rasul Allah*, 369.

39. Ibn Sa'd, *Kitab al-Tabaqat al-Kabir*, 2:37.

40. Al-Waqidi, *Kitab al-Maghazi*, 98. The translation provided in Ibn Ishaq, *Sirat Rasul Allah*, 369 ("marvelous") and al-Tabari, Ta'rikh *al-rusul wa'l-muluk*, I.I, 1373 ("marvel"), would seem to be poorly worded, as these words imply that the concept was magnificent, rather than frightening, which seems to be the true implication here.

41. Ibn Sa'd, *Kitab al-Tabaqat al-Kabir*, 2:39.

42. Al-Tabari, Ta'rikh *al-rusul wa'l-muluk*, vol. 7, n165. Wellhausen translates al-Waqidi's description as a "confederation of Arabs."

43. For details of Watt's analysis see Watt, *Muhammad at Mecca*, 154–57. Watt does support the notion of black slaves being used to fight in this battle based on some hadith evidence. See an-Naisaburi, *Reasons and Occasions of Revelation*, #481.

44. Ibn Sa'd, *Kitab al-Tabaqat al-Kabir*, 2:43.

45. Al-Waqidi, *Kitab al-Maghazi*, 102; and Ibn Sa'd, *Kitab al-Tabaqat al-Kabir*, 2:43.

46. Ibn Sa'd, *Kitab al-Tabaqat al-Kabir*, 2:44.

47. Ibn Ishaq, *Sirat Rasul Allah*, 372.

48. Hamidullah, *Battlefields of the Prophet*, #94, 52.

49. Ibn Sa'd, *Kitab al-Tabaqat al-Kabir*, 2:45.

50. Kahn, *Sahih al-Bukhari*, vol. 5, #423.

51. Ibn Sa'd, *Kitab al-Tabaqat al-Kabir*, 2:45.

52. Ibn Ishaq, *Sirat Rasul Allah*, 372.

53. Al-Waqidi, *Kitab al-Maghazi*, 138. Watt concurs with this assessment; see *Muhammad at Medina*, 22. As for Al-Waqidi, he quotes one of the Makkans after the battle saying, "We were pleased with the victory and decided to return, having learned that Ibn Ubayy with the third part of men and other Madinans in the city were those who remained behind, and we were not safe from an attack" (138).

54. Kahn, *Sahih al-Bukhari*, vol. 5, #394; and Al-Tabari, Ta'rikh *al-rusul wa'l-muluk*, I.I, 1394.

55. Kahn, *Sahih al-Bukhari*, vol. 5, #375.

56. Wise, *Medieval Warfare*, 92–93; and Ayton, "Arms, Armour, and Horses," 203–4. The best effective range of a common bow is only about fifty yards, although it would seem likely that those used by Muhammad's men were more effective than this. See Marcy, *Prairie Traveler*, 221.

57. Hamidullah, *Battlefields of the Prophet*, #96, 52–53. Hamidullah indicates that Hamzah's grave was washed out and his body reburied in its current location. Such a change in an important memorial could also alter where many believed the archers were posted.

58. Al-Waqidi, *Kitab al-Maghazi*, 107–8; and Ibn Sa'd, *Kitab al-Tabaqat al-Kabir*, 2:46.

59. Al-Waqidi, *Kitab al-Maghazi*, 108; and Ibn Sa'd, *Kitab al-Tabaqat al-Kabir*,

2:46. Contrary to the previous two, Ibn Ishaq, *Sirat Rasul Allah*, 373, reverses this order, but al-Waqidi and Ibn Saʿd's accounts would make more sense because Khalid's mission was to turn the Muslim flank. Moreover, there is some confusion regarding who actually commanded the cavalry on each flank. It would appear that ʿAmr bin al-ʿAs was the overall cavalry commander while Ikrimah and Khalid commanded individual cavalry detachments on each flank, although al-Waqidi draws a distinction between Khalid commanding the right "wing" (Ger. Flügel) and Ikrimah commanding the "cavalry" (Ger. Reiterei). If ʿAmr bin al-ʿAs did command some cavalry it would imply a small cavalry reserve. See Ibn Saʿd, *Kitab al-Tabaqat al-Kabir*, 2:46.

60. Ibn Ishaq, *Sirat Rasul Allah*, 373.

61. Ibn Saʿd, *Kitab al-Tabaqat al-Kabir*, 2:46.

62. Al-Tabari, *Taʾrikh al-rusul waʾl-muluk*, I.I, 1214.

63. Ibid., 1398.

64. Ibn Kathir, *Tafsir Al-Qurʾan Al-ʿAzim*, 4:514.

65. Ibn Saʿd, *Kitab al-Tabaqat al-Kabir*, 2:47.

66. Al-Tabari, *Taʾrikh al-rusul waʾl-muluk*, I.I, 1394–95.

67. Al-Tabari relates that ʿAli let Talhah live, only for another to kill him. See al-Tabari, *Taʾrikh al-rusul waʾl-muluk*, I.I, 1396.

68. Ibn Kathir, *Al-Sira al-Nabawiyya*, 3:21.

69. Al-Tabari, *Taʾrikh al-rusul waʾl-muluk*, I.I, 1401.

70. Ibn Ishaq, *Sirat Rasul Allah*, 376. A Sufi legend says that Hamzah refused to wear any armor on the battlefield. When he was told that he was violating the Qurʾanic injunction not to cast oneself wantonly into the hands of destruction (Surah 2:195), he replied that since he was now following the Light of the Prophet, he was no longer a subject of this world, and there was no reason for him not to hasten to death. See Nicholson, *Mathnawi of Jalaluʾddin Rumi*, book 3, 192–96.

71. Ibn Ishaq, *Sirat Rasul Allah*, 379.

72. Ibn Saʿd, *Kitab al-Tabaqat al-Kabir*, 2:49. One author believes that Khalid went to the left, circling the base of Mount Uhud. This would be impossible because the distance is more than twelve miles and would have taken several hours to complete the movement. See Rahman, *Muhammad as a Military Leader*, map after 223.

73. There is some controversy over the issue of the stirrup and when tribes in Arabia actually gained possession of such a piece of equipment. It is possible that some of the men may have been using some form of stirrup by this time because this device was known to cultures to their north and they would have learned of it during their trading. See Haldon, *Warfare, State and Society*, 129. One view indicates that neither the Quraysh nor the early Muslims would have known of the stirrup due to a lack of linguistic information from documents of the era. See Kennedy, *Armies of the Caliphs*, 171.

74. Kahn, *Sahih al-Bukhari*, vol. 5, #394.

75. Ibid., #377.

76. Ibid., ch. 20, 272; and Ibn Kathir, *Tafsir Al-Qurʾan Al-ʿAzim*, 2:296.

77. Ibn Saʿd, *Kitab al-Tabaqat al-Kabir*, 2:49. Some sources like to credit this incident to Iblis, that is the devil, crying out to create more confusion within the ranks of the Muslims. However, many early Islamic sources attribute the malevolent cries of men to the inspiration of the devil, and sometimes to even indicate that the devil

would assume another's physical appearance to deceive men. For one example, see Ibn Ishaq, *Sirat Rasul Allah*, 292. Instead, the declaration could have actually come from one of the Quraysh because it was not an uncommon tactic to declare an enemy general to be slain to dishearten the enemy. See Onasander, *General*, ch. 23. 1–2.

78. Ibn Sa'd, *Kitab al-Tabaqat al-Kabir*, 2:49.

79. Ibn Ishaq, *Sirat Rasul Allah*, 381.

80. Kahn, *Sahih al-Bukhari*, vol. 5, #400.

81. Al-Baladhuri, *Kitab Futuh al-Buldan*, part 1, 92 139. Although also known as Simak bin Kharashah, he should not be confused with another of the same name. See al-Tabari, *Ta'rikh al-rusul wa'l-muluk*, I.I, 2363.

82. Ibn Ishaq, *Sirat Rasul Allah*, 381; Ibn Sa'd, *Kitab al-Tabaqat al-Kabir*, 2:49; and Kahn, *Sahih al-Bukhari*, vol. 5, #393.

83. Ibn Ishaq, *Sirat Rasul Allah*, 381.

84. Kahn, *Sahih al-Bukhari*, vol. 4, #276; vol. 5, #375.

85. Ibn Kathir, *Al-Sira al-Nabawiyya*, 2:59.

86. Clausewitz, *On War*, book 8, 6. B, 605.

87. Ibid., book 1, 1, 2, 75.

88. Sun Tzu, *Art of War*, book 2, 3, 73.

89. Antoine-Henri de Jomini, *Art of War*, 14; Hughes and Bell, *Moltke on the Art of War*, 24; Mao, *On Guerrilla Warfare*, 92; Mao, *Selected Military Writings*, 78–79; and Guevara, *Guerrilla Warfare*, 9–10.

90. Kahn, *Sahih al-Bukhari*, vol. 1, #24, vol. 4, #288, vol. 6, ch. 103, 106; Siddiqi, *Sahih Imam Muslim*, vol. 5, #1780R2; Hasan, *Sunan Abu Dawud*, vol. 2, #2635; Al-Khattab, *Sunan an-Nasa'i*, vol. 1, #702; Ansari, *Sunan Ibn-e-Majah*, #2810; and As-Sanani, *Bulugh al-Maram*, book 11 #1126, 446. This principle of total victory would be echoed by classical and medieval Muslim scholars when discussing the nature of war. See Khadduri, *Islamic Law of Nations* ch. 1, 1, 75–77 (ca. 800); Al-Mawardi, *Al-Ahkam al-Sultaniyya*, 53 (ca. 1100); Ibn Rushd, *Bidayat al-Mujtahid*, vol. 1, sec. 10.1.7, 464 (ca. 1190); Ibn Taymiyyah, *On Public and Private Law*, 135 (ca. 1320); and Ibn Naqib al-Misri, *'Umdat al-Salik*, o9.0, 599 (ca. 1350). Also see Al-Ansari, *Tafrij al-Kurub Fi Tadbir al-Hurub*, 39; and Ibn Khaldun, *Muqaddimah*, 1:287 (ca. 1400).

91. Ibn Ishaq, *Sirat Rasul Allah*, 403.

92. Al-Tabari, *Ta'rikh al-rusul wa'l-muluk*, I.I, 1320.

93. Ibn Ishaq, *Sirat Rasul Allah*, 387.

94. Kahn, *Sahih al-Bukhari*, vol. 5, #404. Onasander noted centuries prior that a defeated general could retrieve his situation by engineering some type of success in the immediate aftermath of defeat. See Onasander, *General*, ch. 36 (2), 3–4.

95. Al-Tabari, *Ta'rikh al-rusul wa'l-muluk*, I.I, 1419.

96. Ibn Sa'd, *Kitab al-Tabaqat al-Kabir*, 2:58–59.

97. Al-Tabari, *Ta'rikh al-rusul wa'l-muluk*, I.I, 1429.

Chapter 5. From the Mountain to the Trench

1. Ibn Ishaq, *Sirat Rasul Allah*, 427–28.

2. Ibn Kathir, *Al-Sira al-Nabawiyya*, 3:92–93.

3. Ibn Ishaq, *Sirat Rasul Allah*, 673–75. Guillaume, the translator of Ibn Ishaq's

work, placed this account out of chronological order, apparently due to the necessity of organizing fragments of Ibn Ishaq's work from other sources.

4. Al-Tabari, *Ta'rikh al-rusul wa'l-muluk*, I.I, 1438.

5. Ibid., 1440.

6. Ibid., 1441.

7. Ibn Sa'd, *Kitab al-Tabaqat al-Kabir*, 2:59.

8. Al-Waqidi, *Kitab al-Maghazi*, 153; and al-Tabari, *Ta'rikh al-rusul wa'l-muluk*, I.I, 1442.

9. Ibn Ishaq, *Sirat Rasul Allah*, 434; Ibn Sa'd, *Kitab al-Tabaqat al-Kabir*, 2:61; and al-Waqidi, *Kitab al-Maghazi*, 153.

10. Ibn Sa'd, *Kitab al-Tabaqat al-Kabir*, 2:65.

11. Ibn Ishaq, *Sirat Rasul Allah*, 434; and Ibn Sa'd, *Kitab al-Tabaqat al-Kabir*, 2:62.

12. Ibn Sa'd, *Kitab al-Tabaqat al-Kabir*, 2:63.

13. Qureshi, *Letters of the Holy Prophet Muhammad*, #12, 36.

14. Ibn Sa'd, *Kitab al-Tabaqat al-Kabir*, 2:39.

15. An-Naisaburi, *Reasons and Occasions of Revelation*, #803.

16. Ibn Ishaq, *Sirat Rasul Allah*, 437.

17. Ibn Sa'd, *Kitab al-Tabaqat al-Kabir*, 2:69.

18. Al-Waqidi, *Kitab al-Maghazi*, 162; Ibn Ishaq, *Sirat Rasul Allah*, 437; and Ibn Sa'd, *Kitab al-Tabaqat al-Kabir*, 2:69.

19. Ibn Kathir, *Tafsir Al-Qur'an Al-'Azim*, 9:545.

20. Al-Waqidi, *Kitab al-Maghazi*, 163.

21. Ibn Kathir, *Tafsir Al-Qur'an Al-'Azim*, 9:545. This fact is excluded from the *sira* literature, such as Ibn Ishaq and al-Tabari, even though it is referenced in the hadith literature.

22. Ibn Ishaq, *Sirat Rasul Allah*, 437.

23. Surah 59:5.

24. Surah 59:2; and Ibn Ishaq, *Sirat Rasul Allah*, 438.

25. Al-Waqidi, *Kitab al-Maghazi*, 164; and Ibn Ishaq, *Sirat Rasul Allah*, 437.

26. Ibn Sa'd, *Kitab al-Tabaqat al-Kabir*, 2:70.

27. Kahn, *Sahih al-Bukhari*, vol. 5, #547, #548.

28. Ibn Ishaq, *Sirat Rasul Allah*, 438.

29. Siddiqi, *Sahih Imam Muslim*, vol. 5, #1757.

30. Surah 59:4. This perspective is reinforced by some early hadith, with the al-Nadir simply showing enmity to the Prophet and Muslims. See an-Naisaburi, *Reasons and Occasions of Revelation*, #802.

31. Ibn Ishaq, *Sirat Rasul Allah*, 445.

32. Ibn Sa'd, *Kitab al-Tabaqat al-Kabir*, 2:72–73.

33. Ibn Ishaq, *Sirat Rasul Allah*, 447.

34. Ibid., 448.

35. Al-Waqidi, *Kitab al-Maghazi*, 175; and Ibn Sa'd, *Kitab al-Tabaqat al-Kabir*, 2:76.

36. Ibn Ishaq, *Sirat Rasul Allah*, 449.

37. Watt, *Muhammad at Mecca*, 10.

38. Ibn Ishaq, *Sirat Rasul Allah*, 450; and Ibn Sa'd, *Kitab al-Tabaqat al-Kabir*, 2:80.

39. Al-Waqidi, *Kitab al-Maghazi*, 191 and n2.

40. Ibid., 191; and Ibn Sa'd, *Kitab al-Tabaqat al-Kabir*, 2:80.

41. Al-Waqidi, *Kitab al-Maghazi*, 191–92.

42. Watt would disagree regarding the numbers, but it is unnecessary to get contentious here. See Watt, *Muhammad at Medina*, 36.

43. Al-Tabari, *Ta'rikh al-rusul wa'l-muluk*, I.I, 1463; and al-Waqidi, *Kitab al-Maghazi*, 191.

44. Hamidullah, *Battlefields of the Prophet*, #124, 64.

45. Al-Tabari, *Ta'rikh al-rusul wa'l-muluk*, I.I, 1469. Muhammad understood the psychology of his people and the need to put his own hand to arduous tasks at a critical moment. See Onasander, *General*, ch. 42 (2), 2.

46. Hamidullah, *Battlefields of the Prophet*, #131, 68–69.

47. Al-Waqidi, *Kitab al-Maghazi*, 195; and Ibn Sa'd, *Kitab al-Tabaqat al-Kabir*, 2:81. The statistics for this were developed from Dept. of the Army, *U.S. Army Field Manual 5–34*, 4–1. The construction of a two-man fighting position was examined to estimate the amount of earth moved. Then, determining that two men could dig ten cubic feet of earth in one hour, this established how much earth could be moved with three thousand men working twelve-hour shifts for six days. Naturally, this is only an estimate. There are numerous variables that could alter this analysis, such as soil quality, the physical fitness of the personnel involved in the operation, and the tools used. The reference in al-Waqidi's *Kitab al-Maghazi* regarding Salman al-Farisi's ability to dig five cubits (ninety feet) in length and five cubits in depth is a useless statistic because it not only excludes the width but also the time in which he could do this. See al-Waqidi, *Kitab al-Maghazi*, 193.

48. Al-Tabari, *Ta'rikh al-rusul wa'l-muluk*, I.III, 229. The claimant was Muhammad bin 'Abdullah, the "Pure Soul" who was a descendent of the Prophet through 'Ali bin Abu Talib. For an overview of this rebellion, see Kennedy, *When Baghdad Ruled the Muslim World*, 21–26.

49. Ibn Sa'd, *Kitab al-Tabaqat al-Kabir*, 2:82; and Ibn Ishaq, *Sirat Rasul Allah*, 453.

50. Al-Waqidi, *Kitab al-Maghazi*, 192.

51. Ibn Ishaq, *Sirat Rasul Allah*, 453.

52. Ibn Sa'd, *Kitab al-Tabaqat al-Kabir*, 2:83.

53. Ibn Ishaq, *Sirat Rasul Allah*, 455.

54. Ibid., 456.

55. Al-Tabari, *Ta'rikh al-rusul wa'l-muluk*, I.I, 1476.

56. Ibn Sa'd, *Kitab al-Tabaqat al-Kabir*, 2:83–84.

57. Ibn Sa'd, *Kitab al-Tabaqat al-Kabir*, 2:84; and Ibn Ishaq, *Sirat Rasul Allah*, 454.

58. Ibn Ishaq, *Sirat Rasul Allah*, 458; and Siddiqi, *Sahih Imam Muslim*, vol. 5, #1739. From the evidence available, it appears that the Prophet said this on a number of occasions.

59. Al-Waqidi, *Kitab al-Maghazi*, 207.

60. Ibn Ishaq, *Sirat Rasul Allah*, 458–59.

61. Ibn Sa'd, *Kitab al-Tabaqat al-Kabir*, 2:85.

62. Ibn Ishaq, *Sirat Rasul Allah*, 469. Slightly different numbers are given in Ibn Sa'd, *Kitab al-Tabaqat al-Kabir*, 2:85–86.

63. Ibn Sa'd, *Kitab al-Tabaqat al-Kabir*, 2:87; Ibn Kathir, *Al-Sira al-Nabawiyya*, 3:158; al-Tabari, *Ta'rikh al-rusul wa'l-muluk*, I.I, 1479; and al-Baladhuri, *Kitab Futuh al-Buldan*, part I, 21, 40.

64. Ibn Sa'd, *Kitab al-Tabaqat al-Kabir*, 2:95. During the siege of the Banu al-Nadir, Muhammad turned on the Banu Qurayzah for reasons unknown. If this was merely to keep them from assisting the al-Nadir, one must ask the question about what kind of agreement even existed at this late date.

65. Al-Waqidi, *Kitab al-Maghazi*, 210.

66. Kahn, *Sahih al-Bukhari*, vol. 5, #443; and Siddiqi, *Sahih Imam Muslim*, vol. 5, #1769.

67. Siddiqi, *Sahih Imam Muslim*, vol. 5, #1769R3.

68. Al-Tabari, *Ta'rikh al-rusul wa'l-muluk*, I.I, 1486.

69. Ibn Sa'd, *Kitab al-Tabaqat al-Kabir*, 2:92. Some sources quoted by Ibn Sa'd say the siege was shorter. See ibid., 94.

70. Al-Waqidi, *Kitab al-Maghazi*, 212.

71. Ibn Sa'd, *Kitab al-Tabaqat al-Kabir*, 2:95.

72. Surah 2:65; 5:60; 7:166; and Ibn Kathir, *Tafsir Al-Qur'an Al-'Azim*, 1:253–54, 4:191–92. It is possible that ancient Hebraic practice allowed for warfare on the Sabbath. When Joshua conquered Jericho it is recorded that his army marched about its walls for seven consecutive days, thus indicating that one of those days was the Sabbath. Under the pressure of the moment, the Jewish leaders of the Qurayzah may have forgotten this, or interpreted this differently. See Joshua 6:6-27.

73. Ibn Ishaq, *Sirat Rasul Allah*, 462.

74. Ibid. Al-Tabari, *Ta'rikh al-rusul wa'l-muluk*, I.I, 1489.

75. Ibn Ishaq, *Sirat Rasul Allah*, 463.

76. Ibid., 464.

77. Al-Tabari, *Ta'rikh al-rusul wa'l-muluk*, I.I, 1497. Sources vary on the number killed, from as low as four hundred to as high as nine hundred. See Ibn Kathir, *Al-Sira al-Nabawiyya*, 3:166; and Ibn Ishaq, *Sirat Rasul Allah*, 464.

78. Watt, *Muhammad at Medina*, 216.

79. Al-Waqidi, *Kitab al-Maghazi*, 221.

80. Khaliyl, *Jami' al-Tirmidhi*, vol. 3, #1260; Kahn, *Sahih al-Bukhari*, vol. 9, #80, #296; and Al-Khattab, *Sunan an-Nasa'i*, vol. 5, #4660.

81. Al-Waqidi, *Kitab al-Maghazi*, 215. For some reason Ibn Sa'd, *Kitab al-Tabaqat al-Kabir*, 2:92, lists two thousand spears. This is possibly a mistake made in the transmission of the source.

82. Ibn Ishaq, *Sirat Rasul Allah*, 480.

83. Kahn, *Sahih al-Bukhari*, vol. 5, #435.

84. Ibid., vol. 4, ch. 122, 139–40.

85. Ibn Ishaq, *Sirat Rasul Allah*, 515. A later tradition provided by the Sufi Rumi supports this contention that Muhammad was being called a king. See Nicholson, *Mathnawi of Jalalu'ddin Rumi*, book 5, 7.

86. The notable exception to this is Jandora, *March from Medina*, 40–41. However, while he raises the issue, he provides no evidence or analysis as to his conclusion.

87. Landau-Tasseron, "Features of the Pre-Conquest Muslim Army," 303, 314n69, 332n164.

88. For example, see the numbers of men attributed to a Persian army when invading Armenia in the fourth century AD. See Garsoian, *Buzandaran Patmut'iwnk'*, book 4, ch. 55, 173. Here, the chronicler notes the Persian army was composed of 5 million men.

89. A good brief discussion of the impact of opportunity cost can be found in Brauer and Tuyll, *Castles, Battles, & Bombs*, 11–15.

90. Rothenberg, *Art of Warfare in the Age of Napoleon*, 129.

91. Caesar, *Gallic War*, 5, 24.

92. Dodge, *Hannibal*, 395–96, 633–34, 639–40. Also see Fuller, *Military History of the Western World*, 1:137.

93. See Record, *Beating Goliath*. However, while Record discusses the need for outside support, he still fails to adequately address the crucial need for outside logistical support for insurgency operations, especially in the early stages.

94. Mao, *Selected Military Writings*, 141.

95. Ibid., 203.

96. Mao, *On Guerrilla Warfare*, 78, 105p, and 102.

97. Ibid., 97. Ibn Taymiyyah stated that when men were tasked to go on a military campaign, the government could compel others who were more adept at farming to work the fields of those who had departed. Therefore, within the early doctrine of Islam, all within the community participated in warfare, either as fighters or as those who support those going into battle. See Ibn Taymiyyah, *Al-Hisba fi al-Islam*, 40.

98. James, *Complete Bolivian Diaries*. For shortage of cash, see: 106; lack of proper shoes, 109; shortage of provisions, 121; need for international monetary support, 127; men weakened and suffering edema, 156; lack of medicine for Che's asthma, 172; and serious lack of water, 200. Even when they did capture supplies and weapons, they often did not have the means to move them and had to leave them behind, 187.

99. Guevara, *Motorcycle Diaries*, 126, 128–33, 138. It is interesting to see his description of Easter Island, where the women did all the work and men did absolutely nothing but laze around (69). Moreover, he describes "good people," who are clearly those who offer to pay his way; at one point he even explains how he had to get his asthma medication by employing the "banal method of paying for it" (141).

100. Shlapentokh, "Revolutionary as a Career," 336–37, 341–43. Peter Stolypin, as interior minister for Czar Nicholas II, strove to crush the revolutionary movements through a series of repressions and reforms. He focused in particular on the funding mechanism for the insurgents prior to his assassination (ibid., 347–48). Moreover, despite Herculean efforts to raise money through criminal activity, the lion's share of the financing came from governments outside Russia (ibid., 350, 352). Regarding a comparison of competitive salaries for revolutionaries, see ibid., 354–56.

101. An analysis of Ibn Sa'd, *Kitab al-Tabaqat al-Kabir*, 2:97–115.

102. Ibid., 2:97.

103. Khalid, *Mukhtasar of al-Khiraqi*, sec. 26.1, 164; and al-Tabari, *Kitab al-Jihad*, sec. 34.1.

104. Hoyt, *Guerilla*, 192–93. The L-59 carried but 311,000 rounds of rifle ammunition, enough to provide just two basic loads of 60 rounds each for Lettow-Vorbeck's men. It also carried machine-gun ammunition and critical medical supplies, and remained aloft for more than ninety-five hours, traveling more than four thousand miles before being recalled by the German High Command over the Sudan. See Banks, *Military Atlas of the First World War*, 285.

105. Lettow-Vorbeck, *My Reminiscences of East Africa*, 220.

106. Ibid., 223, 235, 238, 255, 282.

107. Ibid., 255, 268, 276, 280, 307.

108. Ibid., 261–62.

109. Lawrence, *Seven Pillars of Wisdom*, 274.

110. Ibn Ishaq, *Sirat Rasul Allah*, 487.

111. Al-Tabari, *Ta'rikh al-rusul wa'l-muluk*, I.III, 229.

112. Al-Waqidi, *Kitab al-Maghazi*, 330; and Rehman Shaikh, *Chronology of Prophetic Events*, 114.

113. Adil, *Letters of Hadrat 'Umar Farooq*, #129, 115–16.

114. Kahn, *Sahih al-Bukhari*, vol. 4, ch. 120, 137–38. Muhammad purchased one of his horses for only four hundred dirhams, which was a significant discount. Needless to say, this was a special offer made only to the Prophet. See Ibn Sa'd, *Kitab al-Tabaqat al-Kabir*, 1:581.

115. Hasan, *Sunan Abu Dawud*, vol. 2, #3450.

116. Khaliyl, *Jami' al-Tirmidhi*, vol. 3, #1260; Kahn, *Sahih al-Bukhari*, vol. 3, #693; vol. 8, #707; vol. 9, #80 and #296; Al-Khattab, *Sunan an-Nasa'i*, vol. 5, #4057; vol. 4, ch. 48, 506–7; and Siddiqi, *Sahih Imam Muslim*, vol. 5, #997. Female slaves were valued much less, in one case being sold for 360 dirhams. See Al-Khattab, *Sunan an-Nasa'i*, vol. 5, #4660. However, there is a case where a female slave went for 1,000 dirhams. See Bewley, *Al-Muwatta of Imam Malik ibn Anas*, 31.1.

117. Kahn, *Sahih al-Bukhari*, vol. 3, #459; vol. 9, #109.

118. This figure provides a fascinating comparison regarding the actual level of accumulated wealth between the Muslims and the Sasanid Empire. For example, when Khusrau II was attempting to seize the throne of the empire from his father, he moved 20 million dirhams to the Byzantines to secure their military support for the venture. See al-Tabari, *Ta'rikh al-rusul wa'l-muluk*, I.I, 1000. Later, in AD 607–8, his collected tax revenue exceeded 600 million dirhams. See ibid., I.I, 1042. An additional comparison to demonstrate the monetary assets that the Prophet would have required can be found in Ibn Khaldun's taxation lists for the Muslim Empire during his day, ca. 1300. What Muhammad would have needed to purchase the horses exceeded the tax revenue collections for the Hijaz and Yemen, these two areas bringing in 6.7 million dirhams in one year. See Ibn Khaldun, *Muqaddimah*, 1:365. His financial needs for horses also exceeded more than 140 years of average tax collections taken from Alexandria after its negotiated surrender in AD 641 See al-Baladhuri, *Kitab Futuh al-Buldan*, part 1, 223, 350.

119. Ibn Sa'd, *Kitab al-Tabaqat al-Kabir*, 1:345–421.

120. Hamidullah, *Battlefields of the Prophet*, #199, 100; and Jandora, *March from Medina*, 24.

121. Some sources use "Chosroes" while sources like al-Tabari are translated as "Kisra."

122. Al-Tabari, *Ta'rikh al-rusul wa'l-muluk*, I.I, 1005.

123. Ibid., 1010–13.

124. Dodge, *Alexander*, 59–60.

125. Al-Tabari, *Ta'rikh al-rusul wa'l-muluk*, I.I, 1041. However, it should be noted that the transmitter of this information, Hisham bin Muhammad, was considered untrustworthy regarding some narrations. Yet apparently al-Tabari considered him reliable regarding Khusrau II's activities. See the introduction to Ibn Sa'd, *Kitab al-Tabaqat*, vol. 1, xxi.

126. Cook, "Why Did Muhammad Attack the Byzantines."

127. Al-Tabari, *Ta'rikh al-rusul wa'l-muluk*, I.I, 1848.

128. Kahn, *Sahih al-Bukhari*, 6, #201. There are instances in which the Prophet's words were committed to writing prior, but this was apparently done in very limited form. As an aside, it is interesting to note that there is evidence that some of the Qur'an was soon translated into a Persian dialect. See Hamid, *Companions of the Prophet*, book I, 167.

129. Kahn, *Sahih al-Bukhari*, vol. 4, #275.

130. Al-Baladhuri, *Kitab Futuh al-Buldan*, part 1, 105, 160; and al-Tabari, *Ta'rikh al-rusul wa'l-muluk*, I.I, 1983.

131. Related to this issue of favoritism for the 'Abna, the assassin sent by Muhammad would later launch his own insurgency in an effort to receive the governorship that he, as a faithful Muslim, believed was rightfully his. See al-Tabari, *Ta'rikh al-rusul wa'l-muluk*, I,I 1989–94.

132. Ibn Sa'd, *Kitab al-Tabaqat al-Kabir*, 2:81; al-Tabari, *Ta'rikh al-rusul wa'l-muluk*, I.I, 1465; and al-Waqidi, *Kitab al-Maghazi*, 370. Ibn Sa'd, *Kitab al-Tabaqat al-Kabir*, 2:196. Hamidullah accepts the use of *manjaniq* by the Muslims. Hamidullah, *Battlefields of the Prophet*, #193, 97–98. However, there are those who consider this to have been a different system. See Nossov, *Ancient and Medieval Siege Weapons*, 165. Also see Dennis, *Maurice's Strategikon*, book 11, 1, 113–15. Byzantine Emperor Maurice discusses the fighting techniques of the Persians, and while mentioning the use of a ditch for defense, he says nothing about their use of siege engines. Some even consider Salman to be a fictitious character, a man promoted to be a Persian "saint" later on in an effort to win over Persian support of the Muslim cause. See Noth, *Early Arabic Historical Tradition*, 157. However, this contention is based mostly on speculation.

133. Al-Waqidi, *Kitab al-Maghazi*, 368; and Ibn Ishaq, *Sirat Rasul Allah*, 587.

134. Nicolle, *Medieval Siege Weapons (2)*, 8.

135. Salman al-Farisi merited an entry in Ibn Sa'd's *al-Tabaqat*, vol. 7 (*Men of Madina* vol. 1), 195–96. Muhammad gave Salman an "egg of gold," ostensibly to buy his freedom. The accepted account is that Salman bought his freedom from the Banu Qurayzah with the help of the Muslims in Madinah who assisted him in planting three hundred date palms as part of his purchase price. The remainder is mentioned as the lump of gold offered by the Prophet, but the story could have been a cover for Salman to purchase weapons and horses from an outside source. Regarding the accepted tradition, see Ibn Ishaq, *Sirat Rasul Allah*, 97–98.

136. Sivan, *Radical Islam*, 10; and al-Tabari, *Ta'rikh al-rusul wa'l-muluk*, I.I, 2724.

137. Al-Tabari, *Ta'rikh al-rusul wa'l-muluk*, I.I, 1005–6.

138. Ibn Kathir, *Al-Sira al-Nabawiyya*, 3:365. There appears to be a serious problem in either the accuracy or dating of this incident. According to al-Tabari, *Ta'rikh al-rusul wa'l-muluk*, I.I, 1559–60, the letter would have reached the Persian emperor in April 628, which was more than one month after Khusrau II had been murdered in a coup. See Theophanes, *Chronicle of Theophanes Confessor*, 454–55. Kaegi, *Heraclius Emperor of Byzantium*, 174. Therefore, it is possible the incident is contrived, the letter was dispatched earlier, or it was Khusrau II's son Siroes who read it and tore it up. If the latter, Muslim writers, unaware of Khusrau II's death, assumed it was him who received it and not his son. As it stands, the letter does appear to be genuine.

139. See Kaegi, *Heraclius Emperor of Byzantium*, 122–24 for Khusrau II's letter to the Byzantine emperor, calling him "our senseless and insignificant servant."

140. Al-Tabari, *Ta'rikh al-rusul wa'l-muluk*, I.I, 1005–6.

Chapter 6. The Surge

1. Watt, *Muhammad at Medina*, 133; and Donner, "Mecca's Food Supplies," 254.

2. Ibn Kathir, *Al-Sira al-Nabawiyya*, 3:203. There are disputes about the date of this raid that even Ibn Kathir notes. Nevertheless, Thumamah's capture was still sometime during the first half of 627. Additional details can be found readily in Qureshi, *Foreign Policy of Hadrat Muhammad*, 299; and Ibn Abdul Wahab, *Biography of the Prophet*, 2:578–80.

3. Hamid, *Companions of the Prophet*, book 2, 153–54.

4. Ibn Ishaq, *Sirat Rasul Allah*, 677. Some would imply that Thumamah was fed each day, but the astonishment of the Muslims that he ate so little once released implies that he was left at least without food, for in their eyes he would have been ravenous. This incident is also clearly placed out of order in Guillaume's translation.

5. Kahn, *Sahih al-Bukhari*, vol. 5, #658.

6. Examples of writers who claim that excessive force pushes a populace toward the insurgency abound, but a few can be noted here. Dach Bern, *Total Resistance*, 95; Corum, *Bad Strategies*, 253; and Nagl, *Learning to Eat Soup with a Knife*, 203–4. Nagl asserts that Gen. William Westmoreland's failure in Vietnam was that he was too determined to win the war, yet he quotes Westmoreland earlier in his text stating that the goal in Vietnam was to bring the insurgents to the negotiating table. Negotiations are not a recipe for victory, a point that escaped Nagl's analysis. In insurgency the only time an insurgent wants to negotiate is when they are losing, unless it is for deception purposes. To bring an insurgent to the negotiating table is to stop short of defeating the insurgency; Taber, *War of the Flea*, 13. In contrast to the modern notion of negotiating settlements in insurgency conflicts, insurgencies themselves only negotiate when they are losing and use the respite to renew their efforts in another fashion. Insurgent theorists typically speak of using terror on the local populace to force them to support the insurgent, and yet analysts fail to ask why locals would support insurgents that use terror and brutal force against them but would turn on the government that would use some type of force that inflicts collateral damage on civilians. For example, see Guevara, *Bolivian Diaries*, 151, 164. Today, the ongoing mindset for counterinsurgency is to provide the populace what the insurgents want, or to

"buy off" the populace and insurgents by giving them goodies of tangible economic value. Such a direction is extremely shortsighted and based on Maslow's Hierarchy of Needs, which only describes animal behavior but falls seriously short in dealing with human behavior. The key point to be noted here is that it is necessary to win the war however that war may be defined. Failure courts the loss of support for the effort for plain and obvious reasons that only a massive insurgency propaganda campaign can obfuscate.

7. Two fundamentally differing counterinsurgency strategies exist, the population-centric and enemy-centric strategies. The former is currently in vogue while the latter held sway for thousands of years and is largely the reason why insurgencies were almost universally crushed by counterinsurgency efforts. The two differing positions can be contrasted through two key sources. See Galula, *Counterinsurgency Warfare, Theory and Practice*, for the population-centric view, and Callwell, *Small Wars*, for the enemy-centric view. For an overview of these two positions, see Gentile, "Selective Use of History." It is usually accepted as an article of faith that in the modern world the enemy-centric approach is far too "kinetic," and that public opinion would not support such actions. Yet there are ancient historical examples of counterinsurgencies facing public relations disasters but handling them differently and far more effectively for their cause. For example, during the Riddah, or Muslim counterinsurgency against the apostate tribes in Arabia immediately after Muhammad's death, Khalid bin al-Walid precipitated a scandal by judicially killing a Muslim tribal chief and seizing the dead man's beautiful wife. Despite the general dismay of the Bedouin populace, the first *khalifa* Abu Bakr refused to part with his successful general, even when 'Umar bin al-Khattab lobbied hard for his relief. Instead, Khalid went on to forcefully smash some of the insurgents so thoroughly that their tribes vanished to history. The basic nature of Arabia has never changed since. See al-Tabari, *Ta'rikh al-rusul wa'l-muluk*, I.I, 1921–29.

8. One good example of this myth is Taber, *War of the Flea*, 11, 18.

9. Hasan, *Sunan Abu Dawud*, vol. 3, #4337, #4345; Khaliyl, *Jami' al-Tirmidhi*, vol. 3, #1458; Ansari, *Sunan Ibn-e-Majah*, vol. 4, #2535; and al-Mawardi, *Al-Ahkam al-Sultaniyya*, 60–61.

10. Kahn, *Sahih al-Bukhari*, vol. 4, #220.

11. Ibn Sa'd relates an account of one tribe who decided to engage in one last raid against the Muslims before joining them because once they were Muslims they could not raid other Muslims. See Ibn Sa'd, *Kitab al-Tabaqat al-Kabir*, 1:355.

12. While Ibn Sa'd provides the 220 number (*Kitab al-Tabaqat al-Kabir*, 2:97), al-Waqidi indicates that only 20 men were mounted (*Kitab al-Maghazi*, 226). Al-Tabari accepts that 200 were mounted (*Ta'rikh al-rusul wa'l-muluk*, I.I, 1501).

13. Ibn Sa'd, *Kitab al-Tabaqat al-Kabir*, 2:97.

14. Ibn Ishaq, *Sirat Rasul Allah*, 486.

15. Ibid.; and Ibn Sa'd, *Kitab al-Tabaqat al-Kabir*, 2:100.

16. A fascinating modern example happened to Che Guevara in Bolivia. He and his men would steal cattle and other items, but when soldiers in the area raided one of his hidden caches of stores, he became morally indignant. See Guevara, *Bolivian Diaries*, 154. In contrast, during conventional operations even when one party is hit hard by an enemy, the commander of the former often sees this as a well-conducted attack that

his men could learn from, choosing to view his enemy as a worthy opponent rather than morally lapsed.

17. Ibn Sa'd, *Kitab al-Tabaqat al-Kabir*, 2:100.

18. Ibid.

19. Jandora, *March from Medina*, 19; Hasan, *Sunan Abu Dawud*, vol. 2, #2632.

20. Ibn Sa'd, *Kitab al-Tabaqat al-Kabir*, 2:105.

21. Hourani, *History of the Arab Peoples*, 104–6.

22. An example of this could be seen in the way the Banu Qurayzah spoke of the Prophet. See Ibn Ishaq, *Sirat Rasul Allah*, 461.

23. Kahn, *Sahih al-Bukhari*, vol. 6, #311; Ibn Kathir, *Tafsir Al-Qur'an Al-'Azim*, 7:695–99; and al-Tabari, *Ta'rikh al-rusul wa'l-muluk*, I.I, 1461–62.

24. Kahn, *Sahih al-Bukhari*, vol. 6, #305. In this hadith it is related how Zayd was once named as a son to the Prophet, but then his name was changed when his adoption was nullified by Qur'anic injunction.

25. Al-Tabari, *Ta'rikh al-rusul wa'l-muluk*, vol. 8, fn 1; Ibn Ishaq, *Sirat Rasul Allah*, 214; and Ibn Sa'd, *Kitab al-Tabaqat al-Kabir*, 8:80–81.

26. There are other historical examples of such occurring. A good example is that of the Roman emperor Tiberius, who was envious of his immensely popular adopted son, Germanicus Caesar. Germanicus became successful beyond anyone's dreams as he began to crush the resistant German tribes east of the Rhine River. Before full success was realized, Tiberius astounded everyone even more by transferring him to the backwater of the empire, sending him to the east to oversea provinces such as Syria and Egypt. There Germanicus died, either from natural causes or from poison, a fact to which Tiberius could barely restrain his visible joy. See Tacitus, *Annals*, book 2, xxvi, xliii; book 3, ii–vi. Suetonius at least lends credence to the notion that Tiberius had Germanicus poisoned. See Suetonius *Twelve Caesars*, 3, 52.

27. Al-Waqidi, *Kitab al-Maghazi*, 233; and Ibn Sa'd, *Kitab al-Tabaqat al-Kabir*, 2:107, indicated these were horsemen. This would appear to be in error.

28. Al-Waqidi, *Kitab al-Maghazi*, 235; and Ibn Sa'd, *Kitab al-Tabaqat al-Kabir*, 2:109.

29. Al-Waqidi, *Kitab al-Maghazi*, 236.

30. Ibn Sa'd, *Kitab al-Tabaqat al-Kabir*, 2:110.

31. Ibn Ishaq, *Sirat Rasul Allah*, 665.

32. Ibn Kathir, *Al-Sira al-Nabawiyya*, 4:314.

33. Ibn Ishaq, *Sirat Rasul Allah*, 665; Ibn Sa'd, *Kitab al-Tabaqat al-Kabir*, 2:112; Al-Waqidi, *Kitab al-Maghazi*, 238–39; and Al-Tabari, *Ta'rikh al-rusul wa'l-muluk*, I.I, 1557–58.

34. Ibn Sa'd, *Kitab al-Tabaqat al-Kabir*, 1:352.

35. Al-Tabari, *Ta'rikh al-rusul wa'l-muluk*, I.I, 1901–2.

36. Ibn Sa'd, *Kitab al-Tabaqat al-Kabir*, 2:77.

37. Al-Waqidi, *Kitab al-Maghazi*, 175; Ibn Sa'd, *Kitab al-Tabaqat al-Kabir*, 2:77; Ibn Ishaq, *Sirat Rasul Allah*, 490; and al-Tabari, *Ta'rikh al-rusul wa'l-muluk*, I.I, 1511.

38. Ibn Ishaq, *Sirat Rasul Allah*, 493; and Hasan, *Sunan Abu Dawud*, vol. 3, #3920.

39. Ibn Sa'd, *Kitab al-Tabaqat al-Kabir*, 2:79.

40. Ibn Ishaq, *Sirat Rasul Allah*, 491.

41. Ibid., 492.

42. Ibid.; Kahn, *Sahih al-Bukhari*, vol. 4, #720. However, there was a point when Muhammad did contemplate having ʿAbdullah bin Ubayy killed. See Kahn, *Sahih al-Bukhari*, vol. 8, #655.

43. Ibn Saʿd, *Kitab al-Tabaqat al-Kabir*, 2:112; and Ibn Ishaq, *Sirat Rasul Allah*, 483. That one of the women, who would later look over Abu Rafiʾs body, stated that she heard ʿAbdullah bin ʿAtikʾs voice suggests that he was known in Khaybar.

44. Al-Tabari, *Taʾrikh al-rusul waʾl-muluk*, I.I, 1379.

45. Kahn, *Sahih al-Bukhari*, vol. 5, #372. There is minor disagreement with some sources saying he broke his leg. See ibid., #371; and al-Tabari, *Taʾrikh al-rusul waʾl-muluk*, I.I, 1377. Another hadith quoted by al-Tabari says he merely bruised his leg (1380). To compound the possible confusion, another source says he merely sprained his arm; Ibn Ishaq, *Sirat Rasul Allah*, 483. Suffice it to say, ʿAbdullah bin ʿAtik at least injured himself making his escape.

46. Al-Tabari, *Taʾrikh al-rusul waʾl-muluk*, I.I, 1380.

47. It is noteworthy to contrast this lack of security with the levels of security taken by Christian and Muslim forces during the early Crusades against assassins such as the Nazaris, even when no combatant operations were ongoing. See Harari, *Special Operations*, 91–108, regarding Conrad I of Jerusalem.

48. Burton, *Book of the Sword*, 126–27; and Vegetius, *Military Institutions*, 84. This debate on how to use a sword has raged for centuries. Eastern swords are made for slashing while European swords were designed for thrusting. It is worth noting that Vegetius indicated that thrusting caused more immediate injury than slashing, and that Roman soldiers considered those enemies who slashed with swords to be an "easy conquest." While one may wish to cite the Arab proverb of "death by a thousand cuts," this only applies to patience in various aspects of life, not to an immediate encounter in hand-to-hand combat because it is much more efficient to kill an enemy with one or two thrusts than through scores of slashes.

49. Ibn Saʿd, *Kitab al-Tabaqat al-Kabir*, 2:113. The Arabic here is "amir." Wellhausen translates al-Waqidiʾs usage here as "ihrem haupte," or "their chief." The sense is the same.

50. Ibn Saʿd, *Kitab al-Tabaqat al-Kabir*, 2:114; al-Tabari, *Taʾrikh al-rusul waʾl-muluk*, 9:120n836; and Lane, *Arabic-English Lexicon*, 4:1513.

51. The Prophet used to deliver sermons leaning on either his staff or bow, depending on whether or not he was campaigning. See Hasan, *Sunan Abu Dawud*, vol. 1, #1091; and Ansari, *Sunan Ibn-e-Majah*, vol. 2, #1107.

52. Watt, *Muhammad at Medina*, 43.

53. Kahn, *Sahih al-Bukhari*, vol. 5, #507; and al-Tabari, *Taʾrikh al-rusul waʾl-muluk*, I.I, 1503. The phrase literally means "O, the morning," but was used to warn an entire tribe that a predatory incursion had taken place. Regarding this Arabic idiom, see Lane, *Arabic-English Lexicon*, 4:1642.

54. Kahn, *Sahih al-Bukhari*, vol. 5, #505; vol. 1, #234.

55. Ibn Kathir, *Tafsir Al-Qurʾan Al-ʿAzim*, 3:161–64. This principle was upheld and confirmed by later jurists, though with variations. See Ibn Naqib al-Misri, *ʿUmdat al-Salik*, p22.1, o15.1; al-Mawardi, *Al-Ahkam al-Sultaniyya*, 68–70; Ibn Rushd, *Bidayat al-Mujtahid*, 2:547–49; and al-Marghinani, *Al-Hidayah Fi Sharh Bidayat al-Mubtadi*, 2:279–80.

56. Ibn Sa'd, *Kitab al-Tabaqat al-Kabir*, 2:115. In contrast, see al-Waqidi, *Kitab al-Maghazi*, 241–42. Also see the various hadith in the *sahih* collections regarding the incident, such as Kahn, *Sahih al-Bukhari*, 1:234, 5:505, 507. These do not support Ibn Sa'd's claim.

57. Ibn Ishaq, *Sirat Rasul Allah*, 499.

58. Al-Waqidi, *Kitab al-Maghazi*, 242; Kahn, *Sahih al-Bukhari* vol. 5, #474; #471; 472; #475; 477; Hasan, *Sunan Abu Dawud*, vol. 3, #2759; and al-Tabari, *Ta'rikh al-rusul wa'l-muluk*, I.I, 1529. Regarding the horses, see Ibn Sa'd, *Kitab al-Tabaqat al-Kabir*, 2:118.

59. Kahn, *Sahih al-Bukhari* (vol. 5, ch. 34, 333) cites this as "the Ghazwa of al-Hudaibiya." Ibn Kathir, in his *Tafsir*, states the Muslim column was an army: *Tafsir*, 9:159. Also see Al-Waqidi, *Kitab al-Maghazi*, 242; and Ibn Kathir, *Al-Sira al-Nabawiyya*, 3:224. All concur that the *umrah* was understood to be a military operation.

60. Ibn Sa'd, *Kitab al-Tabaqat al-Kabir*, 2:117; al-Tabari, *Ta'rikh al-rusul wa'l-muluk*, I.I, 1531; Ibn Ishaq, *Sirat Rasul Allah*, 501 (where Muhammad took an arrow from his quiver to puncture the ground to find water); Al-Waqidi, *Kitab al-Maghazi*, 243; and Ibn Ishaq, *Sirat Rasul Allah*, 502.

61. Kahn, *Sahih al-Bukhari*, vol. 5, #495.

62. Regarding Muslim campaigning during sacred months, see Ibn Sa'd, *Kitab al-Tabaqat al-Kabir*, 2:7–9, 34–35, 60–61, 74–75, 91–96, 96–97. The Quraysh tried to violate the sacred months three times after the Muslim violation during the Nakhlah raid, but all were dismal failures. See Ibn Sa'd, *Kitab al-Tabaqat al-Kabir*, 2:33–34, 71–73, 80. The last was the battle of al-Khandaq and can provide an additional explanation why the Quraysh withdrew without a decision.

63. Ibn Ishaq, *Sirat Rasul Allah*, 501.

64. Ibid., 500; and Ibn Kathir, *Tafsir al-Qur'an Al-'Azim*, 9:157.

65. Ibn Sa'd, *Kitab al-Tabaqat al-Kabir*, 2:118.

66. Ibn Ishaq, *Sirat Rasul Allah*, 503.

67. Ibid., 502.

68. Al-Tabari, *Ta'rikh al-rusul wa'l-muluk*, I.I, 1531–32. It is very possible that those reciting hadith regarding this may have confused the action with Khalid's operations during the conquest of Makkah. Nevertheless, this information does not necessarily contradict what the hadith literature later says about Khalid's arrival in Madinah. It may be very possible that his conversion was gradual, and that his role at al-Hudaybiyah was simply to obstruct Ikrimah and Qurayshi operations, coming directly to Muhammad later during the fulfilled pilgrimage a year after the treaty's signing. See Ibn Sa'd, *Kitab al-Tabaqat al-Kabir*, 7:244.

69. Ibn Ishaq, *Sirat Rasul Allah*, 503. Al-Tabari notes that even when the Prophet coughed up phlegm and spat it out, his companions would try to get it on their hands and rub it on their faces to receive a blessing. See al-Tabari, *Ta'rikh al-rusul wa'l-muluk*, I.I, 1537.

70. Al-Tabari, *Ta'rikh al-rusul wa'l-muluk*, I.I, 1535.

71. Kahn, *Sahih al-Bukhari*, vol. 5, #485, #487. There is a minor point of dispute that it was not a pledge to the death, but rather that they would refrain from fleeing if attacked. The difference here would appear to be moot because not running if under

attack by a superior force would necessitate a fight to the death. See *al-Tirmidhi*, vol. 3, #1591 and 1594; and Ibn Ishaq, *Sirat Rasul Allah*, 503.

72. Ibn Ishaq, *Sirat Rasul Allah*, 504.

73. Ibid.; and al-Tabari, *Ta'rikh al-rusul wa'l-muluk*, I.I, 1546–47.

74. Ibn Kathir, *al-Sira al-Nabawiyya*, 3:229.

75. Ibn Ishaq, *Sirat Rasul Allah*, 504.

76. Ibid., 505.

77. Surah 48:1.

78. Ibn Kathir, *Al-Sira al-Nabawiyya*, 3:231.

79. Al-Tabari, *Ta'rikh al-rusul wa'l-muluk*, I.I, 1552; Ibn Kathir, *Tafsir Al-Qur'an Al-'Azim*, 9:167; and Ibn Kathir, *Al-Sira al-Nabawiyya*, 3:240.

80. Al-Waqidi, *Kitab al-Maghazi*, 261.

81. Ibn Ishaq, *Sirat Rasul Allah*, 507.

82. One of the few to see the situation of Abu Basir in this manner was Watt, who noted that "with some words of encouragement from Muhammad he [Basir] left Medina and went to a spot near the coast which commanded Quraysh's route to Syria"; Watt, *Muhammad at Medina*, 61. Both Haykal and Armstrong hint at this, but they are not so clear. See Haykal, *Life of Muhammad*, 357; and Armstrong, *Muhammad*, 227. Other sources completely gloss the issue, such as Bashier, *War and Peace*, 203. However, commentators that do acknowledge Muhammad's subtle hint to allow Abu Basir to flee still do not see Abu Basir as Muhammad's proxy.

83. Ibn Kathir, *Tafsir Al-Qur'an Al-'Azim*, 9:598–99.

Chapter 7. Triumph

1. Ibn Ishaq, *Sirat Rasul Allah*, 485.

2. Al-Tabari, *Ta'rikh al-rusul wa'l-muluk*, I.I, 1601–4; and Ibn Sa'd, *Kitab al-Tabaqat al-Kabir*, 7:244.

3. Ibn Ishaq and al-Tabari imply that Muhammad remained in Madinah for but two months before moving on Khaybar. Ibn Kathir also accepts the earlier date. See Ibn Ishaq, *Sirat Rasul Allah*, 510; al-Tabari, *Ta'rikh al-rusul wa'l-muluk*, I.I 1575; and Ibn Kathir, *Al-Sira al-Nabawiyya*, 3:245–46. However, other evidence suggests a much longer period of time, for Ibn Sa'd and al-Waqidi place the departure date much later. See Ibn Sa'd, *Kitab al-Tabaqat al-Kabir*, 2:131; and al-Waqidi, *Kitab al-Maghazi*, 264. On the basis of the description that the Khaybar workers were planning to harvest dates, this would have placed the raid in August, or in line with Ibn Sa'd's statement. See Rehman Shaikh, *Chronology of Prophetic Events*, 112–13.

4. Ibn Sa'd, *Kitab al-Tabaqat al-Kabir*, 2:134. One source indicates a more precise figure of 1,580 men. See al-Baladhuri, *Kitab Futuh al-Buldan*, part 1, 28, 49.

5. Kahn, *Sahih al-Bukhari*, vol. 5, #508; and Ibn Kathir, *Al-Sira al-Nabawiyya*, 3:247.

6. Ibn Sa'd, *Kitab al-Tabaqat al-Kabir*, 2:131–32; Hamidullah, *Battlefields of the Prophet*, #211, 109. The pace would assume two miles per hour for twelve hours per day. See Burton, *Personal Narrative of a Pilgrimage*, 1:244n1. Had the force been fully mounted, they may have been able to move much faster. For example, T. E. Lawrence was able to move a group of Bedouin insurgents at a pace of about eighty miles per day. See Lawrence, *Seven Pillars*, 293.

7. Al-Baladhuri, *Kitab Futuh al-Buldan*, part 1, 23, 42.

8. Al-Waqidi, *Kitab al-Maghazi*, 273. One of the things prohibited by the Prophet after the battle of Khaybar was the selling of booty before it was distributed. Apparently, some Muslims were selling food items to others and taking advantage of serious logistical difficulties of some of their companions to rake in exorbitant profits. See Ibn Ishaq, *Sirat Rasul Allah*, 512.

9. Hamidullah, *Battlefields of the Prophet*, #210, 108.

10. Al-Waqidi, *Kitab al-Maghazi*, 264, 267. The reference to ten thousand warriors could have included allies such as the Banu Ghatafan, since the Jews were striving to form a coalition. It appears that before Muhammad arrived there were four thousand Ghatafan fighters rallied to support the Jews, but they were turned away. See al-Waqidi, *Kitab al-Maghazi*, 270. One source indicated that the defenders of Khaybar numbered as many as twenty thousand. See Hamidullah, *Battlefields of the Prophet*, #219, 113.

11. Khaliyl, *Jami' Al-Tirmidhi*, vol. 3, #1550. Also see Kahn, *Sahih al-Bukhari*, vol. 5, #510.

12. Watt, *Muhammad at Medina*, 218.

13. This is implied by the hadith literature about moving into the "square" of the city. See Siddiqi, *Sahih Imam Muslim*, vol. 5, #1365R2 and #1365R3.

14. Ibn Ishaq, *Sirat Rasul Allah*, 511.

15. Al-Waqidi, *Kitab al-Maghazi*, 271; and Ibn Ishaq, *Sirat Rasul Allah*, 511.

16. Ibn Ishaq, *Sirat Rasul Allah*, 513.

17. The hadith literature presents some confusion as to who actually killed Marhab. Some cite 'Ali bin Abu Talib but others cite Muhammad bin Maslamah. One position that seems plausible is that Muhammad killed him but 'Ali cut off his head once he was dead. See Ibn Kathir, *Al-Sira al-Nabawiyya*, 3:254–56.

18. Al-Waqidi, *Kitab al-Maghazi*, 273; and al-Tabari, *Ta'rikh al-rusul wa'l-muluk*, I.I, 1576–77.

19. Al-Waqidi, *Kitab al-Maghazi*, 275.

20. Kahn, *Sahih al-Bukhari*, vol. 5, #530, #531; and al-Waqidi, *Kitab al-Maghazi*, 273.

21. Al-Waqidi, *Kitab al-Maghazi*, 274.

22. Ibn Sa'd, *Kitab al-Tabaqat al-Kabir*, 2:133.

23. Ibn Ishaq, *Sirat Rasul Allah*, 515. By doing this Muhammad had given Ibn Maslamah a double bloodwit, for the warrior had already killed Marhab in revenge for his dead brother.

24. Ibn Sa'd, *Kitab al-Tabaqat al-Kabir*, 2:134.

25. Ibn Ishaq, *Sirat Rasul Allah*, 520.

26. Al-Tabari, *Ta'rikh al-rusul wa'l-muluk*, I.I, 1583. Later on, when the Muslims had a demographic advantage, 'Umar bin al-Khattab, as the second *khalifa*, had the Jews expelled from Khaybar and sent to Syria. See al-Tabari, *Ta'rikh al-rusul wa'l-muluk*, I,I, 2594–2695. 'Umar did this largely based on Muhammad's dictum near the end of his life that only one religion, Islam, should remain in Arabia. See al-Tabari, *Ta'rikh al-rusul wa'l-muluk*, I.Im 1590–91; Ibn Sa'd, *Kitab al-Tabaqat al-Kabir*, 2:317–18; Siddiqi, *Sahih Imam Muslim*, vol. 5, #1767; and Khaliyl, *Jami' al-Tirmidhi*, vol. 3, #1606.

27. Ibn Sa'd, *Kitab al-Tabaqat al-Kabir*, 2:139–40.

28. Ibn Ishaq, *Sirat Rasul Allah*, 516; and Ibn Sa'd, *Kitab al-Tabaqat al-Kabir*, 2:133.

29. Al-Baladhuri, *Kitab Futuh al-Buldan*, part 1, #25, 45. A camel-load would be about three hundred pounds. See Engels, *Alexander the Great*, 14.

30. Al-Waqidi, *Kitab al-Maghazi*, 287. A *wasq* is equivalent to about 140 pounds dry measure. It should be noted that 28,000 pounds could feed 38 people at a rate of 2 pounds per day for a year. This would allow select people close to Muhammad to dispense some of their own largess.

31. Muhammad offered the woman her freedom and marriage to himself as the price of her dowry. In this manner, marrying Safiyah actually cost him nothing yet still bound him to the nobility of Khaybar, consummating a significant advantage for the Muslims. See Ibn Sa'd, *Kitab al-Tabaqat al-Kabir*, 2:145.

32. Ibn Ishaq, *Sirat Rasul Allah*, 523; and al-Baladhuri, *Kitab Futuh al-Buldan*, part 1, 31, 53.

33. A question must be asked why the closest companions of the Prophet, such as Abu Bakr, 'Umar bin al-Khattab, and 'Uthman bin 'Affan, did not lead expeditions until very late after the *hijrah*. No answer is being postulated here but merely to ask the question for later analysis.

34. Ibn Sa'd, *Kitab al-Tabaqat al-Kabir*, 2:147.

35. Ibid., 156.

36. Ibn Ishaq, *Sirat Rasul Allah*, 531.

37. Al-Waqidi, *Kitab al-Maghazi*, 300; and Ibn Sa'd, *Kitab al-Tabaqat al-Kabir*, 2:150.

38. Ibn Ishaq, *Sirat Rasul Allah*, 531.

39. Ibn Sa'd, *Kitab al-Tabaqat al-Kabir*, 2:151.

40. Kahn, *Sahih al-Bukhari*, vol. 5, #557, #558; and Siddiqi, *Sahih Imam Muslim*, vol. 4, #1266.

41. Ibn Sa'd, *Kitab al-Tabaqat al-Kabir*, 8:95. The Prophet married her about ten miles outside the city prior to entering the state of *ihram*, or consecration, and before entering Makkah.

42. Ibn Ishaq, *Sirat Rasul Allah*, 531.

43. There is no evidence that any of the Quraysh, save for perhaps al-Abbas, were involved in any kind of commercial affairs to support the Muslims during their stay in the city.

44. Ibn Sa'd, *Kitab al-Tabaqat al-Kabir*, 2:158.

45. Ibid., 158–59.

46. The thesis of David Cook that Muhammad engaged the Byzantines because of the return of the True Cross to them after being held by the Sasanids does not work at this point, for the cross would not be returned until 630. See Kaegi, *Heraclius Emperor of Byzantium*, 205–7; and Mango, *Nikephoros*, 18, 65–67.

47. Muslim poetry suggests that they relied heavily on forage for the feeding of their animals; see Ibn Ishaq, *Sirat Rasul Allah*, 533.

48. Al-Tabari, *Ta'rikh al-rusul wa'l-muluk*, I.I, 1617.

49. Al-Waqidi, *Kitab al-Maghazi*, 311; Ibn Sa'd, *Kitab al-Tabaqat al-Kabir*, 2:159; and Ibn Ishaq, *Sirat Rasul Allah*, 532. Ibn Ishaq says there were two hundred thousand

men in the Byzantine army. Al-Tabari, *Ta'rikh al-rusul wa'l-muluk*, I.I, 1611, says the same.

50. Theophanes the Confessor, *Chronicle of Theophanes*, 466.

51. These two men, though placed in a position of importance in battle, are never seen again in the early sources. Either they are pseudonyms or they may have been killed in the battle, although they are not in the list of dead provided by Ibn Ishaq. See Ibn Ishaq, *Sirat Rasul Allah*, 540.

52. Kahn, *Sahih al-Bukhari*, vol. 5, #560; and Ibn Sa'd, *Kitab al-Tabaqat al-Kabir*, 2:160.

53. Al-Tabari, *Ta'rikh al-rusul wa'l-muluk*, I.I, 1615.

54. Ibid., 1617.

55. Kahn, *Sahih* al-Bukhari, vol. 5 #564.

56. Al-Waqidi, *Kitab al-Maghazi*, 312.

57. Ibn Ishaq, *Sirat Rasul Allah*, 540, cites only eight killed. Compare this with Theophanes's comment that the Byzantines "killed three emirs and the bulk of their army"; Theophanes the Confessor, *Chronicle of Theophanes*, 466.

58. Ibn Sa'd, *Kitab al-Tabaqat al-Kabir*, 2:162.

59. Kahn, *Sahih al-Bukhari*, vol. 5, ch. 64, 454.

60. Ibid., #646, 647; and Ibn Sa'd, *Kitab al-Tabaqat al-Kabir*, 2:163. While not specifically stated, the evidence suggests that the fish was a massive sperm whale.

61. Kahn, *Sahih al-Bukhari*, vol. 5, #595. Many of the tribes waited to see who would triumph.

62. Ibn Ishaq, *Sirat Rasul Allah*, 541.

63. Ibid., 543.

64. Al-Waqidi, *Kitab al-Maghazi*, 323.

65. Al-Baladhuri, *Kitab Futuh al-Buldan*, part 1, 37, 62.

66. Ibn Sa'd, *Kitab al-Tabaqat al-Kabir*, 2:166.

67. Sources say that Muhammad received word from heaven on this issue, but it would seem logical that Muhammad's excellent intelligence service learned of it and reported it to him. See Ibn Ishaq, *Sirat Rasul Allah*, 545; and al-Tabari, *Ta'rikh al-rusul wa'l-muluk*, I.I, 1626.

68. Kahn, *Sahih al-Bukhari*, vol. 4, #251; and Hasan, *Sunan Abu Dawud*, vol. 2, #2645.

69. It is not without cause that Karl Marx and Friedrich Engels, when discussing the dealings that a revolutionary government should have with émigrés, urged that their property be seized. See Marx and Engels, *Communist Manifesto*, 94.

70. Ibn Ishaq, *Sirat Rasul Allah*, 545.

71. Al-Waqidi, *Kitab al-Maghazi*, 330.

72. Ibn Sa'd, *Kitab al-Tabaqat al-Kabir*, 2:167.

73. Ibn Ishaq, *Sirat Rasul Allah*, 547.

74. Al-Baladhuri, *Kitab Futuh al-Buldan*, part 1, 38, 63.

75. Muhammad had pointed out to Abu Bakr that if he saw Abu Sufyan, he was to be beheaded. See al-Waqidi, *Kitab al-Maghazi*, 330.

76. Ibn Ishaq, *Sirat Rasul Allah*, 547.

77. Ibid., 548.

78. Ibn Saʿd, *Kitab al-Tabaqat al-Kabir*, 2:167; and Kahn, *Sahih al-Bukhari*, vol. 5, #577.

79. Al-Waqidi, *Kitab al-Maghazi*, 330. The account stated that the Muslim army had with them a female dog bursting with milk, and the Prophet used this as a metaphor to indicate that it was now the turn of the Quraysh to be milked.

80. Kahn, *Sahih al-Bukhari*, vol. 5, #574.

81. Siddiqi, *Sahih Imam Muslim*, 5, #1780; and Al-Baladhuri, *Kitab Futuh al-Buldan*, part 1, 39, 65.

82. Al-Tabari, *Taʾrikh al-rusul waʾl-muluk*, I.I, 1635.

83. Ibid.; and Ibn Saʿd, *Kitab al-Tabaqat al-Kabir*, 2:167–68.

84. Ibn Saʿd, *Kitab al-Tabaqat al-Kabir*, 2:168. Ibn Saʿd provided a full list of the proscribed, though other sources lower the number.

85. Ibn Ishaq, *Sirat Rasul Allah*, 548–49.

86. Al-Tabari, *Taʾrikh al-rusul waʾl-muluk*, I.I, 1637.

87. Ibid., 1642.

88. Ibn Saʿd, *Kitab al-Tabaqat al-Kabir*, 2:174.

89. Al-Waqidi, *Kitab al-Maghazi*, 345. This is alluded to in a Sufi legend regarding the story of the writer of Qurʾanic revelation who fell into apostasy. However, this account indicates that this apostate was beheaded for his sin, instead of surviving. See Nicholson, *Mathnawi of Jalaluʾddin Rumi*, book 1, 176–79.

90. Ibn Saʿd, *Kitab al-Tabaqat al-Kabir*, 7:307–8.

91. Ibn Ishaq, *Sirat Rasul Allah*, 552–53.

92. Ibn Saʿd, *Kitab al-Tabaqat al-Kabir*, 2:180–81, 194–95.

93. Ibid., 182.

94. Kahn, *Sahih al-Bukhari*, vol. 5, #628.

95. Khalid would later carry tremendous responsibility under the first *khalifa*, Abu Bakr, during the Riddah, or Apostates War, after Muhammad's death. He would engage in further indiscretions to the point that ʿUmar bin al-Khattab would demand that Khalid be relieved of his command and disciplined. However, Abu Bakr would not hear of it. See al-Tabari, *Taʾrikh al-rusul waʾl-muluk*, I.I, 1923–29.

96. Ibn Ishaq, *Sirat Rasul Allah*, 566; and Ibn Saʿd, *Kitab al-Tabaqat al-Kabir*, 2:185. It is curious to note that Ibn Saʿd indicated that the Hawazin "rose in rebellion" as if they were already under Muslim rule.

97. Al-Waqidi, *Kitab al-Maghazi*, 355, indicates that Durayd bin al-Simmah was 160 years old and had for 20 years been famous as a cavalry leader.

98. Ibn Ishaq, *Sirat Rasul Allah*, 566. Malik's use of the women and children is not as reckless as it may sound, for there was historical precedent of doing this to increase the fighting ardor of a force. See Polyaenus, *Stratagems of War*, 2.1.28 and 7.6.1.

99. Al-Tabari, *Taʾrikh al-rusul waʾl-muluk*, I.I, 1656–57.

100. Ibn Saʿd, *Kitab al-Tabaqat al-Kabir*, 2:185.

101. Al-Waqidi, *Kitab al-Maghazi*, 357.

102. Ibid., 358. The numbers provided only add up to 9,450. This can perhaps be explained by the possibility that al-Waqidi had no other information regarding the details of the other 2,500+ in the army and therefore chose to omit any details of these.

103. Ibn Saʿd, *Kitab al-Tabaqat al-Kabir*, 2:186.

104. Kahn, *Sahih al-Bukhari*, vol. 5, #607.

105. Ibn Ishaq, *Sirat Rasul Allah*, 569.

106. Kahn, *Sahih al-Bukhari*, vol. 5, #610.

107. Ibn Sa'd, *Kitab al-Tabaqat al-Kabir*, 2:187.

108. Al-Tabari, *Ta'rikh al-rusul wa'l-muluk*, I.I, 1664; and al-Waqidi, *Kitab al-Maghazi*, 362. Al-Waqidi provides the larger number of the two.

109. Al-Tabari, *Ta'rikh al-rusul wa'l-muluk*, I.I, 1666. Al-Tabari notes that he "had become feeble" with old age; see 1657.

110. Ibn Ishaq, *Sirat Rasul Allah*, 576; and al-Tabari, *Ta'rikh al-rusul wa'l-muluk*, I.I, 1669.

111. Al-Waqidi, *Kitab al-Maghazi*, 366.

112. Ibn Sa'd, *Kitab al-Tabaqat al-Kabir*, 2:188.

113. Hamidullah, *Battlefields of the Prophet*, #190, 96. Al-Baladhuri explained that the town was once called Wajj, but the building of the wall led to the change in name. See al-Baladhuri, *Kitab Futuh al-Buldan*, part 1, 56, 86.

114. Ibn Sa'd, *Kitab al-Tabaqat al-Kabir*, 2:196. Ibn Ishaq, *Sirat Rasul Allah*, 589, gives the longer date. Al-Waqidi indicates it was from fifteen to nineteen days; see al-Waqidi, *Kitab al-Maghazi*, 369. One hadith states the siege lasted forty days; see Ibn Sa'd, *Kitab al-Tabaqat al-Kabir*, 2:197. Al-Baladhuri follows Ibn Hisham in stating it was only fifteen days long; see al-Baladhuri, *Kitab Futuh al-Buldan*, part 1, 55, 85.

115. Al-Waqidi, *Kitab al-Maghazi*, 369.

116. Ibid., 370.

117. Ibn Sa'd, *Kitab al-Tabaqat al-Kabir*, 2:196. Ibn Sa'd claims this exit of slaves was "too much for the people of al-Ta'if to bear" but does not demonstrate how such few giving up would have compelled them to surrender.

118. Ibn Ishaq, *Sirat Rasul Allah*, 589–90.

119. Such techniques have been used throughout history to convince attackers that the besieged had more than enough supplies to outlast an opponent. See Frontinus, *Stratagems*, book 3, xv.

120. Kahn, *Sahih al-Bukhari*, vol. 5, #615.

121. Ibn Ishaq, *Sirat Rasul Allah*, 591.

122. Al-Baladhuri, *Kitab Futuh al-Buldan*, part 1, 56, 87.

123. Ibn Sa'd, *Kitab al-Tabaqat al-Kabir*, 1:369.

124. Ibid., 2:204.

125. Ibn Ishaq, *Sirat Rasul Allah*, 607.

126. Ibid., 602.

127. Kahn, *Sahih al-Bukhari*, vol. 5, #702.

128. Al-Waqidi, *Kitab al-Maghazi*, 391. Ibn Hisham indicates that 'Uthman donated one thousand dinars, or ten thousand dirhams, for the expedition. If this was his one-third, then the question of how Muhammad managed to get up to ten thousand horses looms even larger, for one thousand dinars could purchase only two or three horses at typical market rates. Instead, the cash listed is probably just the liquid wealth he committed to the operation, the rest being in kind. Of course the question could be asked if he may have been the agent for securing the horses from the Sasanids, this being part of his one-third contribution. See Ibn Kathir, *Al-Sira al-Nabawiyya*, 4:3.

129. Khaliyl, *Jami' Al-Tirmidhi*, vol. 6, #3700.

130. Al-Tabari, *Ta'rikh al-rusul wa'l-muluk*, I.I, 1695; Ibn Ishaq, *Sirat Rasul Allah*, 604; and Ibn Kathir, *Al-Sira al-Nabawiyya*, 3:7.

131. Al-Waqidi, *Kitab al-Maghazi*, 394.

132. Ibid., 408; and Ibn Sa'd, *Kitab al-Tabaqat al-Kabir*, 2:205.

133. Ibn Kathir, *Al-Sira al-Nabawiyya*, 4:6.

134. Al-Waqidi, *Kitab al-Maghazi*, 408.

135. Pryor, "Introduction," 20.

136. Ibn Kathir, *Al-Sira al-Nabawiyya*, 4:10.

137. Al-Tabari, *Ta'rikh al-rusul wa'l-muluk*, I.I, 1698.

138. Al-Waqidi, *Kitab al-Maghazi*, 407.

139. This analysis for the Tabuk campaign was previously made by me in another work. See Rodgers, *Fundamentals of Islamic Asymmetric Warfare*, 328–29.

140. Al-Waqidi, *Kitab al-Maghazi*, 403.

141. Ibn Ishaq, *Sirat Rasul Allah*, 608.

142. Ibn Sa'd, *Kitab al-Tabaqat al-Kabir*, 2:205.

143. Ibn Ishaq, *Sirat Rasul Allah*, 609–10; and Ibn Kathir, *Tafsir Al-Qur'an Al-'Azim*, 4:513–16.

Chapter 8. The Generalship of Muhammad, the Prophet of Allah

1. See the Introduction. Also see Qadi 'Iyad, *Ash-Shifa*, part 3, ch. 1, sec. 1, 279–89; sec. 3, 293–95.

2. Al-Mawardi, *Al-Ahkam al-Sultaniyya*, 40.

3. Ibn Kathir, *Al-Sira al-Nabawiyya*, 2:19–20, 22. An interesting Shi'ite tradition cites Hamzah as intervening to protect Muhammad during the early days in Makkah. Some of the Quraysh had thrown the afterbirth of a camel on the Prophet's back. Infuriated, Abu Talib summoned Hamzah, told him to carry his sword, who then took the filthy mess and smeared it on the faces of Muhammad's antagonists. See Kulayni, *Al-Kafi*, book 4, #547.

4. A Shi'ite tradition states that Muhammad blessed those Muslims who moved about in secrecy, known to Allah but unknown as Muslims to the people at large. See Kulayni, *Al-Kafi*, book 5, #1037.

5. Kahn, *Sahih al-Bukhari*, vol. 1, #24; and Hasan, *Sunan Abu Dawud*, vol. 2, #2634.

6. Kahn, *Sahih al-Bukhari*, vol. 4, #196; and As-Sanani, *Bulugh al-Maram*, book 11, #1126.

7. Alinsky, *Rules for Radicals*, 126–30.

8. Ibn Sa'd, *Kitab al-Tabaqat al-Kabir*, 2:52.

9. Frontinus, *Stratagems*, book 1, 12.

10. Employing tricks with treaties was nothing new. The Romans used a unique trick when they made a treaty with the Gauls during the days of the Republic. As part of the agreement, the Romans were to keep one gate into Rome perpetually open. To feign compliance they set up a gate on a deserted rock near the city and kept the doors open to provide a semblance of abiding by the treaty. See Polyaenus, *Stratagems of War*, 8.25.1.

11. Hoffer, *True Believer*, sec. 83, 97–99.

12. Sun Tzu, *Art of War*, book 2, 3; and Clausewitz, *On War*, book 1, ch.1, 2.

13. Clausewitz, *On War*, book 1, ch. 3; and Sun Tzu, *Art of War*, book 1, 17. Sun Tzu here penned his famous phrase, "All warfare is based on deception."

14. Sun Tzu, *Art of War*, book 11, 32, 33, 35; and Clausewitz, *On War*, book 3, ch. 3, 4.

15. Erfurth, *Surprise*, 399.

16. Clausewitz, *On War*, book 1, ch. 3; Luvaas, *Frederick the Great*, 142.

17. Sun Tzu, *Art of War*, book 6, 5; Clausewitz, *On War*, book 3, ch. 9; and Erfurt, *Surprise*, 414.

18. The importance of maps, or lack of them, to military operations is often forgotten when campaigns are analyzed. For an excellent overview of the revolution in military affairs created by cartography, see Black, "Revolution in Military Cartography."

19. Clausewitz, *On War*, book 1, ch. 1, 11.

20. Sun Tzu, *Art of War*, book 5, 14, 15, 20; and Clausewitz, *On War*, book 1, ch. 7; book 3, ch. 1.

21. For a full treatment of personality in war, see Freytag-Loringhoven, *Power of Personality in War*.

22. Frontinus, *Stratagems*, book 4, 1, 16, 17, 23; Bewley, *Al-Muwatta of Imam Malik ibn Anas*, 21.18.43; Kahn, *Sahih al-Bukhari*, vol. 4, #42, #44, #87, #131; Siddiqi, *Sahih Imam Muslim*, vol. 5, #1810; Hasan, *Sunan Abu Dawud*, vol. 2, #2490; #2504; Khaliyl, *Jami' al-Tirmidhi*, vol. 3, #1626, #1637; and Al-Khattab, *Sunan An-Nasa'i*, vol. 3, #3136.

23. Two examples of this pious perspective are Rahman's *Muhammad as a Military Leader* and Rizvi's *Battles of the Prophet in Light of the Qur'an*.

24. Examples include Hamidullah, *Battlefields of the Prophet*; and Schwartz-Barcott, *War, Terror & Peace*, 95–138. Throughout his work, Schwartz-Barcott focuses on Muhammad's operations in light of Qur'anic passages. However, his analysis is based on faulty premises since the author failed to differentiate between recitations in Makkah and Madinah and the change in stages between them.

25. Kahn, *Sahih al-Bukhari*, vol. 5, #8, 9; and Khaliyl, *Jami' al-Tirmidhi*, vol. 6, #3655, #3659. However, there is some evidence to indicate that Abu Bakr may have had much more power and control even during the days when Muhammad was alive. See al-Tabari, *Ta'rikh al-rusul wa'l-muluk*, I.I, 1938–39, which implies that Abu Bakr was ordering assignments for key personnel while the Prophet was alive.

26. For example, see the use of families providing their own supply in the Bible. See I Samuel 17:17–19.

27. Dennis, *Maurice's Strategikon*, book 8, sec. 2. Particularly see paragraph 24, where Maurice discusses the need to either find supply for an army locally or transport the supplies to them on an ongoing basis. Contrast the development of logistical lines with the judgments of early imams regarding the means and method of supplying soldiers in the field. For example, the jurists state that the Muslims would typically travel with their food supplies, and that anything taken in the field was considered supplementary. See Al-Tabari, *Kitab al-Jihad*, sec. 30.1. That the jurists believed that captured food stores belonged to the one who got to them first indicates that there was no organized commissary in the Prophet's army, nor even an effort to organize the plundered food to ensure equal distribution, at least until a campaign was over.

As for logistical support in the Byzantine Empire of the seventh century, see Haldon, *Warfare, State and Society*, 139–43.

28. Adil, *Letters of Hadrat Abu Bakr Siddiq*, #52, 75; #53, 75–76. However, it was clear that Abu Bakr still had much to learn regarding supply and logistics, as one of his forces in the field under Khalid bin al-Walid suffered from severe supply problems. See ibid., #9, 21.

29. Adil, *Letters of Hadrat 'Umar Farooq*, #31, 34, #34, 37–38.

30. Kahn, *Sahih al-Bukhari*, vol. 4, #158, 162. Maintaining adequate security was an issue familiar to many of the great generals in early history; for example, see Polyaenus, *Stratagems of War*, 3.9.17, regarding the great Iphicrates's use of proper security measures.

31. Hasan, *Sunan Abu Dawud*, vol. 1, #435.

32. Polyaenus, *Stratagems of War*, 2.3.7, 9; 6.38.5.

33. Ibn Ishaq, *Sirat Rasul Allah*, 293.

34. For examples of others who turned superstitions to their favor in the ancient world, see Frontinus, *Stratagems*, book 1, xii.

35. Polyaenus, *Stratagems of War*, 2.3.13; 8.23.12.

36. Frontinus, *Stratagems*, book 1.x.3; book 1.xi.8–11; book 1, xii 3, 6,8, 12; book 2.i,17; and Polyaenus, *Stratagems of War*, I. 10; 2.3.12; 6.38.4; 8.23.4.

37. Frontinus, *Stratagems*, book 1.i.13; and Onasander, *General*, ch. 10(9).22.

38. Frontinus, *Stratagems*, book 2.ix.6; 2.i.2.

39. Ibid., book 4.iii.1, 3, 6, 8.

40. Ibid., book 4.v.2.

41. Ibid., book 1.v.18.

42. Ibid., book 2.vii.13.

43. Ibid., book 1.V.22; 1.iv.3; 1.viii.3; 1.i.2; and Polyaenus, *Stratagems of War*, 1.32.3; 7.6.9; 2.1.9.

44. Frontinus, *Stratagems*, book 1.v.12; and Polyaenus, *Stratagems of War*, 2.2.10.

45. Frontinus, *Stratagems*, book 2.iii.1; book 4.ii.6; and Polyaenus, *Stratagems of War*, 2.3.3.

46. Frontinus, *Stratagems*, book 1.x.2; 1.ix.2.

47. Ibid., book I.i.11; and Polyaenus, *Stratagems of War*, 2.3.10.

48. Frontinus, *Stratagems*, book 4.i.4; 4.v.15, 21–22; and Onasander, *General*, 4.1.

49. Frontinus, *Stratagems*, book 1.iii.4; and Polyaenus, *Stratagems of War*, 6.38.1. Polyaenus cites Hannibal's refusal to mutilate dead enemies in an effort to curry favor with them for future negotiation leverage.

50. Polyaenus, *Stratagems of War*, 3.9.3; and Onasander, *General*, ch. 42(8).19–20.

51. Frontinus, *Stratagems*, book 2.xi.5–6; 4.vii.25.

52. Polyaenus, *Stratagems of War*, 2.1.31.

53. Ibid., 1.43.1.

54. Frontinus, *Stratagems*, book I.ii.2; book 3.ii.4; and Polyaenus, *Stratagems of War*, 2.3.1.

55. Frontinus, *Stratagems*, I.ii.5.

56. Polyaenus, *Stratagems of War*, 2.2.8.

57. Other great generals did the same, turning to their strengths at critical mo-

ments in their campaigns, such as Julius Caesar and Alexander. Frontinus, *Strata-gems*, book 2.iii.1–3.

58. Hamidullah, *Battlefields of the Prophet*, #3, 3. A higher casualty list comes from Rahman, *Muhammad as a Military Leader*, 46; and Qureshi, *Foreign Policy of Hadrat Muhammad*, 327. The numbers used by these authors leave out the executed men of the Banu Qurayzah. I have added these to the total war dead.

59. Making such population estimates can be tricky. The population estimates of 50,000–80,000 for the Hijaz region would seem reasonable in light of population estimates for more prosperous regions such as Egypt, Syria, and the Lebanon in the 1300s. See Ayalon, "Regarding Population Estimates."

60. Ibn Saʿd, *Kitab al-Tabaqat al-Kabir*, 2:317–18; Siddiqi, *Sahih Imam Muslim*, vol. 5, #1767; and Khaliyl, *Jami' al-Tirmidhi*, vol. 3, #1606.

61. Wallach, *Dogma of the Battle of Annihilation*, 43. Sun Tzu noted that "those called skilled in war conquered an enemy easily conquered"; *Art of War*, book 4, 10.

62. Freytag-Loringhoven, *Power of Personality in War*, 186.

63. Onasander, *General*, XXII. 1. Khalid led the decisive flank attack against the Muslim forces.

64. Ibn Ishaq, *Sirat Rasul Allah*, 52–53.

65. Hoffer, *True Believer*, sec. 13, 24; sec. 87, 101–2. It should be understood that in making this statement in light of Hoffer's conclusions, I do not endorse the concepts of Adolf Hitler, whom Hoffer quotes in making his conclusion. It must be noted that even though someone like Hitler may say something, it does not always mean it is incorrect simply because of the loathsome nature of the source.

Bibliography

Primary

SCRIPTURE

Pickthall, Mohammad Marmaduke, trans. *The Meaning of the Glorious Qur'an*. Delhi: Kutub Khana Ishayat-ul-Islam, n.d.

Yusuf Ali, Abdullah. *Roman Transliteration of the Holy Qur'an*. Beirut, Lebanon: Dar al Furqan, 1934.

HADITH AND SUNNAH COLLECTIONS

Al-Khattab, Nasiruddin, trans. *Sunan an-Nasa'i*. Vols. 1–6. Riyadh, Saudi Arabia: Darussalam, 2007.

Ansari, Muhammad Tufail, trans. *Sunan Ibn-e-Majah of Imam Abu Abdullah Muhammad bin Yazid Ibn-e-Maja al-Qazwini*. Vols. 1–5. New Delhi: Kitab Bhavan, 2004.

As-Sanani, Muhammad bin Ismail, trans. *Bulugh al-Maram of al-Hafiz Ibn Hajar al-Asqalani*. Riyadh, Saudi Arabia: Dar-us-Salam Publications, 1996.

Bewley, Aisha Abdarrahman, trans. *Al-Muwatta of Imam Malik ibn Anas*. Inverness, Scotland: Madinah Press, 2004.

Hasan, Ahmad, trans. *Sunan Abu Dawud*. Vols. 1–3. New Delhi: Kitab Bhavan, 2005.

Ibn Sa'd. *Kitab al-Tabaqat al-Kabir*. Vols. 1 and 2. Translated by S. Moinul Haq. New Delhi: Kitab Bhavan, n.d.

———. *Kitab al-Tabaqat al-Kabir (The Women of Madina)*. Vol. 8. Translated by Aisha Bewley. London: Ta Ha Publishers Ltd., 1995.

Karim, Al-Haj Maulana Fazlul, trans. *Al-Hadith, Mishkat-ul-Masabih, al-Tabrizi*. Vols. 1–4. New Delhi: Islamic Book Service, 2006.

Khaliyl, Abu, trans. *Jami' al-Tirmidhi*. Vols. 1–6. Riyadh, Saudi Arabia: Darussalam, 2007.

Khan, Muhammad Muhsin, trans. *Sahih al-Bukhari*. Vols. 1–9. Reprint, New Delhi: Kitab Bhavan, 1987.

Kulayni, Mohammed Ibne Yakoob, comp. "*Al-Kafi* Selections, Books 1–8." Translated by Moulana Syed Kalbe Sadeq. http://www.al-kafi.org/. Accessed July 8, 2009.

Siddiqi, Abdul Hamid, trans. *Sahih Imam Muslim*. Vols. 1–8. New Delhi: Idara Isha'at-E-Diniyat Ltd., 2001.

EARLY ISLAMIC HISTORICAL AND COMMENTARY LITERATURE

Adil, Hafiz Muhammad, trans. *Letters of Hadrat Abu Bakr Siddiq*. New Delhi: Kitab Bhavan, 1994.

———, trans. *Letters of Hadrat 'Umar Farooq*. New Delhi: Kitab Bhavan, 1992.

Al-Baladhuri, Ahmad Ibn Yahya. *Kitab Futuh al-Buldan (The Origins of the Islamic State)*. Parts 1 and 2. Translated by Philip Khuri Hitti and Francis Clark Murgotten. Reprint, New York: AMS Press, 1968.

Al-Tabari, Abu Ja'far Muhammad bin Jarir. *Ta'rikh al-rusul wa'l-muluk (The History of al-Tabari)*. Said Amir Arjomand, series editor. Albany, N.Y.: State University of New York Press, 1999.

Al-Waqidi, Muhammad Ibn 'Umar. *Kitab al-Maghazi*. Translated by Julius Wellhausen. Berlin: Druck und Verlag von G. Reimer, 1882.

An-Naisaburi, Abu al-Hassan Ali ibn Ahmad al-Wahidi. *Reasons and Occasions of Revelation of the Holy Quran*. Translated by Adnan Salloum. Beirut, Lebanon: DAR al-KOTOB al-ILMYAH, 1999.

Caesar, Julius. *The Gallic War*. Translated by H. J. Edwards. Cambridge, Mass.: Harvard University Press, 2004.

Ibn Ishaq. *Sirat Rasul Allah (The Life of Muhammad)*. Translated by Alfred Guillaume. Oxford, UK: Oxford University Press, 2004.

Ibn Kathir. *Al-Sira al-Nabawiyya (The Life of the Prophet Muhammad)*. Vols. 1–4. Translated by Trevor Le Gassick. Reading, UK: Garnet Publishing, 2000.

———. *Tafsir Al-Qur'an Al-'Azim*. Vols. 1–10. Edited by Shaykh Safiur-Rahman al-Mubarakpuri. Riyadh, Saudi Arabia: Darussalam, 2003.

Qureshi, Sultan Ahmed, trans. *Letters of the Holy Prophet Muhammad*. New Delhi: Kitab Bhavan, 2003.

EARLY NON-ISLAMIC HISTORICAL LITERATURE

Garsoian, Nina G., trans. *Buzandaran Patmut'iwnk' (The Epic Histories)*. Cambridge, Mass.: Harvard University Press, 1989.

Frontinus. *Stratagems*. Translated by Charles E. Bennett. Cambridge, Mass.: Harvard University Press, 2003.

John of Nikiu. *The Chronicle of John, Bishop of Nikiu*. 1916. Translated by R. H. Charles. Merchantville, N.J.: Evolution Publishing, 2007.

Machiavelli, Niccolò. *The Prince*. Translated by Luigi Ricci. New York: New American Library, 1952.

Dennis, George T., trans. *Maurice's Strategikon.* Philadelphia: University of Pennsylvania Press, 1984.

Mango, Cyril, trans. *Nikephoros Patriarch of Constantinople Short History.* Washington, D.C.: Dumbarton Oaks, 1990.

Onasander. *The General,* Translated by the Illinois Greek Club. Cambridge, Mass. Harvard University Press, 1928.

Polyaenus. *Stratagems of War.* Translated by Peter Krentz and Everett Wheeler. Chicago: Ares Publishers, 1994.

Schaff, Philip, and Henry Wace, eds. *Nicene and Post-Nicene Fathers of the Christian Church.* 2nd series. Vols. 1–8. Reprint, Grand Rapids, Mich.: Eerdmans, 1983.

Suetonius. *The Twelve Caesars.* Translated by Robert Graves. Harmondsworth, Middlesex, UK: Penguin Books, 1965.

Sun Tzu. *The Art of War.* Translated by Samuel B. Griffith. London: Oxford University Press, 1963.

Tacitus. *Annals.* Translated by John Jackson. Cambridge, Mass.: Harvard University Press, 2005.

———. *Histories.* Translated by Clifford Moore. Cambridge, Mass.: Harvard University Press, 2006.

Theophanes the Confessor. *The Chronicle of Theophanes Confessor: Byzantine and Near Eastern History AD 284–813.* Translated and edited by Cyril Mango and Roger Scott. Oxford, UK: Clarendon Press, 2006.

Vegetius. "The Military Institutions of the Romans." In *Roots of Strategy,* book 1, edited by T. R. Phillips, 65–176. Harrisburg, Pa.: Stackpole Books, 1985.

CLASSICAL AND MEDIEVAL ISLAMIC SOURCES

Al-Ansari, 'Umar ibn Ibrahim al-Awsi. *Tafrij al-Kurub Fi Tadbir al-Hurub* (*A Muslim Manual of War*). Translated by George T. Scanlon. Cairo: American University at Cairo Press, 1961.

Al-Duyati, Abi Zakaryya al-Dimashqi, "Ibn Nuhaas." *Mashari al-Ashwaq* (*The Book of Jihad*). Translated by Noor Yamani. http://islambase.co.uk/.

Al-Ghazali, Abu Hamid Muhammad. *The Incoherence of the Philosophers.* Translated by Michael E. Marmura. Provo, Utah: Brigham Young University Press, 2000.

Al-Hujwiri, 'Ali bin 'Uthman al-Jullabi. *Kashf al-Mahjub* (*The Revelation of the Veiled*). Translated by Reynold A. Nicholson. Reprint, Cambridge, UK: E.J.W. Gibb Memorial, 2000.

Al-Marghinani, Burhan al-Din al-Farghani. *Al-Hidayah Fi Sharh Bidayat al-Mubtadi* (*The Guidance*). Vols. 1 and 2. Translated by Imran Ahsan Khan Nyazee. Bristol, UK: Amal Press, 2006–2008.

Al-Mawardi. *Al-Ahkam al-Sultaniyya w' al-Wilayat al-Diniyya* (*The Ordinances of Government*). Translated by Wafaa H. Wahba. Reading, UK: Garnet Publishing, 1996.

Al-Qayrawani, Ibn Abi Zayd. *A Madinan View on the Sunnah, Courtesy, Wisdom, Battles and History.* Translated by Abdassamad Clarke. London: Ta Ha Publishers Ltd., 1999.

Al-Qushayri, Abu'l-Qasim. *Al-Risala al-qushayriyya fi 'ilm al-tasawwuf* (*Al-Qush-*

ayir's Epistle on Sufism). Translated by Alexander D. Knysh. Reading, UK: Garnet Publishing, 2007.

Al-Tabari, Abu Ja'far Muhammad bin Jarir. *Kitab al-Jihad* (*The Book of Jihad*). Translated by Yasir S. Ibrahim. Lewiston, N.Y.: Edwin Mellen Press, 2007.

Ibn al-Arabi. *Futuhat al-Makkiyah* (*The Mysteries of Bearing Witness to the Oneness of God and Prophethood of Muhammad*). Translated by Aisha Bewley. Chicago: KAZI Publications, 2002.

Ibn Khaldun. *The Muqaddimah: An Introduction to History*. Vols. 1–3. Translated by Franz Rosenthal. Princeton, N.J.: Princeton University Press, 1980.

Ibn Khallikan. *Wafayat al-A'Yan Wa Anba' Abna' Al-Zaman*. Vols. 1–7. Translated by M. de Slane. Ed. S. Moinul Haq. New Delhi: Kitab Bhavan, 1996.

Ibn Naqib al-Misri, Ahmad. *'Umdat al-Salik* (*Reliance of the Traveller*). Translated by Nuh Ha Mim Keller. Beltsville, Md.: Amana Publications, 1994.

Ibn Rushd (Averroes). *Bidayat al-Mujtahid wa Nihayat al-Muqtasid* (*The Distinguished Jurist's Primer*). Vols. 1 and 2. Translated by Ahsan Khan Nyazee. Reading, UK: Garnet Publishing, 2006.

Ibn Sallam, Abu 'Ubayd al-Qasim. *Kitab al-Amwal* (*The Book of Revenue*). Translated by Imran Ahsan Khan Nyazee. Reading, UK: Garnet Publishing, 2005.

Ibn Taymiyyah. *Al-Furqan bayna Awliya ar-Rahman wa Awliya ash-Shaytan* (*The Decisive Criteria Between The Friends of Allah and the Friends of Shaytan*). Translated by Abu Rumaysah. Birmingham, UK: Daar us-Sunnah Publishers, 2005.

———. *Al-Hisba fi al-Islam* (*Public Duties in Islam: The Institution of the Hisba*). Translated by Muhtar Holland. Leicester, UK: Islamic Foundation, 1992.

———. *Al-Jawab al-Sahih* (*A Muslim Theologian's Response to Christianity*). Translated and edited by Thomas F. Michel. Delmar, N.Y.: Caravan Books, 1999.

———. *On Public and Private Law in Islam*. Translated by Omar A. Farrukh. Beirut, Lebanon: Khayat Publishing Co., 1966.

Khadduri, Majid, trans. *The Islamic Law of Nations: Shaybani's Siyar*. Baltimore, Md.: Johns Hopkins University Press, 1966.

Khalid, Anas, trans. "The Mukhtasar of al-Khiraqi: A Tenth Century Work on Islamic Jurisprudence." PhD diss., New York University, 1992.

Nicholson, Reynard A., ed. and trans. *The Mathnawi of Jalalu'ddin Rumi*. Books 1–6. Reprint, Cambridge, UK: E.J.W. Gibb Memorial, 2001.

Qadi 'Iyad. *Ash-Shifa*. Translated by Aisha Bewley. Inverness, Scotland: Madinah Press, 2006.

Secondary Sources

Abu Khalil, Shawqi. *Atlas on the Prophet's Biography*. Riyadh, Saudi Arabia: Darussalam, 2003.

Abu Zahra, Muhammad. *The Four Imams: Their Lives, Works and Their Schools of Thought*. Translated by Aisha Bewley. London: Dar Al Taqwa Ltd., 2001.

Ali, Maulana Muhammad. *Muhammad the Prophet*. Lahore, Pakistan: Ahmadiyya Anjuman Isha'at, 1993.

Alinsky, Saul. *Rules for Radicals*. New York: Vintage Books, 1972.

Al-Mubarakpuri, Safl-ur-Rahman. *Ar-Raheeq al-Makhtum* (*The Sealed Nectar*). Madinah, Saudi Arabia: Islamic University al-Madina al-Munawwara, 1979.

Al-Qardawi, Yusuf. *Fiqh az-Zakat: A Comparative Study*. Translated by Monzer Kahf. London: Dar Al Taqwa Ltd., 1999.

Armstrong, Karen. *Muhammad: A Biography of the Prophet*. San Francisco: Harper-One, 1993.

Ashdown, Charles Henry. *European Arms & Armour*. New York: Brussel & Brussel, 1967.

Ayalon, David. "Regarding Population Estimates in the Countries of Medieval Islam." *Journal of Economic and Social History of the Orient* 28, no. 1 (1985): 1–19.

Ayton, Andrew. "Arms, Armour, and Horses." In *Medieval Warfare, A History*, edited by Maurice Keen, 186–208. Oxford, UK: Oxford University Press, 1999.

Banks, Arthur. *A Military Atlas of the First World War*. Barnsley, South Yorkshire, UK: Pen & Sword Books, Ltd., 2001.

Barreveld, W. H. *Date Palm Products*. Rome: Food and Agriculture Organization of the United Nations, 1993.

Bashear, Suliman. *Arabs and Others in Early Islam*. Studies in Late Antiquity and Early Islam, no. 8. Princeton, N.J.: Darwin Press, 1997.

Bashier, Zakaria. *War and Peace in the Life of the Prophet Muhammad*. Markfield Leicestershire, UK: Islamic Foundation, 2006.

Bewley, Aisha. *Glossary of Islamic Terms*. London: Ta-Ha Publishers, 1998.

Black, Jeremy. "A Revolution in Military Cartography? Europe 1650–1815." *Journal of Military History* 73, no. 1 (January 2009): 49–68.

Boissonnade, P. *Life and Work in Medieval Europe*. Translated by Eileen Power. New York: Harper Torchbooks, 1964.

Boutell, Charles. *Arms and Armour in Antiquity and the Middle Ages*. Translated by M. P. Lacombe. Conshohocken, Pa.: Combined Books, 1996.

Brauer, Jurgen, and Hubert van Tuyll. *Castles, Battles, and Bombs: How Economics Explains Military History*. Chicago: University of Chicago Press, 2008.

Burg, David F., and L. Edward Purcell. *Almanac of World War I*. Lexington: University Press of Kentucky, 1998.

Burton, Sir Richard F. *The Book of the Sword*. New York: Dover, 1987.

———. *Personal Narrative of a Pilgrimage to al-Madinah & Meccah*. Vols. 1 and 2. New York: Dover, 1964.

Callwell, C. E. *Small Wars: Their Principles and Practice*. Reprint, London: H. M. Stationery Office.

Cameron, Averil, ed. *The Byzantine and Early Islamic Near East*. Vol. 3, *States, Resources and Armies*. Studies in Late Antiquity and Early Islam, no. 1. Princeton, N.J.: Darwin Press, 1995.

Clausewitz, Carl von. *On War*. Translated and edited by Michael Howard and Peter Paret. Princeton, N.J.: Princeton University Press, 1976.

Cook, David. "Why Did Muhammad Attack the Byzantines: A Reexamination of Qur'an *sura* 30:1–2." Paper delivered at the Association for the Study of the Middle East and Africa conference, April 24–26, 2008.

Corum, James S. *Bad Strategies: How Major Powers Fail in Counterinsurgency*. Minneapolis, Minn.: Zenith Press, 2008.

Crone, Patricia. *Meccan Trade and the Rise of Islam*. Piscataway, N.J.: Gorgias Press, 2004.

Dach Bern, H. von. *Total Resistance*. Translated by Hans Lienhard. Boulder, Colo.: Paladin Press, 1965.

Delbrück, Hans. *History of the Art of War*. Vol. 1, *Warfare in Antiquity*. Translated by Walter J. Renfroe Jr. Lincoln: University of Nebraska Press, 1990.

Department of the Army. *U.S. Army Field Manual 5–34 Engineer Field Data*. Washington, D.C.: Headquarters, Department of the Army, 1987.

D'Este, Carlo. *Patton: A Genius for War*. New York: HarperCollins, 1995.

Dodge, Theodore Ayrault. *Alexander*. New York: Da Capo Press, 1996.

———. *Gustavus Adolphus*. London: Greenhill Books, 1996.

———. *Hannibal*. New York: Da Capo Press, 1995.

Donner, Fred M. "Mecca's Food Supplies and Muhammad's Boycott." *Journal of the Economic and Social History of the Orient* 20, no. 3 (October 1977): 249–66.

———. *Muhammad and the Believers: At the Origins of Islam*. Cambridge, Mass.: Belknap Press, 2010.

———. *Narratives of Islamic Origins: The Beginnings of Islamic Historical Writings*. Studies in Late Antiquity and Early Islam, no. 14. Princeton, N.J.: Darwin Press, 1998.

Ellis, John. *World War II: A Statistical Survey*. New York: Facts on File, 1993.

Engels, Donald. *Alexander the Great and the Logistics of the Macedonian Army*. Berkeley: University of California Press, 1980.

Erfurth, Waldemar. *Surprise*. In *Roots of Strategy*, book 3, 351–554. Harrisburg, Pa.: Stackpole Books, 1991.

Esposito, John, ed. *The Oxford Dictionary of Islam*. Oxford, UK: Oxford University Press, 2003.

Firestone, Reuven. *Jihad: The Origin of Holy War in Islam*. Oxford, UK: Oxford University Press, 1999.

France, John. *Western Warfare in the Age of the Crusades 1000–1300*. Ithaca, N.Y.: Cornell University Press, 1999.

Fraser, David. *Knight's Cross: A Life of Field Marshal Erwin Rommel*. New York: HarperPerennial, 1995.

Freytag-Loringhoven, Hugo von. *The Power of Personality in War*. In *Roots of Strategy*, book 3, 173–350. Harrisburg, Pa.: Stackpole Books, 1991.

Fuller, J.F.C. *A Military History of the Western World*. Vols. 1–3. New York: Funk & Wagnalls, 1954.

Gabriel, Richard. *Muhammad: Islam's First Great General*. Norman: University of Oklahoma Press, 2007.

Galula, David. *Counterinsurgency Warfare, Theory and Practice*. Westport, Conn.: Praeger Security International, 2006.

Gentile, Gian P. "The Selective Use of History in the Development of American Counterinsurgency Doctrine." *Army History*, no. 72 (Summer 2009): 21–35.

Gies, Frances, and Joseph Gies. *Cathedral, Forge, and Waterwheel*. New York: HarperPerennial, 1995.

Gleichen, Lord Edward. *Chronology of the Great War, 1914–1918*. London: Greenhill Books, 2000.

Glubb, Sir John. *The Life and Times of Muhammad*. New York: Cooper Square Press, 2001.

Greene, Robert. *The 48 Laws of Power.* New York: Penguin Books, 2000.

Guevara, Ernesto "Che." *Guerrilla Warfare.* Translated by J. P. Morray. New York: Vintage Books, 1969.

———. *The Motorcycle Diaries: Notes on a Latin American Journey.* Translated by Alexandra Keeble. Melbourne, Australia: Ocean Press, 2004.

Guindi, Fadwa El. *Veil: Modesty, Privacy and Resistance.* Oxford, UK: Berg, 2000.

Haldon, John. *Warfare, State and Society in the Byzantine World 565–1204.* London: Routledge, 1999.

Haldon, John, and Lawrence I. Conrad, eds. *The Byzantine and Early Islamic Near East.* Vol. 6, *Elites Old and New in the Byzantine and Early Islamic Near East.* Studies in Late Antiquity and Early Islam, no. 1. Princeton, N.J.: Darwin Press, 2004.

Hamid, AbdulWahid. *Companions of the Prophet.* Books 1 and 2. London: Muslim Education and Literary Services, 1998.

Hamidullah, Muhammad. *The Battlefields of the Prophet Muhammad.* New Delhi: Kitab Bhavan, 2003.

Harari, Yuval Noah. *Special Operations in the Age of Chivalry.* Woodbridge, Suffolk, UK: Boydell Press, 2007.

Hashi, A. M., M. Kamoun, and D. Cianci. "Feed Requirements of the Camel." International Center for Advanced Mediterranean Agronomic Studies, 1995. http://ressources.ciheam.org/om/pdf/b13/95605343.pdf.

Haykal, Muhammad H. *The Life of Muhammad.* Translated by Isma'il Raji al-Faruqi. Kuala Lumpur, Malaysia: Islamic Book Trust, 2002.

Hill, D. R. "The Role of the Camel and the Horse in the Early Arab Conquests." In *War, Technology, and Society in the Middle East,* edited by V. J. Parry and M. E. Yapp, 32–43. New York: Oxford University Press, 1975.

Hoffer, Eric. *The True Believer.* New York: Harper & Row Publishers, 1966.

Horovitz, Joseph. *The Earliest Biographies of the Prophet and Their Authors.* Studies in Late Antiquity and Early Islam, no. 11. Princeton, N.J.: Darwin Press, 2002.

Hosain, Saiyid Safdar. *The Early History of Islam.* Vols. 1 and 2. Reprint, New Delhi: Rima Publishing House, 1992.

Hourani, Albert. *A History of the Arab Peoples.* New York: Warner Books, 1992.

Hoyt, Edwin P. *Guerilla: Colonel von Lettow-Vorbeck and Germany's East African Empire.* New York: MacMillan, 1981.

Hughes, Daniel, and Harry Bell, trans. *Moltke on the Art of War: Selected Writings.* Novato, Calif.: Presidio, 1993.

Hughes, Thomas Patrick. *Dictionary of Islam.* Chicago: KAZI Publications, 1994.

Ibn Abdul Wahab, Shaikh Abdullah ibn al-Shaikh Muhammad. *Biography of the Prophet.* Vols. 1 and 2. Translated by Sameh Strauch. Riyadh, Saudi Arabia: Daussalam, 2006.

James, Daniel, ed. *The Complete Bolivian Diaries of Che Guevara.* New York: Stein and Day, 1969.

Jandora, John. *The March from Medina: A Revisionist Study of the Arab Conquests.* Clifton, N.J.: Kingston Press, 1990.

Jomini, Antoine-Henri de. *The Art of War.* London: Greenhill Books, 1996.

Kaegi, Walter. *Heraclius Emperor of Byzantium*. Cambridge, UK: Cambridge University Press, 2003.

Kennedy, Hugh. *The Armies of the Caliphs: Military and Society in the Early Islamic State*. London: Routledge, 2001.

———. *When Baghdad Ruled the Muslim World*. Cambridge, Mass.: Da Capo Press, 2005.

King, G.R.D., and Averil Cameron, eds. *The Byzantine and Early Islamic Near East*. Vol. 2, *Land Use and Settlement Patterns*. Studies in Late Antiquity and Early Islam, no. 1. Princeton, N.J.: Darwin Press, 1994.

Lancaster, William, and Fidelity Lancaster. "Concepts of Leadership in Bedouin Society." In *The Byzantine and Early Islamic Near East*. Vol. 6, *Elites Old and New in the Byzantine and Early Islamic Near East*. Edited by John Haldon and Lawrence I. Conrad, 29–61. Studies in Late Antiquity and Early Islam, no. 1. Princeton, N.J.: Darwin Press, 2004.

Landau-Tasseron, Ella. "Features of the Pre-Conquest Muslim Army in the Time of Muhammad." In *The Byzantine and Early Islamic Near East*. Vol. 3, *States, Resources, and Armies*, edited by Averil Cameron, 299–336. Studies in Late Antiquity and Early Islam, no. 1, Princeton, N.J.: Darwin Press, 1995.

Lane, Edward W. *An Arabic-English Lexicon in Eight Parts*. Beirut, Lebanon: Librarie Du Liban, 1968.

Lawrence, T. E. *Seven Pillars of Wisdom*. Garden City, N.Y.: Garden City Publishing, 1938.

Lecker, Michael. *The "Constitution of Medina": Muhammad's First Legal Document*. Studies in Late Antiquity and Early Islam, no. 23. Princeton, N.J.: Darwin Press, Inc 2004.

Lettow-Vorbeck, Paul von. *My Reminiscences of East Africa*. Uckfield, East Sussex, UK: Naval & Military Press, n.d.

Luvaas, Jay, trans. *Frederick the Great on the Art of War*. New York: Da Capo Press, 1999.

Mao Tse-Tung. *On Guerrilla Warfare*. Translated by Samuel B. Griffith. Baltimore, Md.: Nautical & Aviation Publishing Company of America, 1992.

———. *Selected Military Writings of Mao Tse-Tung*. Peking: Foreign Language Press, 1963.

Marcy, Randolph B. *The Prairie Traveler*. Reprint, Bedford, Mass.: Applewood Books, 1993.

Martin, George. *The Red Shirt and the Cross of Savoy: The Story of Italy's Risorgimento (1748–1871)*. New York: Dodd, Mead and Company, 1969.

Marx, Karl, and Friedrich Engels. *The Communist Manifesto*. Translated by Samuel Moore. New York: Washington Square Press, 1974.

McCudden, James. *Flying Fury: Five Years in the Royal Flying Corps*. London: Greenhill Books, 2000.

Nagl, John A. *Learning to Eat Soup with a Knife: Counterinsurgency Lessons from Malaya to Vietnam*. Chicago: University of Chicago Press, 2005.

Nicolle, David. *Medieval Siege Weapons (2): Byzantium, the Islamic World, and India AD 476–1526*. Oxford, UK: Osprey Publishing, 2003.

Norman, A.V.B., and Don Pottinger. *English Weapons and Warfare 449–1660.* Englewood Cliffs, N.J.: Prentice-Hall, 1979.

Nossov, Konstantin. *Ancient and Medieval Siege Weapons.* Guilford, Conn.: Lyons Press, 2005.

Noth, Albrecht, with Lawrence I. Conrad. *The Early Arabic Historical Tradition: A Source-Critical Study.* Studies in Late Antiquity and Early Islam, no. 3. Princeton, N.J.: Darwin Press, 1994.

Omar, Abdul Mannan. *Dictionary of the Holy Qur'an.* Hockessin, Del.: NOOR Foundation, 2005.

Ostrogorsky, George. *History of the Byzantine State.* New Brunswick, N.J.: Rutgers University Press, 1957.

Pryor, John H. "Introduction: Modelling Bohemond's March to Thessalonikē." In *Logistics of Warfare in the Age of the Crusades,* edited by John H. Pryor, 1–24. Aldershot, UK: Ashgate Publishing Ltd., 1988.

Qureshi, Muhammad Siddique. *Foreign Policy of Hadrat Muhammad.* New Delhi: Kitab Bhavan, 1991.

Rahman, Afzalur. *Muhammad as a Military Leader.* London: Muslim Schools Trust, 1980.

Ramadan, Tariq. *The Messenger: The Meanings of the Life of Muhammad.* London: Penguin Books, 2007.

Record, Jeffrey. *Beating Goliath: Why Insurgencies Win.* Washington, D.C.: Potomac Books, 2007.

Rehman Shaikh, Fazlur. *Chronology of Prophetic Events.* London: Ta Ha Publishers Ltd., 2001.

Rickenbacker, Edward V. *Fighting the Flying Circus.* New York: Edward A. Stokes Company, 1919.

Rizvi, Sayyid Ameenul Hasan. *Battles of the Prophet in Light of the Qur'an.* Jeddah, Saudi Arabia: Abul-Qasim Publishing House, 2002.

Rodgers, Russ. *The Fundamentals of Islamic Asymmetric Warfare.* Lewiston, N.Y.: Edwin Mellen Press, 2008.

Rogerson, Barnaby. *The Prophet Muhammad, a Biography.* Mahwah, N.J.: Hidden Spring, 2003.

Rothenberg, Gunther E. *The Art of Warfare in the Age of Napoleon.* Bloomington: Indiana University Press, 1980.

Sawaya, W. N., J. K. Khalil, A. Al-Shalhat, and H. Al-Mohammad. "Chemical Composition and Nutritional Quality of Camel Milk." *Journal of Food Science* 49(1984): 744–47.

Schwartz-Barcott, T. P. *War, Terror, and Peace in the Qur'an and in Islam.* Carlisle, Pa.: Army War College Foundation Press, 2004.

Sedgwick, Mark J. *Sufism, the Essentials.* Cairo, Egypt: American University in Cairo Press, 2000.

Sheppard, Steven ed. *The Selected Writings of Sir Edward Coke.* Vols. 1–3. Indianapolis, Ind.: Liberty Fund, 2003.

Shlapentokh, Dmitry V. "Revolutionary as a Career." *Communist and Post-Communist Studies* 29, no. 3 (1996): 331–61.

Siddiqui, Abdul Hameed. *The Life of Muhammad*. Kuala Lumpur, Malaysia: Islamic Book Trust, 1999.

Sivan, Emmanuel. *Radical Islam: Medieval Theology and Modern Politics*. New Haven, Conn.: Yale University Press, 1990.

Steingass, Francis Joseph. *English-Arabic Translator Dictionary*. London: W. H. Allen and Company, 1882.

Strange, L. A. *Recollections of an Airman*. Reprint, London: Greenhill Books, 1989.

Taber, Robert. *War of the Flea: The Classic Study of Guerrilla Warfare*. Washington, D.C.: Brassey's, Inc., 2002.

Udet, Ernst. *Mein Fliegerleben*. Berlin: Ulstein A. G., 1935.

Von Mises, Ludwig. *Theory and History: An Interpretation of Social and Economic Evolution*. Reprint, New Rochelle, N.Y.: Arlington House, 1969.

Wallach, Jehuda L. *The Dogma of the Battle of Annihilation*. Westport, Conn.: Greenwood Press, 1986.

Watt, W. Montgomery. *Muhammad at Mecca*. Oxford, UK: Oxford University Press, 2004.

———. *Muhammad at Medina*. Oxford, UK: Oxford University Press, 2004.

Wise, Terence. *Medieval Warfare*. New York: Hastings House Publishers, 1976.

Index

Budayl bin Warqa, 211, 215
al-Bukhari, 18, 19, 105, 256
Buwat, 79, 82
Byzantines/Byzantine Empire, 24–26,
    141, 144, 163, 165, 195, 221, 237,
    281nn118,132; 283n139; boycott of
    hostile Arab tribes, 162; logistics
    and, 240, 295n27; Muhammad's
    raids against, 164, 166, 206–7, 227,
    230; Mu'tah, battle of, and, 208–9

Caesar, Germanicus, 285n26
Caesar, Julius, 15, 155, 188, 240, 245,
    273n22
Camels: as transport, 76; cost of
    75–76; not for mounted
    combat, 76
Cannae, battle of, 247
Cavour, Camillo, 264n41
Charlemagne, 74
Clausewitz, Carl von, 3, 129, 157
Cook, Michael, 7, 21
Counterinsurgency: American Indians
    and, 5; buying off populace by,
    283n6; force, use of during, 169,
    171, 283n6; fortifications as, 173;
    insurgency to be destroyed by, 248;
    insurgent vulnerability due to small
    numbers, 60; and Maslow's Hierar-
    chy of Needs, 284n6; population-
    and enemy-centric views of, 284n7;
    severe punishments as form of, 185
Covenant of Madinah, 55–58, 60, 65,
    115, 137, 138, 145; provisions of, 56
Crone, Patricia, 7

Damascus, 112
Descriptive Approach, 6
Dhal al-Salasil, 160, 195
Dhat Atlah, 195, 206
Dhul al-Qassah, 170
Dhu Qarad, 170, 173–74
Diya (definition), 33
Donner, Fred, 5–9, 11, 13–14, 16,
    255n3

Dumat al-Jandal, 134, 141, 170, 178, 221,
    230
Durayd bin al-Simmah, 220, 223

East Africa, 158
Egypt, 26
Emanuele, Vittorio, 264n41
Epaminondas, 245

Fadak, 170, 178, 195, 203–4
Fatima, 203
Fay, 140, 203
Fazarah (tribe), 170, 178–79
Feisal, Prince, 159
Fihr (tribe), 83
Foco, 157
Frontinus, 11, 117
Frumentius, 44
Fudul, 37
Furat Ibn Hayyan 111–12, 273n27

Gabriel, Richard, 263n27
Garibaldi, Giuseppe, 264n41
Ghalib bin 'Abdullah al-Laythi, 106,
    195, 204
al-Ghamr, 170
Ghassan (tribe), 162, 207–8
Ghatafan (tribe), 106, 107, 138, 140,
    142–43, 147–48, 170, 173, 174, 175,
    178, 184, 195, 196, 198, 204, 244
Ghaylan bin Salama, 165
Ghazwah (definition), 78
Goats in Islamic law, 158
Goldziher, Ignaz, 7
Guevara, Ernesto Che, 129, 156–57,
    171, 284n16; supply shortages and,
    280n98
Guillaume, A., 18, 20
Guynemer, Georges, 12

al-Hajjaj bin 'Ilat al-Sulami, 202
Hamidullah, Muhammad, 58, 130, 144,
    197
Hamzah, 42–43, 45, 79, 81–82, 95–96,
    124, 130, 218, 232, 275n70

186–87, 193, 209, 217, 220, 221, 230, 248, 275nn 59, 72, 284n7

al-Khandaq, battle of, 70, 134, 143, 145–48, 236, 245; consequences of, 153–54, 166–67

al-Kharrar, 79, 81

Khaybar, 170, 181–82, 184; described, 72; siege of, 160, 195–200, 245; siege analyzed, 201, 233

al-Khazraj (tribe), 46–47, 54–57, 59, 64, 66, 67, 110, 118, 122, 138, 149, 181–82

Khurasan, 12

Khusrau II, 26, 162–63, 166–67, 187, 283n138

Khuza'ah (tribe), 131, 141, 143, 172, 179–80, 187, 189, 211–12, 216

Kinanah bin al-Rabi bin Abu al-Huqayq, 200–201, 203

al-Kudr, 106–7

Kurz bin Jabir al-Fihri, 79, 83, 170, 185, 218

Lawrence, T. E., 158–59

Lettow-Vorbeck, Paul von, 158–59

Lex talionis, 32–33, 40, 43, 45, 109; and Hebraic Law, 258n31

Lihyan (tribe), 134, 160, 170, 172–74, 242

Liwa' (war banners), 28

Logistics: analysis of Muhammad's raids and, 158; Byzantine and Muslim, 295n27; Byzantine and Sasanid concepts of, 240; and interpretive approach to early Islamic sources, 16–17; Madinah as base of, 71–76; Muslims' weak, 211, 240, 296n28; need for in insurgency, 71; outside support and, 155, 157; paid leadership and, 157

Ma'bad al-Khuza'i, 131–32, 141

Machiavelli, 64

Madinah: described, 52, 54; divisions in, 54–55; food production and consumption, 72; population of, 58, 60;

preaching of Islam in, 47; Prophet as judge of, 56; siege of. *See also* al-Khandaq, battle of

Mahmud bin Maslamah, 199

Makhzum clan, 88, 90

Makkah: agriculture in, 29; described, 26–27; falls to Muhammad, 216–19; grain embargo against, 169; rise of merchants in, 26–27; place between great empires, 24; politics of, 40–41; population of, 45

Maktum, 84

Mala', 26, 40–41, 51, 213, 216

Malik bin 'Auf al-Nasri, 220, 222, 224

Malik (tribe), 223

Manjaniqs, 200, 282n132; Muslim use of, 165, 225

Mansur, 144

Mao, Tse-Tung, 129, 157

Marhab, 196, 199

Marthad al-Ghanwi, 134

Maslow's Hierarchy of Needs, 284n6

Mawla (definition), 31

Mayfa'ah, 195

al-Miqdad bin al-Aswad, 95

Mirba' bin Qayzi 118–19

Mises, Ludwig von, 14

Moltke, Helmuth von, 129

Mu'adh bin Amr 97–98

Muhajirun: defined as emigrants, 58; joined with Ansar, 60

Muhammad: and 'Abdullah bin Ubayy, contemplates assassination of, 286n42; 'Abdullah bin Ubayy, as possible contrived opponent, 63–69; adopted son leads multiple raids 175, 177; age for fighting determined by, 89; Alinsky's rules and, 234, 236; Apostle, Messenger, or Prophet, 19; assassination attempts on, 50, 203; assassination of Abu Sufyan authorized, 133, 135; assassinations authorized by, 105, 107, 113, 165; called King of Hijaz, 153; camels, supply of, 75; casus belli sought

Muhammad—*continued*

against Qaynuqa, 109; chain of command first created by, 207; coup d'oeil of, 237; date palms destroyed by, 139; death penalty for apostasy declared by, 171; decree against Jews declared by, 115; distribution of plunder altered by, 257n18; economic plight in early life, 36; embargo against the Quraysh, 169; enemies mocked by poets, 141; fear prayer established by, 140; feint prior to attacking Makkah, 215; fifth column in Makkah, 214–15; fighting permitted by, 49; first raid a failure, 82; food supplies and, 71, 73; horses, possible source of, 161; horses, supply of, 75; ill-prepared to be raided, 174; incites Quraysh at al-Hudaybiyah, 190; initiative retained by, 236; intelligence service of, 76; isolates followers in Madinah, 71; Jews, efforts to co-opt, 69; al-Khandaq, stratagem at battle of, 147; Khaybar, Jews of subjugated, 202; kunyah of Abu al-Qasim, 176; kunyah used in ridicule, 259n41; logistical weakness of, 240; *maktum*, use of, 84; as merchant and small banker, 23; moral inversion and, 108, 213; Mudhammam pejorative of, 269n45; mutilation of enemy dead prohibited by, 130; night movement initiated by, 81–82; non-delegator, 239; non-Muslim help refused, 118; offensive warfare and, 81; operational techniques of, 244; operational tempo controlled by, 238; outside support sought by, 45; overestimates own capabilities, 241; overextended, 188; personality, force of, 238; plunder offered by, 96; political supervision used by, 210–11; prayer toward Jerusalem and Makkah initiated by, 69; preachers sent to Madinah, 47; predictability of operations, 243; prisoners executed by, 100; prisoners tortured by, 169, 200; proscription list of, 218; proxies used by, 191, 226; punitive attacks by, 168, 175, 178, 179, 204, 207, 211; Quraysh deceived by, 201; raids, logistical analysis of, 158; religious freedom ended in Makkah by, 219; revelation cited to violate treaty, 192; rumors, possible use of, 107; sacred months and fighting, 86; self-defense posture taken by, 43; staff functions performed by, 239; surprise attacks by, 204; surprise, vulnerable to, 241; surprised at Badr, 93; tactical advice sought by, 93; tactical weakness of, 242–43; tax collectors dispatched by, 226; terror used by, 172; threat worse than action, 236; and three stages of war, 232; total victory and, 233; transport camels, alters sacrifice to preserve, 205; trench excavation in Madinah, 143, 278n47; unique title of, 257n38; vineyards burned by, 225; vulnerable to popular opinion or superstition, 242; weapons and, 74–75

Muhammad bin Maslamah, 106, 113–14, 118, 169–70, 175, 199, 201

Muharib, 106, 170

Mulawwih, 195

Mulawwih (tribe), 206

Munafiqun, 65, 68, 76–77, 180, 228; defined, 63

al-Mundhir bin ʿAmr, 134, 136

al-Muraysi, 170, 180

Murrah (tribe), 195, 204

Musʿab bin ʿUmayr, 47, 122, 151

Musaylimah bin Habib, 226

Muslim, Imam, 18, 256n34

Muslims: "believers" as possible early name, 255n3; defections among, 49; individual military skill lacking in, 114, 183; Khaybar, first offensive siege of, 201; logistical weakness of, 211; migration to Abyssinia, 43; migration to Madinah, initial, 58; nation at arms, 238; persecutions in Makkah, 40; private warfare and, 268n34;

recruitment for raids of, 61; sacred months violated by, 287n62; security improved during Crusades, 286n47; strength in Makkah, 45; warfare, attitude toward, 146; warfare, breadth of in Islam, 105
al-Mustaliq (tribe), 66, 170, 175, 179–80, 240, 244
Mu'tah, battle of, 160, 195, 207–9, 227, 239, 244
al-Mut'im bin 'Adiy, 260n66
al-Muttalib, 30

al-Nadir (Jewish tribe), 54, 57, 59, 66, 70, 73, 110, 112–13, 115, 134, 137, 142, 144, 148, 149, 200, 203, 225, 233, 245, 277n30, 279n64; expelled from Madinah, 138–40
al-Nadr bin al-Harith, 100
Na'im (Khaybar fort), 199, 201
Najd, 111, 136, 159, 195
al-Najjar clan, 262
Nakhlah, 33–34, 76, 79, 84, 86, 87, 89, 90, 130, 177
Napoleon, 129, 155
an-Nasa'i, 19
Naufal, 30
Negus, 43–44, 162, 188
Noth, Albrecht, 10–13, 15; military movements and, 256n24; themes and, 8–9; topoi and, 11
Nu'aym bin Mas'ud bin 'Amr, 147

Onasander, 276n94

Persia, 13, 15, 26, 165–67
Persian Empire, 25–26, 51, 144, 251, 282n132. *See also* Sasanid Empire
Polyaenus, 11, 296
Pony Express, 15
Prisoners of war (handling), 99, 273n22
Prophet, status of, 34
Protection and allegiance, 40; cross-cultural, 260n58
Puritans, 268n29

Qamus (Khaybar fort), 199
al-Qara (tribe), 133, 135–36
al-Qaradah, 106, 111–12
Qaribah (singing girl), 218
Qaylah (tribe), 54
Qaynuqa (Jewish tribe), 54, 58–59, 65–66, 70, 104, 106, 151, 245; expelled from Madinah, 108–10
Qays bin Abu Sa'sa'a, 95
Qays bin al-Musahhar, 179
Quda'ah, 195
Quda'ah (tribe), 210
al-Qurada, 170
Quraysh (tribe of Makkah): coalition organized, 142; concept of war 128, 129, 146; defections to Islam from, 194; embargo against, 169; failure at al-Hudaybiyah, 190; government as democratic republic, 41; horse cavalry of, 160; Makkah's defenses and, 215; mercenaries and, 116; Muhammad's departure from Makkah and, 52; negotiation and, 172; origin of term, 260n60; risk aversion of, 248; tolerance and diversity among, 40, 248; victory eludes, 248; violations of sacred months, 268n30, 287n62; weaknesses of, 247, 249
Qurayzah (Jewish tribe), 54, 58–59, 70, 107, 110, 115, 134, 138–39, 144–48, 153, 194, 245, 279nn64, 72; destruction of, 149–52, 167
Qureshi, Sultan Ahmed, 55
Qusay, 28–29, 30, 36–37, 38, 42, 219, 232, 260n60
Qutbah bin Qatadah 208–9

Rabigh, 79
Razzia (definition), 32
Rehman Shaikh, Fazlur, 20, 79, 104
Riddah (Apostates War), 26, 196, 231, 240, 284n7
Rifadah, 28–30, 37, 39, 219
Rothenberg, Gunther, 155
Rumi, Jalalu'ddin, 261n73
Russian revolutionaries, 280n100

Russ Rodgers is currently command historian with the U.S. Army and former adjunct professor of history. His previous publications include *Fundamentals of Islamic Asymmetric Warfare: A Documentary Analysis of the Principles of Muhammad, The Rise and Decline of Mobility Doctrine in the U.S. Army, 1920–1944,* and a chapter on suicide bombers in *Terrorism's Unanswered Questions.*